THE LATER
THIRTY YEARS WAR

**Recent Titles in
Contributions in Military Studies**

A Navy Second to None: The History of U.S. Naval Training in World War I
Michael D. Besch

Home by Christmas: The Illusion of Victory in 1944
Ronald Andidora

Tides in the Affairs of Men: The Social History of Elizabethan Seamen, 1580-1603
Cheryl A. Fury

Battles of the Thirty Years War: From White Mountain to Nordlingen, 1618–1635
William P. Guthrie

A Grateful Heart: The History of a World War I Field Hospital
Michael E. Shay

Forged in War: The Continental Congress and the Origin of Military Supply
Lucille E. Horgan

Tricolor Over the Sahara: The Desert Battle of the Free French, 1940–1942
Edward L. Bimberg

Henry Lloyd and the Military Enlightenment of Eighteenth-Century Europe
Patrick J. Speelman

United States Military Assistance: An Empirical Perspective
William H. Mott IV

To the Bitter End: Paraguay and the War of the Triple Alliance
Chris Leuchars

Guns in the Desert: General Jean-Pierre Doguereau's Journal of Napoleon's Egyptian Expedition
Rosemary Brindle

Defense Relations between Australia and Indonesia in the Post-Cold War Era
Bilveer Singh

THE LATER THIRTY YEARS WAR

From the Battle of Wittstock to the Treaty of Westphalia

William P. Guthrie

Contributions in Military Studies, Number 222

GREENWOOD PRESS
Westport, Connecticut • London

Library of Congress Cataloging-in-Publication Data

Guthrie, William P., 1953–
  The later Thirty Years War : from the Battle of Wittstock to the Treaty of Westphalia / William P. Guthrie.
    p. cm.—(Contributions in military studies, ISSN 0883-6884 ; no. 222)
  Includes bibliographical references and index.
  ISBN 0-313-32408-5 (alk. paper)
  1. Thirty Years' War, 1618-1648. 2. Europe—History, Military—1492-1648. 3. Peace of Westphalia (1648). I. Title. II. Series.
D258.G89 2003
940.2'442—dc21   2002023547

British Library Cataloguing in Publication Data is available.

Copyright © 2003 by William P. Guthrie

All rights reserved. No portion of this book may be reproduced, by any process or technique, without the express written consent of the publisher.

Library of Congress Catalog Card Number: 2002023547
ISBN: 0-313-32408-5
ISSN: 0883-6884

First published in 2003

Greenwood Press, 88 Post Road West, Westport, CT 06881
An imprint of Greenwood Publishing Group, Inc.
www.greenwood.com

Printed in the United States of America

The paper used in this book complies with the Permanent Paper Standard issued by the National Information Standards Organization (Z39.48-1984).

P

In order to keep this title in print and available to the academic community, this edition was produced using digital reprint technology in a relatively short print run. This would not have been attainable using traditional methods. Although the cover has been changed from its original appearance, the text remains the same and all materials and methods used still conform to the highest book-making standards.

To My Mother

Contents

Preface   ix

1. The Early Thirty Years War   1

2. Baner's War and the Battle of Wittstock   37

3. Bernhard Sax-Weimar: The Battle of Rheinfelden   77

4. Torstensson's War, 1642–45: Second Breitenfeld and Jankow   105

5. The Battle of Rocroi: The War in Flanders and France   157

6. Mercy and Turenne: The Battles of Freiburg and Second Nordlingen   197

7. The Battle of Zusmarshausen: The End of the Thirty Years War   233

Glossary   269

Bibliography   273

Index   279

Index of Units   295

Preface

In the preface to *Battles of the Thirty Years War*, I expressed the intention to complete the war in a second volume. Together that book and this one form the first detailed study of the military aspects of the war as a whole.

The Thirty Years War began as a civil war in Bohemia and Germany to determine the religious policy of those entities. However, the wider implications of the conflict lured foreign powers to try fishing those troubled waters, notably, the Danes, the Swedes, and the French. Although the purely German conflict had been resolved by the compromise Peace of Prague (1635), the national interests of Sweden and France forced the fighting to continue.

The period 1440–1690 saw the replacement of muscle-powered feudal arrays with regular armies relying on firearms; the Thirty Years War, 1618–48, was an essential link in this chain of development. The first half of the conflict, 1618 through 1635, was marked by the eclipse of the "tercio" system, as exemplified by Tilly, by the linear system, associated with the meteoric career of King Gustavus Adolphus of Sweden. The task for their successors during the later part of the war was to apply the new theories in practice. The war, which had briefly seemed so "Napoleonic," became a drawn-out battle of attrition between evenly matched opponents. Under these circumstances, the emphasis was less on brilliant battlefield victories, although these still played their part, and more on campaigns and the patient erosion of enemy power. In the growing devastation, logistics became a constraint.

As in the first volume, I have used the most common English name and spelling in the text, to the extent that such exist; thus, Gustavus Adolphus rather than Gustav Adolf, Wallenstein rather than Waldstein, Vienna rather than Wien, Hapsburg rather than Habsburg. In the biographies, more complete forms are presented. This approach has necessarily led to inconsistencies: thus, Cologne rather than Koln, but Regensburg rather than Ratisbon. Personal names were a thornier problem: if one uses Aldringer instead of Aldringen, or Aldring, should one change Hofkirchen and Klitzing to Hofkircher and Klitzinger? In each case, I have tried to stick to the more common form, accepting the inconsistencies.

As Dr. Bonney has kindly pointed out, the date given for Wolgasr in *Battles* (p. 143) was in Old Style; the New Style date would be September 2, 1628.

1

The Early Thirty Years War

BACKGROUND OF THE WAR
The 17th century in Europe was a stage of uneasy transition from a medieval patchwork of hundreds of autonomous and semiautonomous polities, to a "modern" system of a couple of dozen fully sovereign states.[1] The precise difference between an independent country and a lesser jurisdiction was not agreed on, and many localities, municipalities, provinces, individuals, and groups laid claim to varying degrees of sovereignty, rights, and privileges vis-à-vis their ruler or country. Loyalty to a king included both the king's own "sacred" person and a more general allegiance to the royal dynasty. But this was not incompatible with loyalty to one's own group or class, and/or insistence on traditional privileges and limiting the king to his "proper" role. Thus, it was not uncommon to assert one's loyalty to the king even while leading a revolt.

Such revolts were, in fact, a serious danger to even the most powerful states. At this time, most administration was in the hands of local authorities, minor nobility, and town councils. Standing armies were few, and even those that existed were small by modern standards. Weapons were in common possession by all classes; the ability of disgruntled subjects to resist oppression was still relatively high.[2]

It was not remarkable that these differing values occasionally came into conflict, but—and this was a point that no 17th century decision maker could overlook—there was another, equally divisive loyalty: religion.

When Martin Luther ignited the Protestant Reformation in 1517, he unleashed centrifugal forces that were to wrack Europe for over a century. The Protestant movement soon split into Lutheran and Calvinist branches, the Lutherans in turn splintering into Gneislutherans and Philippists, while the Calvinists fissioned between Gomarists and Arminians. Other sects such as Zwinglians, Socinians, and Anabaptists found adherents, and even Catholics divided along national and factional lines. This would have been of marginal importance in a more secular or pluralist society, but the whole basis of 16th century political theory was the "divine right" of kings. Events were soon to indicate that a monarch whose religion differed from that of his subjects or even a substantial minority of them wore an uncertain crown. This was aggravated by radical theories that a ruler of "erroneous" religious views might legitimately be deposed by his subjects, which in turn engendered increased emphasis on established churches and religious conformity. Successful minority takeovers were necessarily followed by the elimination of the former majority religion. To some extent it was a self-sustaining process: in reaction to real or feared persecution, a religious minority would throw a country into civil war, in turn feeding the fears of religious conservatives, who reacted by persecuting minorities, resulting in more revolts.

There were three important religious groups in Western Europe in 1618: Catholics, Lutherans, and Calvinists. The Catholics were the most numerous, dominating the important kingdoms of Spain and France, Italy, and much of Germany, Poland, and Hungary. Catholics tended toward conservatism but maintained the hope that Europe's former religious unity might eventually be restored. The Lutherans dominated Scandinavia and northern Germany; radical revolutionaries in the mid-1500s, their very success had by now inclined them toward moderation. The Calvinists were scattered: a tolerated minority in France, an illegal majority in Scotland, enclaves in Germany, Switzerland, and Transylvania, but their political center was Holland, more properly, the United Provinces of the Netherlands or Dutch Republic. The Calvinists were the "radicals" of the period, feared and loathed by Catholic and Lutheran alike. The Dutch had evolved into a Protestant counterweight to the hegemony of Catholic Spain; in this "Eighty Years War," they had developed a policy of alliance with Lutherans against the common enemy, Catholicism. In its early 17th century form, this "Protestant International" included, more or less informally, not only the Calvinist states and at least half of the Lutherans but several Catholic countries whose policies were hostile toward Spain. Another Protestant power was the British monarchy, an unhappy union of Calvinist Scotland, Catholic Ireland, and divided England under a minority Anglican church.

All of the decision makers of the Thirty Years War were guided, to varying degrees, by four considerations: personal, dynastic, national, and religious. It was a fortunate statesman who, like Gustavus Adolphus, found these values mutually reinforcing. Some, like Richelieu, easily emphasized the dynastic over the religious, while most, like Christian IV of Denmark or Johann Georg of Saxony, were torn between contradictory demands of dynasty, religion, and nation.

The epitome of European divisiveness was the unique polity called "The Holy Roman Empire of the German Nation," more simply, "the Empire" or "Germany." It has become customary to refer to this body as "Neither holy, nor Roman, nor even an Empire."[3] Actually, it was very much what a late medieval would have called an "empire": a loose association of semiautonomous states owing allegiance to a common monarch, an overall system of laws, and a shared sense of nation. By modern standards, the Empire fell somewhere between anarchy and chaos. It was a heterogeneous collection of independencies, ranging from large, well-organized states to individual villages ruled from a castle with all the sizes in between. There were princes, dukes, archdukes, margraves, landgraves, counts, barons, knights, and even a king or two, not to mention free cities, bishops, archbishops, monasteries, priories, and some jurisdictions that defy classification.

The titular head of this aggregation was the Holy Roman Emperor, who was chosen for life by seven electoral princes (titled "electors"): the archbishops of Mainz, Cologne, and Trier (all Catholic), the duke of Saxony and the margrave of Brandenburg (both Lutheran), the Count Palatine of the Rhine (Calvinist), and the king of Bohemia. To become an elector was the ambition of every German dynast. By 1618, the Imperial title had long been hereditary in the Austrian Hapsburg dynasty (Catholic), but the Protestants dreamed of someday gaining a majority in the electoral college and choosing their own emperor.

Germany had been the first region hit by religious warfare, with continuous fighting after 1524. The Lutherans had quickly established themselves in the north and east of the Empire, but Catholicism stubbornly maintained itself to the south and west. In an effort to halt the growing chaos, the two factions agreed to a compromise, the Peace of Augsburg, 1555, and this treaty was thereafter the legal basis of religion in the Empire. Its guiding principle was *cujus regio ejus religio* "the one who rules determines the religion of his subjects." The choice was restricted to Catholicism and Lutheranism, Calvinism and more exotic sects being excluded. Unfortunately, the peacemakers were unable to reach agreement on all points. The Lutherans held that some Catholic countries had to tolerate Protestant minorities but that no Protestant was required to tolerate Catholicism. The Catholics held that the remaining "Church Lands," that is, territories where the rulers were officers of the Catholic Church, were required to remain in Church possession, whereas the Lutherans held that they could be "secularized" (Protestantized) if certain legal forms were observed. These points were left open in the final draft.

The Protestant rulers did not observe the restrictions of the settlement, continuing to expand their territories for several decades, mostly at the expense of Church Lands. When a territory was "secularized," Catholic worship was prohibited; the inhabitants had to adopt the new creed or emigrate.[4] This was a grievance to the Catholics, who regarded their own Protestant minorities with increasing disapproval. Nevertheless, by 1580 or so, the Lutherans had become sufficiently well established to desire stability more than conflict. Unfortunately, at about the same time, several important Lutheran princes were converted to the more aggressive Calvinist faith and reopened the whole issue. Calvinism regarded Catholicism as its principal enemy, but most Calvinist gains were at the expense of the Lutherans. The whim of a prince could determine the religion of a country. The uncertainty of the situation bred distrust and paranoia. Every religious minority was regarded as a potential "fifth column"; these minorities in turn reacted with hostility and disloyalty.

The German Catholics had maintained a defensive, even passive stance throughout most of the 16th century. Although numbering nearly half of the population of the Empire, not quite equal to the Lutherans and Calvinists combined, the Catholics were at a disadvantage because most of the magnates were Protestant. Of the great princes, only the Austrian Hapsburgs and the dukes of Bavaria still held the old faith; most Catholics lived under minor nobles or in Church territories. However, by 1600, the Catholics were adopting a more determined stance. This was partially due to the religious reinvigoration of the Counter-Reformation and partially as a reaction against Protestant inroads. There followed a series of clashes: the Cologne War of 1583–88, the Donauwerth Incident of 1606–9, the Julich Conflicts of 1609–10 and 1614–15, and the Gradisca War of 1615–18. These crises may be viewed, in retrospect, as so many steppingstones to total war, or simply as occasional outbreaks of "cold war" hostility. However, their natural effect was to heighten tensions.

The Donauwerth affair epitomized the level of paranoia and the cycle of reaction-counterreaction in prewar Germany. Donauwerth had been one of the towns designated as open to both religions, but the Lutherans had marginalized the Catholics, excluding them from government and restricting their freedom of worship. In 1606, the Catholics attempted to hold a religious procession. The Protestants assumed that the Catholics were planning to seize power. A mob was organized to smash the procession, and similar attacks were to follow. In 1607, Imperial commissioners were dispatched to enforce the law, but they were unable to restrain even greater disorders. The town council made no effort to restrain the mob, nor would they obey an Imperial order to restore freedom of worship.[5] Faced with direct defiance, Emperor Rudolf authorized Duke Maximilian of Bavaria to intervene by force.[6] Maximilian occupied and later annexed the town, proscribing the Lutherans in turn.[7] Protestants argued that Maximilian's action was illegal, because he was head of the Bavarian circle, and Donauwerth lay in the Swabian circle.[8] But Swabia was headed by the Lutheran duke of Wurtemberg. The whole fiasco was taken as proof by the Protestants that the Catholics were planning to restart the religious wars. They split into two factions: the extremists, led by the Calvinist Elector Palatine, organized a "Protestant Union" (1608)[9] to oppose Catholic designs. The moderates, loosely aligned under Johann Georg of Saxony, hoped to remain neural. Maximilian, in turn, organized a Catholic League (1609) to protect against attack by the Union.

This conflict should not be vulgarized into a simple "good guys-bad guys" dichotomy. Both, or one may say all, of the sides involved had legitimate apprehensions and aspirations, as well as ambitions that were less so. The pervading atmosphere of paranoia exaggerated even minor differences into incomprehensible gulfs.

THE HAPSBURGS, BOHEMIA, AND THE OUTBREAK OF WAR

Austria was itself a particularly egregious example of the German condition. Although theoretically overlords of all Germany, this was little more than a formality. The emperors' actual power derived from the hereditary lands of the Hapsburg dynasty. They were a heterogeneous collection. German provinces included the archduchies of Lower Austria, Upper Austria, Inner Austria, Tyrolia, and the Oberland. Then there was the Kingdom of Hungary, at the time reduced to Pressburg and Croatia.[10] Finally came the Kingdom of Bohemia, divided into the four provinces of Bohemia, Moravia, Silesia, and Lusatia. Each of these 10 realms had a different legal status, a separate nobility, and its own estates, the only unifying factor being the court at Vienna. Although the Spanish Hapsburgs had become the recognized champions of Catholicism in Europe, their Austrian cousins were unequal to the challenge. Under the mad Emperor Rudolf II (1576–1612) and the weak Matthias (1612–19) so many concessions were made that Austria became the most divided territory in the Empire. In Lower Austria, the Lutherans held a majority of the nobility, although not the population as a whole; the same was true of Hungary. In Upper Austria, Lutherans and Calvinists held a clear majority between them. On the other hand, the much more populous Inner Austria and Tyrol were overwhelmingly Catholic.[11] In Bohemia, the confusion reached its peak. Silesia and Lusatia were Lutheran, but Bohemia proper was divided between Lutherans, Calvinists, and Catholics, the Lutherans being split between pro- and anti-Hapsburg elements. It is difficult to be certain, but all the Protestants together probably held a majority of the population; in any case, they dominated the estates. Moravia was similarly divided; there the Catholics may have held a slight edge.

Emperor Matthias having no direct heir, the Hapsburg family had agreed on his nephew Ferdinand as successor. The transfer of power, begun in 1617, was a complicated and lengthy process but routine except in Bohemia. The estates there claimed the power to elect their king, and it was feared that the Protestant majority, under a Count Thurn, would refuse to accept the candidate. This did not occur; Ferdinand won by a lopsided vote. He was formally crowned, handed the regency over to two local Catholics, and returned to Vienna.

Almost immediately, Thurn decided to take over. On May 23, 1618, he and his supporters broke into the palace and threw the regents out of a window.

For such an impromptu coup, it went very smoothly. The estates assumed complete control of the government, Prague was secured, Catholicism was proscribed, both Church and royal properties were seized. Not all Bohemians were pleased at this turn of events: aside from the Catholic minority, a few Protestants felt loyalty to the Hapsburgs. Several towns, most importantly Pilsen and Budweis, declared for Ferdinand. But, inside of a month, the rebel regime was in effective control of the country. Their first step was to send to Moravia, Silesia, and Lusatia for support; their second was to organize for war. Meanwhile, in Vienna, the Imperial government was assembling what forces it could find and petitioning Spain for assistance. This local rebellion was the spark that ignited the Thirty Years War.

THE POLITICS OF THE WAR

The Thirty Years War was a most complicated struggle, one of the more involved conflicts in history. One reason is the sheer number of participating states and decision makers and the complexity of their motivations. The war cannot be narrowed down to two sides with definable war goals; even the closest of allies followed independent policies and would seek their own advantage without undue concern for their friends. A second is the length of time involved, with radical shifts in the overall situation. Third are the many peripheral wars and conflicts loosely grouped around the German war. Finally, there is the irregular character of the politics; a country might enter the war, fight a few years, then go back to neutrality. Many shifted from side to side according to events. Some countries were allies in one area and enemies in another. Nonbelligerents were *not* bound by modern rules of neutrality and might support one side or the other with money, troops, or supplies, free passage of troops, even bases.

That being understood, it is possible to lay out the *important* participants without too much ambiguity.

The Imperial or Catholic alliance centered on the Austrian Hapsburgs of Vienna, ruled by Emperor Ferdinand II (1619–37) and later his son Ferdinand III (1637–57). Their principal allies were the Catholic League under Maximilian of Bavaria (1597–1651) and the Spanish Hapsburgs. Although primarily interested in wars with Holland and France, Madrid gave Vienna a good deal of financial and military support. Spanish decision makers in the war were King Philip III (1598–1621), his son Philip IV (1621–65), and premier Olivares (1621–43).

The Protestant or anti-Hapsburg cause was first represented by the Bohemian rebels under Thurn; they were soon joined by German Protestants under Elector Friedrich of the Palatinate (1610–32) and Prince Christian of Anhalt (1595–1620). King Christian IV of Denmark (1588–1648) was drawn into the war (1625–29). After his withdrawal, the Protestant cause was championed by Sweden under King Gustavus Adolphus (1611–32) and Chancellor Oxenstierna (1612–54). The Dutch Republic, which was embroiled in a long-term war with Spain (1567–1648), gave assistance to the Protestant cause up until the mid-1630s but thereafter lost interest.

The third corner of the anti-Hapsburg triangle was France; dynastic rivalry with Spain had driven this Catholic country to ally itself with Protestants.[12] French leaders were King Louis XIII (1610–43), Cardinal Richelieu (1624–42), and Cardinal Mazarin (1642–61).

The German Protestant moderates under Johann Georg of Saxony (1611–56) failed to remain neutral. They were mainly aligned with Sweden 1631–35 but switched to the Imperials 1636–48. Other German leaders were the Calvinist and very anti-Imperial landgraves of Hesse-Cassel, the opportunistic Duke Georg of Brunswick-Luneburg, and the Lutheran extremists: Georg of Baden-Durlach, Christian of Brunswick, and the Sax-Weimar brothers.

Several of the lesser powers are worthy of mention. Poland was aligned with the Hapsburgs throughout, but maintained a show of neutrality. Most of Italy, especially Genoa, was pro-Spain. Venice was aligned with France against Spain but took no active part in the war. Savoy, caught between Spain and France, shifted from side to side trying to gain some slight advantage for itself. Transylvania, under Princes Bethlen Gabor (1613–29) and George Rakoczy (1630–48) followed a pro-Protestant (Calvinist) policy, but there was a long period (1629–42) when internal disorder precluded intervention.

The Papacy was a special case. Although most of the wartime popes, Paul V

(1605–21), Gregory XV (1621–23), and Innocent X (1644–55), were pro-Hapsburg, the one who reigned longest, Urban VIII (1623–44), was pro-French and anti-Hapsburg. Thus emerged the paradox that the spiritual head of Catholicism was an indirect ally of the Protestant cause.

The war is divided into five distinct phases: (1) the Bohemian War, 1618–20, centering on the original rebellion; (2) the German (or Dutch-German) War, 1621–24, carried on by diehard supporters of Elector Friedrich; (3) the Danish War, 1625–29; (4) the Swedish War, 1630–35; (5) the French or French-Swedish War, 1636–48, which saw a near-united Germany under attack by both Sweden and France.[13]

THE COURSE OF THE WAR, 1618–29

The first years of the war, 1618–19, saw a deadlock between Imperials and rebels. The Bohemians, joined by Silesia, Lusatia, and Upper Austria, were able to expand into Moravia and part of Lower Austria, but they were unable to capture Vienna or win the war. Spanish assistance to the Imperials was only partially balanced by Dutch and Transylvanian aid to the rebels. Elector Friedrich assumed leadership of the rebellion, but the Protestant Union as a whole remained neutral.

In 1620, the deadlock was broken. Both Lutheran Saxony and the Bavarian-led Catholic League intervened on the Imperial side. The Catholic-Imperial army under Tilly crushed the Bohemians at the Battle of White Mountain (November 8, 1620). Protestant partisans Baden, Brunswick, and Mansfeld attempted to carry on the fighting in Germany, but were defeated by Tilly's League Army. Baden was routed at the Battle of Wimpfen (May 6, 1622); Brunswick at the Action of Hochst (June 20, 1622) and the Battle of Stadtlohn (August 6, 1623). By 1624, the Protestant forces had been entirely eliminated.

This one-sided outcome did not sit well with the anti-Hapsburg powers of France and Holland. A strange alliance was cobbled together, Denmark, Sweden, France, England, the Netherlands, Brandenburg, Transylvania, and Venice to invade Germany and undo the Catholic victory. It soon became apparent that the real burden of the war would rest on Denmark, under King Christian, and the remaining Protestant extremists, including Baden, Brunswick, and Mansfeld.

From 1621 to 1624, the Imperial Army had been little more than an auxiliary to Tilly's League forces. But the crisis of the Danish invasion had induced the emperor to organize a new, more significant army, under the enigmatic genius Wallenstein. Wallenstein's army soon dwarfed Tilly's and assumed a political status outweighing its military one. Against these two strong opponents, Christian was at a disadvantage. Tilly defeated Christian himself at the Battle of Lutter (August 27, 1626), while Wallenstein achieved the lesser triumphs of Dessau (April 25, 1626), Kosel (August, 1627), Heiligenhofen (September, 1627), and Wolgast (August 24, 1628). King Christian had no choice but to admit defeat (Peace of Lubeck, May 22, 1629).

This first phase of the war was dominated by the traditional "tercio" style army of Tilly, which, despite its historical obsolescence, was overwhelmingly successful against the more "modern" armies of the Bohemian, German, and Danish Protestants. Tilly's victories were not accidents; neither were they the result of a "superior" Catholic military system. Rather, in each case Tilly had more and better troops and was himself a better general. In 1629, Tilly was the most experienced commander in Europe.

TILLY'S ART OF WAR

As in any period, the organization of war was defined by its weapons. For the infantry, these were pike and musket[14]; for cavalry, sword, pistol, and arkebus.

A pike, of course, is no more than a long spear. Some had butt-spikes and a few armored shafts, but the majority were simple poles with spearheads. The standard length was 18 feet, but there were plenty in the 14–16 foot range and some as short as 12 feet. Contemporaries distinguished between "heavy armed" and "naked" (i.e., unarmored) pikemen, the former wearing the corselet, breastplate, backplate, thigh-pieces, brassarts, tassets, and helmet. In fact, armor was already losing ground, and many "armored" pike wore only the breastplate. A unit might contain a dozen gradations between "fully armed" to "naked," including partial armor, helmets only, and buff (i.e., heavy leather) coats. The older or better paid a unit, the higher the proportion of armor among the pikemen, half-and-half being a rough average.

In action, the pikes formed a solid block called a battalion, twice as wide as deep. These battalions were 20–30 ranks deep, depending on the size of the unit. The officers and NCOs, what was called the "prima plana," were in the pike battalion, while the "shot," the musket-armed troops, grouped more loosely around this core. Veteran file-leaders, forming the first rank, wore the heaviest armor, protection declining in each succeeding rank. Only the first five ranks were expected to directly contact the enemy; rearward elements acting as reserve and moral support. A steady battalion could defy any number of cavalry, and, advancing shove aside lighter infantry. Only another pike block could meet them head-on. Such collisions were *not* conducted at a full-tilt charge although some critics thought they should be. If (as did not always happen) the defending battalion stood its ground, and contact was made, the front-rank men on both sides would duel, one on one, with the next four ranks in support. In this sort of fighting, armored men had a real edge. An actual melee would be a confused affair, with half-pikes stabbing, broken pikes being swung, and supporting shot using clubbed muskets. Good swordsmen could chop the heads from pikestaffs. But as long as the battalion maintained formation, no penetration by hostiles was possible. Because of the morale effects of deep formations and armor, a pike melee was more likely than, for example, a Napoleonic bayonet clash, but they were never really common, and there were plenty of cases where battalia retired or broke before actual contact.

Firearms were of three types, matchlock, wheellock, or snaphance. These refer to method of detonation. In a matchlock, the powder charge is ignited by a length of slow-burning cord, the "match." A wheellock uses a spring-wound wheel to strike pyrites against steel, producing sparks. The snaphance was a primitive flintlock. Both wheellocks and snaphances could be called firelocks.

The matchlock was clumsy and awkward to use. It took too long to prepare a shot, the match required continual readjustment, more cord was burned than powder, and the misfire rate was double that of a firelock (20% as opposed to 10%). But it was sturdy, comparatively cheap, and easy to make. The wheellock was both expensive and mechanically delicate. The snaphance was still little used outside Holland; such "advanced technology" was not yet widely understood. For such reasons, the matchlock remained the principal infantry firearm well after the war, the wheellock being used mainly by horse.

The infantryman's matchlock was called a musket, although technically this term applied to the heavier weapons requiring a rest. Musket design was a trade-off between effective range, hitting power, weight, length, and rate of fire.[15] The massive "heavy" or "Spanish" musket, what the English called a "double musket," was over five feet long and fired a 2-ounce ball. The "Dutch" or "standard" musket was more like 55 inches with a 1.35-ounce ball. The "light" or "half" musket was about four feet in length and 14 or 15 balls to the pound. Strong men could use the lightest half muskets without a rest. Next came the heavy infantry arquebus, the type the English called calivers, at maybe 45 inches and 1 ounce/ball. These required no rests and vaguely resembled the Brown Bess muskets of the 18th century. There were still lighter arquebuses. Average rates of fire ran from three minutes per shot for double muskets to 1/1 for very light arquebuses, but well-drilled troops could shave these times.

Table 1.1
Infantry Firearms

Type	Ball/Lb	Length"	Wt/Lb	Min/Shot	Rg/Yd	Rest?
Double Musket	8	65+	20	3	250	Yes
Standard Musket	10–12	55	16	2.5	225	Yes
Half Musket	14–15	48	12–14	2	200	Option
Caliver	16	45	12	1.5	150	No
Arquebus	20–24	35–40	10–12	1	100	No
Snaphance	16	45	12	3/4	150	No
Swede Musket	10	48	10–11	2	200	Yes
Fusil (flintlock)	16–20	42	10–12	1/2	150	No

These were not standardized sizes so much as rough classifications. All weapons were handmade and varied to a greater or lesser degree. The "ideal" firearm was a matter of professional debate. Catholics, influenced by Spain, tended to favor a mixture of muskets and arquebuses. Protestants, equally influenced by Holland, were inclined to standardize either the Dutch standard musket or the smaller half musket. Some favored division by role, with battalion shot carrying muskets, and detached shot, arquebuses. However, as arms were rarely procured or issued systematically, the variations even in the same unit could be considerable.[16] Differences in armaments would tend to cancel out.

Firearm-equipped infantry, what the Germans called musketeers and the English simply "shot," were normally supplied with 12 rounds of ammunition, the "twelve apostles." These consisted of measured charges of gunpowder, about the same weight as the ball, carried on a shoulder bandoleer in individual wooden flasks, seven in front, five behind. The priming powder was carried in a separate horn or flask, the bullets in a pouch or pocket or in the mouth. Paper cartridges, such as those used in the 18th century, were known but still rare. Critics disliked the bandoleer flasks because their rattling could betray surprise, but they remained common practice throughout the period. As most musketeers had only 12 shots and none more than 20, they could quickly exhaust their ammunition. In lengthy battles, it was necessary to replenish supply, either by looting the fallen or from battalion barrels. Thus powder wagons were often placed close behind the troops; these were highly explosive and a hazard to their own side. It was preferable to place single powder barrels (about 100 pounds each) along the battle line. These were dangerous too, as contact with the burning cord of a matchlock would set off the powder.

Some elite infantry, scouts, artillery train, and ammunition guards carried firelocks. Not only were these safer around black powder, but they were more effective. The firelock, invariably of caliver/arquebus size, had double the rate of fire of an equivalent matchlock. It was preferred for ambushes and night operations because the glowing match of the musket could give it away.

Most musketeers wore ordinary clothing, but some added sleeveless buff jackets, and a few had helmets. Shot operating on their own without pike support were called "forlorns" or "forlorn hopes." They were more mobile than pike battalions but very vulnerable to horse.

Both pikemen and musketeers normally carried a short sword, but those given to common foot were of poor quality. A musketeer usually fought hand-to-hand with clubbed musket.[17]

The mounted troops available to Tilly were heavy cavalry, medium cavalry, light or irregular cavalry, and dragoons.

Heavy cavalry were cuirassiers, in German *kyrysser* or *kurassiere*, abbreviated KUR.[18] These were distinguished by the cuirass, heavy body armor. The "true" or ideal cuirassier wore three-quarters armor—covering everything but seat, legs below the knee, and forearms—heavy cavalry boots, and long gauntlets. Helmet and breastplate should be at least "pistol proof." They were armed with at least two pistols and a heavy "armor-smashing" sword.

Medium cavalry were arkebusiers (archbusiers, ARK), so-called from their weapon, the arkebus (cavalry version of the infantry arquebus). Arkebusiers and dragoons both originated in the mounted arquebusiers of the 16th century but evolved in opposite directions. The arkebusiers became true cavalry, incapable of dismounted combat; the dragoons pure mounted infantry, using their horses only for movement. In theory, arkebusiers were armored only in leather jackets; their weapons were the arkebus, one or more pistols, and a light sword. Aside from boots and gloves, dragoons were identical to foot musketeers.

Both theorists and practitioners spent a good deal of thought on the relative merits of cuirassiers and arkebusiers. Cuirassiers were supreme on the battlefield; their weight and invulnerability could crush any lesser cavalry. With their superior mobility, maneuverability, and longer-ranged weapon, arkebusiers were valuable in skirmishes and smaller fights, what were called "actions." The problem lay in their relative proportions and their optimal coordination. Some favored mixed units; others, regiments of a single type. In the former case, the arkebusiers could range ahead of the cuirassiers to fire, but form behind them in battle. In the latter, a similar result was achieved by expedients. So-called "demi-cuirassiers" with less armor and an arkebus could act in the skirmish role. Likewise, some "heavy" arkebusiers were equipped with breastplate and helmet to play a battlefield role. There was, of course, always considerable variation between individual troopers. The best of the arkebusiers might be as well armed as a demi-cuirassier. In all cases, the best-trained, best-armed men would form the front rank, with diminution in each succeeding row.

The principal cavalry weapon was the wheellock pistol. This was a sturdy, clublike weapon between one and two feet long, of 20–24 balls to the pound of lead. After firing, they could be used as bludgeons or thrown, although this would damage the mechanisms. These sizable weapons were carried in large saddle-holsters. The wheel was located on the right side, a delicate spring wound with a key. It was advisable to wind it shortly before use, as keeping the wheel wound too long (e.g., overnight) could ruin the elasticity of the spring. Ideally, the pistoleer would turn his mount 90 degrees to the left and extend his right arm toward the enemy straight out, turning his hand sideways so that the wheel was on top. This posture avoided disturbing the horse and maximized the efficiency of the wheellock. However, the trooper often simply fired ahead, the explosion scorching the horse's ear.

Both arkebusiers and dragoons carried wheellocks. These varied from short-barreled "dragons" (hence, "dragoon") with heavy balls, to longer weapons with smaller bullets. In Germany, the arkebusiers tended toward shorter weapons, the dragoons, toward full-size arquebuses.

Table 1.2
Cavalry Wheellocks

Type	Balls/Lb	Length/Inch
Dragon	15	30
English Carbine	15–16	34
German Arkebus	20–24	32–36
Dragoon Firelock	16–24	36–48

Pistols were employed at up to 25 meters and arkebuses at 50 or more, although true accuracy was doubtful. Dismounted dragoons, of course, enjoyed as much accuracy as infantrymen.

Light irregular cavalry, mostly of East European origin, were common in the Imperial armies of the period. These were of three basic types. The Croats were similar to light arkebusiers; their weapon was the arkebus. The hussars or Hungarians relied on the saber; the Cossacks or Poles on the lance. These irregulars were skillful in skirmishing, raiding, looting, and general harassment but unreliable in formal battle. Aside from their national weapons, they carried a heterogeneous array of axes, swords, knives, bows, and pistols. They wore little armor, not even helmets or buff jackets. Their mounts were light but fast. Although fierce and mobile, they were lacking in order.

Map 1.1
The Empire ca. 1640

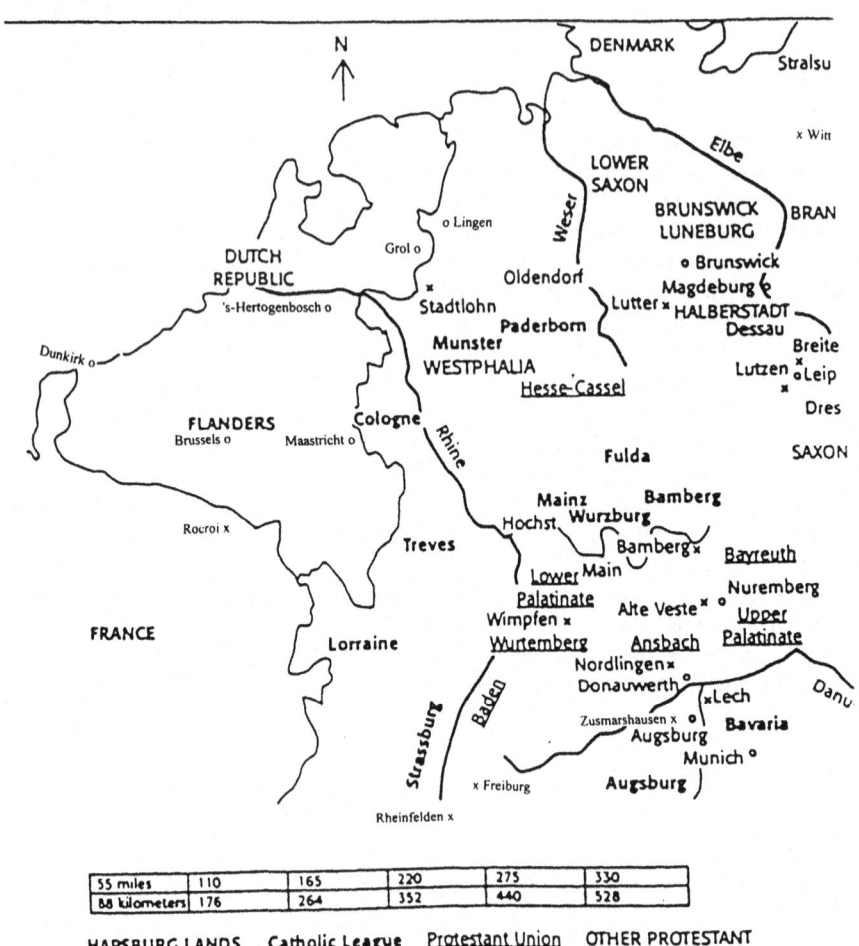

55 miles	110	165	220	275	330
88 kilometers	176	264	352	440	528

HAPSBURG LANDS Catholic League Protestant Union OTHER PROTESTANT

The Early Thirty Years War

By 1600, the once-common lance had virtually disappeared from Western Europe—aside from a few bodyguards, the lance appears only in Polish hands.

Artillery defies easy classification. Every gunner was a technical expert, every gun, a unique work of art. Reformers had attempted to standardize calibers, but with little success. The problem was a trade-off between durability, range, accuracy, hitting power, mobility, and cost; every commander had different ideas about the ideal combinations. Further, the guns cast by private manufacturers for general sale aggravated the confusion.

Guns of the period may be divided into two main categories, cannon (the German term was *Karthaunen*) and culverins (German: *Schange*). The cannon was a relatively short-barreled, thin-walled piece, while the culverin had a longer barrel and much thicker tube. The culverin was valued for its superior range,[19] accuracy, and safety, while the cannon threw a heavier projectile. Because of the metal involved, a culverin might be twice as heavy as a cannon of the same caliber.

Within each category, guns were classed by caliber, specifically, the weight of (iron) ball thrown.[20] The prevalent systems were heavily influenced by the ideas of Maurice of Nassau. This Dutch leader had standardized his calibers at 48, 24, 12, and 6 pounds. Note that he standardized ball size, not gun type; cannon and culverins of the same caliber fired the same ball. It was generally acknowledged, at least in Germany, that a 48-pound ball was the right size for a (full or whole) cannon and 24 pounds, at least in theory, for a culverin. Larger pieces, of up to 75 pounds, were "royal" or "double" cannon. More important were the subdivisions, the "half" cannon (demicannon) of 24 pounds, the quarter cannon of 12 pounds, and the demiculverin, also a 12 pounder. Full cannon (48 pdr) were strictly siege guns; they were too heavy, awkward, and slow firing for the battlefield. Both demiculverins and quartercannon (12 pdr) were medium/heavy field guns, while demicannon (24 pdr) served in both battle and siege roles.

In the lighter calibers, the differences between culverins and cannon were less, but the variety was even greater. The English spoke of minions, sakers, falcons, drakes, and robinets; the Germans of falcons, falconets, demifalconets, *schlangels*, "field guns," and *singerins*. There were guns cast in every pound and half pound between one and 10. Many commanders, Maurice, Baden, Christian IV, Gustavus Adolphus, fancied themselves artillery experts and tried to design the "ideal" light gun. Others, like Tilly, were content to use whatever happened to be available.

Table 1.3
Artillery

Type	Lb (nom)	Lb (act)	Wt (lb)	Shots/hr	Horses
Cannon/Kartaunen	48	30–60	4500–7000	8	9–20
Demicannon	24	20–36	3000–4000	10	8–16
Quarter-cannon	12	10–15	2000	12	5–10
Demiculverin	12	7–12	2000–3400	12	5–12
Falcon/Schlangel	6	3–6	1000–1400	15	4–8
Falconet	2	1–3	500–1000	15–20	2–6
Regimental Gun	3	3	500	20–30	1–2

Guns were supposed to be bronze or brass, but some were of heavier, less reliable, but cheaper iron.

Demicannon and demiculverins could fire ball effectively up to 1500 meters; the smaller guns, rather less. These guns were as accurate as their Napoleonic descendants, but their rate of fire was lower. They were heavy, inefficient, and had no elevating screws. The crew had to run the gun up after each shot, and 17th century carriages were built for durability rather than speed. They had to be laid for each shot, a tedious process involving handspikes and wedges.

Although their range and accuracy with ball were up to later standards, the same was not true of canister. The use of wired charges was still new, and the technology was poorly understood, so the effective range of grapeshot was not yet much over 100 meters. Also, smallshot damaged the inside of the barrel. Thus, even the lightest guns used ball at comparatively short ranges, and the larger rarely fired anything else.

Mortars were short-barreled, high-trajectory weapons designed to throw an explosive shell. Their limited accuracy and low rate of fire relegated them to siege work. They were, however, popular in that role and were cast in sizes varying from 3 to 200 pounds.

When the war broke out in 1618, there were barely three standing armies in Western Europe: France, Spain, and the Dutch Republic. In the whole of Germany, there were only a few scattered garrisons and guards, divided among a dozen great princes. Some principalities, like Bavaria and Saxony, had well-organized militias. The Catholic League and its opposite number, the Protestant Union, had theoretical organizations, but there were no actual troops. When the fighting started, both sides scrambled to form armies from nothing, partially by borrowing from Spain or Holland but mostly by contracting. So-called military enterprisers received contracts from their respective princes, "warlords" (*kriegsherren*), to raise, equip, and lead regiments of infantry or cavalry. These men should not be thought of as mercenaries, as they operated under the license of a specific government. The regiments that fought the Thirty Years War were very rarely the mercenaries that they are often called but the formal property of the warring princes. At worst, they were units made up of mercenaries. It was unknown for a unit, as opposed to individuals, to simply switch sides. The colonels had "proprietary rights" in their regiments but not true ownership; the men felt some attachment to their warlord or their cause. There were no "free" mercenary bands that would auction their services to the highest bidder. Battles were the preserve of formally organized units officially belonging to the warlords. Purely local units engaged in "partisan" warfare are less easy to classify. There were, in addition, unofficial bands of marauders, but these had no interest in actual combat.

The average owner-colonel would be a man of some military experience, having served in Flanders, Hungary, or Germany and risen to captain or higher. Such men were mostly from the officer class, the nobility. After receiving his commission, from emperor or League, he would collect a cadre of officers and experienced NCOs and fill the ranks with recruits. All commissioned officers had to be confirmed by the warlord, but this was often a formality. Some owners were uninterested in actual command. Some had higher responsibilities—nearly every general owned a regiment—some held posts in the civil government, and some preferred to attend the Imperial court in Vienna. This was more common in the Imperial army than the Bavarian. They would delegate to an experienced lieutenant colonel. Units were sometimes classified according to their areas of recruitment, High (South) Germans being considered more warlike than Low (North) Germans, Walloons more effective than Germans, and so on.

As the war dragged on, it became possible for would-be careerists to rise through the ranks as if in a regularly organized army and even be promoted to colonel in a regiment originally owned by someone else. The warlords held the power to dismiss the original owner and take over his unit or to assume control of a unit whose colonel had died or retired. Nevertheless, military enterprisers continued to raise and own regiments right up to the end of the war.

A regiment, whether of horse or foot, consisted of 10 companies. There were many exceptions: some units had 2, 3, or 4 companies, and one monster had 31. But these were less common; of the 53 infantry regiments (IRs) in the Imperial *Krieglisten* for 1631, 44 were of 10 companies, and 5 of 5 each (half-regiments). There were no subdivisions between regiment and company, but it was not uncommon to detach 4 or 5 companies under the lieutenant colonel or major. An infantry company had 300 men at full strength; a cavalry, 100, thus an infantry regiment would be 3000, and a cavalry regiment, 1000. Actual field strengths were much lower, especially in the Imperial army. At Breitenfeld the League infantry regiments averaged a bit over 2000, and the Imperials, around 1000.

In theory, the infantry was equally divided between pike and shot. In fact, it varied from time to time and unit to unit, generally to the advantage of the shot. Again in theory, the best and strongest men were to be pikemen. The lighter, more agile men were to bear musket or arquebus. However, many colonels ignored these rules. Part of the problem was that while pikes were indispensable in former battles, shot were superior in skirmishes, actions, and sieges—and these were far more common. During the period 1618–32, the proportion of pike to shot fluctuated between 1:1 and 1:2.

Table 1.4
Infantry Proportions 1601–1627

Nationality	Year	Pike			Shot		
		Cadre	Armd	Unar	Muskt	Arqs	Shot
Spanish	1601	646	1047	954	1237	2117	56%
Walloon	1601	375	1125	694	1237	1242	53%
German	1601	665	5651	692	1194	700	21%
Walloon	1619	152	857	0	1435	424	65%
Cath.Leg	1625	121	1000	200*	1500	300	58%
Cath.Leg	1625	4+	80	10*	201	0	68%
Cath.Leg	1627	150	300	350*	1500	0	65%

*= Halberds.
Armored; Unarmored; Musketeers; Arquebusiers.

As noted earlier, the core of an infantry formation was the "battalion" of pikes. These were normally formed in "double battalion," two files per rank;

thus the depth of the formation varied according to its size. This practice was somewhat antiquated in 1631. The Protestant reformers favored a fixed depth 5–10 ranks. Similarly, the Imperial FM Basta had suggested that each infantry regiment of 3000 be divided into three battalions of 500 pike and 500 shot each and that the pikes be formed 12 deep and 40 wide. Wallenstein seems to have experimented with such shallower formations. However, Tilly, who believed in mass, favored the older style.

The shot were divided into three groups and placed around the pike battalion.[21] Two equal wings, called "sleeves,"[22] of musketeers went on each side of the pikes; their depth was equal to that of the battalion. Tilly wrote that these sleeves should never exceed 20 files, as the outlying men would be too far away to be protected by the pikes. Three to five more ranks of shot were placed front of the whole mass; those before the pikes should be light arquebuses. The whole would comprise a solid block of men, the pike center surrounded on three sides by shot. This massed formation was called the *tercio*, after the Spanish term for regiment.

Table 1.5
Tercio Formations

208 shot 13x16	96 shot 32x3	208 shot 13x16		442 shot 17x26	176 shot 44x4	442 shot 17x26
	512 pike 32 x 16				968 pike 44 x 22	
Imperial Tercio (1024)				League Tercio (2028)		
	58 x 19				78 x 26	

Musketeers employed a system called the countermarch. The man in front would fire, then go to the rear of the formation and reload, while the next man would step forward and fire in turn. By the time the last man in the file had fired, the first had finished reloading and was ready to fire again. As a rough rule of thumb, for every minute that the weapon required to load, five ranks were needed—that is, five ranks fired per minute. Thus, arquebuses should be 5 to 8 deep, and double muskets, 15.

In the Dutch army, each rank, having fired, would split and file off to both sides. Catholics seem to have preferred a single file around the flanks. Another style, sometimes used by the French, was to doublespace the shot so that individuals could countermarch within the formation.[23]

There were other versions. In the advancing countermarch the first man remained in place while reloading, and successive ranks moved in front to deliver fire. The formation could advance firing some 20–40 meters a minute. In the retiring countermarch, favored by the Dutch, each rank after firing would move back to reload, but the next man would fire in place, instead of moving forward. Thus, they would be falling back some 10–20 meters a minute. In both cases the pike would move correspondingly.

The tercio followed an opposite principle. The pike were the formation, the shot around them were supporting skirmishers. They were expected to move to accommodate the pike. Unlike their Protestant opponents, the Catholics did not form their shot in regular ranks. It appears that they merely grouped themselves around the pike in loose files, and each man took as much time reloading and firing as he needed. There was no attempt to systematize the weapons for uniform fire. Usually the heavier, slower weapons lined up closer to the pikes, and the lighter farther out on the sleeves, with the lightest actually in front of the battalion, but that was all. The officers were inside the pike battalion and made little effort to direct or supervise fire. Every man fired as he could, selecting his own target. As a tercio's sleeves might be 25 ranks deep or more, it could maintain a steady fire for over an hour. The excess depth meant that any given discharge was only 60% the theoretical maximum; however it also compensated for inefficient organization of shot. As it had a 40% "firepower cushion," the tercio could fire while advancing in a way impossible to a more efficient, shallower formation.

When the Spanish invented the tercio in the 1530s, it had appeared an ideal combination of arms. The pike would ward off cavalry and deal with enemy pike, and the shot would deliver a steady stream of fire. When the enemy was sufficiently weakened, the battle would be resolved with push of pike and butt of musket. On the defense, the shot could punish the enemy, falling back behind the pikes if threatened by cavalry. For this reason, the pike had to maintain at least a 4:6 ratio to the shot, and the sleeves could not be too wide or there wouldn't be enough pikes to shield the shot. The tercio was awkward, moving about 60 meters a minute, but it could freely fire on the move. Each tercio could act on its own, independently of the other battalions in the line. It somewhat resembled a Napoleonic bayonet column surrounded by skirmishers.

By 1590, the tercio was looking old-fashioned. As compared to a 10-rank Dutch formation, it was inefficient. It had only about 60% firepower efficiency, only 25% of the pike were actually utilized, and its solid mass was extremely vulnerable to firepower. However, it still had its virtues. A Dutch battalion required extensive training; at least 60% of the men had to know what they were doing. For the tercio, a reliable cadre would suffice; the rearward ranks might never see the enemy. Training was "on the job" as recruits started out in back and gradually worked their way forward, becoming veterans in the process. The tercio had resilience and could endure more punishment, with less loss of effectiveness, than its competitors. The solid mass of the tercio represented a morale power encouraging to its members and demoralizing to its enemies. For all the efficiency of his linear battalions, Maurice of Nassau never challenged the Spanish tercios on even terms. His "retiring" countermarch maximized his firepower while avoiding close contact where solidity would become a factor.

Tilly was a conservative in tactics. He believed that the traditional virtues of morale and solidity, which had been winning battles for a century, were just as valid in 1631 as in 1531. He had impressive evidence to back his claim: a matchless string of victories. White Mountain, Wimpfen, Hochst, Stadtlohn, Lutter—in each case the tercios had proven impervious to attack and had shattered thinner, more brittle formations.

In battle, the tercios normally formed in three "checkerboard" lines (echelons), with wide intervals between, the battalions in the second line covering the gaps in the first and those in the third covering those in the second. The intervals between tercios were about 75–100 meters, those between echelons 100–200 meters. The tercios being so awkward and clumsy, spacing facilitated movement and maneuver. In the event of actual contact with the enemy, the second line could fill in the gaps in the first, the third acting as reserve. Nevertheless, the tercios were not designed for cooperation and mutual support; each battalion moved on its own and fought as an individual.

As noted before, the cavalry were heavy cuirassiers and lighter arkebusiers. A cavalry company consisted, nominally, of 100 horse. As with the infantry, the ideal cavalry regiment mustered 10 companies, but deviations were more common. Of 39 Imperial cavalry regiments, only 19 had 10 companies, and none of the 11 League regiments did.

Tilly, as might be expected, organized his cavalry in old-fashioned dense formations, 10 ranks deep. Thus a League cavalry regiment of 800 would be 80 files wide by 10 ranks deep, cuirassiers in front, arkebusiers behind. Dutch and German Protestants preferred 300-man squadrons, 6 deep by 50 wide. Under Basta's influence, Wallenstein had directed that Imperial cuirassiers form 8 deep and arkebusiers only 6.

The battle tactic of these cavalry was called the caracole, an attack with pistols. There were four main varieties that may be called the simple caracole, the true caracole, the limacon, and the Protestant caracole. All consisted of a mounted fire attack without direct contact. The "simple" caracole involved the formation closing to range, then halting. The first rank fired, then filed to the rear to reload, while the second rank fired, exactly like an infantry countermarch. In theory, this could be kept up indefinitely, but in practice, the units seem to have disengaged after one or two complete discharges. The "true" caracole was much the same, except that the unit halted about 50 meters from the target, and each individual rank closed range to shoot in turn. Thus, at any given time, the main body was behind as an intact support. The "limacon" or "snail" was similar to the true caracole, except that fire was delivered by file rather than rank. Each left-hand file in turn would approach the target, turn right, place themselves parallel to the enemy front, deliver their fire, then ride behind the main body, resume their original position, and reload. This maneuver was particularly popular among arkebusiers. The "Protestant" caracole involved the whole unit closing to range, only the first rank firing their pistols, then the unit wheeling sharply to the left so that the right-hand file could fire. Sometimes the unit would continue to wheel, turning around completely, so that the leftmost file could fire as well. The Protestant caracole was considered suitable for units not well trained enough for the more complex maneuvers, or if the commander intended to close to contact after the initial discharge; however, the exposure of the flanks during the wheel must be considered a disadvantage.

In view of the universal condemnation accorded the caracole for the last 350 years, it is necessary to point out the virtues of the tactic. The caracole, as opposed to the cavalry charge with cold steel, was "unaggressive" in that "Instead of relying upon the impact of the mass of man and horse, the cavaliers of western Europe were reduced, in battle, to a debilitated popping of pistols." In the words of Roberts, "...the whole performance was nearly as futile as it was elaborate."[24] that is, it employed weak mounted firepower instead of direct shock. Yet the caracole had struggled against cold steel throughout the 16th century and had come off the victor.

As du Picq, Keegan, Griffith,[25] and others have pointed out, the real force of a cavalry charge is moral, not physical. Sword and lance are inefficient killing instruments; even the most casual exchange of fire will produce more losses than a mounted melee. Cold steel may break and scatter a unit; it will not produce many casualties. Similar considerations governed the replacement of pike by musket.

Charging cavalry do not crash into each other like medieval knights at a tournament. There are, in fact, four main outcomes to a cavalry collision. First, one or the other side will break before contact. The victor may pursue. If the defender withdraws to safety in good order, and the attacker does not pursue, it is simply "bounced." Second, both halt at a distance, often a very short one. They may skirmish, exchange shots, or disengage. Third, the two may open ranks and actually pass through each other, trading swordstrokes in passing. Fourth, the two come together and stop, striking with cold steel. They may even become intermingled in a wild, "Hollywood style" melee. After 5–15 minutes, the loser may break and rout, or both may lose interest and separate. During the 18th and 19th centuries, the first result was by far the most common; the fourth, the least. The situation was somewhat different in 1600. The deep formations favored by Tilly had a double effect on morale. As only 10% of the men were in the first rank, these would be the men least likely to shrink from contact. Further, the multiple ranks behind inhibited withdrawal. As has been pointed out by du Picq and Keegan, in such masses, the men in front *cannot* flee until the men behind do. Second, the heavy armor worn by the first rank made contact rather less dangerous. Thus, the pre-contact rout first case was less common in 1615 than 1815.[26] Similarly, the depth of formations made case three less likely as well (although there were examples). The caracole was predicated on one and two constituting the norm. By the time the aggressor has closed to pistol range, a weaker unit would probably already have broken. If it stood (i.e., case two), a well executed caracole might expect to send a wavering unit over the edge. If it was sufficiently prepared to stand and return fire, then cold steel would probably not have broken it either. Even then, the pistols would inflict loss. If the enemy did waver under fire, the cuirassiers could draw their "armor-smashers" and finish him. The morale impact of arkebusiers was less because they fired at a much longer range: 50 meters as opposed to 10.

The caracole *did* have very real drawbacks. The "moral impact" was less than that of a charge with sword or lance. Troops accustomed to caracole were often reluctant to close (i.e., cases three and four) and could be intimidated by opponents who did. Also the wheeling maneuvers rendered a formation vulnerable to counterattack. On the plus side, a trot was much easier to control than the flat-out gallop. What we may call the "mathematics" of the cavalry charge were not fully worked out until the 19th century, and poorly executed charges were not uncommon. Even after the caracole was discarded, such generals as Conde, Montecuccoli, and Cromwell preferred to trot.

In battle, the bulk of the cavalry was placed on the wings, with some in reserve behind the infantry. Most authorities favored a checkerboard deployment similar to that of the infantry, but Tilly preferred a more solid line, with minimum gaps.

Artillery was deployed as a loose line in front of the foot, with 10–20 meter intervals between guns. There was little effort to coordinate the fire of different guns and no battery organization. There was an overall artillery officer, but his duties were more administrative than operational.

Although they had their political differences, militarily the Imperials and the Catholic Leaguers were as one. Officers often held commissions in both services simultaneously, mixed forces were common, and individual regiments were traded back and forth between the two allies and Spain as well. Friction in Tilly's army was more a product of personal rivalries than interservice feuds or mercenary motivations.

SWEDISH INVASION, 1630

Emperor Ferdinand II had hoped for a general peace settlement 1629–30, but he was outmaneuvered by French diplomacy (under Cardinal Richelieu) and that of his trusted ally, Maximilian of Bavaria. He was forced into a series of concessions of which one, the dismissal of Wallenstein, was intended to restore his dependence on the League, while the other, the Edict of Restitution, alienated the hitherto neutral Protestant moderates, including Johann Georg of Saxony.

On May 11, 1630, Swedish diplomats presented the Imperials with an ultimatum. On July 20, King Gustavus Adolphus landed on the German mainland. On August 24, Wallenstein was dismissed from command. Tilly, suddenly appointed joint commander of both Imperial and League armies, had to bring his scattered forces together while repelling an invasion by the most dangerous of the Protestant armies.

THE MILITARY REFORMS OF GUSTAVUS ADOLPHUS

Gustavus Adolphus has been celebrated as a brilliant innovator, but his true genius lay in synthesizing the best of contemporary practice into a coherent doctrine. Basically, Gustavus combined Maurice of Nassau's idea of a linear, well-trained infantry battalion with the Polish system of shock cavalry charges, modified by his own ideas on firepower and synergistic combination of arms.

His 19th and 20th century admirers were prone to credit Gustavus with virtually every innovation introduced prior to 1800, making him a preview of Frederick or even Napoleon. In fact, of course, he belonged to the 17th century, not the 18th (and early 17th at that). Gustavus Adolphus did *not* abolish the pike, shorten the pike,[27] introduce the bayonet, introduce the paper cartridge,[28] abolish the musket rest,[29] equip all his shot with firelocks,[30] introduce the flintlock, or abolish body armor. He did experiment with uniforms, but not systematically.

Gustavus was interested in the "shock" aspect of battle, as opposed to the attritional. This placed him against the prevailing current of military reform as represented by Maurice; in a sense, he was actually closer to Tilly. But while Tilly clung to traditional formations, Gustavus attempted to adapt the new style to fit his theories. Unlike Maurice, he did not de-emphasize the pike; in theory at least, his regiments had as many pikes as the Catholics. The pike and the musket would no longer play separate roles but work together.

Gustavus believed that rapidity of fire, mobility, and hitting power were more important than range or durability; this was manifested in his new "Gustavan" musket. This was a matchlock about four feet long, weighing 10–11 pounds, with a light stock and a bore of 10 balls to the pound. It did require a rest, and had a rate of fire of about two minutes per shot. It was a departure from both Spanish and Dutch models. The comparatively short barrel increased ease of loading and rate of fire,[31] and the weight was less than that of a normal half musket, yet the heavier ball compensated for loss of impact.

The new musket would have a unique role in the tactical synthesis, a role based on shock rather than attrition. Gustavus devised or borrowed a new idea, the infantry volley. This was an offshoot of the Maurician countermarch. Under the tercio system, each musketeer shot individually, then let the next man fire while he reloaded. Maurice envisioned a formed line of musketeers firing as one, then filing back as a group to let the next line fire. This was more efficient, as it permitted a 10-deep formation to maintain a steady fire (five rounds to the minute). Gustavus carried the idea further: what if not 10% of the shot fired as one, but 33%, 50%, even 100%? What if the shot thinned to 3 ranks depth, and everyone fired at once? The moral shock would be enormous!

This volley system was to prove popular and, when adapted to flintlocks, was to dominate European tactics for 150 years. When employed by matchlocks, it had problems, specifically, the low rate of fire. This was a continuing drawback; the musketeers were defenseless between shots. Later armies divided battalions into from two to four platoons, each firing separately, so that there would always be one ready. This, of course, weakened the volley impact. But to Gustavus, this was no problem; protecting the shot was what pikes were for. If attacked while reloading, the musketeers could shelter behind the pike.

Contrary to myth, the volley was not a more efficient "killing machine" than the countermarch. If anything, it was less: the stress on speed meant no aiming was possible, and the fire of the third rank was largely wasted. Per man accuracy may have been as low as half that of the countermarch,[32] but the whole loss was inflicted in seconds, not spread out over two or three minutes, and it was accompanied by a terrifying roar.[33] The moral impact was greater than the physical damage.

In an ideal "Gustavan" clash, the musketeers would disrupt the enemy with a massed volley, and the pikes would then charge and exploit their confusion, winning the fight with a minimum of attrition. In both attack and defense, pike and shot were to work in coordination.

The king applied these principles to cavalry as well. One of his stranger innovations was to intersperse small detachments of shot, "platoons," between his mounted squadrons. When standing on the defense, the Swedes were to wait until the enemy was within range,[34] then all the musketeers were to volley, along with the pistols of the first two ranks of horse. Then the cavalry would draw their sabers and execute a short, controlled dash, "bouncing" the enemy while they were still disordered from the volley.

On the attack, the cavalry were to draw swords and pistols and launch a flat-out charge at the gallop. This sacrificed the support of the shot and tactical control for greater impetus and moral impact. Because of the scattering and disorder that inevitably resulted, such charges were timed to decide the issue then and there; in any case there should be a reserve line behind to salvage setbacks and exploit successes. The charging units could not be expected to reform for further action; even if they did, they would probably be exhausted.

Pursuant to his emphasis on battlefield combat-power and shock over fire, Gustavus abolished the arkebusiers; all of his cavalry were cuirassiers, expected to charge and strike. This turned out to be premature; his heavier, charge-oriented horse were at a disadvantage in skirmishing. So in 1631, he reorganized his dragoons to fire and fight while mounted as well as afoot, combining the roles of both arkebusiers and dragoon. Gustavus seems to have regarded the armor of the German cuirassiers as too heavy and too variable; his Swedish regulars had more standardized suits of cuirass and helmet over buff coat and high boots. Arm and leg armor was mostly discarded. However, this does not apply to his German cavalry.

The same principles of mobility and speed were applied even to the artillery. Gustavus fancied himself an expert artilleryman, and in fact he was not far short. He could lay a piece as well as a master gunner and had interesting ideas about massed salvos and rapid concentrations of fire—the "shock" of gunfire. However, his influence was less marked than on the other arms. The new Swedish guns were much the same as their Dutch progenitors. Gustavus abolished the 48 pdr full cannon, believing that its lack of mobility and low rate of fire outweighed its superior hitting power. The 24 pdr demicannon was adequate to siege work and could serve on the battlefield as well.[35] The king's approach to siege operations emphasized bluff, storm assaults, and displays of artillery technique, rather than the methodical reduction of defenses of the Dutch-Spanish school (later perfected by Vauban).

Having abolished the "full" cannon, Gustavus standardized his calibers at 24 and 12 pdrs—note that while all the 24 pdrs were demicannon, the 12 pdrs included both demiculverins and quarter-cannon. These were heavy guns, deployed in batteries on the battlefield.

There were minor innovations in their design. Sweden being Europe's chief producer of copper, there were no iron guns. Swedish gunmetal was copper-rich, slightly softer than most. Excess metal was trimmed from the barrels to reduce weight, and lighter carriages, with larger wheels, were used. This reduced durability but allowed greater mobility with fewer horses per gun. Better training and the use of premeasured charges gave the Swedes a higher rate of fire than their opponents. Nevertheless, the differences between the king's guns and the emperor's remained minimal.

Gustavus's better-known invention concerned the ongoing search for the perfect infantry support gun. Gustavus, again, believed that lightness, ease of use, and rapidity of fire outweighed effect as such. His first entry was the infamous "leather gun," a weapon so light that its thin copper tube had to be reinforced with a leather sheath. This weapon saw action in Poland, but its weak firepower rendered it ineffective, and it was abolished. The leather gun as such was *not* used in Germany.[36]

Its replacement was a 3 pdr, the regimental gun,[37] Gustavus's true brainchild. Its short barrel of light copper alloy weighed only 500 pounds; it could be pulled by three men or one horse. Although manned by infantrymen under an assistant gunner, this weapon could, using prepared charges, load and fire "faster than musketeers."[38] Pulled by a single horse, it could keep up with cavalry or detached shot.[39] It could be used effectively—against massed targets—at up to 1000 meters. This gun was the "superweapon" of 1630, its only serious weakness being its fragility.

It is often stated that the regimental gun was intended as a grapeshot-sprayer, like a modern machinegun. This cannot be true, as its effective canister range did not exceed 100 meters. Monro tells us that the regimental guns fired during the preliminary bombardment at Breitenfeld, this was certainly ball. Against an Imperial tercio approaching at 60 meters a minute, the 3 pdr would get off 5 to 10 balls as opposed to one or two charges of grape. Similarly, the assertion that the 3 pdr was good only for 30 shots must be rejected; they fired more than that at Breitenfeld alone, and there is no reason to assume that it wore the guns out. The 30-shot limit refers to canister, which was more likely to damage the bore. The ratio for solid shot would be much higher.

Unlike Maurice, who adapted his tactics to fit his troops, Gustavus decided to redesign his army to fit his tactics. When he came to the throne in 1611, Sweden had no army aside from a few garrisons; the armed forces consisted of semifeudal "noble" cavalry and an infantry militia of conscripted peasants. This was not uncommon; most of the European powers had militias of some kind. These militias were strictly distinguished from the (in theory voluntary) regular or "mercenary" armies in that they could not be required to serve outside their own province.[40] However, Gustavus simply reorganized the peasant militia as a standing army recruited by conscription—the first in Europe. So great was the king's charisma and political acumen that this radical program encountered virtually no opposition. Considering the failure of much milder reforms in England, Spain, France, and Denmark, this must be considered his most remarkable success.

Gustavus's ideas on infantry tactics were incarnated in the "skvadron,"[41] his version of Maurice's infantry battalion. A skvadron consisted of 556 men, 264 officers and pike, 192 battalion musketeers, and 100 detached musketeers.[42] In action, it would form a battalion 76 wide by 6 deep, supported by skirmishers in front. The shallow depth, less than Maurice's 10, was based on the idea that only the first 5 ranks of pike could actually reach the enemy, plus a 6th rank as a reserve. Gustavus believed that thoroughly trained men—like Maurice, he spent a lot of effort in training—could fight as effectively in 6 ranks as less prepared men in 25. Note that he determined an ideal depth by the theoretical limitations of the pike, unlike Maurice who based his formation on the countermarch of the musket. Gustavus's musketeers had two options: they could employ a "Swedish countermarch," actually a hybrid volley, of three fires of 2 ranks each,[43] or they could extend their line, halving their depth to three ranks, and fire as one. This tactical system was reflected in his new model regiment of 1200 men divided into two skvadrons of 600.[44] Unfortunately, Gustavus's units were perennially understrength, so the ratio of two skvadrons per regiment seldom applied—even when the detached shot were added to fill the ranks. Also, this necessity reduced his planned proportion of pikes to shot, boosting firepower at the expense of shock. Finding the individual skvadron too weak to stand up to serious attack, Gustavus hit on the idea of grouping them into "brigades" of three or four battalions. This formation, three battalions in line—the middle one is depicted as slightly forward, like a flattened arrowhead—grouped under the command of a senior colonel, combined the efficiency and firepower of the line with the flexibility of the tercio.[45]

Gustavus established conscription districts in Sweden and Finland corresponding to different regiments. Ideally, new recruits would be dispatched to a garrison battalion in Livonia, where they would learn the basics of drill, and then be sent to a field regiment (of 1200) to fight in battle. Their service completed, the now-experienced veterans would be returned home to form a reserve regiment that could be mustered at need. Thus, each "land-regiment" would incorporate garrison, field, and reserve regiments. Between attrition and the demanding wars, this ideal could not be recognized.

Table 1.6
Gustavan Formations: Theory

3 pdr	100 skir	3 pdr
96 mskt	266 pike	96 mskt
16x6	44x6	16x6
Skvadron (556)		

Horse
125x4
Cav Sqd
(500)

	ll	
ll	mppm	ll
mppm		mppm
Brigade (1668)		

Practice

	3x3pdr	
270 M	200 P	270 M
45x6	37x6	45x6
Mackay & 2 small IR (740)		

Horse
100x4
Smaland CR

	lll	
ll	mpm	ll
mpm	Spens	mpm
Green		Mackay
Green Brigade		

	2 x 3pdr	
154 M	201 P	154 M
26x6	37x6	26x6
Bn of Teuffel IR (509)		

Horse
75x4
Finn Sqd

	ll	
ll	mppm	ll
mpm		mpm
Yellow Brigade (1526)		

P/p Pike; M/m musket; ll two 3 pdr.

Even with excessive conscription, tiny Sweden could not satisfy the king's appetite for infantry; thus, he formed a "mercenary" (i.e., foreign) regular force. The Yellow, Blue, and Red German infantry regiments and the Scottish Green Regiment were the oldest of these. Gustavus expanded his numbers with new, mostly German, enterpriser-type units—these would not have enjoyed the extensive training of his peacetime troops. Gustavus once remarked that German troops with Swedish training actually fought better than Swedes (of course, the Germans were volunteers) and that Sweden would lose little even if "not a bone" returned from Germany. What this meant in practice was that the actual fighting was carried out primarily with Germans, while the Swedish conscript units acted as garrisons, supports, or stiffening. Gustavus's use of conscription was therefore entirely opposite to that of the mass armies of the Napoleonic period. At Breitenfeld, only one of eight brigades was Swedish.

The king's ideas on cavalry paralleled those on infantry. The cavalry would fight in 4-deep squadrons of 500 sabers each.[46] Therefore, his horse would be formed in regiments of 1000, to consist of two squadrons each. The cavalry were the elite of Sweden, the best men the country had, and, after rigorous training, the best battlefield cavalry in the world. Although peerless in formal battle, the Swedish horse sometimes found themselves at a disadvantage in minor actions.

As with the infantry, the cavalry were seldom up to full strength, so that at Breitenfeld most of the cavalry regiments formed a single squadron instead of the theoretical pair. The national horse constituted a much larger proportion of the total cavalry than their infantry counterparts and were always the king's most trusted troops.

Gustavus is credited with being the first to organize his artillery into regular military units. This was less a unique departure than the formalization of Dutch practice, also the crews did not become ordinary soldiers but retained the old "craftsman" ranks of master gunner, gunner, and assistant gunner (or mattross). The new organization, of six companies under Lennart Torstensson, included light and heavy guns, engineers, and miners (sappers). Although Torstensson had administrative control over all the guns, in battle he commanded only the battery guns, while the regimental pieces were seconded to the infantry. These attachments were temporary; the light pieces could be switched around, massed, or detached depending on the mission.

A much-praised reform of Gustavus was to cut the army's baggage to increase strategic mobility, but this was a diminishing asset. As time drew on, his forces were swollen by untrained recruits, and his veterans lost contact with their homes and bases; baggage gradually accumulated. Also, his vaunted lack of impedimenta no doubt aggravated his chronic logistical problems.

The king believed in cooperation among the various weapons, much like modern combined arms doctrine. Not only were pike and shot to work together, but both would be supported by artillery as well. Similarly, the horse would not only be assisted by shot, but would assist the infantry brigades. In any case, Gustavan doctrine called for an infantry center composed of three or four brigades. Each brigade was formed into three battalions (skvadrons), each of which had two regimental guns in support. The heavy guns would be placed in battery in front of the foot. The flanks were made up of cavalry, with 200-man platoons of shot deployed between each squadron. A small body of horse was placed in close reserve behind the infantry, ready to intervene in their support. A second, reserve, line would be positioned some 200 meters behind the first line, a slightly weaker twin. This second echelon would have fewer regimental guns, no heavies at all, and there would be no shot between the squadrons. Unlike the standard checkerboard pattern, both echelons would be fairly solid lines—there were intervals between the brigades. To this extent, Gustavus's battle order prefigured those of the linear period.

GUSTAVUS'S WAR, 1630–32

Upon landing, Gustavus found his initial target, the Baltic provinces of Pomerania and Mecklenburg, held by about 20 Imperial strongpoints, fortified towns, castles, and fortresses. None of them were very strong, and they did not coordinate their defense, but they required a good deal of time and effort. Not until March 1631 was this base area secured. Tilly had chosen to eliminate Gustavus's inland allies first, notably, the town of Magdeburg (fell May 20, 1631). The two generals sparred cautiously at Neu-Brandenburg (March 1631) and Werben (August 1631), but both deemed it too uncertain to risk a major battle. At about the same time, the Protestant moderates under Johann Georg finally made their move, attempting to secure the areas Swabia-Hesse-Saxony. Their raw recruits were scattered by secondary Imperial forces, and Tilly himself marched on Saxony. Reinforced with the Saxons, Gustavus was at last strong enough to meet Tilly in the open. In the subsequent Battle of Breitenfeld (September 17, 1631), Tilly suffered his first and greatest defeat, losing both his veteran army and his reputation.

At a stroke, the Imperial dominion in Germany collapsed. The ebullient Protestants rose up everywhere, while Catholic morale evaporated. Within a couple of months, Gustavus found himself in control of over two-thirds of the Empire. The Swedish armies multiplied, threatening every Catholic district with their now-overwhelming numbers. Tilly did what he could with his weakened forces to slow the Swedish advance, striking back at the minor Action at Bamberg (March 9, 1632), but he was finally defeated and killed by Gustavus at the Battle of the Lech (April 14–16, 1632).

Unfortunately for Gustavus, the Imperials had taken more effective means to restore the balance. Wallenstein had been restored to his former position, with full authority to rebuild and restore the Imperial Army, and Pappenheim had assumed command of Catholic forces in the Westphalia theater.

Almost single-handedly, Pappenheim reversed the situation in northwest Germany, defeating secondary Swedish-Protestant forces in the actions of Madgeburg, Hoxter, Stade, Volksmarsen, 2nd Hoxter, Wolfenbuttel, and Hildesheim. At the same time, Wallenstein was able to hold Gustavus's main army, rebuffing his advances at the Action of Alte Veste (September 1–2, 1632). Gustavus succeeded in catching Wallenstein with his forces divided and in the open at the Battle of Lützen (November 16, 1632). However, the new-style Imperial Army fought the Swedish veterans to a bloody draw, and Gustavus himself was among the dead.

WALLENSTEIN'S NEW IMPERIAL ARMY

The army of Alte Veste and Lützen was radically different from that destroyed at Breitenfeld. Whatever his flaws, Wallenstein was a first-class organizer, and there was no aspect that remained unaffected. Wallenstein tried to assimilate the best of tercio tradition, contemporary theory, and Gustavus's innovations into a workable whole; he succeeded well enough that his new model set the Imperial style for the rest of the war. In a very real sense, it was designed to stand up to Gustavus on his own terms.

The infantry battalion was reduced to 1000, two-thirds musketeers, one-third pike. The depth of the pike was reduced to seven, with three ranks of musketeers in front and the rest in the flanking sleeves, 10-deep. Given 100 officers, the pike block would be roughly 57 wide by 7 deep, the sleeves 21–22 by 10, for a total 100 by 10. This was still deeper than the Swedes, but much shallower than the tercio, with more firepower. "The enemy's army was ordered like ours," commented a Protestant eyewitness.[47] The new battalion maintained the same depth, whether of 1000 or 500, the units adjusting their width proportionately.

Wallenstein was familiar with the volley but, given his 10-deep formation, cannot have relied on it. The post-Wallenstein army seldom used volley fire.

Wallenstein's cavalry reforms were less radical. The squadron depth was set at 6, intermediate between the 8–10 of 1631 and the 4–5 that became standard by 1636. The caracole was now restricted to arkebusiers; cuirassiers were to advance at a steady trot, fire pistols at pointblank, then close with swords.[48] Wallenstein's squadrons were, like Tilly's, quite large, of 500–800 men, one per regiment, and his cuirassiers were as heavily armored. He had no leaders between regiment and wing commander—Holk and Piccolomini acted as ad hoc brigadiers.

Wallenstein's approach to artillery was more systematic than Tilly's but not up to Gustavus's standards. He attached two light guns (2–6 pdr) to each infantry battalion, and his placement of batteries was good, both at Alte Veste and Lützen, but he didn't grasp the use of artillery as a mobile base of fire. He was familiar with the salvo, but at Lützen its value would have been limited.

Wallenstein understood the theory of combined arms, placing his foot, horse, and guns in close mutual support in imitation of Gustavus, but he lacked the king's knack of coordinating them in practice.

THE SWEDES WITHOUT GUSTAVUS, 1633–35

Although the king's unexpected death left the Swedes grossly overextended and divided in command, this was counterbalanced by Wallenstein's growing insanity and unfitness to command. Despite a major mutiny in the Swedish army, the Swedes and Imperials fought out 1633 on even terms. The solitary Imperial success at Steinau (October 10, 1633) was outweighed by Swedish victories of Oldendorf (July 8, 1633) and Pfaffenhofen (August 11, 1633). Wallenstein being killed by his own troops after a bungled coup, Imperial command devolved onto Gallas. Imperial strategy in 1634 took advantage of the Swedes' weakness and the support of a major Spanish army under the Cardinal Infante and Leganes. Despite initial Swedish successes, the actions of Liegnitz (May 8, 1634) and Landshut (July 22, 1634), the Imperial counteroffensive threatened to shatter the Protestant alliance. Quarreling co-commanders Horn and Bernhard Sax-Weimar agreed to attack the combined Imperial-Spanish-Bavarian army with a smaller force. The resultant defeat, the Battle of Nordlingen (September 6, 1634), proved as disastrous to the Swedish cause as Breitenfeld had been to the Imperials. An Imperial diplomatic offensive, cumulating in the Peace of Prague (May 30, 1635), brought Saxony and most of the German moderate Protestants into the anti-Swedish alliance. The anti-Hapsburg forces were reduced to Sweden and Hesse-Cassel. Unwilling to see Austria victorious, France entered the war (May 21, 1635), beginning the French-Swedish phase (1636–48).

THE STRATEGIC CONSTRAINTS

A typical campaign year would begin with the opposing armies breaking quarters in March or April; the side that went first would gain the initiative, but starting too soon would entail logistical drawbacks. The two sides would spend several months feeling each other out with skirmishes and outposts. After a while in contact, the generals would realize which side was stronger and which weaker. The weaker side would assume a defensive posture; the stronger, the offensive. In general, the offensive army would be trying to advance into enemy territory, to capture enemy strongpoints, and to force the defenders to accept battle at a disadvantage. The weaker army would attempt to minimize enemy gains and to offer battle only when holding counterbalancing advantages of position and entrenchments. As mobility was inversely related to strength, the weaker army would normally be able to retreat more quickly and avoid undesired battle (unless surprised). It might become necessary to accept risks to defend friendly territory. Before a battle, the aggressive general would evaluate the strength of the defender's position and adjudge whether his army was capable of attacking it successfully. If not, he would not attack. These professional evaluations were generally right, and the attacking side normally won the battle.

Table 1.7
Selected Battles, 1620–48

Block	Siege	Retreat	Surprise
White Mountain	Oldendorf	Wiesloch	Heiligenhofen
Wimpfen	1st Nordlingen	Hochst	Lützen
Fleurus	Rheinfelden	Stadtlohn	Tuttlingen
Bamberg	Rocroi	Lutter	Mariendorf
1st Lech		1st Breitenfeld	
Pfaffenhofen		Zusmarshausen	
Steinau			
Wimpfen			
Freiburg			
Jankow			
2nd Nordlingen			

Whether or not a battle was fought, operations were broken off in November or December, and both sides would retire into winter quarters. Sieges might be

prolonged into the winter. Battles, and many lesser actions as well, tended to fall into four categories:
(1) the defender had assumed a defensive position in order to block an advance; (2) the defender was attempting to relieve a fortress under siege; (3) the defender was attempting to retreat; (4) the defender was surprised.

Strategy in the Thirty Years War differed from both that of the linear period and that of the Napoleonic period in vital respects. There is no greater error than to concoct Napoleonic concepts into a "true" or "universal" strategy and to judge other eras by their adherence to this supposed norm. There were major differences in scale, logistics, and fortification, and these differences dominated the way that generals went about waging their wars.

The armies of 1618–48 were necessarily smaller than those of 1660–1780 or those of 1790–1820. A typical army of 1620 was set at 25,000—20,000 foot and 5000 horse—as opposed to 50,000–100,000 for the linear period and 100,000–200,000 for the Napoleonic. In the 1640s, 20,000—10,000 foot and 10,000 horse—was more common. This upward limit was logistically inflexible: while larger concentrations could be achieved for a few days or a week, it was impossible to maintain them over an extended period.[49] This lesser scale had an important impact on operations. Comparatively small countries like Bavaria, Denmark, and Sweden could meet the Great Powers of Europe on near-even terms. Siege operations were more difficult and chancier. Large armies, like Gustavus's of 1632, were split up into smaller, logistically viable forces, each fighting a local war in a limited theater, with little possibility of overall coordination.

Prior to the development of the railroad, armies were supported by local supply and stored reserves. This applies to *all* forces, ancient, medieval, 17th century, linear, and Napoleonic. Land transportation was slow and awkward; it was a fortunate commander who could utilize ships to transport his stores to his armies. Linear armies were well supplied by prestocked magazines and the establishment of field bakeries at regular intervals, but this was at the expense of flexibility.[50] Napoleonic armies employed both magazines and foraging, gaining mobility at the expense of security. The armies of the Thirty Years War relied almost exclusively on local supply, what was called "kontribution."[51]

The concept of "kontributions" was as important to Thirty Years War logistics as foraging to Napoleon or supply lines to Patton. Kontribution is defined as "a cross of traditional estate-approved war taxes (contributions) with what the Germans call *Brandschatzung*…a ransom paid for property that could be looted and burned under the existing laws of war."[52] that is, a cross between taxation and extortion. Kontribution represented a synthesis of taxes paid in kind, tax deductions for supplies given to the army, quartering of troops, property ransoms in enemy territory, living off the enemy's land, and pay deductions to cover food supplies.

In 16th century theory, a soldier would receive a recruitment bonus when he joined the army, from which he was expected to supply his own weapons and equipment. He was thereafter entitled to a monthly wage that had to cover his food, clothing, and necessities. During the Eighty Years War (1567–1648), both the Spanish and the Dutch found it desirable to supply food directly to the troops and deduct the cost from their pay. Food supplied by communities was applied against their tax liability. Raiders would "tax" enemy-held areas for cash and goods.

During the early part of the Thirty Years War, neither side had enough money to pay their troops, and the soldiers were forced to plunder for mere subsistence in friendly, enemy, and neutral territory alike. It may have been Tilly who first set this looting on a systematic basis. Finding himself operating in areas that could neither be defined as clearly friendly nor actively hostile, Tilly advised the local authorities that if they supplied specified amounts of food to his army, he would grant "safeguards" against casual looting. In friendly territory, the supplies would be deducted from their taxes (contributions); in neutral areas, they fulfilled their obligation to support the emperor's troops, and hostiles who paid wouldn't be burned out. Under Tilly's system, the food would count for one-third the soldier's pay, the remainder to be paid in cash. As his army was relatively small, about 20,000–30,000 men, and he was at that time receiving regular subsidies from the Catholic League, Tilly's system worked well in practice.

In 1624, Tilly occupied the hostile Landgraviate of Hesse-Cassel. Having some idea of passive resistance, the ruling landgrave ordered his subjects not to cooperate. Tilly's men were, however, able to force compliance on a local basis, showing that kontributions could be levied without legal sanction.

In 1625, the Imperial Generalissimo Wallenstein devised a more lucrative system of kontribution. As the emperor's treasury was empty, kontributions would be levied to cover both subsistence and wages. Kontributing communities would be liable for both food and money. As Wallenstein's army exceeded 100,000 men, these demands inflicted considerable hardship over a wide area. Under the Wallenstein system, food was considered to be worth one-half the soldier's pay, the other half being owed in cash.

Not surprisingly, Gustavus Adolphus was at the same time developing a very similar approach. Under Gustavus's system, kontributions in food were issued to the troops as subsistence; they were counted as one-half their owed wage. Kontributions in cash were used to recruit more soldiers. The owed cash wages were "deferred" to a later date when all the arrears would be paid in full. Kontributions were levied on the king's authority in friendly, enemy, and neutral regions alike.[53]

By the late 1630s, the ability of the countryside to support the war had declined. Every commander levied such kontributions as he could, with little regard for the overall situation or political niceties. Food could be reckoned at as much as two-thirds of the wage; the dwindling cash portion was subject to deductions for clothing and arms. Many troops "did not know what pay was"; that is, they had received no cash subsequent to their recruitment bonuses.[54] However, as long as kontributions supplied food, the armies were able to keep fighting. By the same token, it was impossible to campaign in areas incapable of maintaining the armies. Therefore, a theater had to be logistically viable. This attention to kontribution potential has led certain historians to deride Thirty

Years War operations as "stomach strategy," as opposed to the supposedly purer strategy of a Frederick or a Napoleon. The limitation imposed by fortifications is perhaps the most difficult to grasp. It was possible for Napoleon to win a "decisive" battle and overrun whole nations, detaching small corps to screen the few fortresses obstructing him. It was possible for Frederick to conquer a province with two or three sieges. This was never an option for Tilly or Gustavus.

The strongpoints of 1620–48 Germany were formidable in their numbers, rather than their defenses. When Frederick the Great invaded Silesia, there were about half a dozen fortresses opposing him and perhaps a dozen more in the rest of Austria. When Napoleon invaded Germany in 1806, there were about two dozen fortresses in the whole country. These were modern Vauban-type fortresses, each capable of withstanding siege. In 1630, there were only a few places in Germany comparable to the superfortresses of Holland and Flanders — Ingolstadt, Breisach, Stade, Philipsburg. But there were many places of secondary and tertiary strength. A record from 1648 gives the anti-Hapsburg alliance no fewer than 222 garrisoned strongholds in Germany.[55] Given those held by Austria, Bavaria, Saxony, neutrals, and local forces, the grand total would be 400–500. But this was probably not the wartime high. Every important target had defenses. Any attempt to sweep past the enemy defenses, Napoleon-style, in search of a nonexistent soft rear area would thrust the army into the middle of a network of hostile garrisons, with no available supply or effective mobility. Sound strategy required the isolation or reduction of enemy garrisons in an area before advancing through it.

By the same token, battles could not be "decisive" in the sense of an Austerlitz, a Jena, or a Waterloo. No matter how total the defeat, the enemy could retire into his fortified heartland and rebuild. This was accentuated by the relative isolation of the centers of power, France, Spain, Holland, Austria, Sweden, from the theaters of war. No degree of Imperial success could actually force Sweden to surrender, as it was protected by the Baltic. On the other hand, the increasing exposure of Austria to attack in the last years of the war was undoubtedly a factor in the final peace settlement. These considerations did not protect the minor powers in the same way: Bohemia was overthrown by a single "decisive" battle; the Palatinate was simply conquered, and Denmark, Saxony, and Bavaria were all, at some point, forced to accept harsh terms.

When Gustavus landed in Germany in 1630, he was confronted by a dozen garrisons, ranging from outposts to fairly strong places, along the Baltic coast alone. It was more difficult for him to reduce the tiny province of Pomerania than for Frederick to conquer Silesia or for Napoleon to overrun all Prussia.

THE EVOLUTION OF WEAPONS, 1630–48

Throughout the 16th century, the proportion of pike to shot had been gradually shifting in favor of the shot, as firearms became more effective on the one hand, and pike formations less willing to melee on the other. The ratio in 1618–29 fluctuated between 1:1 and two muskets per pike. The Gustavan phase, 1631–32, saw a radical increase in the proportion of firearms; at Lützen some of

Gustavus's brigades were more than 80% musket. This, however, seems to have marked a high point. The fact was, shot unsupported by pike were virtually helpless against cavalry, so the abandonment of the pike in 1632 was premature.[56] There seems to have been a sort of pike revival after 1634. Montecuccoli, writing in 1641, states that the ratio of pike to shot was 1:2, which matches the regulations of the Imperial Army at the time, but that a higher proportion of pike was desirable in battalions.[57] As late as 1687, Vauban set the proportion of pike in the shot-oriented French Army at 20–25%[58]

The pike itself was changing. The original 18-foot length had been intended to give an advantage over the 11-foot lances of the 16th century gendarmes. But heavy lancers had virtually disappeared by 1600. After 1635, the pike began to shrink, dwindling to 13–14 feet by 1680.

The decline of body armor ran parallel to that of the pike. As hand-to-hand fighting and the push of pike grew uncommon, and the danger from fire increased, armor became less and less "cost-effective." By 1660, infantry body armor had disappeared, even for pikemen. Among cavalry, who retained the use of cold steel, helmet and breastplate were considered useful up to the end of the 19th century.

In his "Swedish musket," Gustavus had tried to maintain a balance between rate of fire and hitting power, but it proved merely another stage in the diminution of the musket. The half musket, of 14–15 caliber, enjoyed a brief vogue; it was sufficiently light that a strong man could fire it without a rest. But the overall trend was toward smaller weapons (caliber 16–20) that anyone could fire freely. The last matchlocks (ca. 1660) were the same size as the flintlocks that succeeded them. The absurd catchphrase that musketeers "abandoned the rest after Breitenfeld" is a misunderstanding of this evolution.

The *fusil*, believed to be the first true flintlock,[59] began to appear in France and Italy around 1610–30. Like all flintlocks, it was of the smaller type without a rest. This early version saw service, along with snaphances, in the Dutch Army, and was used in significant numbers by the French. However, its advantage in rate of fire was largely negated by the 5–8-deep formations still in use. The flintlock did not show its true superiority until the introduction of the 3-deep battalion line and the platoon volley system (ca. 1685).[60] The reduction in misfires, from about 20% to 10%, was a minor advantage of the flintlock over the matchlock.[61]

The pike was able to survive, despite its declining popularity, simply because musketeers on their own could not effectively defend themselves from cavalry. The period 1635–70 saw a number of experiments to overcome this flaw, including arming musketeers with boar spears, swine-feathers, and caltrops. Around 1640, the French started to use the plug bayonet, a development of an old hunter's trick of placing a knife in the musket muzzle to improvise a spear. It saw some popularity, but the fact that a musketeer could not fire while the bayonet was readied greatly limited its use. In 1687, Vauban introduced the socket bayonet, dooming the pike. The bayonet was a poor weapon, inferior to the pike in every respect, but it provided a means whereby shot could defend itself from cavalry. The pike, long in disfavor, was no longer needed and had effectively disappeared, except as a ceremonial arm for cadre, by 1720.

APPENDIX A: CURRENCIES OF THE WAR

The chief currencies in use at the time were the (silver) florin (of 20 groschens or 60 kreuzers; kr) and the (silver) taler or Reichstaler (90 kr). The Austrian gulden was interchangeable with the florin (not to be confused with the gold florin, the Italian florin, or the Flanders florin). The taler was equal to the Danish rigsdaler and the Swedish rixdaler (which were not the same as ordinary dalers). Other important foreign moneys were the Dutch guilder, equal to 60% of a florin, and the French livre, which was 60% of a florin in 1630 but had dropped to a half by 1640.

Spanish finances were based on the real, equal to 10 kr. The Spanish unit was variously called the escudo, the ducat (not to be confused with the Venetian or Hungarian ducats), or the ducado and was worth, depending on context, 10, 11, or 12 reales. Some prefer to dub the 10 real unit the escudo and the 11 the ducat, but this is anachronistic.

Table 1.8
Values in Kreuzer (kr)

Florin = 60 kr	Guilder = 36 kr
Gulden = 60 kr	Livre = 30–36 kr
Taler = 90 kr	Rigsdaler = 90 kr
"Escudo" = 100 kr	Rixdaler = 90 kr
"Ducat" = 110 kr	Venetian Ducat = 88 kr
"Ducado" = 120 kr	Hungarian Ducat = 180 kr
Flemish florin = 40 kr	English pound = 400 kr

NOTES

1. A few of these old microstates—Monaco, San Marino, Andorra—survive to this day.
2. Although the trend was running in favor of standing armies and nation-states; the last successful old style revolt in Western Europe was the Portuguese secession of 1640.
3. From an 18th century joke by Voltaire.
4. It was a pleasant feature of the religious quarrels of Germany that outright massacres were rare. As Germany was divided between all three religions, the offending minority was simply persuaded to move to another territory.
5. Of course, they were Lutheran themselves and probably involved. Certainly they would have shared the fears of their violent compatriots.
6. Bavaria had eliminated its own Protestants in the 1560s and had replaced the Hapsburgs as defenders of Catholicism in Germany.
7. He does not seem to have actually expelled them; at least Donauwerth was still mostly Protestant in 1632.
8. The Empire was administratively divided into 10 "circles," each headed by the most prominent member.
9. Although headed by a Calvinist, most of the members were Lutherans. Insofar as that goes, not all Calvinists were extremists; some were even pro-Imperial.
10. This was free or royal Hungary, consisting of less than a third of the kingdom. Hungary proper was ruled by the Ottoman Turks, while Protestant Transylvania maintained some autonomy.
11. A rough population estimate would be 600,000 for Upper and Lower Austria; 2 million for Inner Austria and the Tyrol; less than 1 million for Hungary, and upwards of 3

million for Bohemia. But see Geoffrey Parker, *The Thirty Years' War* (London: Routledge, 1984), p. 4, for a slightly different count.

12. This could lead to some odd situations; at one point the French were assisting Dutch Calvinists against Spain while waging war against their own Calvinist minority.

13. The present study covers only the last phase, but see William P. Guthrie, *Battles of the Thirty Years War* (Westport, CT: Greenwood, 2002).

14. The sword-and-buckler of the 16th century had by this time almost disappeared.

15. Modern-day critics contend that no smoothbore can fire accurately at ranges exceeding 150 meters, but the effect of individual inaccuracy is reduced when the target is a mass 100 men wide and 50 deep. According to Sir Roger Williams, the heaviest muskets could be employed effectively at over 500 yards.

16. The same applies to *all* equipment.

17. Thus the expression "Push of pike and butt of musket."

18. Referring to cuirassiers in general and KUR regiments in particular.

19. So contemporaries thought; modern ballistics experts disagree.

20. Unfortunately, the weight of a "pound" varied from country to country and region.

21. In the 16th century, the pike battalion was often square, with four equal blocks of shot at each corner. This practice was considered obsolete by 1600.

22. As sleeves were worn on the sides of the "body" of pike.

23. Hence the assertion that matchlock muskets required a 6-foot frontage.

24. Michael Roberts, *Gustavus Adolphus: A History of Sweden 1611–1632*, vol. 2 (London: Longmans, 1958), p. 179–80.

25. C.J.J.J. Ardant du Picq, *Battle Studies* (Mechanicsburg, PA: Stackpole, 1958), pp. 179–96; John Keegan, *The Face of Battle* (New York: Vinetage, 1977), pp. 144–50; Paddy Griffith, "Cavalry Melees," *Courier*, vol. 6, no. 6, p. 20; Rory Muir, *Tactics and the Experience of Battle in the Age of Napoleon* (New Haven: Yale University Press, 1998), pp. 113–37.

26. Which is *not* to say that it never happened; the difference is between as much as 50% of cases for Napoleon as opposed to perhaps 25% for Tilly.

27. His regulations set the pike at 17.5 feet, as opposed to 16–18 for Wallenstein.

28. He conducted tests with paper cartridges, but they were expensive for common use.

29. The Swedish army retained the rest into the 1690s.

30. The "Gustavan" or "Swedish" musket was a matchlock.

31. Of course, no matchlock was really easy or fast.

32. The 19th century Prussian kriegspiel made the first two ranks 70% and the third nil.

33. If, as was preferred, the volley was held until pointblank range, the accuracy differential would be less.

34. 50–100 meters. The phrase "don't fire until you see the whites of their eyes" was Gustavus's; C.R.L. Fletcher, *Gustavus Adolphus* (New York: Capricorn, 1963), p. 190.

35. Gustavus's decision was justified by the relative weakness of German fortresses. Had he been campaigning in Flanders, things might have been different.

36. Imperial humorists suggested that the guns had been eaten by the hungry Swedes!

37. That is, a gun used in direct support of an infantry regiment, rather than as battery.

38. One shot per two minutes in sustained fire or double that in a crisis. Gustavus was unable to address the more technical aspects limiting his artillery, such as lack of an elevating screw. A 3 pdr of 1800 would have had at least five times this rate of fire.

39. Cavalry at a walk; the gun crew was on foot. This was the ideal; at Breitenfeld, 29 of the 3 pdrs were drawn by one horse, twelve by two, and one beauty required seven!

40. Militiamen as individuals could be, and often were, conscripted into regular forces.

41. This terminology was unique to Gustavus. More usually, an infantry unit was called a "battalion," and the term "squadron" was reserved for a cavalry formation.

42. These might be used as skirmishers, as forlorns, or placed with the cavalry.

43. Or six of one. Gustavus used an advancing countermarch, each new line 10 paces in front of the last.

44. The theoretical total of 1200 applied to royal regiments, like the Swedes or the elite Yellow and Blue infantry regiments. Most of his infantry were raised by enterprisers, and were allowed up to 14 "dead pays" per company. Thus a regiment might muster only 1088 at full strength.

45. This idea was too far ahead of its time.

46. Like Tilly and unlike Maurice, Gustavus favored a large squadron, although his were shallower than either Dutch or Catholic ones.

47. Roberts, *Gustavus Adolphus*, p. 253, n. 1.

48. See Montecuccoli's remarks in Thomas Barker, *The Military Intellectual and Battle* (Albany, NY: SUNY Press, 1975), pp. 108–09, 146–47; also Brent Nosworthy, *The Anatomy of Victory* (New York, NY: Hippocrene, 1990), pp. 121–22.

49. Most notoriously, Gustavus's 1632 concentration at Nuremberg. Of his original 45,000, 11,000 disappeared over a two-week period. Logistics were rather better in the Flanders theater, and both Dutch and Spanish fielded armies in the 30,000–35,000 range.

50. The exemplar being the "five march system." Even linear armies relied on "green forage" for their horseflesh. It seems that the larger size of the linear armies made it impossible for them to subsist on local supply even if they had wanted to, see John A. Lynn, *Feeding Mars* (Boulder, CO: Westview, 1993), pp. 140–43.

51. Dutch, Spanish, and French armies made use of magazines and hired contractors to supply bread to the field forces. This worked well in the narrow Flanders theater, less so elsewhere. This was undoubtedly the origin of the later magazine system.

52. Fritz Redlich, *The German Military Enterpriser and his Work Force* (Wiesbaden: Steiner, 1964), p. 149.

53. Hence his famous maxim, "War must support war."

54. Redlich, *Enterpriser*, pp. 483–514. Note that a recruitment bonus was always cash.

55. There were 127 Swedish, 52 French, and 43 Hessian, see Parker, *Thirty Years War*, pp. 154, 267.

56. However, King Christian of Denmark is credited with abolishing the pike as early as 1630. Christian seems to have been motivated by the utility of firearms in sieges.

57. Barker, *Military Intellectual*, pp. 104–06. His ideal army numbered 17,024 shot to 7120 pike, a firearm proportion of 70%, but this does not seem to include officers and NCOs, which would increase the number of pike.

58. John A. Lynn, *Giant of the Grand Siècle, The French Army, 1610–1715* (Cambridge: Cambridge University Press, 1997), p. 457.

59. There were a number of minor changes before it assumed its final form by 1700.

60. The paper cartridge, although known as early as the 16th century, was not widely adopted until the 18th, for what we would call reasons of cost-effectiveness. It is *not* true that cartridges halve the loading time of a smoothbore; it is more a matter of shaving 5–10 seconds. For a flintlock with a rate of fire of two shots per minute, the use of paper cartridges could increase it to three, a very respectable gain of 50%. For a matchlock with a rate of two shots in five minutes, the gain was a meager 7%, which did not justify the higher cost.

61. The developed flintlock musket of 1680–1720 had a rate of fire (by trained men) of not quite two rounds a minute. After the introduction of paper cartridges and the iron ramrod, the rate improved to three rounds per minute, where it remained until the smoothbore was replaced by the rifle.

2

Baner's War and the Battle of Wittstock

The disaster of Nordlingen and consequent Peace of Prague effectively eliminated the Protestant alliance as a vehicle of Swedish power. Those German officers in Swedish service divided, some sticking with Sweden (e.g., Vitzthum, Pfuhl), some following the princes in switching to the emperor (Sperreuter), and some joining Bernhard's independent "Weimarian" army (Taupadel, the Rhinegrave). The situation in the south collapsed: Bernhard's little army got the "bums' rush" from Frankfort and survived in Alsace only by joining the French. Duke Georg's defection swung Westphalia firmly into the Imperial camp, and that of Saxony and Brandenburg had a similar effect in the northeast. Baner found himself the sole Swedish bastion amid general dissolution.

Even in Sweden there were those who favored peace—after all, they argued, the dangers that had seemed so real in 1630, the destruction of German Protestantism and the loss of the Baltic, were removed. The emperor had renounced his menacing ambitions, and the Germans whom they were supposed to be rescuing had abandoned them. But peace would require disgorging their German conquests and with them their own wider claims. Gustavus was dead, but his lieutenant, Chancellor Oxenstierna, now ruled in Stockholm; he would not abandon the dream of a Baltic empire. The war continued, no longer a struggle of idealism and religion, Protestant against Catholic, but a campaign of loot and conquest, Protestant Sweden and Catholic France against Germans of both faiths.

FM Baner, formerly the least of the king's paladins, now found himself supreme representative of Sweden in Germany. Baner's attitudes differed radically from those of Gustavus or even Horn, and conditions had changed equally radically. It is clear in retrospect that the period between Breitenfeld and Nordlingen, 1631–4, represented a sort of interregnum or transition between the early war, dominated by Tilly's tercios, and the late war now unfolding.

BANER'S ART OF WAR

The "late war" style was not solely attributable to Baner, as parallel evolutions mark Bernhard's army and the Imperial forces. In part, these changes represent the assimilation of Gustavus's reforms; in part, their adaptation into usable form; in part, reversion to previous ideas, and, perhaps most of all, the continuation of trends that the king had tried to resist or modify. Both Tilly and Gustavus had opposed the tendency toward firepower dominance, Tilly by his emphasis on massive units, shock, and morale, Gustavus by his attempts to fuse gun, musket, pike, and saber into a combined arms attack. Able as they were, both failed to arrest the trend.

Baner's break with his mentor is most conspicuous in basic tactics. When Gustavus had adapted the small, Dutch-style battalion, he had cautiously grouped them into large brigades of 1500–2000 men, a counterweight to massive tercios and superior cavalry. But by 1636, the tercio was dead,[1] and the Swedes could count on superior cavalry. The late king had envisioned a synergistic coordination of pike and musket, the musketeers disrupting the enemy with devastating volleys as preparation for the pike charge. The action would be decided by push of pike and butt of musket.

Baner and his contemporaries fell into the trap of regarding fire alone as the (infantry) battle-winner. Pikes were merely a support, a moral stiffening, at best a protection against horse or hostile pikes. Each pikeman in line was a potential musketeer wasted. Fast-loading smallarms and volley fire were merely better methods for killing the enemy, not preparation for hand-to-hand combat. Baner's new brigade/regiment has been described as two of Gustavus's old battalion/skvadrons put together, but this is misleading. The new formation was simply a double-sized battalion, 700–1000 strong; it moved and fought as a single unit, pike in the center, shot on both wings, a single line of 5 or 6 ranks. Aside from the "Gustavan" depth, it more closely resembled the earlier Dutch or German Protestant battalions. It was also very close to the "new style" Imperial battalions devised by Wallenstein, except that the Imperials retained the tercio practice of placing several ranks of shot in front of the pike (see Table 2.1).

Table 2.1
Infantry Formations

180 shot 18x10	102 shot 34x3 238 pike 34 x 7	180 shot 18x10		216 shot 36x6	218 pike 36x6	216 shot 36x6
Imperial Brigade (700)				Saxon Brigade (650)		

296 shot 49x6	300 pike 50x6	296 shot 49x6		284 shot 47x6	288 pike 48x6	284 shot 47x6
Swede Brigade (892)				Blue Brigade (856)		

The impact on cavalry tactics was at once less radical and longer lasting, that is, the division of regiments into uniform squadrons as tactical units. The squadron unit can be traced back to the Middle Ages, but now appeared the developed "linear" form, which was to survive right up to the World War I. Use of squadrons of 100–300 men, 6 to 10 ranks deep, had been a staple of the Spanish-Dutch "Flanders" systems, but more battle-oriented commanders, like Henry of Navarre or Tilly, preferred to employ large, cohesive units comprising whole regiments, 300–500 strong or more. Gustavus seems to have inclined the same way, envisioning units of 500 sabers, 4 deep. He made very limited use of squadrons. At Breitenfeld, 13 of 18 regiments fought as units, and only 5 divided. At Lützen, only 1 regiment of 27 was split up, but most of the regiments were already very small. At Wittstock, by way of contrast, 20 of 30 regiments were divided into squadrons, and 7 of the remaining 10 were squadron-sized, 150–175. At 2nd Breitenfeld all of the cavalry regiments were so split, and at Jankow, 21 of 26. A parallel pattern appears among the Imperials. Croats aside, there were no squadrons at Breitenfeld or Lützen, but at Wittstock, at least 6 of 17 cavalry regiments are divided, at 2nd Breitenfeld 14 of 30, and at Jankow 13 of 14. Much the same is true of Saxons, Bavarians, and Weimarians.

The ideal squadron was 50–60 files, so a 3-rank Swedish squadron should run 150–180, and the 4- to 5-rank Imperials, 200–300.[2] In practice there was still much variation, more than in later periods, with room for idiosyncratic judgment and personal choices by generals and colonels. Strength and quality were factors; an unreliable unit might be formed deeper and stronger, while a trusted one might be spread thinly or split into tiny "squadronettes." Baner's squadrons at Wittstock varied from 112 to 250, Hatzfeld's from 104 to 454 (?). At Jankow, the Swedish squadrons ran 112–312.

The new smaller, thinner squadrons were optimized for the cavalry charge. Gustavus had hesitated between two concepts; while using the true charge, such as Baner's counterattack at Breitenfeld, he was aware of the loss of control involved. Thus, he also employed a more passive arrangement whereby horse were supported by musket detachments and countered the enemy advance with short, controlled rushes.[3] Baner's preference for the charge led to the decline of musket support. The Imperials also adopted the shock attack, but, fearing loss of control, they charged at the trot, rather than the gallop. The relative merits of different paces became a European controversy, gallop, fast trot, and slow trot. The Swedes and their pupils, the English Royalists, favored the gallop. Cromwell conquered Britain using the slow trot but then switched to the charge. The French were divided, Turenne favoring the gallop, Conde and Luxembourg the trot. The Imperials were torn between fast and slow trots. Montecuccoli implied that heavy horse should advance at a slow trot to maintain control but that they should speed up just before contact.[4]

At the slow trot, pistols were discharged at pointblank just prior to contact, whereas the charge relied on cold steel, pistols being used only as melee weapons. The fast trot fell between, some firing before impact, others strictly forbidding the use of firearms.[5]

The new, shallower formations contributed to the decreased "steadiness" of cavalry. After 1632, it became increasingly common for units being charged to break prior to contact. This phenomenon came as an unpleasant surprise; the dissolution of Hofkirchen at Brandeis and Puchheim at 2nd Breitenfeld were major scandals. By 1690, such outcomes were unremarked, even commonplace. At the same time, the infantry, now deployed in shallow lines and deprived of their pikes, were increasingly vulnerable to cavalry, particularly on their narrowed flanks.[6]

During the period 1636–48, Gustavus's notion of fast, fragile artillery was gradually abandoned in favor of slower, sturdier types, but it is not clear whether this was deliberate policy or simply failure to replace Gustavan pieces as they wore out. Neither Baner nor Bernhard was a notable artilleryman, but Baner's successor, Torstensson, was to prove the most effective gunner of the war. Both sides imitated the king's artillery tactics, heavy pieces in battery with light guns as infantry support, but with decreasing skill and effectiveness.

These tactical changes were matched by shifts on the strategic level. From the first, the armies had survived primarily by foraging. In the realest possible sense, the men lived off the country. However, the war itself was destroying its own logistical underpinnings by devastating the German economy. Up until 1631, fighting had been confined to comparatively limited areas. Thus, while Bohemia was devastated by 1620, the Rhineland by 1622, and Westphalia by 1626, the bulk of the Empire remained relatively intact. When fighting shifted to a new theater, the ruined province had time to recover. In 1632, Gustavus's "Grand Strategy" launched simultaneous offensives in a dozen fronts. Armies and Imperial counter-armies were scattered from the Alps to the Baltic. The king's victory program for 1632 called for 200,000 men; he actually fielded about 150,000. Wallenstein's second armada boasted 102,000. Had Gustavus conquered, it would have been a brilliant masterstroke. Failed, it was an Empire-wide ruination.

Not coincidentally, 1633 saw the first logistical disaster, the collapse of Holk's army in Saxony. Thereafter, Germany was in a state of continuously worsening desolation. The destruction of the civilian economy translated to military hardship. Pay rates declined, when the troops were paid at all. Rations deteriorated in both quantity and quality. The armies shrank in size—an average army of 1636–48 ran about 10,000–15,000, although this was somewhat offset by the practice of combining two or three armies for major battles. As the capacity of the countryside to support the men declined, the soldiers became increasingly brutal and merciless plunderers—and they had been no choirboys to begin with!

The ruin of so much of Germany led to a new emphasis on logistics, as commanders had to anticipate the current capacity of target regions to support operations. Errors, like those of Gallas in Lorraine and, later, Denmark, could "wreck" an army. Only commanders who could adapt to these circumstances—men like Baner, Torstensson, Turenne, Piccolomini, Montecuccoli, and Mercy—could hope for success.

Nineteenth century historians were to sneer at such concerns as "stomach strategy," alleging that mere subsistence had superseded war aims, a drastic degeneration from Gustavus. True strategy, they contended, lay in the elegant aggression of a Frederick the Great or Napoleon.

This is not particularly useful. "Stomach strategy" represented a long-drawn-out attritional approach. Major battles became less "decisive" as logistics and maneuver limited gains and losses; but it was rare for commanders to lose sight of "national" goals. The aim of strategy is winning the war, not impressing future historians with flashy operational victories. The extended duration of the final stage of the war was due not to faulty strategy so much as to the balance between the opponents, the growing importance of defensive strongholds, and sudden reversals of fortune. For all its "Napoleonic sweep," Gustavus's 1632 strategy ended in failure. Adroit use of stomach strategy enabled such men as Baner (in 1637) and Piccolomini (in 1640 and 1645) to avert apparently certain defeat. Of course, it must be kept in mind that whatever its purely military virtues, stomach strategy was invariably disastrous for the unfortunate civilians inhabiting the theaters of war.

Baner's army of 1636 was separated by only five years from Gustavus's heroes, but it was an altogether different creature. How much of this was due to the changed political situation, how much to Baner's character, and how much to the necessities of stomach strategy? After the Peace of Prague and the resolution of religious differences, most of Germany, Catholic and Protestant alike, had rallied around the emperor. Stripped of its religious pretensions, the Swedish cause stood revealed as naked ambition: plunder and conquest. Aside from a few exiles and fanatics, most of whom joined Bernhard, the German "anti-Imperials" were purely mercenaries. Those who remained with Baner—and they made up 70% of his army—were the dregs. The situation was aggravated by Baner's command policies. After the collapse of 1635, the Swedes distrusted all Germans as potential defectors and excluded them from senior rank. Aside from Vitzthum, who had remained "loyal," and Baner's brother-in-law, Pfuhl, there were no longer any German generals. This greatly benefited the Scots in Swedish service. Of eight generals at Wittstock, three were Swedes, four Scots, and only one German. Baner deliberately encouraged dissension between his subordinates, down to individual regiments. The army had become a nation of nomads with two or three camp followers for every soldier. Baner regarded his "nation" with distrust and contempt; they responded with mingled fear and loathing.

Gustavus's army has enjoyed a reputation for discipline and good conduct that was not always deserved. It did look good next to Wallenstein's crowd. Baner's crew, on the other hand, were the most dreaded fiends of the period: cynical, merciless, and wholly devoid of idealism. They were, however, very good troops, brave, stubborn, and well trained.

A final characteristic of the late war period was the changed composition of armies. Not only were they smaller, the proportion of cavalry relative to infantry was radically increased. Up to 1632, the cavalry had been relatively stable at 20–30% of the total. After 1635, it was 50% (see Table 2.2).

The increased proportions of musketeers to pikemen and cavalry to infantry went hand in hand with increased emphasis on "small war" (*kleine krieg*), raid, ambuscade, skirmish, outpost, and scouting. There was an equal impact on battlefield tactics, as outcomes were determined more and more by the cavalry wings. The strategic repercussions were still greater. The prosecution of sieges was almost exclusively an infantry role. With the decline of infantry, not merely proportionately but even more so in raw numbers, a field army's ability to reduce a fortress was considerably reduced. Sieges were conducted "on the cheap," with assaults replacing systematic approach and outposts substituting for lines of circumvallation.[7] The new, smaller armies had rather poor siege records. For example, in 1631, Tilly reduced Leipzig in less than a week; in 1637, Baner besieged it for a month, unsuccessfully, with a loss of 1000 men. Bernhard's siege of Breisach occupied his whole army for a year. In 1632, Prague fell twice, and was considered almost indefensible against serious attack. In 1640, 1645, and 1648, it repelled major Swedish armies.

Table 2.2
Infantry-Cavalry, 1620–45

Battle	Army	Infantry	Cavalry	% Cavalry
White Mountain (1620)	Catholic	18,800	6,000	24%
	Bohemian	11,600	5,100	30½%
Wimpfen (1622)	Catholic	13,000	5,000	28%
	Protestant	9,400	3,300	26%
Hochst (1622)	Catholic	18,000	10,000	36%
	Protestant	13,000	8,300	39%
Stadtlohn (1623)	Catholic	15,300	5,400	26%
	Protestant	11,600	4,400	27½%
Lutter (1626)	Catholic	16,960	7,457	30½%
	Dane	16,000	5,000	24%
Breitenfeld (1631)	Catholic	21,000	10,000	32%
	Swede	26,842	13,289	33%
Lützen (1632)	Imperial	12,570	9,200	42%
	Swede	12,786	6,210	33%
Nordlingen (1634)	Imperial	5,000	7,000	58%
	Bavarian	3,000	3,000	50%
	Swede	16,000	9,700	38%
Wittstock (1636)	Imperial	8,500	10,122	54%
	Swede	7,750	10,250	57%
2nd Breitenfeld (1642)	Imperial	10,000	16,000	61½%
	Swede	10,000	10,000	50%
Jankow (1645)	Imperial	5,000	10,000	67%
	Swede	6,135	8,530	58%

THE 1635 CAMPAIGN

The awkward process of disentangling the Swedes from their defecting ex-allies was not completed until October, leaving much hard feeling on both sides. Baner abandoned Saxony and Silesia altogether, to concentrate on holding Pomerania, Mecklenburg, Magdeburg, and part of Brandenburg.

Johann Georg of Saxony had pulled together his own army, plus 3 Brandenburg cavalry regiments, near Leipzig, a paper total of 25,000 men and 31 guns. To these were added 7000 Imperials under Marrazino. Baner mustered some 15,000 men and 49 guns at Magdeburg, pivot of the middle Elbe. His second-in-command, Torstensson, had another 4500 foot and 2500 horse, and an even smaller detachment retained Bremen as a foothold in Westphalia.

The Germans divided into two groups. Marrazino's corps, reinforced with 2 Saxon cavalry regiments and the Brandenburgers, operated on the Lower Oder toward Pomerania. The Saxons, under Baudissin, were to advance down the Elbe. Baudissin was a curious choice as lieutenant general. A veteran of the Protestant cause, he had been court-martialed by Christian IV but had served Gustavus adequately, if not brilliantly. An unabashed alcoholic,[8] he was often too intoxicated to command. History records how Johann Georg, arriving to confer with his general, had been "forced" into a drinking bout, leaving both too senseless to discuss strategy. Baudissin's predecessor, Arnim, had resigned in protest against the Peace of Prague, which he thought unfair to Sweden. He changed his mind when Baner had him arrested as an enemy of the Protestant cause! He died before he could reclaim command.

Fighting resumed with an unsuccessful Saxon attack on Havelberg. The Saxons were more successful in a surprise assault of Werben (October17). Meanwhile, Baner was feinting against Georg at Luneburg. His real purpose was to ambush a Saxon detachment not far from Lauenburg (Action at Ludershausen, October 25—1600 Saxons killed or captured). Baudissin attacked the Domitz bridgehead with 4265 men and was not only beaten off but ambushed as well. Baner had sent a detachment, 400 horse and 1000 musketeers, under a Scot, MajGen Ruthven. The Rout of Domitz was the worst Saxon disaster of the whole war (and that is saying something!). Only 665 cavalry escaped Ruthven, including, unfortunately, Baudissin. Undaunted, he and the elector then laid siege to Magdeburg (December 4–January 24, 1636), then defended by 4 infantry regiments under Lohausen. Baner rounded out the year by retaking Werben (December 25, with 1200 prisoners) and relieving Magdeburg. The Saxons went into winter quarters at Wittenberg; the Swedes, at Magdeburg.

Torstensson had successfully obstructed Marrazino's operations against Pomerania, October through December. Then, as the Imperials returned south to reinforce the elector, he ambushed their column of march (Action of Kyritz, December 17). Two hundred Germans were made prisoner. Rejoining Baner, he then captured Barby near Magdeburg (January 28).

THE 1636 CAMPAIGN

Baner now organized his field troops into three armies: the main force (12,000) at Magdeburg, facing the Saxons; a corps of 6000 under Leslie (another Scot), against Georg in Westphalia, and 6000 more in Pomerania under Wrangel (a Swede), to keep an eye on Marrazino.

The allied Germans had plans of their own. The emperor had managed to scrape up another 15,000 men (paper strength) from Westphalia and the Lower Rhine; these were dispatched to Saxony under FM Hatzfeld. Baudissin having retired, Hatzfeld would also act as lieutenant general of Saxony. The combined army mustered 25,000, plus another 6000 in Marrazino's corps.

Baner broke quarters April 2 but was content to move aggressively around Aschersleben before returning to Magdeburg (April 13). Hatzfeld, having linked up with Johann Georg at Eisleben (April 11), now outnumbered Baner 2–1. The allies marched directly on Magdeburg. Baner pulled back (May 5), leaving 2000 men to hold the citadel. He lay at Werben with only 9000, having detached garrisons to Alt-Brandenburg and Rathenow.[9] Magdeburg was placed under siege, June 18–July 13, and surrendered under honors of war.[10]

Marrazino re-invaded Pomerania (April 11–August 28), with his usual lack of success.

Hatzfeld's success at Magdeburg did not encourage him to overconfidence; he remained there until August 12. Baner's small force was equally inert at Werben, even after the arrival of 3350 reinforcements in July. On August 12, he left for Westphalia and Leslie. He had realized that it was futile to oppose the allies with such inferior numbers. He could no longer count on Baudissin's bungling, and all his small war successes counted for nothing if he couldn't face Hatzfeld on equal terms. His new plan was to combine his force with Leslie's and strike at each opposing army in turn, a strategy of interior lines. After linking up with Leslie (August 22), the garrisons would defended occupied territory, while the combined field force moved aggressively against Luneburg.

Although unaware of Baner's departure, Hatzfeld had nevertheless resumed the offensive the same day, August 12. On the 14th, he reached Tangermunde, where he learned of Baner's westward thrust. He hesitated, unable to decide whether to match Baner by joining Duke Georg at Luneburg or to take advantage of his absence to liberate Brandenburg. Hatzfeld detached a Saxon corps under Klitzing to Brandenburg, while the main army constructed a bridge of boats at Tangermunde. Klitzing seized both Werben and Havelberg without difficulty (August 23–26), so Hatzfeld and the elector decided to take the army to Luneburg.

Baner's thrust against Georg had been, in fact, only a feint,[11] and he was already on his way back to Saxony. Unexpected by either, the two armies nearly collided at Salzwedel (August 31). Both recoiled, Baner to a fortified position at Luchow (which covered Domitz, his last Elbe bridgehead) and the allies back to the middle Elbe. Hatzfeld was worried about supplies and hoped that riverine transport could feed his men. Also, he feared that focusing all his efforts on Baner would risk the gains around Havelberg.[12] His new plan was a scaled up version of the August success. Klitzing would again be detached, to overrun Alt-Brandenburg, Rathenow and Berlin. The pontoon bridge would be dismantled and floated down to Sandau. The main army would act as a covering force.

Klitzing set off September 4, and Hatzfeld reached Havelberg on the 6th. At the same time, he directed Marrazino to add his corps to the main army. All went well, at first. Klitzing's 4000 men took Rathenow without difficulty (September 12) and moved against Alt-Brandenburg (September 21). Hatzfeld assumed a very strong position at Perleburg (September 13). For some reason (perhaps to avoid ambush?), Marrazino decided to dribble his troops in by detachments and regiments, rather than moving as a single group.

Baner, of course, was less than pleased with this turn of events; also he was afraid that Hatzfeld and Georg might combine to eliminate the Domitz bridgehead. Aggressive as always, he marched directly on Perleburg. He seems to have assumed that the Germans, whose strength he overestimated, would willingly come out and fight. Given the arrival of reinforcements from Pomerania[13] and Klitzing's continued absence, the odds were, he thought, as favorable as they were going to get. Baner drove in the Imperial outposts[14] and offered battle on September 25. Secure in his entrenchments and protected by marsh and woods, Hatzfeld declined the invitation. The immediate area, he knew, was too wasted to sustain the Swedes for long. Baner retired on the 27th, leaving behind a virtual desert.

Up to this point, Hatzfeld had had the better of their duel. Baner formed a new plan, to bypass the enemy position and strike at the much-disputed strongpoints of Werben and Havelberg. Luck was with him; Havelberg fell at once (September 28) with much of the allies' supplies, exposing the pontoon bridge. The bridge, then at Sandau, was protected only by a weak Saxon detachment. Three Swedish cavalry regiments[15] easily overran them, and the bridge, the mainstay of Hatzfeld's logistics, was destroyed. Werben put up more resistance, so Baner placed it under siege.

The loss of both the bridge and the supplies at Havelberg rendered the Perleburg position untenable (stomach strategy again!). Hatzfeld and Johann Georg had been wavering between a move north, to Plau in Mecklenburg, and retiring south, back to Saxony. Now they agreed to rejoin Klitzing at Ruppin, marching via Pritzwalk and Wittstock.

The allies broke camp at dawn, September 29; Baner, at Werben, was informed before dark. He determined to intercept them before they reached Klitzing, even if it meant forcemarching the whole way. Klitzing, still besieging Alt-Brandenburg, was unaware of the situation. Baner left Werben at 8:00 A.M. on the 30th. He reached Kyritz October 1 and, on the 2nd, crossed the Dosse at Wusterhausen and made Katerbow. There he was joined by the Alt-Brandenburg garrison.[16] On the 3rd, he arrived at Fretzdorf, where his scouts made contact with Hatzfeld's outposts. In the same time, the allies had merely moved from Pritzwalk to Wittstock. Baner had won the race.

THE COMMANDERS

Field Marshal Johan Baner (1596–1641) was one of the most detestable characters of the war—and this is in competition with people like Mansfeld, Wallenstein, and Georg of Luneburg. One of the few commoners to rise to high command, he was throughout his life obsessed with his lack of social status, regarding his superiors with paranoia and his subordinates with distrust and contempt. Added to a naturally abrasive personality and alcoholism, this made him difficult to deal with; aside from Torstensson, he was practically incapable of cooperating with anyone.

Gustavus's military expansion of the 1620s made it possible for men like Baner, born outside the traditional military class, to become officers. His ability soon brought him to the king's personal attention; he was selected as one of Gustavus's inner circle, the "paladins." Baner commanded the right wing at Breitenfeld, leading the decisive charge, and was appointed to the Elbe army, 1631–32. His Elbe command was brief and unsuccessful—it was at this time that his alcoholism was first remarked—due to his inexperience and attitude. Baner remarked at the time that if he combined forces with Wilhelm Hesse-Cassel, he could beat Pappenheim, but if they did, all the credit would go to the prince, none to the commoner. After Thurn's defeat in 1633, he assumed command of the Silesia army. In that purely military campaign, he did well. After the disaster of Nordlingen (1634), he found himself at the head of the only major force left to Sweden. Oxenstierna persuaded his colleagues in regency to accept Baner as supreme commander.

Baner's style of command reflected his character. He seems to have deliberately embroiled his colonels in a web of feuds, Swede against Scot, both against Germans. He played favorites, exalting certain officers, notably, Pfuhl, above the other Germans, and pet regiments, like Alt-Blau, above the rest. Resentful, divided, and at the mercy of his violent mood swings, his men were thoroughly under his thumb—but the moment he died, they mutinied.

Baner's generalship was active and aggressive. His men were in constant motion, exerting continuous pressure on the enemy: skirmishes, raids, sudden strikes, and ambushes. His love of surprise was reflected in repeated winter operations and forced marches; these certainly hurt the Imperials, but the strain on his own forces must have been enormous. Baner's boldness hid a certain calculation; despite seemingly reckless moves, notably in 1636 and 1637, he was always quite aware of enemy capacity and never blundered into such disasters as overcame Christian of Brunswick or Bernhard Sax-Weimar. Baner was a master of "small war," skirmishes and small actions, but Wittstock, his only major battle, betrays an uncertain grasp of the operational.

Wholly self-interested and at the head of an army of mercenaries, it was feared that Baner would become a Swedish Wallenstein, even usurp the throne. Unlike his Imperial counterpart, these fears were groundless. While Baner had no "loyalty" as such, his firm grasp of the realistic justified Oxenstierna's faith in him.

Baner was cynical, brutal, alcoholic, a womanizer, and an unabashed social climber. He was paranoid, trusting no one but Torstensson, Oxenstierna, and Pfuhl. Unlike Mansfeld or Gallas, his failings and obsessions seldom affected his military judgment.

Field Marshal Count Lennart Torstensson (1603–1651), opposite to his friend Baner, had been marked for advancement from the first. Unusually for a noble, he made his name as an artillery expert and commanded the guns at Breitenfeld, the Lech, and Alte Veste. Captured at the last, his subsequent imprisonment left him broken in health and embittered in mind. From 1635, he acted as Baner's right hand, succeeding him in 1641. He led the army to 1645, winning the battles of 2nd Breitenfeld and Jankow.

Youngest of Gustavus's paladins, Torstensson was the also the most capable, displaying a remarkable flair for the operational and unsurpassed brilliance as an artilleryman. He was the perfect number two for Baner, their cynical characters meshing precisely. Although less Machiavellian than his friend, he did nothing to "morally" regenerate the army from Baner's degradations.

Field Marshal Torsten Stalhansk (1594–1644) was of slightly less obscure origins than Baner. His lack of background seems to have hampered his advancement, but unlike Baner, he wasn't sensitive about it. Although Gustavus's best cavalryman, he was never invited into the inner circle. He had a squadron at Breitenfeld, led a brigade at Lützen and Oldendorf, and acted as deputy wing commander at Wittstock and wing commander at 2nd Breitenfeld—invariably with success. No genius, he was very good at what he did.

Major General Count Hans Vitzthum von Eckstadt (ca. 1595–1648) was a Saxon Lutheran of the very military Vitzthum family—he had brothers and cousins in the Imperial and Saxon armies. He long served the Protestant cause and was a colonel under Christian of Denmark before joining Gustavus. He led the White Brigade at Breitenfeld with success and managed to escape the disaster at Nordlingen. He was one of the few German leaders to stick with Sweden after the Peace of Prague. He was a cautious general and hated Baner personally, which made him a poor choice as reserve commander.

Alexander Leslie (1573–1651), John King (1589–1652), Patrick Ruthven (1573– 1651), and Walter Karr were all Scottish "soldiers of fortune." Although Scottish mercenaries have received a bad name in the war, most of them fought for "Protestant" causes most of the time. Leslie, King, and Ruthven later rose to high rank during the English Civil War, Leslie with the Scots Convenanters, King (Baron Eythin) and Ruthven (Earl of Forth and Brentford) for the Royalists. They were all competent, if over-cautious officers, but not fit for supreme command.

Lieutenant General Count Melchior von Hatzfeld (1593–1658) was a Hessian Calvinist, but from a family closely aligned with the Hapsburgs (his brother became a Catholic bishop). He served as an Imperial officer 1621–32, progressively in Alt-Saxon Infantry Regiment, Holstein Cuirassier Regiment, Alt-Saxon Cuirassier Regiment, and Neu-Saxon Cuirassier Regiment,[17] becoming a colonel (cuirassiers) during Wallenstein's 1632 reorganization. His promotion thereafter was rapid: lieutenant-field-marshal in 1633, general of artillery 1634, field marshal in 1635, and lieutenant general of Saxony in 1636. He later became lieutenant general of the Empire (1645). A career officer, thoroughly loyal to the Hapsburgs, he backed Gallas in 1634 and served under him 1634–39. He was later killed leading an Imperial army in Poland. Although reliable and a competent strategist, Hatzfeld lacked operational ability and lost control of his army at both Wittstock and Jankow. He was a whiner, constantly blaming colleagues and subordinates for everything that went wrong, and he lacked the strength of character to enforce his will over unruly underlings. On the other hand, his mild, diplomatic manner won approval at court.

Duke Johann Georg Wettin, Elector of Saxony (1585–1656), was the leader of the "moderate" German Protestants. Well-meaning and essentially loyal to the Empire, he was hampered by limited ability and alcoholism. Alienated by Imperial policies, he backed Gustavus in 1631 but returned to loyalty in 1635. He supported the Imperials through numerous defeats but signed a separate peace in 1645.

Proud, touchy, and a poor judge of men, Johann Georg was able to raise armies but not to lead them to victory. He preferred to leave operations to subordinates but managed to be present at the routs of Breitenfeld and Wittstock. Hatzfeld blamed him for the defeat: either the general was excusing himself, or he was too weak to argue with his sovereign's ally.

Field Marshal Count Rudolfo Giovanni di Marrazino (AKA Rudolf Morzin) (ca. 1585–1645), of an Italian military family, served the emperor from 1620, helped oust Wallenstein, and did well at Nordlingen. Sent to support Saxony in 1635, his "soldierly manner" offended the elector; at the same time, he embroiled himself in a pointless feud with Baudissin. Thus, he was superseded by the courtly Hatzfeld. He was subsequently defeated and captured at the action of Chemnitz (1639). A brave and reliable subordinate, he was poorly suited to independent command and wholly out of his depth against Baner.

The lesser German leaders included GWM Ulhefeld, commanding the left wing; Col. Wildberg, leader of the center cavalry; Col. Montecuccoli, who led the rearguard, and Saxon major generals Taube and Dehne. Gen. Monnier of Saxony commanded the artillery.

THE ARMIES

There are no agreed on figures for the forces at Wittstock. Baner set his own army at 16,378 and the allies at 25,000. Hatzfeld made it 20,200 Swedes to 12,000 German. Another Imperial source gave Hatzfeld 13,500–14,000. Tingsten, following the Swedish accounts, said 15,398 Swedes to 21,000 allies. Schmidt estimated 17,438 Swedes to 22,000–23,000 Germans. Delbruck revised the Swedes upward to 21,000 and the allies down to 18,000. The best modern estimates place both sides at about 18–19,000.

Imperial-Saxon Army—Hatzfeld (see Appendix A)

Vanguard: 1000 dragoons in 10 sqd

UNIT	DATE	COY	ESTSTR	NOTES
Bissinger DR	1632	3	100?	IMP; Persinger; 1 sqd?
Gall a Burke DR	1633	10	400	IMP; AKA Hall; 4 sqd?
Leslie DR	1633	6	200	IMP; 2 sqd?
Marrazino DR	1631	8	300	IMP; 3 sqd?

Right Wing—1st Echelon—Marrazino: 1440 cav in 9 sqd

Marradas KUR	1616	10	314	IMP; Sp; 3 sqd of 105 ea
Vitzthum CR	1632	10	200	Saxon CR#8; 1 sqd
Schierstadt CR	1632	10	175	" CR#6; 1 sqd
Kalkstein CR	1632	10	200	" CR#7; 2 sqd of 100 ea
Trauditsch CR	1634	-	251	" CR#10; 1 sqd
Strein CR	1631	10	300	" CR#4; 1 sqd.

Right Wing—2nd Echelon—Kalkstein: 1304 cav in 6 sqd

Alt-Taube CR	1631	10	175	Saxon CR#3; Leib; 1 sqd
Bose CR	1635	12	175	" CR#19; 1 sqd
Wolframsdorf CR	1635	9	150	" CR#17; Ramsdorf; 1 sqd
Rochau CR	1633	16	350	" CR#16; Strachow;2 sqd
Wintz KUR	1631	8	454	IMP; Ger; Winz; 1 sqd

Center—1st Echelon—4900 inf in 7 "brigades" (bns) & 30 guns

BRIGADE	IRs	COY	STR	NOTES
Goltz	Goltz	9	600	IMP; Bohemian-German
	Pappenheim	7		IMP; Pappenheim-Alzheim
Thun	Thun	10	700	League; Bavaria
	Westfalen	5		" Westphalia
	Werth	6		" Bavaria
Manteuffel	Manteuffel	6	800	IMP; High German
	Enkefort	12		IMP; High German
	Gonzaga	9		IMP; Italian
Enan	Enan	10	700	IMP; Spanish-German
	Bonninghausen	3		IMP; Westphalia
	Lombardi	8		IMP; Italian.
Bunau	Bunau	10	800	Saxon; IR#11
	Zehmen	10		Saxon; IR#10
	Trandorf	10		Saxon; IR#1
Wallenstein	Alt-Waldstein	4	600	IMP; LG; Max Waldstein
	Jung-Waldstein	10		IMP; Ger; Ladislas Waldstein
Colloredo	Colloredo	15	700	IMP; German
	Harrach	7		IMP; High German
	Niedrumb	4		IMP; German

Artillery: 5x 24pdr, 6x 8pdr, 2x 6pdr, 4x 4pdr, 1x 3pdr, 12x "small"

Center—2nd Echelon—Wildberg: 1322 cav in 7 sqd

UNIT	DATE	COY	ESTSTR	NOTES
Kalkreuter CR	1632	10	300	Saxon; CR#9: 2 sqd of 150
Baudissin CR	1631	10	250	" CR#1: 2 sqd of 125 ea
Gersdorff CR	1631	5	200	" CR#11; 1 sqd
Hanau CR	1631	10	255	" CR#2; 1 sqd
Ruck KUR	1632	10	317	IMP; German; 1 sqd

Center—3rd Echelon—3600 inf in 6 "brigades"(bns)

BRIGADE	IRs	COY	STR	NOTES
Bourre	Bourre	10	600	IMP; High German
	Mansfeld	5		IMP; High German
Hatzfeld	Hatzfeld	10	500	IMP; High German
Schleinitz	Schleinitz	12	700	Saxon; IR#3
	Brink	5		" DR#7
Pforte	Pforte	8	600	" IR#2
Bose	Bose	10	700	" IR#4
	Darmstadt	-		Hesse-Darmstadt
Strassoldo	Strassoldo	6	500	IMP; Italian
	Zweyer	6		IMP; High German
	Herrera	6		Spanish-German

Center—4th Echelon—1134 cav in 5 sqd

UNIT	DATE	COY	ESTSTR	NOTES
Rittberg KUR	1631	8	284	IMP; German; 1 sqd
Falkenstein KUR	1631	8	307	IMP; German; 1 sqd
Puchheim KUR	1634?	-	243	IMP; German; 1 sqd
Alt-Burgsdorf CR	1632	-	150	Brandenburg; 1 sqd
Duke Franz Karl	1632	10	150	" 1 sqd

Left Wing—1st Echelon—Hatzfeld: 2031 cav in 8 sqd
Unit	Year	Coy	Str	Notes
Wildberg KUR	1626	9	438	IMP; Ger; 2 sqd of 219 ea
Hatzfeld KUR	1625	10	645	IMP; Ger; 2 sqd of 322 ea
Polniskow KUR	--	10	243	IMP; 1 sqd
Schonickel KUR	1634	6	268	IMP; German; 1 sqd
Del Maestro ARK	1632	10	437	IMP; Austria; 2 sqd of 218

Left Wing—2nd Echelon—Ulhefeld: 1891 cav in 8 sqd
Unit	Year	Coy	Str	Notes
Ulhefeld KUR	1630	10	409	IMP; Ger; 2 sqd of 204 ea
Mansfeld KUR	1633	2	163	IMP; German; 1 sqd
Montecuccoli KU	1626	5	254	IMP; Low German; 1 sqd
Harrach KUR	1634	9	286	IMP; German; 1 sqd
Bissinger KUR	1632	10	536	IMP; Ger; 2 sqd of 268 ea
Darmstadt KUR	1634/6	5	243	Hesse-Darmstadt; 1 sqd

Total: 8500 inf in 13 bn; 9122 cav in 43 sqd; 1000 drag, 30 guns = 18,622 men.

Swedish Army—Baner (see Appendix B)

Right Wing—1st Echelon—Torstensson: 950 cav in 4 sqd, 500 inf & 7 guns
UNIT	COY	ESTSTR	NOTES
Gadau CR	4	225	Swede; Uppland CR; 1 sqd
Klingsor CR	4	225	Swede; East Gothland CR; 1 sqd
Bjelke CR	8	500	Finn CR; 2 sqd of 250 ea
Musketeer Dets		500	7x 3pdrs

Right Wing—2nd Echelon—Baner: 1350 cav in 7 sqd
Kurland CR	8	300	Balt; 2 sqd of 150 ea
Livonia CR	10	450	Balt; 2 sqd of 225 ea
Wachtmeister CR	12	600	German; 3 sqd of 200 ea

Right Wing—3rd Echelon—1325 cav in 6 sqd.
Franz Henrich C	8	375	German; 2 sqd of 187 ea
Krakau CR	8	400	" 2 sqd of 200 ea
Schlang CR	8	550	" 2 sqd of 275 ea

Center—Leslie & Karr: 4344 inf in 5 "brigades" (bns), 1450 cav & 40 guns
Swedish Brigade	24	892	Adams, Drake, Ermis IRs
Scots Brigade	24	800	Karr, Lindsey, Cunningham IRs
Blue Brigade	16	856	German; Alt-Blau & Munda IRs
Leslie Brigade	8	900	Scots; Leslie IR
Sabelitz Brigade	20	896	German; Sabelitz & Goltz IRs
Baner Leib CR	12	600	German; 2 sqd of 300 ea
Torstensson CR	6	300	" 1 sqd
Smaland Sqd	4	250	Swede; 1 sqd
Wurzburg CR	8	300	German; 1 sqd.

Artillery: 20 heavy (12–24pdr) & 20 light (3pdr) guns

Left Wing—1st Echelon—Stalhansk: 1675 cav in 9 sqd & 3 guns
Wittenberg CR	8	500	Finn CR; 2 sqd of 250 ea
Stalhansk CR	10	500	German; 2 sqd of 250 ea
Dewitz CR	8	250	" 2 sqd of 125 ea
Bruneck CR	8	150	" 1 sqd; AKA Birkenfeld
Boy CR	8	225	" 2 sqd of 112 ea

Left Wing—2nd Echelon—King: 1475 cav in 9 sqd

Glaubitz CR	8	275	German;	2 sqd of 137 ea
Beckermann CR	-	175	"	1 sqd
Hoditz CR	8	275	"	2 sqd of 137 ea
King CR	8	250	"	2 sqd of 125 ea
Wopersnow CR	4	300	"	1 sqd
Stuart CR	4	200	"	1 sqd

Reserve—Vitzthum & Ruthven: 2886 inf in 4 "brigades," 2025 cav & 10 guns

Thomasson Brigade	8	438	Swede; Nerike & Wormland IRs
Wrangel Brigade	28	738	Ger; Wrangel, Jescwizki & Gun IRs
Ruthven Brigade	24	698	" Ruthven, Hansson & Bengtsson IRs
Bauer Brigade	47	1012	" 6 small IRs
Douglas CR	8	225	German; 2 sqd of 112 ea
Goldstein CR	8	500	" 2 sqd of 250 ea
Jens CR	8	375	" 2 sqd of 187 ea
Duval CR	8	250	" 2 sqd of 125 ea
Pfuhl CR	8	400	" 2 sqd of 200 ea
Berghofer CR	8	175	" 1 sqd
Jarotzky CR	8	100	" 1 sqd

Artillery: 10 light (3pdr) guns
Total: 7730 inf in 9 brgs; 10.250 cav in 52 sqds; 60 guns = 17,980 men.

MARCH TO BATTLE

In order to move more quickly, Baner had left behind his heavy baggage—but not his guns—guarded by a detachment under Col. Mortaigne. Shortly thereafter, Jens reinforced him with 1000 foot from Alt-Brandenburg; half of these were detailed to garrison the castle guarding the Fretzdorf bridge. These detachments reduced his effective force from over 20,000 to some 18,000. This did not unduly worry Baner because the troops in question were infantry, and he relied on his 10,000 cavalry for victory.

Hatzfeld was somewhat aware of Baner's approach, although not his exact position or intentions. He therefore assumed a strong defensive position near the town of Wittstock. His line ran along a plateaulike ridge running east–west, called the Schreckenberg. This ridge dominated the area to the south, the Natte Heide (or heath), a low-lying plain broken up with marshes and small woods. Hatzfeld's left (east) was protected by hills (the Scharfenberg), a larger woods (the Fretzdorfer Heide), and the Dosse River; his right rested on the Heiligengrab Forest. The southern face of the ridge was fortified with redoubts, entrenchments, obstacles, wooden barriers, and heavy wagons chained together; however no especial effort was made to secure the flanks or rear. Defended by 7 brigades of foot and all the guns, the Schreckenberg position was very strong. A direct attack from the Natte Heide—which was, in any case, unsuitable ground for an offensive—would have been suicidal, much worse than Horn's assault at Nordlingen.

Some have questioned why Hatzfeld expected Baner to attack such a formidable line. Probably he didn't. Most likely, he assumed that Baner, seeing the Germans so strongly emplaced, would retire, as at Perleburg.

Unlike Gallas at Nordlingen or Mercy at Freiburg, Hatzfeld did not place his entrenched foot ahead and hold back the horse in reserve. Rather, he deployed as an ordinary line of battle, infantry in the center, cavalry on the flanks. Only the infantry center benefited from the earthworks. His line extended merely along the ridge; the hills on the left were not occupied or even patrolled. There was a so-called "vanguard" of 10 squadrons of dragoons—perhaps 1000 skirmishers—posted inside the southern edge of the Scharfenberg woods. Like the main defense, this outpost was focused on the Natte Heide. South of the "vanguard," the Dosse angled west at Fretzdorf. Hatzfeld made the bridge there unusable but did not destroy it completely, nor did he occupy the castle on the east bank.

The Dosse is a very minor river, but at that particular time it was swollen with heavy rainfall, with marshy, difficult banks. It could be crossed only by bridge. Before encamping on the night of October 3, Baner had the Fretzdorf bridge restored to service. The whole Swedish army would cross that single span to intercept the Germans.

Some cavalry were thrown across at the same time, to scout toward Hatzfeld and place outposts, while the bulk of the army slept on the east bank. Baner began crossing early on the 4th, but the bridge was so narrow that it was after noon before he had finished. The Swedes then had to move several miles through the Fretzdorfer Heide, so it was after 1:00 P.M. before their deployment was complete. Baner had hoped to cut off the 1000 dragoons of the vanguard, but these hastily fell back onto the flanks of Hatzfeld's line. Only now, about 2:00, did Baner get a look at the German position. He realized at once that it was too strong to attack, but he also guessed at weaknesses. On no more basis than this, he formed a bold, even reckless plan. He would divide his army into four corps: the right, under Torstensson and himself, 4125 strong; the center, under Leslie and Karr, 5794 men; the left under King and Stalhansk with 3150 horse, and a reserve of 4911 under Vitzthum and Ruthven. The right would move north between the woods and the Dosse, the center following. The left would swing west in a wide circling movement and engage the German far right. The reserve would support the right and center.[18]

It appears that Baner originally envisioned a double envelopment, the right curling around Hatzfeld's left, the center moving through the woods to fix his front, and King striking his right. It did not develop that way.

Baner's intuition regarding Hatzfeld's position was essentially correct, but he had not anticipated the difficulty involved in coordinating four separate elements 5 miles apart. His very expertise in small war had misled him; what would have worked very nicely with a few thousand horse proved much trickier with a mixed force of 18,000. Also, his guesstimate of the ground was not wholly accurate.[19]

Be this as it may, Baner separated his four corps between Fretzdorf and Dessow, about 4 miles southeast of the German position. King swung wide to the left, between the Scharfenberg woods and the Fretzdorfer Heide, while Baner proceeded north along the Dosse past Bohnenkamp, turning west just south of Wittstock town.

Baner's War and the Battle of Wittstock 53

Map 2.1
The Battle of Wittstock, October 4, 1636

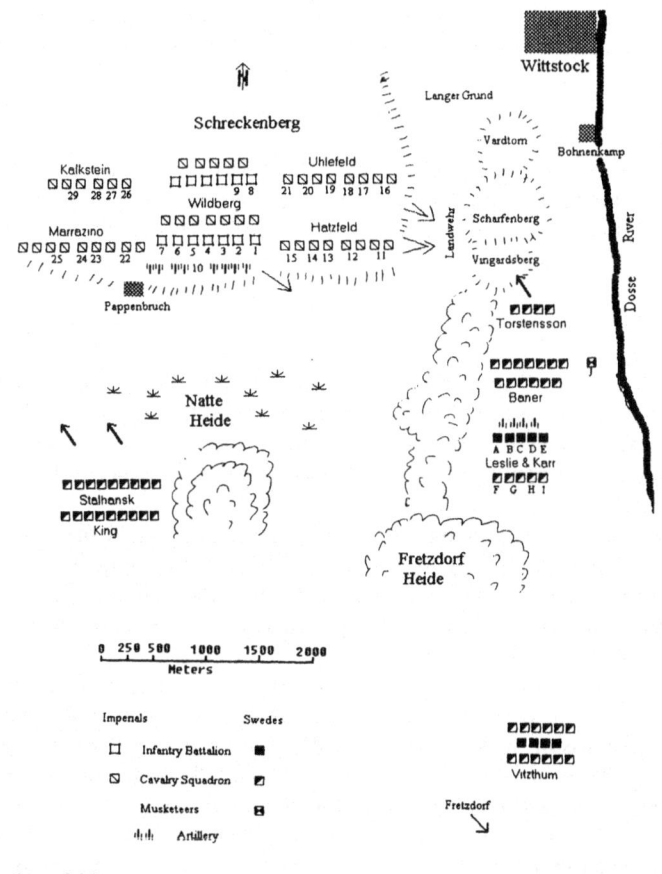

[Map showing troop positions at the Battle of Wittstock. Features labeled include: Wittstock, Langer Grund, Vardtom, Bohnenkamp, Schreckenberg, Kalkstein, Uhlefeld, Wildberg, Marrazino, Hatzfeld, Scharfenberg, Landwehr, Vingardsberg, Pappenbruch, Torstensson, Baner, Natte Heide, Leslie & Karr, Stalhansk, King, Fretzdorf Heide, Dosse River, Vitzthum, Fretzdorf. Numbered positions 1–29 for Imperial units and lettered positions A–J for Swedish units. Scale 0–2000 meters.]

Legend:
Imperials — Infantry Battalion, Cavalry Squadron, Musketeers, Artillery
Swedes — Infantry Battalion, Cavalry Squadron, Musketeers, Artillery

Imperials (Hatzfeld)
1 - Goltz
2 - Thun
3 - Manteuffel
4 - Enan
5 - Bunau
6 - Wallenstein
7 - Colloredo
8 - Bourre
9 - Hatzfeld
10 - Guns & Redoubts

11 - Wildberg
12 - Hatzfeld
13 - Polniskow
14 - Schonickel
15 - Del Maestro
16 - Ulhefeld
17 - Mansfeld
18 - Montecuccoli
19 - Harrach
20 - Bissinger
21 - Darmstadt
22 - Marradas
23 - Vitzthum
24 - Schierstadt
25 - Kalkstein
26 - Alt-Taube
27 - Bose
28 - Wolframsdorf
29 - Rochau

Swedes (Baner)
A - Leslie
B - Blue
C - Scots
D - Swedes
E - Sabelitz

F - Torstensson
G - Baner
H - Smaland
I - Wurzburg
J - Musketeers

THE BATTLE OF WITTSTOCK, OCTOBER 4, 1636

Between 2:30 and 3:00, Hatzfeld, on the German left, spotted some Swedes "sneaking" through the Langer Grund, the open area between the Schreckenberg, the Vardtorn, and Wittstock.[20] They fell upon the Saxon train encamped there, pioneers, wagoners, siege guns, and ammunition, and quickly put the defending foot[21] to the sword, scattering the noncombatants and seizing the transport.

Baner's advance had been hidden from Hatzfeld's vantage by a ridge of three hills. The northernmost, the Vardtorn, lay about a mile south of Wittstock; next came the Scharfenberg, and south and east of that was the Vingardsberg, "Vineyard Hill." South of these hills lay the Scharfenberg woods, which, together with the Fretzdorfer Heide, formed a belt of trees as far as Fretzdorf. A ravine-like depression, the Landwehr, separated the Schreckenberg and the Scharfenberg.

Hatzfeld had been so confident of the impassability of the woods, the marshiness of the Dosse, and the steepness of the Scharfenberg that he had not even bothered to post a lookout on the eastern ridge—this omission is difficult to understand. As a result, Baner had been able to move unnoticed as far as the Langer Grund.

The moment that he spotted the enemy, Hatzfeld realized that the situation was radically altered. The key to victory was now not the Schreckenberg but the Scharfenberg. Gathering the units nearest to him, the Wildberg, Hatzfeld, and Polniskow cuirassier regiments,[22] he personally led them to secure the hill, ordering the rest of the left wing to follow.

Baner had subdivided his corps into three brigades, a vanguard under Torstensson, the main body of 7 veteran squadrons, and 6 more behind as a reserve. Torstensson had 4 elite squadrons, Swedes and Finns, plus 500 musketeers. These had been deployed in 7 small detachments to support the cavalry, but while dividing the army, Baner had combined them into a single forlorn hope. Torstensson's vanguard was apparently acting as left flank guard next to the Scharfenberg. Baner had not occupied the hills, even though other Swedes had reached the Langer Grund; presumably, he wished to avoid alerting Hatzfeld of his movements.[23] Looking west, Torstensson could see "great masses of enemy cavalry shining" as they climbed the Scharfenberg.

Torstensson reacted at once, knowing that if the Germans secured the Scharfenberg, Baner would be pinned between the steep slope and the marshy riverbank. Trotting up the gentler gradient of Vineyard Hill, he was able to forestall Hatzfeld and seize the Scharfenberg. The forlorn hope occupied the woods by the southern face.

Torstensson had 950 elite sabers to Hatzfeld's 1300. These should have been reasonable odds, given the Swedes' superior quality; nevertheless, they were worsted. Either they were exhausted by their dash up the hill, or the Imperials were better than their reputation. Gadau was wounded, Bjelke captured, and the brigade driven back onto Vineyard Hill. It seemed as though Baner's rash move might end in disaster, with his right driven into the Dosse.

At this critical juncture, fate, or Hatzfeld's sloppiness, intervened. The fourth cavalry regiment in his line, Schonickel Cuirassier Regiment, had not followed the first three eastward. Schonickel had been beaten in a skirmish a few days before and had either lost confidence in his men,[24] or considered himself unfairly overburdened. Not only did he not move himself, he blocked the movement of the rest of the wing. Since Hatzfeld was at the head of his men, there was no wing commander present to clear up the resultant confusion.[25]

Meanwhile, Baner with his 1350 cuirassiers was scaling the Scharfenberg to renew the fight. The 1325 of the reserve moved up Vineyard Hill, relieving Torstensson's battered survivors. Because of Schonickel, there were no reinforcements for Hatzfeld. Outnumbered 2-1 by fresh troops, he found himself cut off and fighting for his life. Baner drove him back over the Scharfenberg, down into the Landwehr, and onto the slope of the Schreckenberg. Baner went, in fact, too far. Fighting fiercely against impossible odds—the Imperials engaged suffered 15% casualties—Hatzfeld had won enough time for Gen Ulhefeld to put the German left back into order. Now they fell upon Baner's wearied victors, 2600 strong with more coming up from the center and right.

Slowly, the Swedes were pushed back over the Scharfenberg onto Vineyard Hill. Baner, reinforced only by Torstensson's regrouped remnants, at least six times managed to gather squadrons for local counterattacks. Nevertheless, he could not withstand "triple his numbers." He remarked afterward that he'd never been in such a heated, desperate fight. Messengers were dispatched to Leslie and Vitzthum. And what had happened to King?

The battle had been nearly won and lost in not much more than an hour, and the three corps leaders were wholly unaware of Baner's plight. Although he exaggerated the Germans' numbers—only part of the center squadrons were yet engaged, and the right not at all—his position was bad and rapidly getting worse. His horse had suffered heavily and were exhausted besides. His repeated, frantic counterattacks only aggravated the situation. At the same time, 4 German brigades of foot,[26] with more close behind, had arrived and were trying to outflank the Swedish left in the woods. This woodland was relatively open, with large, century-old oaks widely spaced and little underbrush; the 500 musketeers of the forlorn were not enough to block the advancing foot. To top it all off, a rumor began to spread through the line that Baner was down—captured or killed, like Gustavus at Lützen.

At this crucial moment for the Swedish cause, Leslie suddenly appeared with the center. He had been about a mile back, between Goldbeck and Dessow, waiting for Baner's signal. When the order came, he forcemarched forward, arriving in the nick of time. His 4 squadrons[27] charged the Imperial infantry so fiercely that the outflanking maneuver was abandoned. Leslie spread his 5 brigades, each with supporting regimental guns, on a wide front to allow Baner's horse to fall back behind them and take a "breather." Hatzfeld's foot seem to have done the same for their cavalry. Despite superior numbers and the presence of a few Saxon light guns, the German infantry were at a distinct disadvantage in this duel of cannon and musketry. Throughout the battle, the Swedes tried to employ their reserve as solid striking forces, while Hatzfeld tended to dribble his in, a unit or two at a time.

The Imperial foot were weakening under Leslie's fire, when a fresh cavalry force[28] fell upon the Swedish flank. Two of Leslie's best units, the Swedish brigade and Karr's Scots brigade, were cut to pieces, the Swedes losing 65% of their strength.

The infantry on both sides then drifted south into the woods for a long-drawn-out firefight at long range, while the cavalry, now somewhat rested and again battleworthy, resumed their interrupted melee on the hills. The Swedish heavy artillery had been dragged up behind Leslie and was rather awkwardly placed east of Vineyard Hill. The German heavy guns were still on Schreckenberg ridge, entirely useless.

Vitzthum had remained immobile, ignoring both the clearly audible cannonfire and Baner's direct order. At Nordlingen, his caution had enabled him to escape when the army was destroyed; now, he assumed, Baner's recklessness had spawned a similar disaster.

Baner was later to emphasize the superhuman courage of his cavalry in this lengthy conflict. However, it would appear that this second melee was much less fierce than that which had preceded Leslie's intervention. Both sides had lost their edge. Hatzfeld, it seems, was counting on bringing up his right wing cavalry, 2750 strong, as a last reserve to decide the battle. He was under the impression—no doubt fostered by the broken terrain and woods—that the troops he was fighting, Baner and Leslie, were the whole Swedish army. This perhaps explains his cautious, methodical approach. For his part, Baner had despaired of Vitzthum, let alone King, and hoped only to hold out until darkness would enable him to break off and disengage. Hatzfeld was confident of success, and the Saxon artillery on the Schreckenberg had begun to "Shoot Victory!" as token that the day was won.[29]

At 6:30, two cannon shots sounded behind the German line. This was the prearranged signal to Baner; King and Stalhansk were at last in position and ready to attack. Their lengthy delay is easily explained; the route around the German right was both longer and more difficult than Baner had hoped. Given his extremely sketchy idea of the local geography, he was lucky that they showed at all.

As if he'd been waiting for them, Vitzthum suddenly appeared behind Baner. Abruptly, it was a whole new battle, and Baner cursed the dusk he'd just been praying for.

Stalhansk surged forward with the 1675 sabers of the 1st echelon and rolled over a German group of "1000 musketeers" (Pforte and Bose?) who tried to stop his advance. At the same time, Berghofer and 3 squadrons[30] charged the Imperial horse harrying Baner's far right. He was killed, but the Germans were halted. Vitzthum's infantry relieved Leslie's line, while Stalhansk made contact with Marrazino. However, it was getting too dark for serious fighting, and little loss ensued. Hatzfeld had been outmaneuvered, but his army was not "swept from the field."

If Vitzthum had hoped to steal the glory of Baner's humiliation by covering the retreat of his broken wing, he had timed his arrival exactly. Unfortunately, King's simultaneous appearance discredited him.

Light skirmishing continued during the night, while Hatzfeld and the elector summoned an emergency council of war. The German situation was not good: the train and baggage were largely lost, Stalhansk had overrun the heavy artillery, their line was hopelessly turned, and their reserves were gone. Disheartened soldiers had begun deserting, slipping away in ones and twos under cover of darkness. The Swedes, on the other hand, still had almost half their forces uncommitted. A successful defense in the morning was still conceivable, but the council's decision to withdraw is understandable.

The retreat began around midnight. Montecuccoli was given 4 cavalry regiments to act as rearguard. The operation was hampered by the weariness of the infantry and the numerous wounded. Fortunately, Baner didn't realize what they were up to until dawn. Too late, he dispatched King and Stalhansk in pursuit. They spent Sunday October 5 harassing Montecuccoli and the retreat. Much equipment and baggage was lost—notably the remaining guns and the elector's silver—but few casualties were inflicted.

AFTERMATH

The Imperial-Saxon allies suffered about 27% casualties, 2000 dead, 2000 prisoners, the 1000 musketeers, plus 151 flags and all 31 guns. Baner's claims, repeated by Barker,[31] that another 5000 were lost in the retreat, are incompatible with the casualty returns. The real figure was less than 500. The total Saxon loss is set at 463, while the Imperials may be estimated at 1200 cavalry and over 3000 infantry.

The Swedes lost more heavily in dead, but hardly any prisoners: 3313 in all. The losses were unevenly distributed among the corps: King lost 293; Vitzthum, 345 foot and 65 horse, while Baner and Leslie suffered 2610 of their original 9419, some 28%. They also lost 15+ flags, but no guns. Baner's victory was costly, though hardly pyrrhic; Montecuccoli rightly termed it indecisive.

Characteristically, Baner blamed his officers for everything that had gone wrong, while claiming all credit for himself. King and Leslie were both criticized, but Vitzthum, reasonably enough, received the full force of his wrath. The Saxon was never to command in the field again.

While Baner's basic strategy—concentrating against a divided enemy—was perfectly sound, his tactical implementation was risky in the extreme. If he really believed his own estimate of 25,000 Germans, then his actions would be indefensible. His inability to coordinate his four separated columns was a major weak point in his whole concept.

Both Baner and Hatzfeld chose to lead their cavalry in person, and, hardly coincidentally, both lost operational control of their forces. Baner, of course, benefited by leading from the front in his accustomed skirmishes and raids. In this case, however, this approach effectively eliminated any possibility of proper coordination. Leslie and Vitzthum needed closer direction—especially because of his own divisive leadership style. Under such circumstances, it was unrealistic to expect them to show much initiative. He should have delegated the right wing to Torstensson, and moved between right, center, and reserve as circumstances dictated.

Hatzfeld was guilty of three errors, which together cost him the battle. First, he neglected to secure his flanks, allowing Baner to envelop not one but both wings. Better scouting, outposts, even a lookout on the Scharfenberg would have averted this. In the next phase, he was alert enough to recognize Baner's threat and reacted quickly enough to forestall it. Had he been merely a cavalry brigadier, he could not be faulted. But by leading the counterattack himself, he allowed the wing behind him to fall into disorder, and the opportunity was wasted. Indeed, he was lucky to overcome Torstensson and avoid destruction by Baner. He would have done better to have appointed Ulhefeld or Montecuccoli to lead the counterattack. His most grievous error was his failure to crush Baner in detail—the Swede gave him repeated opportunities. He simply didn't realize it. Perhaps he was too caught up in the cavalry melee to grasp the overall situation and "couldn't see the forest for the trees." Hatzfeld blamed the Saxons for his "risky" strategy, but his own command failure, not Saxon bungling, handed Baner a victory that his recklessness had forfeited.

For "daring" and "vision," not to mention a fortunate outcome, Wittstock has been compared to Torgau and even Cannae. Americans may notice a slight resemblance to 2nd Bull Run.

The defeated Hatzfeld retired via Pritzwalk and Werben to Halberstadt. The Saxons remained there, while the Imperials decided to continue back to Westphalia.

BANER'S WINTER OFFENSIVE, 1636–37

Baner's fondness for winter operations must have been almost as dangerous to his own men as to the enemy. In this case, he seems to have assumed that his hard-won victory had opened Saxony itself to conquest. Unfortunately, his army wasn't quite up to the job.

He began his offensive by retaking Werben, then driving into Saxony-Thuringia. After capturing the key center of Erfurt, contact was made with the French-allied Hessians. The Saxons[32] were routed in minor actions, and Torgau[33] surrendered without a fight. Finally, Baner laid siege to Leipzig (January 11, 1637). The town was weak but actively defended by the obstinate Col. Trandorf. Despite the employment of heavy siege guns, mortars, and a mine, Baner made no headway. The siege was lifted February 6, with the loss of 1000 Swedes. After a little futile maneuvering around Naumburg, Baner took up winter quarters at Torgau (March 15). The only real gain of the offensive was Erfurt.

GALLAS'S OFFENSIVE OF 1637–38

In June, Gallas, as Imperial lieutenant general, set off from the Rhine with 20,000 men. On the 28th, he joined Marrazino and the much-reduced Saxon army at Pretzsch (on the Elbe, midway between Torgau and Wittenberg). Their total came to 45,000 on paper, although 30,000 seems more likely. Baner, still at Torgau, was down to 14,000 (9 brigades of foot, 50 mounted squadrons, and 80 guns). Gallas immediately conceived a bold plan to cut Baner off and destroy him en toto—it had been careless of the Swede to allow so superior an enemy to get so close. There ensued a race north, which Gallas won, reaching Kustrin first and trapping Baner between the Oder and the Polish border.

Formidable in desperation, Baner feinted east, then forcemarched west, crossed the Oder at Gorlitz, then hurried to the Baltic. Baner's genius was hailed throughout Europe, while Gallas became a laughingstock.[34] This often repeated judgment is false: Gallas's plan was correct; Baner had been trapped by his own carelessness. His escape was due in equal parts to boldness, clever maneuver, and good luck, but the danger need not have occurred at all.

Baner had escaped, but wars are not won by evacuations. Gallas, moving in pursuit, defeated the small army of Wrangel, while a corps of Saxons and Brandenburgers under Klitzing gobbled up the remaining Swedish garrisons in the area (including Werben and Havelberg). Baner and Wrangel fell back into the strong fortress of Stettin (July 21).

As Wallenstein had discovered in 1628, the Baltic strongholds, situated in a barren region and easily supplied by sea, were practically impossible to secure. The logistical position was much worse in 1637, as the ravages of war and the onerous Swedish occupation had impoverished Pomerania. Given their control of the sea, the Swedes were hard to dislodge, but found it easy to return. For the moment though, Baner with his inferior forces[35] could only watch helplessly as Gallas devoured each fortress in turn.[36] The Imperials spent summer and fall overrunning Pomerania, then wintered in Mecklenburg (stomach strategy again). By spring of 1638, Baner was down to Stettin and Stralsund in Pomerania plus Wismar and Warnemund in Mecklenburg. Aside from now-isolated Erfurt, all the gains of Wittstock had been lost.

Similar reverses attended the other Swedish fronts. Leslie in Westphalia was reduced to four strong places (Minden, Nienburg, Osnabruck, Vechta), while Hanau, Sweden's last foothold on the Main, fell to the Imperials February 13, 1638. The French still threatened the Rhine, but, on the whole, early 1638 represented a last peaking of Imperial power. Both victories and defeats were still to come, but the Hapsburg star was never to shine quite so brightly again.

Baner remained trapped in Stettin until July, when a reinforcement of 9000 Swedes and 5000 Finns revitalized his army.

Gallas's subsequent bungling has obscured his very real accomplishments in 1634 and 1637. Despite Baner's escape from the Oder, Gallas made effective use of superior numbers to eliminate the Swedish dominion in northern Germany. Given the disparity in numbers, Baner did well to preserve his force intact. The 1637 campaign reflects credit on both commanders.

BANER'S LAST OFFENSIVES, 1638–41

Baner's counterattack began on August 10, with 21,000 men—10,000 foot in 11 brigades and 11,000 horse in 31 regiments. Gallas's army was so reduced by attrition, garrisons, and detachments that he had only 15,000 available. The logistical constraints, stomach strategy, gave the Swedes an unbeatable advantage on the Baltic coast. If Gallas concentrated his forces, they starved. If he dispersed them, they were taken in detail. Now it was his turn to watch as his gains disappeared. Marrazino blundered into another one of Baner's traps—as usual—losing 2400 men at Neukloster (November 30). By this time, the Swedes had regained all Pomerania. Baner briefly went into winter quarters (December 8–31), before initiating yet another winter offensive (January 1, 1639). He quickly overran Mecklenburg and Lauenburg, then thrust into Johann Georg's Saxony with 18,000 men. A small German corps (4–5000 men) under Saxon Col. Trauditsch was shattered at the action of 2nd Lützen.[37] The minor towns of Zwickau and Chemnitz were taken, and Freiburg besieged (March 3–20). Baner threw away 1000 men in an unsuccessful storm before the surprise appearance of an Imperial corps under Marrazino forced him to break off. Unfortunately, poor Marrazino then proceeded to fall into yet another of Baner's ambushes, the action of Chemnitz (April 4), losing 2500 men. Baner made a halfhearted second attempt at Freiburg, then switched to the less determined pass outpost of Pirna (April 26–May 3). He had a new, decisive scheme in mind, the conquest of Bohemia. Leaving 3000 men to hold Pirna, he took his main body of 26,000 through the Elbe Pass. An Imperial covering force dispatched by Gallas was routed at Brandeis (May 29); Prague itself was bombarded. However, Gallas positioned his main force to defend the city; Baner was too weak to attempt an assault.

While all this was going on, Swedish Gen Lilliehook with Wrangel's old corps was reducing the remaining German garrisons in Brandenburg, while a similar detachment under Torstensson menaced Saxony. He was opposed by an Imperial contingent under Hatzfeld. Their ongoing struggle degenerated into a series of sieges around Bautzen in Lusatia, the town ending up in Swedish hands.[38] A third detachment, under Stalhansk, overran most of Silesia, so that in mid-1639, Baner appeared on the verge of strategic victory. The Swedes had not been so well positioned since Nordlingen.

The success was illusionary. The projected conquest of Bohemia had degenerated into fruitless maneuver and skirmish. Reinforcements were sent from all over the Empire, bringing Gallas's army, now under Archduke Leopold, the emperor's brother, to over 30,000 by July. The logic of stomach strategy had turned against Baner. With characteristic braggadocio he advised Oxenstierna that although he'd "destroyed every village between Prague and Vienna" he still couldn't feed his men. Both sides were melting away, but the Swedes much faster than the Imperials.[39] The Swedes resorted to ruthless plundering; their depredations were to be remembered for centuries. The arrival of Piccolomini from Flanders with 15,000 more men (October) rendered the Swedish position absolutely untenable. Still fixated on the prospect of total victory, Baner stubbornly refused to admit this. The Imperials began a winter offensive of their own (January 26, 1640), fielding 13,400 foot and 8350 horse. In this sort of fighting, the irregular Croats were worth two of the Swedish heavies. Baner was forced to abandon his plans, falling back to Saxony with a mere wreckage of his once-powerful array.

Irrepressibly, the Swedish commander bounced back almost immediately. His new plan called for a strike against the Danube based on Erfurt. Stalhansk would continue operations in Silesia, while Axel Lillie[40] assumed responsibility for Brandenburg and Saxony. On May 16, 1640, Baner effected a junction with the

Hessian and Franco-Weimarian armies, giving him a grand total of 16,000.[41]

Unfortunately for him, Piccolomini had occupied Saalfeld, southwest of Erfurt, with 10,000 men (May 6), blocking the road to Bavaria. When Baner arrived, he found them dug in and ready for his attack. After Wittstock, Baner had lost his taste for assaulting entrenched armies. A confrontation (May 17–20) was followed by retreat. The Swedes and their allies moved aggressively against the Rhine. Piccolomini followed cautiously, until the arrival of 15,000 Bavarians under Mercy brought him up to 25,000. The allies separated; Baner and his Swedes returned to Erfurt (June 23).

He was still far from beaten. As it happened, the Imperial Diet was meeting at Regensburg, key to the Danube. He resolved to essay yet another daring winter offensive, swoop down on the unsuspecting councilors, and at once cut short their deliberations and secure the strategic city. Baner had expected the support of 6000 Franco-Weimarians, but they failed to materialize, so he began the operation (December 16) with fewer than 10,000 men. He achieved initial surprise, but by the time he reached Regensburg (January 26, 1641), it was well garrisoned and prepared for defense. Thwarted, he fell back on Bamberg (February 16–March 20).

Not expecting so successful a defense, the Imperials had directed Archduke Leopold, Piccolomini, and Mercy to form an army of relief. Together (February 21), they mustered 9000 foot; 13,000 horse, and 40 guns. They attempted to cut off and destroy the retreating Swedes; only the sacrifice of Schlang's detachment at Neunburg enabled Baner to escape. The Swedes were forced to retire, pursued by the Imperials as far north as Halberstadt.

There Baner met with the double-dealing Georg of Luneburg, who was interested in changing sides again. Unfortunately, negotiations were aborted when both Baner and Georg died of food poisoning (May 20, 1641).

Shocked, half-disbelieving, Baner's embittered veterans celebrated his passing with a general mutiny.

SOURCES

The best English account of Wittstock is Barker (1975); Delbruck is worth a look. German sources include Schmidt's *Die Schlacht bei Wittstock* (1876) and Krebs's *Aus der Leben des kaiserlichen Feldmarschalls Grafen Melchior von Hatzfeld* (1910–26). Swedish sources are Tingsten (1932) and Bjorlin (1914). The "Quartermaster's List" is reprinted in Schmidt (1876); the Hatzfeld diagrams and casualty list in Krebs. Bjorlin has a version of the Baner diagram.

APPENDIX A: THE IMPERIAL ARMY AT WITTSTOCK

There are three sources for Hatzfeld's army, his own account, the Imperial casualty lists, and the "quartermaster's list" captured by the Swedes, to which three may be added the units mentioned in Wrede. However, the "quartermaster" seems to include troops detached with Klitzing and may exclude some of Marrazino's. The Hatzfeld list is certainly incomplete—he seems to be deliberately understating his force—nevertheless, it can be relied on as far as it goes.

As regards unit strengths, the cavalry can be estimated with fair accuracy from the casualty reports, but the infantry provide only an approximate global figure. These were formed into composite "brigades" (actually battalions) of several infantry regiments each. No doubt Hatzfeld intended the battalions to be roughly equal when he brigaded them, but this still allows for wide variation. The "10 squadrons" of the vanguard probably included the Imperial dragoons. Although not mentioned in the cavalry casualty reports, these "squadrons" cannot have been much less than 100 each. Some of the missing cavalry, such as Kracht, may have been with them.

Unit	Date	Coy	Est Str	Notes
Goltz IR	1626	9	350	Bohemian-German
Pappenheim IR	1631	7	250	HG; Pappenheim-Alzheim
Manteuffel IR	1626	6	200	High German
Enkefort IR	1631	12	350	High German
Gonzaga IR	1633	9	250	Italian
Enan IR	1635	10	350	Spanish; AKA Ennon
Bonninghausen IR	1634	3	100	Ex-League; Westphalia
Lombardi IR	1635?	8	250	Italian; AKA Lambardi
Alt-Wallenstein IR	1629	4	200	LG; Max Waldstein
Jung-Wallenstein IR	1633	10	400	Ger; Ladislas Waldstein
Colloredo IR	1625	15	400	German
Harrach IR	1626	7	200	HG; AKA Harrich, Horrich
Niedrumb IR	1633	4	100	German; AKA Niedrum
Bourre IR	1631	10	400	High German; AKA Bourri
Mansfeld IR	1625	5	200	High German
Hatzfeld IR	1632	10	500	Low German
Strassoldo IR	1631	6	200	Italian
Zweyer IR	1634	6	150	High German
Herrera IR	1635	6	150	Spanish-German
Thun IR	1620	10	350	League; Bavaria
Westfalen IR	1631	5	150	" Westphalia
Werth IR	1633	6	200	" "
Darmstadt IR	1634/6	?	350	Hesse-Darmstadt
Bunau IR	1633	10	250	Saxon IR #11
Zehmen IR	1633	10	250	Saxon IR #10; AKA Zehme
Trandorf IR	1631	10	300	Sax IR #1; AKA Drandorf
Schleinitz IR	1631	12	327	Saxon IR #3
Brink IR	1635	5	373	Saxon DR #7
Pforte IR	1631	8	600	Saxon IR #2
Bose IR	1631	10	350	Saxon IR #4
Marradas KUR	1616	10	314	Spanish-German; oldest CR
Wintz KUR	1631	8	454	Ger; AKA Winz, Vinz.
Ruck KUR	1632	10?	317	Ger;ex-Lg; LtCol Mansfeld
Rittberg KUR	1631	8	284	Ger; Riedburg; ex-ARK.
Falkenstein KUR	1631	8	307	Rhine; ex-ARK; Col KIA
Puchheim KUR	--	?	243	Ger; not in Wrede
Wildberg KUR	1626	9	438	Ger; Col KIA
Hatzfeld KUR	1625	10	645	Ger; AKA Hatzfeldt
Polniskow KUR	--	10	243	"Prince of Poland"
Schonickel KUR	1634	6	268	Ger; Col court-martialed
Del Maestro ARK	1632	10?	437	Austrian; Col wounded
Ulhefeld KUR	1630	10	409	LG; AKA Uhlfeld;
Mansfeld KUR	1633	2	163	German; LtCol Wippart
Montecuccoli KUR	1626	5	254	Low German

Unit	Year	Coys	Men	Notes
Harrach KUR	1634	9?	286	Ger; AKA Harrich, Horrich
Bissinger KUR	1632	10	536	" AKA Basinger, Bissengen
Darmstadt KUR	1633/6	5	243	Hesse-Darmstadt
Alt-Burgsdorf CR	1632	?	150?	Brandenburg
Franz Carote CR	1632	10	150?	Franz Karl Sax-Lauenburg
Vitzthum CR	1632	10	200	Saxon CR #8; MajGen
Schierstadt CR	1632	10	175	Saxon CR #6
Kalkstein CR	1632	10	200	Saxon CR #7
Trauditsch CR	1634	?	251	Saxon CR #10
Strein CR	1631	10	300	Saxon CR #4
Alt-Taube CR	1631	10	175	Saxon CR #3; Leib CR
Bose CR	1635	12	175	Saxon CR #19
Wolframsdorf CR	1635	9	150	Sax CR#17; AKA Ramsdorf
Rochau CR	1633	16	350	Sax CR#16; AKA Strachow
Kalkreuter CR	1632	10	300	Saxon CR #9
Baudissin CR	1631	10	250	Saxon CR #1
Gersdorff CR	1631	5	200	Saxon CR #11
Hanau CR	1631	10	255	Saxon CR #2
Gall a Burke DR	1633	10	400?	German; AKA Hall
Leslie DR	1633?	6	200?	"
Bissinger DR	1636	3	100?	" note: 7 coys & 200 men
Marrazino DR	1631?	8	300?	" part of CR?

Guns: 5 Demicannon (24pdr), 2 Demiculverins (8pdr), 6 falcons (2x6pdr; 4x4pdr), 12 "small guns" (2-4pdr), 1 falconet (3pdr), 4 mortars, 8 petards.

To these forces can probably be added 2 Saxon coys:

Unit	Year	Coys	Men	Notes
Elector Household	1631	1	100?	Elector's personal escort
Schwalbach DR	1635	1	161	Firelocks; guarded artillery

Wrede lists 3 cuirassier regiments that do not appear in Hatzfeld, the casualty lists, or even the Quartermaster:

Unit	Year	Coys	Men	Notes
Ratkay KUR	1634	?	?	Possibly Puchheim?
Lobkowitz KUR	1632	?	?	Part of Marrazino's corps
Kracht KUR	1636	6	?	Low German; Lutheran

Kracht was formed out of troops originally raised for Gustavus by Georg of Luneburg. Most of them deserted to Baner after Wittstock. They could have been with the vanguard.

The "Quartermaster's List" shows a number of units not mentioned by Hatzfeld. Most of them were probably detached or with Klitzing:

Unit	Year	Coys	Men	Notes
Arnim IR	1631	12	?	Saxon IR #5
Wolfersdorf IR	1631	12	?	Sax IR #6; AKA Wilsdorf
Taube IR	1631	12	?	Saxon IR #7; Leib
Schneider IR	1632	6	945?	Saxon IR #9
Ponickau IR	1631	5	456	Sax IR #13; AKA Ponikaw
Schleinitz CR	1631	5	?	Saxon CR #5
Dehne CR	1634	10	?	SaxCR#12; Dene-Rothfelsen
Milbe CR	1633	6	?	Saxon CR #13
Jung-Taube CR	1633	9	?	Saxon CR #14; 2nd Leib CR
Masslehner DR	1635	5-6	497	Saxon DR #3; "Hungarian"

Klitzing therefore had upward of 3000 foot and 1000 horse.

Also listed are 2 IMP regiments:
Wolkenstein IR   1634   ?   ?   Tyrol
Zaradeszky ARK   1633   ?   ?   Silesia

Zaradeszky had been with Marrazino but was sent to Silesia before the battle. Wolkenstein's location is unclear; it was a very weak unit and may have already been disbanded.

APPENDIX B: BANER'S ARMY AT WITTSTOCK

Schmidt and Mankell place the Swedes at 7288 foot and 9150 horse; this estimate rests entirely on the contemporary history of Chemnitz. But, as pointed out by Delbruck, the (at least) equally reliable Grotius and Frankfort report place them rather higher. None of the lists include the 840 dragoons they had in July.

	Schmidt	Delbruck
Baner	10,438	10,438
Leslie	4,000	7,000
Neu-Brandenburg	(1,000??)	1,000
Pomerania	2,000	ca. 3,350
Total	16,438	21,788

Thus, the range of estimates runs 16,438–22,628. From this total was subtracted 500 infantry to garrison the castle and upwards of 1000 (Mortaigne) to guard the train. Schmidt and Mankell failed to allow for these guards and the 500 musketeers in the detachments. Adding 1000 men from Neu-Brandenburg would cover the garrison and detachment, but not the train. Adding the dragoons as well would approach the figure.

The number and type of guns are unknown. Extrapolating from other figures, I approximate 8 demicannon, 11 demiculverins, and 40 falconets.

The Swedish lists fail to properly distinguish between Stalhansk's former Finn cavalry regiment (Wittenberg) and his newly formed German cavalry regiment. Smaland Cavalry Regiment is mentioned, but does not appear in the O.B.; Wurzburg isn't mentioned but does appear. Slang and Jarotzky are not in the O.B. but are in the July lists.

Mankell	#288 (Oct 1)		#284–287 (July 17)	
Brigade	IR	Str	Coy	Str
Swedish	Drake	892	8	500
	Ermis		8	150
	Sal Adams		8	400
Scots	Kunigham	800	8	400
	Karr		12	400
Blue	Abel Moda	856	4	100
	Baner		12	600
Sabelitz	Goltz	896	8	400
	Sabelitz		12	600
Leslie	Leslie	900	8	200
Thomas Thomasson	Thomas Thomasson	438	8	700
Wrangel	Jeschwitzki	738	12	600
	Wrangel		8	300
	Gun		8	100
Ruthven	Hansson	698	8	300
	Ruthven		8	350
	Bengtsson		8	748 (Pilefeld)
Bauer	Peter Linds	1012	4	128
	Herberstein		10	200

			Str	Coy	Str
	Kriegbaum			8	100
	Bauer/Bagge			12	500
	Strahlendorf			5	150
	Forbes			8	100
Total			7228 Inf		
CR			**Str**	**Coy**	**Str**
Gadau (Uppland)			200	4	250
Klingspor (East Gothlnd)			200	4	250
Bjelke (Abo Finns)			500	-	--
Wittenberg (Abo Finns)			500	-	--
Wachtmeister			600	12	500
Livonian			450	10	300
Kurland			300	8	300
Krakau			400	8	400
Duke Franz Henrich			350	8	300
Baner Leib			600	12	600
Torstensson			300	6	200
King			250	-	--
Hoditz			250	-	--
Beckermann			150	-	--
Glaubitz			250	-	--
Boy			200	-	--
Birkenfeld			150	-	--
Dewitz			250	8	250
Jens/Jensson			350	8	400
Goldstein			500	8	500
Stalhansk (newly raised)			550	10	1200
Berghofer			150	8	200
Pfuhl			400	8	200
Duval			300	8	250
Douglas			200	8	400
Wopersnow			300	4	320
Stuart			200	4	302
Wurzburg			300	-	--
		Total	9150 cav		
			16,378 in all		
Schulmann (Wurzburg?)				8	200
Schlang				8	600
Jarotzky				6	100
Smaland				4	500
Dragoons	Gustafson			4	400
	Hansson			8	300
	Hay			4	140

APPENDIX C: IMPERIAL RECORDS

Baner discovered the "Quartermaster's List" among the captured Imperial baggage:
Infantry
Hatzfeld's Corps   Saxon Corps
7 Pappenheimb   7 Harruch

12 Enckeforth
8 Lambardi
10 Hatzfeld
6 Jean de Weert
6 Manteuffel
3 Bonighause
10 Enan
10 Salis (=Thun?)
9 Goltz
10 Wolkenstein
10 Bawer
6 Zweyen
5 Manssfeld
5 Westphael
9 Gonsago
6 Strasoldo
6 Herrere
3 Persinger DR (Bissinger)
141 Coys in 19 Regts

15 Colloredo
4 Wallenstein
10 Jung Wallenstein
12 Taubens or Leib
12 Wilsdorff
12 Schleinitz
4 Niedcrumb
8 Pfordte
10 Bose
6 Schneider
10 Traendorff
12 Arnheim
5 Ponikaw
127 Coys in 14 IRs

Artillery & Dragoons
6 Maschleiner Hungarian DR
133 Coys in 15 Regts

Cavalry
Hatzfeld's Corps
9 Wildberg
10 Bosingers KUR
9 Schunickels
10 Hatzfeld
10 Prinz Polnischkaw
5 Monte Cuculi
8 Falckenstein
5 Darmstadt
8 Alt Rittberg
2 Manssfeldt
88 Coys in 10 CRs

Saxon Corps
6 Geersdorf
5 Schleinitz
10 Lieutenant-General
10 Alt Taube
9 Jung Taube
5 Seidlitz
10 Ralckstein
10 Schierstett
10 Hans v. Strachaw
9 Stramssdorff
6 Multe
10 General Vitzthums
12 Bose
10 Duke Frantz Carok
122 Coys in 14 CRs

Marrazino's Corps
10 Marazini
8 Winse
10 Don Baltasar
8 Sarradetzky
8 Trausse
10 Hanaw
10 Schablitzko
10 Strein
10 Daen
84 Coys in 9 CRs
Dragoons
10 Hall
6 Lessle
8 Marazini
24 Coys in 3 DRs

Note the presence of Imperial units with the Saxon corps and Saxon units with Marrazino. The "quartermaster" seems to have envisioned Marrazino's force as all mounted.

Hatzfeld drew up three diagrams of the battle. The first seems to illustrate his initial deployment:
    Left Wing, 1st Echelon=6 sqds (left to right): illegible; Wildberg; Wildberg; Hatzfeld; Hatzfeld; Prince of Poland.
    Left, 2nd Echelon=7 sqds: Dragoons; Ulhefeld; Ulhefeld; Montecuccoli & Mansfeld; Bissinger; Bissinger; Darmstadt.
    Center Infantry, 1st Echelon=7 bns: Goltz & Pappenheim; Thun-Westfalen-Werth; Manteuffel-Enkefort-Gonzaga; Enan-Bonninghausen-Lombardi; Bunau-Zehme-Trandorf; Jung & Alt-Wallenstein; Colloredo-Harrach-Niedrumb.
    Behind the 1st Echelon=7 cav sqds (names blank)
    Center, 2nd Echelon=5 bns: Bourre & Mansfeld; Hatzfeld; Schleinitz & Brink; Bose & Darmstadt.
    Behind the 2nd Echelon: Artillery Train

Behind the Train=5 cav sqds (blank)

Right Wing, 1st Echelon=6 sqds: Marradas; Marradas; Marradas; Vitzthum; Schierstadt; Kalkstein.

Right Wing, 2nd Echelon=7 sqds: Leib CR; Bose; Wolframsdorf; Rochau; Rochau; Dragoons; (blank).

There is a sqd (blank) between the two echelons, behind Kalkstein.

A note between Colloredo Infantry Regiment and Marradas indicates that there were eight K (quarter-cannon?), four K (demicannon?), falcons, and assorted minor pieces in the 1st echelon.

Hatzfeld's second diagram appears to illustrate the situation at some unknown point in the fighting. It shows 35 squadrons (cavalry & dragoon) in 2 groups of 2 echelons each, the units in each group numbered 1–17.

The 1st echelon, under Marrazino (left to right): Montecuccoli (8); Horrich (7); Bissinger (6); ? (5); Marradas (4 & 3); Strein (2); Trauditsch (1).

2nd echelon, under Kalkstein: Rochau (17 & 16); Wintz (15); ? (14); Kalkstein (13 & 12); Ramsdorf (11); Puchheim (10).

Note that Falkenstein (9) and "Dragoons" are between the echelons, to the left of Montecuccoli and Rochau.

3rd echelon, under Ulhefeld: Ulhefeld (1 & 2); Del Maestro (3); Del Maestro & Wippart (4); Schonickel (5); Wildberg (6 & 7); Hatzfeld (8 & 9).

4th echelon, under Wildberg: Kalkreuter (10); Kalkreuter & Ulhefeld (11); Hoffmann (12 & 13); ? (14)); Hanau (15); Ruck (16); Rittberg (17).

A unit marked Dragoon (9) is between, and right of Hatzfeld and Rittberg.

It seems likely that this represents the cavalry deployment very late in the day, possibly during the disengagement. A 2-echelon disposition is likely, but it is unclear whether we should read Marrazino's group as the left wing and Ulhefeld's the right, or Marrazino the 1st line and Ulhefeld 2nd.

The third diagram is a remarkably accurate reconstruction of Baner's formation, with estimates of unit strengths:

Left Wing, 1st echelon=3350 horse in 14 sqds (left to right): Stalhansk, 1000 horse in 2 sqds; Dewitz, 450 in 2; Bruneck, 150 in 1; Boye, 250 in 2; Glaubitz, 300 in 2; Beckermond, 200 in 1; Hoditz, 400 in 2; King, 600 in 2.

Left Wing, 2nd echelon=1300 horse in 6 sqds: Douglas, 450 in 2; Goldstein, 450 in 2; Gens, 400 in 2.

Center, 1st echelon=5200 foot in 6 brigades: Leslie, 1400; Baner Infantry Regiment & Moda, 1000; Kunnihoj-Karr-Lindse, 900; Thomas Thomasson, 500; Hans Drake & Salomon Adams, 900; Goltz & Sabeltiz, 500.

Center, 2nd echelon=1100 horse in 4 sqds: Torstensson, 200 in 1; Baner Leib, 900 in 3.

Center, 3rd echelon=3500 foot in 4 brigades: Kniphausen & Forbes, 900; Bauer & Strahlendorf, 800; Sangon & Ruthven, 900; Jungl-Jeswitzky-Gunn, 900.

Right Wing, 1st echelon=4000+ horse in 16 sqds: Duke Franz Henrich, 550 in 2; Krak, 550 in 2; Kurlanders, 600 in 2; Livonians, 1 sqd; Wachtmeister, 900 in 3; Slang, 700 in 2; Finns, 700 in 2; Swedes, 2 sqds.

Right Wing, 2nd echelon=1050 horse in 6 sqds: Dautz, 300 in 2; Jarotsky, 150 in 1; Pfuhl, 300 in 1; Berghofer, 300 in 2.

Total: 10,900 cavalry & 9300 infantry.

Note that Hatzfeld apparently allowed 600 infantry for the musketeer detachments.

Aside from a tendency to round up instead of down, Hatzfeld's figures are close to Baner's own. Clearly, Hatzfeld came away from the battle with a much more accurate idea of his enemy than Baner did.

APPENDIX D: ACTIONS & FORCES 1635–41

Marrazino's corps in 1635 included infantry regiments Harrach, Colloredo, Alt- and Jung-Wallenstein, and Niedrumb; cuirassier regiments Marrazino, Wintz, and Marradas; Zaradeszky Arkebusier Regiment, and dragoon regiments Gall a Burke, Leslie and Marrazino. To these were added Saxon CRs #5 (Schleinitz) and #10 (Trauditsch). At this time, Baudissin had IRs #1–14, CRs #1–19 (less 5 & 10), DRs #3–7, a coy each of Household horse and foot, 31 guns, and 300 gunners plus 3 Brandenburg cavalry regiments (Franz Karl, Alt-Burgsdorf, and Jung-Burgsdorf). Infantry regiments 8–12 and 14 were probably in garrison.

Torstensson's corps

Unit	Coy	Str	Notes
Torstensson CR	1	150	German
Axel Lillie Coy	1	154	" governor of Pomerania
Schulmann CR	4	580	"
Johann Printz CR	4	595	"
Klingspor CR	4	600	"
Gadau CR	4	589	"
		2659 cavalry	
Drake IR	8	1200	Swedes
Bagge IR	8	700	German
Gun IR	12	700	"
Musketeer Detachments		1000	"
		3600 infantry	
Ruthven IR	8	900	Scots?
Fleetwood IR	8	850	"
Gordon IR	4	460	"
Schutte IR	7	730	German?
		2940 infantry en route to Wolgast	

Gallas's army of 1637–38 included at least:
    9 infantry regiments=Leslie, Grana, Goltz, Alt-Wangler, Salis, Webel, Zuniga,* Gonzaga,* Moulin*;
    22 cuirassier regiments=Marradas, Bruay, Gonzaga, Pompeji, Altheim,* Jung, Puchheim, Mislik, Borneval,* Bredow,* Lobkowitz,* Montecuccoli, Lamboy, Hussmann,* Sparenberg,* Munster, Sieghofer, Burksdorf,* Kracht,* Gissenburg,* Schutz*;
    1 arkebusier regiment=Maestro*;
    3 dragoon regiments=Gall a Burke, Grana, Carasco, Schonkirchen*;
    1 Croat regiment=Losy;
plus the support of the Saxon and Brandenburg forces. The number of units destroyed or disbanded during this campaign (marked *) was unusually large.

Baner's army (Mankell 293) seems much too small:

Unit	Coy	Str	Unit	Coy	Str
Drummond IR	11	800	Baner Leib CR	1	100
Fels IR	8	500	Swede CR	4	300
Kinnemund IR	8	400	Cappuhn CR	6	150
Guntersberg IR	8	400	Wopersnow CR	6	150
Sincklers IR	8	200	Stuart CR	4	150

Gordon IR	4	200	Kerberg CR	4	150	
Infantry		2500	Schulmann CR	4	125	
Baner Dragoon Coy	1	80	Cavalry		1125	
Free Dragoon Coys	3	220				
Dragoons		300				
Total: 3925						

Baner assembled a larger force for his 1638 breakout from Stettin (Mankell 302):

23 infantry regiments in 11 brigades: Alt-Blau, Baner Leib & M. Hansson; Torstensson, Fels & Braun; Sabelitz & East Gothland (Swedes); Col Baner & Mortaigne; E. Hansson; Jeschwitzki; Lindsey, Kinnemund, Cunningham & Fleetwood (Scots Brig); Green, Yellow & Nieroth (Hesse-Cassel); Stenbock (Swedes); A. Hansson; Osterling & Flotow.

31 cavalry regiments: Wrangel (Uppland Swedes); Oxenstierna (East Gothland Swedes); Stakes (West Gothland Swedes); Bjelke Finns; Wittenberg Finns; Stalhansk Finns; Stalhansk German; Baner Leib; Torstensson Leib; Pfuhl; Duval; Duke Franz Henrich; Livonia; Kurland; Wachtmeister; Dewitz; Leslie; Jens; Douglas; Hoking; Wurzburg; Slang; Witzleben; Hoditz; Cratzenstein; Glaubitz; Konigsmarck; Knyphausen; Eberstein (Hesse-Cassel); Dalwigk (Hesse-Cassel); Eppen (Hesse-Cassel).

Action at Chemnitz, April 4, 1639

Marrazino's army consisted of:

Unit	Date	Coy	Est Str	Notes
Leslie IR	1619	10	?	IMP
Colloredo IR	1625	15	?	IMP
Gonzaga IR	1625	9	?	IMP; ex-Grana
Goltz IR	1626	9	?	IMP
Alt-Wangler IR	1628	10	?	IMP
Bourre IR	1631	10	?	IMP
Webel IR	1632	?	?	IMP
Schlick IR	1632	?	?	IMP
Puchheim KUR	1630	10	?	IMP
Mislik KUR	1631	?	?	IMP; 340 captured
Salis ARK	1636	?	?	IMP; heavy loss
Tergouschlitz CR	1631	5	?	IMP; Croats
Trauditsch CR	1631	?	143	Saxon CR #3
Hanau CR	1631	?	248	" CR #4.
Jung-Schleinitz CR	1632	?	191	" CR #10
Reuchel CR	1635	?	154	" CR #4
Masslehner CR	1635	5–6	66	" CR #9
Dragoons	1635	?	70	" DR #3?

52 coy mounted, 18 on foot.
Total: approximately 5000 men.

Baner's attack force included the Baner Leib, Torstensson, Wachtmeister, Wittenberg, Stalhansk, and Pfuhl cavalry regiments, and a sqd of Konigsmarck. Both sides lost 500 killed and wounded, but Baner took 1500 prisoners, of whom 300 were officers. Marrazino survived court-martial but never commanded again.

Action at Brandeis, May 29, 1639

Having entered Bohemia via the Elbe Pass, Baner intended to ford that river near

Brandeis. Gallas dispatched 10,000 men under Hofkirchen to block him. When they arrived, Baner was already across, 18,000 strong. Given the superiority of the enemy, Col. Montecuccoli urged Hofkirchen to withdraw; instead he ordered an immediate pell-mell advance (to push the Swedes back over the Elbe?). The Imperial cavalry, leading the attack, collided head-on with their Swedish opposites. The Imperials recoiled from contact, breaking into rout after "firing fifty pistol shots." The infantry, close behind, and many officers were abandoned to the Swedes. Baner lost 600 men in all; the Imperials suffered 1000 dead and wounded plus 400 captured, including both Hofkirchen and Montecuccoli.

Siege of Neunburg, March 19, 1641

After the disastrous failure of his raid on Regensburg, Baner was able to escape only because of the delaying action of MajGen Schlang. Throwing himself into the small town of Neunburg, he stubbornly held out against ten times his numbers. There was, however, no escape; he surrendered with 1600–1700 horse and 180 musketeers.

The Imperial-Bavarian army, under Archduke Leopold, Piccolomini, Mercy, and Geleen, included:

Caretto IR	IMP	Archduke Leib KUR	IMP	
Suys IR	"	Braganza KUR	"	(ex-Marradas)
Souces IR	"	Alt-Piccolomini KUR	"	
Hunoldstein IR	"	Gonzaga KUR	"	
Harrach IR	"	Nicola KUR	"	
Gunter IR	?	Spiegel KUR	"	
Mercy IR	Bavaria	De Vera KUR	"	
Hasslang IR	"	Ester CR	"	
Spork ARK	"	Rodoan CR	"	
Kolb ARK	"	Gayling KUR	Bavaria	

APPENDIX E: THE SAXON ARMY 1631–48

In peacetime, the Saxon Army had consisted of a few guards (household and escort) supplemented by stored weapons in the arsenal (artillery), and a militia of 9360 infantry, 1586 cavalry, and 1500 pioneers. As part of the mobilization of the Evangelical Union (1631) a "regular" army was raised: 7 infantry regiments, and 5 or 6 cavalry regiments, plus a train of four 24 pdrs, six 12 pdrs, and six 6 pdrs. In 1632, as part of Gustavus Adolphus's grand mobilization, 2 infantry, 4 cavalry, and 2 dragoon regiments were added. In the post-Gustavus years 1633–34, 2 infantry and 7 cavalry regiments were raised. After rejoining the Imperial alliance 1635–36, 3 infantry, 3 cavalry, and 7 dragoon regiments were raised against the Swedes.

The Saxon Army 1631–36 (Belaubre):

	1631	1632	1633–34	1635	1636
IR 1	Schwalbach			Trandorf	
IR 2	Starshadel	Pforte			
IR 3	Loser			Schleinitz	
IR 4	Arnim	Bose			
IR 5	Klitzing		Sax-Lauenburg		
IR 6	Solms	Wolfersdorf			
IR 7	Schaumburg	Taube			
IR 8		Vitzthum			
IR 9		Schneider			Markenser
IR 10			Jg Vitzthum	Zehmen	

IR 11			Bunau		
IR 12				Monnier	
IR 13				Ponickau	
IR 14				Mitzlaff	
CR 1	Sax-Altenburg			Baudissin	
CR 2	Bindauf	Holstein	Sx-Launbg?	Hanau	
CR 3a	Taube				
CR 3b	Arnim		reformed		
CR 4	Hoffkirch		Geiso	Strein	
CR 5	Steinau	Sx-Altenbg	Rauchhaupt	Schleinitz	
CR 6		Anhalt	Schierstadt		
CR 7		Kalkstein			
CR 8		Alt Vitzthum			
CR 9		Jung Vitzthum		Wolfersdorf	Kalkreuter
CR 10			Trauditsch		
CR 11			Gersdorff		
CR 12			Dehne		
CR 13			Milbe		
CR 14			Jung Taube		
CR 15			Seidlitz		
CR 16			Rochau		
CR 17				Wolframsdorf	
CR 18				Reuchel	
CR 19				Bose	
CR 20					Masslehner
DR 1		Kalkstein	reformed (to IR #9)		
DR 2		Taube	converted to infantry		
DR 3				Masslehner	
DR 4				Schwalbach Coy	
DR 5				Bose Coy	Schleinitz
DR 6				Bose	
DR 7				Brink	
DR 8					Kluge Coy
DR 9					Vitzthum Co

Electoral Household KUR (1 coy)
Elector Leib Coy (KUR?) 1635-37
Electoral Household Foot (firelock?)
3 Free Coys Schlieben   Wagner
Dresden City Guard (325)
Militia CR 1 Loser (1631)
Militia CR 2 Pfugh (1631)
Not included are the Brandenburg regiments.

In 1637-8, the Saxon Army was reorganized, decimated units being broken up or combined. CR #3 became 1st Leib CR; #14, 2nd Leib; CRs #1, 8, 10, and 17 became CR #3; CR #2 was absorbed into #4; 13 and 19 into CR #5; 9 into 6; 11 and 18 became #7; 12 and 16, #8; and CR #20 (the old DR #3) was renumbered #9. IR #15 was broken up between 1st and 2nd Leib. IRs 6, 7, and 12 became IR #1; the old #1, #2; 10 and 13, #3; 2 and 9, #4; 3, 4, 14, IR #5; 5, #6, and 4, #7. There were now only four DRs: #1 was the artillery train escort; #2 a coy attached to CR #5; #3 was the old DRs #5 and 9, now a single squadron-sized unit, and #4, the old #8, still one coy. DR #7 switched to Brandenburg as Klitzing Dragoon Regiment.

The Saxon Army 1637–48 (Belaubre):

Unit	Colonel	Notes
IR 1	Grubbach	Leib IR
IR 2	Trandorf	
IR 3	Zehmen	To IR #5 1639
IR 4	Pforte	To IR #5 1639
IR 5	Schleinitz	
IR 6	Arnim	
IR 7	Bose	To IR #5 1639
CR 1	Callenberk	1st Leib;
CR 2	Knoche	2nd Leib
CR 3	Trauditsch	To CR #6 1640
CR 4	Hanau	
CR 5	Alt-Schleinitz	To CR #2 1639
CR 6	Jung-Schleinitz	Seidewitz in 1647
CR 7	Reuchel	To CR #4 1640
CR 8	Rochau	To CR #2 in 1639
CR 9	Masslehner	Hungarian; only 2 coy; unit destroyed 1642
DR 1	Lehmann	Artillery escort
DR 2	Schleinitz	1 coy (leib)
DR 3	Haugwitz	
DR 4	Kluge	

Electoral Household KUR (1 coy); AKA Leib Corps
3 Free Coys Wagner (to 1645)

| CR 10 | Jung-Schleinitz II | Formed 1642 with 688 men; later combined with CR #6? |
| CR 11 | Neu-Leib Sqd | Formed 1643 with 4 coys; AKA Rickert |

In 1640, the army was estimated at 2326 cavalry in 43 companies (4 regiments of 10, 1 of 2, and the Household), the infantry at 3552 foot in 4 regiments and 3 free companies, and the dragoons at 770, of which only two-thirds were mounted.

As regards the later Saxon artillery: for the 1641 siege of Gorlitz, the Saxons fielded 26 guns, 2 mortars, 161 wagons, 517 drivers, and 1034 horses. For the recapture of Chemnitz in 1643, they had two 42 pdr cannon, two 24 pdr demicannon, two 12 pdr demiculverins, two 8 pdr falcons, and two 3 pdr regimental guns, with 445 horses.

The army was demobilized after the peace, except for

Leib Coy	121 cavalry
Leib IR	510 infantry
3 Free Companies	558 infantry
3 garrison detachments	120 men
Artillery	143 men

APPENDIX F: THE ACTION OF VLOTHO, OCTOBER 17, 1638

In 1637, the English government decided to finance a scheme to restore the elector palatine. The claimant, Karl Ludwig (eldest son of the late Elector Friedrich, and nephew of King Charles I of England), would form an independent army in Westphalia, then advance through Hesse to liberate the Palatinate by force. With English funding, Karl Ludwig succeeded in raising a few thousand men, a mixture of English volunteers, raw Germans, and deserters from the real armies. Baner loaned him 1000 Swedes under LtGen King, the same King who commanded the left wing at Wittstock. They did not follow their original strategy; the Swedes instead persuaded Karl Ludwig and Lord Craven to besiege the minor Imperial stronghold of Lemgo in Westphalia. Baner's thinking is clear: whatever the final fate of Karl Ludwig's little army, Lemgo would represent a solid gain in the ongoing war of skirmishes.

Palatinate Army—Karl Ludwig, Craven & King

Unit	Coy	EstStr	Notes
Craven IR	10?	1200	Palatine Leib
Loe CR	6?	600	" CR #1
Ferentz CR	6?	600-	" CR #2
Rupert CR	6?	600	" CR #3
Craven DR	2	200	"
King IR	8	300+	Swedish; Scottish-German
King CR	12	400	" " "
Konigsmarck CR	3	200	" German
Guns		?	

Total: 1500 infantry & 2500 cavalry=4000 men.

Lemgo was placed under siege October 15, 1638. However, FM Hatzfeld, who had been transferred to Westphalia after his defeat at Wittstock, quickly assembled a mobile column.

Imperial Army (Westphalia)—Hatzfeld

Unit	Date	Coy	EstStr	Notes
Hatzfeld IR	1632	10	900	IMP; High German; LtCol Carasco
Soye IR	1637	?	900	IMP; Cologne
Hatzfeld KUR	1625	10	600?	IMP; Ger; LtCol Fingerling
Westfalen KUR	1632	10	400?	IMP; Westphalia; ex-ARK; LtCol Lippe
Krafft KUR	1634	?	400?	IMP; Krafft-Lammersdorf; German
Beck KUR	1634	?	400?	IMP; Westphalia
Alt-Nassau KUR	1635	?	400?	IMP; Nassau-Dillenburg
Leittersheim KUR	1636	10?	400?	IMP; Hanensee auf Bottensee; Cologne
Hanensee KUR	1636	?	400?	IMP; Luneburg
Gotz ARK	1632	10	300?	IMP; German
Deveroux DR	1631	?	300?	IMP; German
Westerhold CR	1632	6	400?	League; Westphalia

Total: 1800 inf & 4000 cav=5800 men.

Scouts reported his approach on the 16th. The Protestants estimated his force at over 8000. The commanders decided to retreat at once to the Swedish fortress at Minden. They had to choose between two routes, the Rinteln bridge or the west bank of the Weser via Vlotho (favored by King). The Rinteln route would place the river between them and Hatzfeld, but they would be exposed to attack while crossing. The Vlotho road was shorter and easier, but they would be vulnerable until they reached Minden. Some have questioned the decision to take the Vlotho route, but this was not their real problem. Burdened as they were by baggage and artillery, Hatzfeld's flying column would have overtaken them whichever way they chose.

In the event, when they reached Vlotho, they found that Hatzfeld had cut them off; he was ready and waiting for them. The Palatiners were strung out in line of march, baggage in front, the cavalry following, with the infantry and field guns bringing up the rear. King directed that the cavalry form a defensive line on a small hill, the Eiberg, while he went back and brought up the infantry. Cautiously, he also took the opportunity to send his own baggage safely away, a bit of defeatism that later raised questions.

No sooner had he left, than Konigsmarck proposed an alternative plan. The cavalry would advance from the Eiberg up a narrow valley toward the Imperials. The valley, he said, would act as a defile, preventing Hatzfeld from using his superior numbers. Karl Ludwig and Craven agreed to his suggestion and sent him ahead with the cavalry. They remained on the Eiberg with the dragoons waiting for King.

The defile was only wide enough for 1 cavalry regiment at a time, so Konigsmarck placed Loe in front, Ferentz next, and Rupert third (this was under Prince Rupert, Karl Ludwig's brother and later a famous commander in the English Civil War), with his own Swedes acting as reserve.

When he saw the enemy advancing, Hatzfeld counterattacked with 2 of his own cavalry regiments; at the same time, he dispatched 800 horse under Westerhold and Lippe to envelop their right. As this movement was concealed by the low hills surrounding the valley, it was almost a miniature of Baner's envelopment at Wittstock.

Loe Cavalry Regiment broke before the Imperials, sweeping away Ferentz as well. Seeing the Imperial advancing, Rupert ordered an attack, a "flat-out" Swedish-style charge, of the sort he was later to make famous in England. Whether due to elan, tactics, or the enemy's exhaustion, Rupert succeeded where Loe failed. Col. Gotz was killed, and the Imperials thrown back right out of the valley. Rupert pressed after them in pursuit.

Unfortunately for him, as he emerged from the defile, Hatzfeld surrounded him on both wings.

Konigsmarck had remained inert as he watched the drama, but Craven decided to intervene with his only reserve, the 2 troops of dragoons. Perhaps he hoped to rally the remnants of Loe and Ferentz, support Rupert's advance, and save the battle. It was not to be. No sooner had he joined Rupert than GWM Westerhold's group emerged from the hills, neatly trapping the Palatiners against Hatzfeld.

Konigsmarck now decided to withdraw, his troops unbloodied. King, returning too late, abandoned his men to flee the field with Karl Ludwig.

Rupert, Craven, and the others fought bravely. Westerhold was killed springing the trap. But it was hopeless, and all four colonels, Rupert, Craven, Loe, and Ferentz, were taken prisoner. They did manage to hold Hatzfeld long enough for Konigsmarck to extricate the Swedish contingent safely.

Hatzfeld demonstrated a cool professionalism in this minor action, which was not in evidence at Wittstock or Jankow. The Swedish veterans King and Konigsmarck, on the other hand, outdid themselves in ineptitude. King, unfairly, blamed Rupert for the defeat; the two were still feuding 10 years later. Konigsmarck escaped all censure and later became one of Torstensson's most trusted officers.

NOTES

1. Except in Spain.
2. Montecuccoli indicated that a superior Imperial squadron (4 deep) should be 200 strong and an inferior one (5 deep), 250–300, Barker, *Military Intellectual*, p. 91. By 1690, a typical squadron was 165 sabers, 3 deep.
3. Roberts, *Gustavus Adolphust*, pp. 256–57.
4. Barker, *Military Intellectual*, pp. 146–47. This controversy was still raging as late as the Napoleonic wars, eventually being resolved in favor of the gallop, see Nosworthy, *Anatomy of Victory*, pp.121–33.
5. They hoped to combine the control of the trot with the impact of the gallop.
6. The bayonet was still a half-century off.
7. This was not true of Flanders, where infantry retained their earlier importance.
8. Baudissin, Johann Georg, Marrazino, and Baner were all notorious alcoholics, even by the none-too-stringent standards of the 17th century!

9. He was later to claim that he had deliberately allowed the Imperials to exhaust themselves in siegework; given the discrepancy in numbers, he had had little choice.
10. It was defended by Swedish colonels Drake and Saloman Adams. 1470 of the garrison opted to rejoin Baner, and 300 Germans to enlist with Hatzfeld.
11. Alternatively, Baner could simply have decided that Luneburg was too hard a nut to easily crack, or, equally possibly, the rapid loss of Werben and Havelberg may have shaken him. Anyway, he suddenly abandoned the Westphalia operation and moved east.
12. To whom? Wrangel?
13. 3800 men under Vitzthum and Stalhansk, but see Appendix A. They joined Baner at Parchim, September 22.
14. Most notably in the action at Wolfshagen, September 24. 6 Saxon cavalry regiments under a Col. Unger were routed by the Swedish vanguard.
15. Boy, Pfuhl, and Berghofer. Hatzfeld called the loss, for which he blamed the Saxons, "a disgraceful error."
16. 1000 men under Col. Jens. They had surrendered to Klitzing October 1 and received free passage back to Baner.
17. These Lutheran regiments seem to have formed a sort of "Protestant Corps" inside the Imperial Army.
18. This plan has been compared with Frederick the Great's attack at Torgau.
19. Compare map with Baner diagram.
20. Who these Swedes were, moving ahead of Baner, is unclear. They could have been outriders from Torstensson's group or the missing 840 dragoons (see Appendix B).
21. Schwalbach's company? See Appendix A.
22. Krebs says Hatzfeld, Bissinger, and Del Maestro, but I find his argument unconvincing.
23. Swedish accounts gloss over this; Baner never admitted that his original scheme had miscarried. Also they confuse Torstensson's brigade with the looters at the Saxon train, 2 miles away.
24. Given the outcome, 20% captured during the battle, he may have been right!
25. Schonickel was subsequently court-martialed and stripped of his regiment. Hatzfeld was to suffer a similar command failure at Jankow in 1645.
26. Probably Goltz, Thun, Manteuffel, and Enan.
27. Baner Leib, Torstensson, and Smaland CR.
28. Probably Rittberg, Falkenstein, and Puchheim.
29. Wittstock was the most melodramatic of battles, with repeated crises and radical reversals of fortune.
30. His own cavalry regiment plus Pfuhl's.
31. Barker, *Military Intellectual*, p. 211.
32. 4 cavalry regiments under Col. Dehne.
33. Held by Saxon Infantry Regiments #5, 6 and 7 and Cavalry Regiments #12 and 16, under Col. Wolfersdorf. The town was not strong, but the terms allowed the defenders to evacuate safely. Both Dehne and Wolfersdorf lost their ranks for these failures.
34. Caricatures showed him holding an empty sack, while Baner escaped through a hole in the bottom.
35. Baner was now down to 10,000; Wrangel had 5000; there were 9000 men garrisoning strongholds in Pomerania, and another 1200 in Mecklenburg: a total of 25,200 of whom only 15,000 were mobile. Gallas had 20,000–30,000 plus strong detachments under Marrazino and Klitzing.
36. Vitzthum partially redeemed his reputation by the heroic defense of tiny Sax-Hausen.
37. February 20: 1400 Germans KIA, 600 captured.

38. Hatzfeld had partially redeemed himself from the onus of Wittstock by defeating a Swedish detachment at Vlotho (October 17, 1638). See Appendix F.

39. Possibly due to the unexpected hostility of the local peasantry. Baner had assumed, no doubt based on his experience in Silesia, that the Bohemians would be Protestant partisans, as in 1618-20, and would rise in his support. But the religious situation had changed radically, and his marauders were unwelcome.

40. Not to be confused with Lillichook.

41. 23 infantry battalions and 80 cavalry squadrons. This was the first joint operation of all three armies.

3

Bernhard Sax-Weimar: The Battle of Rheinfelden

In retrospect, the French entry into the war seems almost inevitable.[1] From his rise to power in 1624, Richelieu had followed a consistently anti-Spanish policy; under the circumstances, it was necessarily an anti-Austrian policy as well. Leaving aside such diplomatic moves as attempting to alienate Bavaria from the emperor and the bungled Valtelline[2] operation of 1625, France had deliberately encouraged and financed the two attacks on Germany by Denmark and Sweden.[3] Imperial troops had fought French during the Mantuan War of 1628–31. The period of Swedish predominance, 1631–34, had been cynically exploited by the Richelieu regime to expand into Germany without apparent risk. In December 1631, Imperial garrisons west of the Rhine were overrun; in January 1632, the pro-Hapsburg duchy of Lorraine was subverted; in April–August, Trier was occupied despite Spanish resistance, and French forces intruded into Austrian Alsace.[4] By 1633, Alsace had become a nightmarish patchwork of Imperial, Spanish, Lorrainer, Swedish, and French garrisons. After Gustavus's death at Lützen, the French assumed a still more blatant role, paying pensions to Protestant officers and trying to become "protectors" of both the old Catholic League and of Sweden's Protestant alliance, the Heilbronn Bund. Angered at Duke Charles's intransigence, the French decided to occupy Lorraine outright, taking the capital-fortress of Nancy September 20. By the end of 1634, most of Lorraine was overrun, and French armies had pushed to the Rhine.

The Swedish disaster at Nordlingen altered the whole strategic situation. The Rhine Protestants handed over many fortresses to French garrisons. By January 1635, French armies were openly fighting Imperials in Heidelberg, Spires, and Philippsburg. Supported by the Imperials, Duke Charles had returned to liberate Lorraine. In March, the Spanish reoccupied Trier, ejecting the French.

Richelieu was presented with an unpalatable choice: either he back down and abandon his ill-gotten gains or directly enter the war. In February, he concluded an agreement with the Dutch for a joint attack on Spain. In April, a similar agreement was made with Sweden. March and April also saw a French army dispatched against the Valtelline; about the same time, their forces along the Flanders frontier assumed an aggressive attitude. On May 21, 1635, in a surprisingly medieval ritual, a French herald threw down the gauntlet at the Spanish court in Brussels; the official declaration against the emperor was not to follow until March 1636, but effectively France was at war with the house of Hapsburg.

The French seemed in good shape militarily; they had gradually built up their army 1628–34, and mustered (on paper) over 120,000 men, not to mention Dutch allies and German Protestants. They hoped to score a knockout blow against Spain, striking simultaneously over half a dozen fronts. The main force, in combination with the Dutch, struck at Brussels, others operated in Italy, Gascony, Catalonia, Lorraine, the Valtelline, and Alsace. In general, the French strategy was a failure.[5] The course of the Franco-Spanish War (1635–59) is of interest here because of its impact on the Thirty Years War, specifically in the Rhine-Alsace-Lorraine theater.

BERNHARD AFTER NORDLINGEN

As the sole senior commander to survive Nordlingen, Duke Bernhard received the task of rebuilding the ruined army, an impossible task made harder by the Swedes' withdrawal north and the mass defection of Protestant ex-allies. Holding the Upper Rhine as both Swedish general and commander for the allied Protestants, Bernhard found himself caught between the renascent Imperials and the ambitions of his ostensible allies, the French.

In the months following Nordlingen, the Protestant cause was as a house built on sand, aggressive Imperial columns overrunning towns, fortresses, and strongholds. It was Gustavus after Breitenfeld in reverse. Bernhard assembled his new army in the Frankfort area, while the Rhinegrave bartered his Alsace fortresses to France for protection. Gallas and Hatzfeld led the main Imperial army westward. In December, a French army under La Force crossed the Rhine and relieved Heidelberg. Nevertheless, the French garrison of Philippsburg had to surrender (January 14, 1635). Shortly thereafter, Werth drove across the frozen Rhine, secured Spires, and scourged the nearby French outposts. Late in February, Werth joined Duke Charles in an attempt to regain Lorraine, but French general Rohan drove them out again. Bernhard, still independent of the French, launched a feeble counterattack, regaining Spires (March 1). Rohan's departure for the Valtelline saw a reshuffling of French generals, La Force taking over in Lorraine, while La Valette assumed the German command. La Force wasted the rest of the year in futile offensives against the Spanish Franche-Comte, while the unenterprising La Valette went on the defensive. The conclusion of the Peace of Prague (May 20) shifted the balance in Germany toward the emperor—even as the French declared war (May 19). Frankfort and Strassburg rudely ejected Bernhard's partisans, while Gallas retook Spires, then Worms, Zweibrucken, and Bernhard's base at Kaiserlautern (late June–early

July), finally laying siege to Mainz. Bernhard managed to relieve it (July 24), he and La Valette threatening to restore the situation (August). They skirmished against Hatzfeld (September 4), then were nearly cut off by Gallas, escaping to Metz by a forced march (September 6–18). Hogendorf in Mainz was forced to surrender. Gallas pursued them into Lorraine, confronting the Franco-Weimarian army at Dieuze. After a series of indecisive skirmishes (October 12–November 1), lack of supplies[6] forced Gallas to fall back into Alsace. Minor fighting there, notably around the much-disputed stronghold of Hagenau, dragged on until 1636.

More important was the treaty between Bernhard and the French government. Negotiations had begun in late 1634, but the French had been reluctant to meet Bernhard's demands. His obstinacy, abetted by the deteriorating military situation, paid off. On October 27, 1635, he formally entered French service.[7]

FRENCH SERVICE: 1636–37

French plans for 1636 were much the same as for 1635, but this time, the Hapsburgs had a plan of their own, a combined offensive by Spanish and Imperials.[8] Bernhard started the year well, snatching the strong place of Sauverne, northwest of Strassburg, from under Gallas's nose. Meanwhile, the elder Conde[9] attacked into the Franche-Comte, laying siege to Dole. In August, however, Gallas and Duke Charles appeared with a large force,[10] marched south through the Belfort Gap into Franche-Comte, and relieved Dole. Conde's army was pushed back into Burgundy proper. Gallas then threatened Dijon, capital of French Burgundy, but was rebuffed by the tiny fortlet of St Jean de Losne. Bernhard assumed a defensive position at Langres, while Conde dug in at Dijon. It was 1635 all over again and worse. Gallas was unwilling either to attack or to withdraw; he planned to go into winter quarters in Burgundy. His unfortunate army, already afflicted by the enemy and the autumn flooding, now suffered logistical breakdown. The countryside was too wasted to support one army, let alone three. Plague broke out, and desertion ran rampant. Gallas's wretched remnants struggled back to Alsace, and wits in Vienna started to dub him "The Army-Wrecker."

The year 1637 was quiet, chiefly notable for the death of the old emperor.[11] Bernhard first defeated a Catholic force under Duke Charles and a new general named Mercy at Gray-sur-Saone in the Franche Comte (August), then drove north into Alsace. Surprisingly, the Alsatian peasantry rose in favor of the Hapsburgs; this "guerrilla" resistance would plague the French to the end of the war. The appearance of a Spanish army under Piccolomini plus a Bavarian one under Werth forced Bernhard into another of his rapid retreats. He maintained his Rhine foothold, taking up winter quarters in Basel. The Imperials took the precaution of occupying Wurtemberg. A Wurtemberger officer, Wiederhold, commandant of the Bodensee fortress of Hohentwiel, sold his position, including the garrison, to Bernhard for 20,000 talers—a bargain![12]

THE 1638 CAMPAIGN

Bernhard, as noted, had gone into winter quarters 1637–38 in the bishopric of

Basel, placing him in an excellent position to resume his Upper Rhine offensive in 1638. He got off to a flying start by breaking quarters at the start of February and seizing the minor towns of Sackingen, Waldshut, and Laufenburg (as Laufenburg was a Rhine crossing, he garrisoned it with the Schonbeck Infantry Regiment). He then (February 5) began the siege of Rheinfelden, key to the Upper Rhine.[13] Pushing the attack with his usual enthusiasm, Bernhard exploded three mines on February 15, 16, and 23, opening a sizable breach, and by the 28th had made another. A major storm was planned for March 1. Bernhard's siegework may have been hampered by his unbalanced force, only 2000 foot to 4000 horse, and his relatively weak artillery—he had, at best, three siege guns and two 12 pdrs.

The Catholic command was not unaware of the situation. Werth, assisted by Generals Enkefort, Furstenberg, and Sperreuter, hastily assembled a relief force at Augsburg. Marching west, they were joined by an Imperial detachment out of the Franche-Comte under Savelli. This improvised corps moved south and west to approach Rheinfelden from the right or north bank of the Rhine.

Rheinfelden proper is on the left or south bank, the two sides connected by a bridge. The Rhine is impassable at this point, and the bridge constituted the chief strategic value of the stronghold. Bernhard had prepared his operations with some care, first securing the next nearest bridge, 13 miles east at Laufenburg. Then he established a ferry at the nearby hamlet of Bucken. Finally, he gained control of the Rheinfelden bridge itself and isolated the defenders with outposts on the north bank. His main army, on the south bank, was engaged in preparations for the next day's assault when the northern outposts reported the approaching enemy.

The Imperial-Bavarian army was apparently a bit weary from their rapid march. In any case, Bernhard's outposts managed to repel their initial probe. This seems to have given Bernhard an entirely misleading idea of their strength. He decided that it would be possible to beat them off without releasing his grip on Rheinfelden. He would defeat them, he thought, with such forces as could quickly cross and form before the enemy reached the siege line.

Meanwhile, on their second try, Savelli and Werth made short work of the outposts. They had given Bernhard warning and time to cross, but he was now opposing an enemy who outnumbered him by over 2-1.

THE COMMANDERS

Duke Bernhard von Sachen-Weimar (1604–1639) was a scion of the Ernestine Wettins, one of the oldest and noblest of German dynasties. A century before, his ancestors had been leading princes, wealthy and powerful. Political mistakes and repeated partitions among too many offspring had ruined them; by Bernhard's birth they were both poor and politically insignificant. Bernhard felt deeply the discrepancy between noble birth and actual poverty and resented those whom he blamed for it: the Imperial Hapsburgs and the elector of Saxony, leader of the Protestant moderates. Thus, it was natural when war broke out, that Bernhard and his brothers were drawn toward the ultra-Protestant fanatics, even though they were themselves ordinary Lutherans, not even particularly bigoted.

Bernhard himself was characterized by two traits, a greedy ambition for wealth and a realm of his own and a violent personal arrogance considered extreme even in his own day. This made him difficult to deal with; he quarreled with Gustavus, Horn, Baner, Birkenfeld, and the Rhinegrave, while the French found his need to constantly reaffirm his "independence" a real hindrance. Some of his outbursts resembled "temper tantrums."

After Nordlingen, Bernhard saw all his gains of 1631–34 disappear; he even managed to lose his personal treasure. It should come as no surprise that he rejected the Peace of Prague—he had nothing to gain from peace and little to lose from war. Like Mansfeld before him, his army was his fortune. His arrangement with the French was directed toward his great goal, his own principality. He was a surprisingly good financier for a prince; practically broke in 1635, he left an estate of about 350,000 talers in 1639.

Judged as a soldier, it is necessary to stress his over-aggressiveness, the rashness that he displayed at Lützen, Nordlingen, and Rheinfelden. However, it is only fair to point out that he was not completely insensate; during the Rhine campaigns he made quite a specialty of rapid retreats from awkward situations. Of course, a more cautious general would not have found himself in such danger to begin with! Bernhard shows a real development in command, from the berserker of Lützen and Nordlingen to the scientific reduction of Breisach. He retained his charismatic "up front" style of leadership to the end, despite declining health—his insistence on personally leading the cavalry both inspired the men and hampered the proper use of reserves. Around 1635–36 Bernhard contracted an intestinal disorder, possibly similar to the one that killed his older brother, and this, plus his exhaustion from the 1638 campaign, weakened his resistance when the "plague" (typhus?) broke out.

Major General Georg Christoph von Taupadel (ca.1600–1647) was one of Gustavus's leading colonels (although not one of the king's inner circle) and one of the survivors of Nordlingen, but he did not rise to high rank until joining Bernhard. Captured at Wittenweier, he was not exchanged until 1640. Thereafter, he served France loyally. A capable cavalryman, he lacked capacity for overall command and was eventually superseded by Erlach.

Field Marshal Jan de Werth, AKA Johann von Werdt (1591–1652), was the most noteworthy Catholic "upstart," that is, a commoner who rose to high rank. A Protestant peasant from the village of Weert—hence his name—Werth enlisted as a trooper in Spinola's cavalry in 1622, transferred to the League Eynatten Cavalry Regiment, and somehow worked his way up to colonel (1633). He conducted numerous successful small actions in south Germany 1632–34—Taupadel and Sperreuter were among his victims—and took part in the victory of Nordlingen in 1634. That same year, he converted to Catholicism—a wise career move—and was promoted to general and made a Bavarian noble. He fought Bernhard and the French 1634–38. Captured at Rheinfelden, he remained a prisoner until exchanged for Horn in 1642.

Werth was an able cavalry leader and a brilliant exponent of "small war"—his career is a list of successful raids, skirmishes, and ambushes—but his record in more formal pitched battles was poor. Fearless and an able leader and tactician, he lacked operational grasp of the overall battlefield.

Duke Frederico Savelli, Prince of Albano (ca.1595–ca.1660) was the opposite of Werth, being an absolutely incapable officer raised to army command entirely through social background and influence. A high noble of Italy, Savelli joined Wallenstein's first armada as a colonel in 1629. He acted as commander of Mecklenburg 1630-31, where his inept defense against Gustavus's second assault (February 1631) drew sharp criticism from Tilly. After Gallas was transferred to face Baner, Savelli took over as Imperial commander against the French. After his defeats at Rheinfelden and Wittenweier only his rank saved him from court-martial. He was transferred to the diplomatic service, where his talent for disaster enjoyed less scope. Remarkably enough, he was later appointed army commander by Pope Urban VIII, and his incompetence helped the Papacy lose the Castro War (1642-44).

Savelli has been suggested as Gallas's chief rival for the title of "Greatest Army Wrecker of the Thirty Years War," however his record hardly justifies this charge. Gallas was blamed for "wrecking" armies, that is, leading them into areas where they could not subsist, then keeping them there until they disintegrated—Burgundy in 1636, the Baltic in 1638, Jutland in 1644. Savelli was repeatedly defeated, but he didn't "wreck" armies in that particular manner. Not only incompetent, Savelli lacked courage as well. A Swedish quip ran that the duke was a "clotheshorse, not a soldier." Supposedly, Savelli's subordinates, complaining to Vienna of his incompetence, were instructed to report only the good things about him. Savelli's conduct at Rheinfelden and Wittenweier contrasted sharply with the reckless courage of Werth and Gotz. Tilly had suspected him of cowardice after his surrender of Demmin to Gustavus.

Major General Klaus Dietrich Sperreuter (ca.1595–ca.1665), a native of Mecklenburg, was one of Gustavus's leading colonels and was made a general in 1632. He operated in the south 1632-34, where he was defeated by Werth and took part in the disaster of Nordlingen. In 1635, he briefly commanded the Swedish army in Westphalia, but when Mecklenburg accepted the Peace of Prague, he transferred to Imperial service. He was a Weimar prisoner 1638-40, then joined the Bavarian army, becoming Generalwachtmeister in 1646. After 1647, he took service with Venice. Sperreuter was a respected officer, but perhaps not quite as good as his reputation.

THE ARMIES

Imperial-Bavarian Army—Savelli & Werth (see Appendix B).

UNIT	DATE	COY	ESRSTR	NOTES
Gayling KUR	1620	9	770	Bavarian
Billehe KUR*	1620	13	1000	Bav-Wurzburg
Horst ARK	1620	8	396	Bav
Werth ARK	1621	9	593	Bav
Metternich ARK	1632	10	300	Bav-Wurzburg
Neuneck ARK	1633	8	277	Bav
Wolf Dragoons	1638	6	294	Bav
Pappenheim IR	1622	9	700	Bav
Wahl IR	1624	11	800	Bav
Gold IR	1638	8	600	Bav

Lamboy KUR*	1632	10	300	IMP; German, ex-ARK	
Sperreuter CR*	1636	?	300	IMP	
Salis ARK	1636	?	400	IMP	
Henderson IR	1628	?	500	IMP; Low German	
Rejkovics Croat	1631	2	180	IMP	

* not present at 2nd Rheinfelden

4810 cavalry; 2600 infantry = 7410 Total.

Weimarian Army—Bernhard Sax-Weimar

CAVALRY	INFANTRY
Bernhard Leib Coy (Cav)	Bernhard Leib Coy (Inf)
Potbus CR	Forbus IR
Wurtemberg CR	Hattstein IR
Nassau CR	2 Bn = 2000 Inf
Bodendorf CR	
Rosen CR	Artillery:
Taupadel CR	4 x 12 pdr, 8 x 3 pdr, 2 x 24 pdr
Kanoffsky CR	
Ohm CR	
Caldenbach CR	
Rhinegrave CR	

10 CR = 4000 Cav (20 sqd of 200 each)
4000 cav in 20 sqds; 2000 inf in 2 bns; 14 guns = 6000 Total

The Imperial corps, being a hastily assembled, highly mobile, relief force, had no artillery, a serious lack. The Weimar field word was, as Gustavus had used, "Gott mit uns." The Imperials used, in both actions, "Jesus Ferdinandus," in compliment to the new emperor, Ferdinand III.

BATTLE: FIRST RHEINFELDEN, FEBRUARY 28, 1638

The force that Bernhard brought over the bridge consisted of 600 musketeers detached from their regiments, 6 cavalry regiments, and 8 light guns, not many more than 3000 in all. The terrain of the north bank was constricting, a narrow (about a mile wide) stretch of open ground running along the riverbank, then forest. Bernhard decided to try to stop the Imperials in the woods before they reached the cleared area. The broken, divisive ground split the battle into two or more separate actions, units fighting individual opponents in clearings and trails and through the trees. Bernhard divided his army into two wings, he commanding the left and Taupadel the right. The Imperials did the same, Savelli and Sperreuter taking the right and Werth the left; thus, Savelli was facing Bernhard, and Werth, Taupadel. The composition of each division cannot be ascertained, except that the Taupadel and Nassau cavalry regiments were with Taupadel, and that the Rhinegrave and Bodendorf cavalry regiments were present, probably with Bernhard. The Imperial contingent was probably all with Savelli, plus some of the Bavarians. Wolf Dragoon Regiment was with Werth. The French general Rohan, who had joined Bernhard as a volunteer,[14] placed himself at the head of Nassau Cavalry Regiment.

A confused struggle resulted, as Werth contacted Taupadel's van, Rohan and

Nassau. First the Bavarians had the advantage; Rohan was struck down and captured, while Nassau Cavalry Regiment was pushed back. Then Taupadel counterattacked, regaining the lost ground. After not quite an hour's fighting, Rohan was freed and the Bavarians were pushed back in disorder.

The combat on the other wing was opposite. Somehow, Savelli and Sperreuter managed to brush Bernhard aside and reach the open ground. Immediately, Savelli surged forward and secured the bridge. Now Bernhard found himself in a very disadvantageous position, his right victorious, his left defeated, his infantry outnumbered and under heavy pressure, and, worst of all, entirely cut off from the other half of his army. Reluctantly, he gave the order to retire on Laufenburg.

The Weimarians lost 150 in all and 10 cornets. Rohan and the Rhinegrave were mortally wounded, and Colonels Erlach, Schaffelitzky, and Bernhold were captured. Three guns were abandoned in the retreat. The principal Bavarian loss was Dragoon Colonel Wolf, one of the bravest officers in their army, captured in Taupadel's counterattack. Werth was slightly wounded in a "battle-duel" with Colonel Nassau.

The Catholics marched triumphantly into Rheinfelden, assuming the threat banished. They could not have been more wrong.

SEQUEL: SECOND RHEINFELDEN, MARCH 3, 1638

Instead of following up their victory with a sharp pursuit, Savelli and Werth assumed quarters at Rheinfelden. They have—rightly—been criticized for this inertia, but it is hardly incomprehensible. The army had just completed a forced march in late winter, the men were tired and cold, moreover, Werth's corps, their most cohesive and aggressive element, had been battered and scattered in the action. Equally understandable is their decision to disperse for foraging; at that time of year, both food and fodder were in short supply, and there certainly couldn't have been much left in the fort. Clearly, they should have sent a scouting force to keep an eye on Bernhard, but they no doubt considered that it would take time for him to recover from defeat, the loss of Wolf reduced their reconnaissance capacity, and their outposts would warn them of approaching danger.

Bernhard, with the same obstinacy that he showed at Lützen and Nordlingen, refused to concede defeat. Retiring, he found his route blocked by an Imperial outpost near Sackingen; he stormed it, wiping out 300 men (March 1). Then the separated halves of his army were reunited at Laufenburg (March 2). He spent the balance of the day resting and reanimating his men, then crossing them to the north bank and moving somewhat toward the enemy, to Bucken.[15] By the 3rd, he was ready to strike.

About 7:00 A.M., March 3, 1638, Savelli's outposts spotted the approaching enemy. Like his mentor, Gustavus, Bernhard had his men up and moving while it was still dark; needless to say, Bernhard's 6000 warriors were much easier to form and set in motion than the great hosts of Breitenfeld and Lützen. Werth, Savelli, and Sperreuter responded with commendable, if belated, energy, hastily pulling their scattered forces into some kind of battle formation. Considering the lack of time, they did not do badly; only 3 of their regiments did not arrive in time to take part. Unfortunately, these were 3 of their best units, the Billehe and Lamboy cuirassiers, and Sperreuter Cavalry Regiment. Of the heavy cavalry, only Gayling Cuirassier Regiment was available.

As he retraced his steps from the 28th, Bernhard received an unexpected bonus, the 3 guns lost in the earlier action, still lying where they'd been abandoned. This was inexcusable; no doubt the guns were useless to Savelli, who had no artillerymen with him, but he could have borrowed some from Rodel, or, at the very least, have had them dragged inside the fortress.

The advancing Weimarians were deployed in two wings and two echelons. The right, under Taupadel, consisted of the 3 cavalry regiments Potbus, Wurtemberg, and Nassau, in the first line and Taupadel and Rhinegrave in the second, 10 squadrons in all, the regiments of the second echelon fronting the intervals between those of the first. The left wing, under Bernhard, comprised the 2 battalions Forbus and Hattstein and the 2 cavalry regiments Bodendorf and Rosen in the first line, thus, right to left, Potbus, Wurtemberg, Nassau, Forbus, Hattstein, Bodendorf, Rosen; Potbus flanking the woods and Rosen the Rhine. There were 5 light guns attached to Forbus and the two 12 pdrs to Hattstein. The recovered guns were added to the array as well. The second echelon consisted of Kanoffsky Cavalry Regiment (between the 2 battalions), Ohm Cavalry Regiment (between Hattstein and Bodendorf), and Caldenbach Cavalry Regiment (between Bodendorf and Rosen).

Savelli based his defense on a crooked drainage ditch perpendicular to the Rhine, his right resting on the river, his left on the woods near—slightly behind—a village called Nolligen. The Imperials deployed in 3 echelons. The first, immediately behind the ditch, comprised, right to left, Neuneck Arkebusier Regiment in 2 squadrons, the Henderson, Pappenheim, and Gold infantry regiments (1 battalion each), the 2 squadrons of Werth Arkebusier Regiment, and, against the trees, the battalion Wahl Infantry Regiment. In the second echelon were 6 squadrons, 2 each of Gayling Cuirassier Regiment, Horst Arkebusier Regiment, and Salis Arkebusier Regiment. Gayling faced the two intervals flanking Henderson, Horst the same for Gold, and Salis the intervals between Wahl and Werth's 2 squadrons. In the third line Metternich Arkebusier Regiment's single squadron faced between Horst's 2, and the third Gayling squadron faced between the first 2. The now-leaderless Wolf Dragoon Regiment lay right and behind Neuneck, against the riverbank, one company of Croats behind Wolf and adjacent to the second line and the other behind the first, adjacent to the third line. About half of the musketeers were placed in the ditch, in front of the main line. Savelli took command of the right, Neuneck and Gayling; Sperreuter, the infantry in the center, and Werth, the left wing, including Wahl Infantry Regiment.

The Weimarians advanced in good order—in contrast to the hastily formed Imperials. Forbus, Hattstein, and Bodendorf moved against the infantry behind the ditch, while Rosen dealt with Neuneck. Taupadel's wing singled out Werth's division for attention. Ignoring the fire of the skirmishers, the 2 battalions reached the ditch then delivered repeated volleys at pointblank range. Three times the 11 guns poured death into the Imperial line. The target was not the scattered musketeers protected in the ditch but the densely packed infantry battalions behind. Without cannon and masked by their own skirmishers, the defenders were at a disadvantage replying. Hundreds fell in this one-sided exchange. The Imperial foot broke, the 3 battalions dissolving into flight, even while the victorious Weimarians stormed into the ditch. The skirmishers, as one would expect, at once joined the formed troops in flight. The cavalry, seeing their center broken in panic, followed their example, abandoning the field without firing a single pistol.

Savelli and Sperreuter, seeing the way things had gone, abandoned the fight for lost. Werth did not. Wahl Infantry Regiment, which had escaped the fury of Bernhard's fire, had held together when the rest of the line broke. With reckless courage, Werth tried to rally the fleeing cavalry around this strong point. Meanwhile, on the riverbank, the bridge was clogged by a formless mass of 2000 horse, including Savelli himself. Only a few got across.

Bernhard's cavalry, barely engaged, took up the role of pursuers. Hundred of routed infantry were rounded up. The bulk of the horse at the bridge were taken as well—those who fled along the bank mostly got away. Taupadel, moving through the woods on the right and the vacuum on the left, surrounded Wahl and Werth—Bodendorf was killed hitting their rear. Despite their courage, their position was hopeless; they had to surrender en masse on the field.

Werth's stand no doubt helped some of the defeated to escape, but the Imperial army had effectively ceased to exist. Over 500 were dead and 3000 captured—1200 horse and 1800 foot—plus 36 flags. All the generals were taken, Savelli, Werth, Sperreuter, and Enkefort, plus 10 colonels, including Neuneck, Gold, and Henderson.[16] The remnant of the Imperials, mostly cavalry, retired to Tübingen.

AFTERMATH: BREISACH AND WITTENWEIER

After the victory, Bernhard found himself at the head of 9000 men, his original 6000 plus the prisoners. This reinforcement was vital to his subsequent successes, so that the small Rheinfelden battle turned out to be the decisive action of the Alsace campaign.

Bernhard detached a corps under Taupadel and Rosen to operate to the north, while he, with the main body, resumed the interrupted siege of Rheinfelden. Rodel capitulated March 22, on good terms—he and his 600 men were given passage to Breisach. The prisoners from 1st Rheinfelden, notably, Erlach and Schaffelitzky, were recovered with the surrender of their prison.

Taupadel and Rosen had conducted an extensive raid, first through the Freiburg-Breisach area, then east toward Stuttgart, capturing the tiny strongpoint of Aurach and finishing up with a strike against the Imperial remnants at Tübingen.

With the Imperial field army eliminated, Bernhard's next target was the Breisgau, the province just east of the Rhine from Alsace. Its conquest would complete his control of the Upper Rhine. The capital was Freiburg, but far more important was the near-impregnable Rhine bank fortress of Breisach. Freiburg was held by 200 men and as many militia under Colonel Bunnigen; it was besieged April 1–11, surrendered on terms, and was placed under Kanoffsky. Nevertheless, even with reinforcements (5 French regiments under Guebriant) Bernhard knew that Breisach would be a harder nut to crack; also his problems had just doubled.

Field Marshal Gotz, the acting commander of the Bavarian army,[17] was at this time (March 9) in the relatively inactive theater of Westphalia. Gotz decided to take most of the field forces there to the Rhine, gathering other corps along the way, and restore the situation. He left Dortmund March 21, picking up Truckmuller corps from Frankfort (4 regiments), Salis's corps from Bamberg (4 cavalry regiments, 3 infantry regiments), and the Redetti Cavalry Regiment at Nassau, March 28–30. By April 1, he had 12,000 men; Schnetter brought in more on the 7th, but Metternich and the artillery did not arrive until May 17. On May 21, Gotz took the field (at Billigen); it had taken him two months to assemble his 15,000.

Bernhard, at this time, had 15,960 men available, 5200 cavalry, 6600 infantry, 660 dragoons, Guebriant's 3500 French, and 23 guns (4 siege, 12 field, 7 light). Leaving 7 cavalry regiments under Taupadel to watch Gotz, he marched on Breisach, investing it on June 15.

Breisach, as noted before, was an almost impregnable position, a cliff fortress on the east bank of the Rhine. It was held by Reinach, a competent and very determined officer, with 3000 men and 152 guns. Despite an aggressive siege, the only sure way of reducing the place was starvation.

Gotz attempted to interfere with the siege, advancing to Kenzingen (June 26), 12 miles northeast of Breisach, and he succeeded in throwing some supplies into the fortress. Then he decided that the best way to dislodge Bernhard—without a fight—was to cut off *his* supplies. He crossed the Rhine into Alsace, hoping to secure the harvests intended for Bernhard.

Unfortunately for this plan, Taupadel crossed too, and shadowed Gotz in a very aggressive manner, blocking his operations and cutting off detachments. Gotz was not able to make any impression on Bernhard's garrisons in Alsace, Colmar, Schlettstadt, and Benfeld. On the contrary, Taupadel had the better of him in several minor actions. On July 9, he ambushed the Corpes Croat regiment near Benfeld, capturing their colonel, their baggage, and 7 cornets. Despite total loss of less than 20, the unit was crippled. A bit later, 400 of Taupadel's horse surprised Harthausen Cavalry Regiment at Ottenheim, cutting it up so badly as to leave it a mere fragment of a unit. Gotz had to recross the river (July 12) and retire to Wurtemberg to reorganize his unsatisfactory army.

In August, Bernhard received a reinforcement of 1900 more French under Turenne (later to be a leading commander) and the news that Gotz was on his way back. He apparently concluded that Breisach could not be reduced with Gotz hovering about, smuggling in food and munitions, so he decided to intercept him. Leaving Breisach uncovered, he concentrated his available forces at Kenzingen (August 7). On the 8th, he crossed the Schutter rivulet to the village of Friesenheim. Gotz, now joined by Savelli with 4000, approached nearby and assumed a defensive position. Some skirmishing resulted, but between hills, ditches, and woods, the ground was judged, by Gotz at least, unsuitable for battle.

Bernhard spent the night in preparation. At dawn, immediately after morning prayers, the Weimarians departed for the insignificant hamlet of Wittenweier. Gotz and Savelli were also at morning services when the news arrived that the enemy had disappeared. At once—too late?—the army was ordered in pursuit. Around noon, while the Imperials were still blundering behind, Bernhard took up a defensive position at Wittenweier, an advantageous site for an ambush.

The Action of Wittenweier (August 9, 1638) was a much larger affair than Rheinfelden, with 16,000+ men on each side, but it was not considered a pitched battle. Bernhard had deployed so that the Imperials would have to pursue him through constricting passages. Gotz therefore divided the army into 2 bodies, vanguard and rearguard. He then made the mistake of entrusting the critical vanguard to Savelli. The armies were composed thus:

Vanguard—Savelli: 4 battalions + 14 squadrons = 8205

UNIT	DATE	COY	ESTSTR	NOTES
Lamboy KUR	1632	10?	300	IMP
Nicola KUR	1628	?	300	IMP
Sperreuter CR	1636	?	300	IMP
Seneschal KUR	1636	?	300	IMP
Weyer CR	1636	?	300	IMP
Wevin Cav	1638?	?	300	IMP
Grana IR	1627	2	200	IMP; with Wallenstein
Wallenstein IR	1629	10?	700	IMP; 1 bn of 1000
Henderson IR	1628	1	100	IMP; with Wallenstein
Enkefort IR	1631	5	500	IMP; 1 bn of 1000
Burgundian Inf	1638?	?	500	IMP; with Enkefort
Gallas DR	1632	10?	200	IMP
Kratz DR	1623?	?	100	IMP
Wartenburg CR	1632	10	350	Bavaria
Metternich KUR	1636	10	300	Bavaria
Neuneck ARK	1633	8	277	Bavaria
Meissenger CR	1635	5	218	Bavaria; Col KIA
Albert IR	1620	10	1000	Bavaria; Col KIA
De Puech IR	1620	9	985	Bavaria; 1 bn of 1210
Schnetter IR	1633	5	225	Cm KIA
Limbach DR	1633	10	400	Bavaria; Col KIA
Neu-Werth DR	1634	6	350	Bavaria; Cmdr KIA

3 falcons (4 pdr) & 2 demicannon (24 pdr)

Rearguard—Gotz: 4 battalions + 12 squadrons = 7894

Gayling KUR	1620	9	770	Bavaria
Horst KUR	1620	8	396	Bavaria; Cmdr KIA
Kolb KUR	1634	9	483	Bavaria
Gotz KUR	1635	10	800	Bavaria; LtCol KIA
Alt-Werth ARK	1621	9	593	Bavaria
Truckmuller ARK	1632	2	150	Bavaria
Harthausen CR	1634	6	5	Bavaria; Col KIA

Bernhard Sax-Weimar

UNIT		ESTSTR	NOTES
Vehlen CR	1635 7	70	Bavaria
Redetti CR	1635 6	50	Bavaria; Cmdr KIA
Metternich ARK	1632 10	25	Bavaria
Gotz IR	1620 10	1392	Bavaria
Reinach IR	1620 10	1143	Bavaria
Metternich IR	1620 8	785	Bavaria
Hasslang IR	1631 8	574	Bavaria; 1 bn of 1232
Edlinstetten IR	1633 8	658	Bavaria; with Hasslang

8 demicannon, 4 demiculverins (12 pdr), 15 light guns (3, 4 & 6 pdrs),
3 mortars, the artillery train, and the baggage train
Army Total = 16,099

Weimarian Army—Bernhard Sax-Weimar

UNIT	COY	ESTSTR	NOTES
Leib Coy	1	100	
Rosen CR	8	650	"Leib CR"; heavy loss
Taupadel CR	8	500	Col captured
Nassau CR	8	600	
Kanoffsky CR	8	500	
Ohm CR	8	550	
Caldenbach CR	8	460	
Rhinegrave CR	8	550	LtCol Schon?
Potbus CR	8	450	
Witersheim CR	8	500	ex-Wurtemberg?
Rotenhan CR	8	450	ex-Bodendorf
Berg CR *	8	550	LtCol Rosen
11 CR	81	5860	5200 Cavalry + 660 Dragoons
Guebriant CR		1000	French
Turenne CR			
Vattronville CR			
Tracy CR			
Du Hallier CR			
5 CR			
Leib Coy (Inf)	1	300	
Forbus IR	10	900	
Hattstein IR	12	900	
Schonbeck IR	16	1750	
Flersheim IR	8	1000	
Hodiowa IR	9	850	
Kanoffsky IR *	9?	600	
Moser IR *	9?	300	
Schmidtberg IR	12	1000	
8 IR = 7 Bn	77	7600	Infantry
Batilly IR	12	700	French
Vardy IR	12	700	
Castelmoron IR	12	700	
Melun IR	12	700	
Volunteers IR	12	600	
Leslie IR	12	500	Scots (France)
Sinot IR	12	500	Irish (France)

7 IR = 3 Bn   84   4400   French Infantry
Kluge   4 x 24 pdr (demicannon), 10 x 12 pdr (demiculverin), 18 x 3–6 pdr
Total: 6860 cav; 12,000 inf in 10 bns; 32 guns = 18,860
*- at least part of Kanoffsky was left at Freiburg; Moser and Berg may have been left at Breisach.

Bernhard deployed in 3 divisions. Taupadel, with a dozen squadrons, commanded the right wing; Nassau and Guebriant, with the rest of the Weimar cavalry and 3 French squadrons, took the left. Ohm commanded the center, 5 battalions strong. Kanoffsky led the center 2nd echelon, 2 battalions. Turenne had the 3rd echelon, of 3 French battalions and 2 French squadrons. Bernhard himself took post on the left, near Guebriant. A detachment of 200 musketeers lay hidden in the woods.

It would seem from this deployment that Bernhard was prepared to fight a pitched battle, but his opponents' carelessness made this unnecessary. Bernhard's field word was, as always, "Gott mit uns," which the French rendered as "Emmanuel." The Imperials used "Ferdinandus" for Emperor Ferdinand III.

Savelli, with the same casual disregard that he'd shown at Rheinfelden, blundered after the "fleeing" Weimarians without bothering to scout ahead or keep contact with Gotz behind. Thus, the van emerged from the passage rather too far ahead of the rearguard. Bernhard, in an army-sized ambush, fell at once upon the outnumbered Imperials, shattering their flank. As at Rheinfelden, Savelli gave the action up for lost and decamped, so that when Gotz appeared, he found his vanguard reduced to a leaderless mass, disorganized and demoralized. The routed corps poured around him, sweeping away his light cavalry and part of his foot.

Gotz rose to the situation with lionlike courage. Setting himself at the head of his 4 cuirassier regiments, Gayling, Horst, Kolb, and Gotz, he improvised a counterattack against the enemy, his 4 battalions following in support. Amazingly, his attack was a success; Taupadel's wing, exhausted and scattered in their success and pursuit, broke in their turn, streaming backwards in rout. Taupadel himself was struck down and captured. Gotz then fell upon Bernhard's center, retaking the 5 guns abandoned by Savelli and pushing back the enemy foot. The Weimarians directed their deadly artillery against him—Gotz had lost his own gunners in the panic. Nevertheless, Gotz led repeated attacks, holding his ground for five hours against 3-1 odds. At one point, he had even overrun Bernhard's main battery. Finally, at 10:00 P.M., he conceded defeat—by then he was down to only 2000 men in all—and slipped away under cover of darkness. His stand had not been in vain, however, for the rest of the army had already escaped while he held Bernhard.

Gotz wrote a few feeling words on the battle:

"When the enemy saw Savelli emerge from the passage so far ahead and separated from the rearguard, they took him in flank, overwhelming his corps, so that when the rearguard arrived, he was already beaten. I rushed with the rearguard to the rescue, gathering up the rest of the vanguard, and hurled myself on the enemy right wing, whipping them from the field. Then I charged against the left wing, head over heels, to retake Savelli's two demicannon and keep them from firing at us. What still was left of Savelli's corps took to their heels with my own light horse, so only my five infantry and four cuirassier regiments, themselves somewhat shaken, remained. The train drivers had fled, leaving our baggage, artillery, and provisions. Around ten, the Weimarians were attacking again, slaughtering our troops, and I was unable to rally the routed, Savelli's or my own. I now had fewer than 500 cuirassiers and 1600 foot with me. Besides, Savelli and the other generals, with their people, had abandoned the field. I therefore had to retire, carrying such of our wounded as I found as I retreated."[18]

Savelli was recalled to Vienna, where he narrowly escaped court-martial.

The Imperial-Bavarian army lost 1500 dead, 1300 captured, 83 flags, and 11 guns—Savelli's five plus four 3 pdrs and 2 heavy mortars. Among the dead were Colonels Albert, Limbach, Harthausen, and Meissenger; the lieutenant colonels of the Albert, Schnetter, Gotz, Redetti, and Neu-Werth regiments, plus the major of Horst Cuirassier Regiment. Bernhard lost 700 in all, mostly from the Taupadel and Rosen cavalry regiments, and 40 flags. Taupadel was the only important prisoner; the Rhinegrave, Rosen, Nassau, and Rotenhan were wounded.

What Gotz lacked in acumen, he made up for in determination. Falling back to Rottweil, he began reassembling his army for a third relief attempt.

Bernhard was now ready to encircle Breisach with an unbreakable line of circumvallation, to begin the reduction in earnest. The sufferings of the starving garrison were terrible. Every crumb was devoured; every animal, dog, cat, or rat inside the fortress was hunted and eaten. Still worse off were their Weimarian prisoners there—these unfortunates were unable to get around to hunt rats! Several starved to death and were at once torn apart and eaten by their cellmates. Despite these horrors, Col. Reinach remained obdurate, still hoping for an army of relief.

By October, Gotz's efforts had borne fruit. Not only had he reassembled much of his earlier army, Imperial General Lamboy had arrived from Flanders with 5000 men, and Duke Charles of Lorraine had put together 4000. In all, the Imperials had mustered well over 20,000. Unfortunately, they were unable to agree on how to use them. Gotz was determined not to repeat his previous blunders, which led to Lamboy accusing him—unfairly—of delay, even cowardice. Eventually, they decided on a plan. Gotz, with the main force, would make his way up to Bernhard's siege line and draw his attention with a violent assault, at which Duke Charles would force his way in from the west, over the Rhine, with food and munitions. It was a plausible scheme but would require close coordination to bring off properly.

At Breisach, Bernhard formed a mobile strike force[19] and set out to intercept Charles (October 13). He caught the Lorrainers, 1500 horse, 2500 foot, and 5 guns, and routed them in a sharp, fast-moving ambush, the Action of Traun (AKA Sennheim, October 15, 1638). Only a few were killed, but 600 (400 foot, 200 horse) were taken, including a general and 2 colonels, along with all the guns, the baggage and supplies, and 44 flags. Bernhard's losses were light, but Col. Witersheim was killed, and Nassau wounded.

Gotz, apparently unaware of Charles's defeat, went on with the plan. October 22-24, he fell upon the southern face of Bernhard's line with 14,000 men—4000 cavalry, 10,000 infantry, and 8 guns. He was successful at first, taking an outwork[20] and one of the three bridges Bernhard had thrown across the Rhine. It appeared possible that he would force his way in, through the defenses. Bernhard launched a counterattack in three groups,[21] retook the work, and thrust Gotz back out. The Imperials retired—Gotz to be court-martialed. Bernhard lost less than a thousand men, including Batilly (killed), Schonbeck (wounded), and Leslie (captured). Gotz lost 1000 dead plus 1000 wounded or captured.

November was quiet except for a few minor skirmishes, one (November 20) with the irrepressible Duke Charles. It was by now clear even to Reinach that no help would be coming for Breisach, but he was quite prepared to go on starving unless he was granted honors of war. Bernhard offered very good terms. On December 17, 1638, Reinach handed over the town. He and his handful of survivors—450 men of whom 50 were sick—marched away proudly, flags flying, muskets loaded, 2 cannon dragged behind them. They left for Bernhard, 135 "great" guns, 15 smaller ones, 150 wall pieces, a large supply of muskets and ammunition, plus a million talers in cash.

Bernhard was so enraged when he saw the Weimarian prisoners—the ones reduced to cannibalism—that he threatened to abrogate the surrender and imprison Reinach and his men. He did not carry out the threat.

Bernhard spent the next seven months securing and consolidating his Rhine "kingdom." He garrisoned Breisach with 2317 men under Erlach. Around this time, the emperor dispatched Savelli—of all people!—to appeal to Bernhard's "patriotism"; by turning Alsace over to France, he was betraying the whole German Volk. Bernhard threw one of his characteristic tantrums; he "needed no lessons in patriotism from any Eye-talian duke!" Nevertheless, the mission may have had some effect. In February 1639, he advised the French that he was assuming personal control of the Rhineland.

Bernhard had been careful to garrison each strongpoint with troops loyal to him personally; the French corps was in no position to interfere. In the long run, of course, his situation was untenable; no general, however brilliant, could set up an independent Rhine state in the teeth of both France and the emperor. But, for the moment, Richelieu and Guebriant could only plead.

What was Bernhard up to? Was he planning to switch sides? Had he some scheme involving Baner and the Swedes? Was he just positioning himself for "hardball" negotiations with France? Or had he simply lost his mind? No one will ever know. Plague broke out in the army, and Bernhard declined to leave the troops. He died July 18, 1639.

In his will, Bernhard left his army to his four most favored officers, Erlach, Rosen, Nassau, and Ohm,[22] with instructions to auction it off between France, Sweden, the emperor, the count palatine, and his brother Wilhelm. Under the circumstances, this came down to France versus the emperor. Richelieu carried the auction with a modest 1,200,000 livres (= 400,000 talers) in cash and a much larger sum in promises (these promises were not kept). There is no excuse for the emperor's inertia in this matter. No doubt the French could always have outbid him; nevertheless, the combined Austrian, Spanish, and Bavarian exchequers should have been able to put together a respectable bid. If they couldn't match Richelieu, they could at least make him pay for his victory.

What did Richelieu get for his 1,200,000 livres? Not only did he obtain some 17,000 veteran soldiers, he also secured the Rhine, Alsace, Basel, and the Breisgau. Soon Breisach had a French garrison, and French commanders occupied Alsace (which remains French to this day). Wasting this opportunity hurt the Hapsburg cause fully as much as the defeats of Rheinfelden, Wittenweier, and Breisach.

SOURCES

The principal sources for Bernhard are two biographies, by Droysen (German, 1885), and Noailles (French, 1913). The 1638 chapter of Heilmann's *Kriegsgeschichte* (1868) is invaluable, especially for Rheinfelden.

There are no good English accounts of the campaign. Wedgwood went into some detail, but her grasp of military matters was limited. Redlich has much important background on Bernhard and his army. There is a contemporary English account of Rheinfelden, Overton's *True and Brief Relation of the Bloody Battle* (1638), originally bound with other German "news" and available on microfilm.

APPENDIX A: THE BAVARIAN ARMY

The Bavarian, or Catholic League, forces at Rheinfelden consisted of 3 infantry and 7 cavalry regiments.

		No. Coy/ Strength Reported in:			
Unit	Date	1635	1640	1642	Notes
Pappenheim IR	1622	9/700	--	9/702	ex-Springen, Hubner
Wahl IR	1624	11/2000	--	9/800	ex-Erwitte, Gallas
Gold IR	1638	--	--	8/590	New
Billehe KUR	1620	13/1000	--	--	Wurzburg;ex-Schomb
Gayling KUR	1620	6/500	9/770+111*	--	ex-Cronberg, Keller
Horst ARK	1620	8/300	8/396+180*	--	ex-Erwitte.
Alt-Werth ARK	1621	18/1000	9/593+210*	--	ex-Eynatten, Salis
Metternich ARK	1632	10/300	--	--	Another Wurzburg CR
Neuneck ARK	1633	5/400	8/277+164*	--	Ex-Kratz, Busch
Wolf Dragoons	1638	--	6/294+287*	--	New

* - Mounted + Dismounted

Given these limitations, any strength figures can only be estimates. We know that Bernhard had around 6000, and that Savelli had about the same or a bit more. The contemporary report gives 2000 infantry, while Noailles says 3–4000. The infantry loss, 1800 captured, effectively put Pappenheim, Wahl and Gold out of action for the rest of 1638, but the Imperial Henderson Infantry Regiment escaped virtually intact. Nevertheless, the possibility that Wahl was larger than estimated cannot be excluded.

As regards the horse, Billehe was very likely not at full strength, but it didn't take part at 2nd Rheinfelden anyway. Gayling is listed at 3 squadrons, Horst, Werth, and Neuneck at 2, Metternich at 1 or 2 (?). Neuneck may, therefore, have been larger than estimated, Metternich smaller.

Gayling, Alt-Werth, Metternich, Neuneck, and Horst, but not Billehe, Wolf, or the infantry, were at Wittenweier. Horst seems to have been reclassified as cuirassier. Gotz had 10 other cavalry regiments and 8 infantry regiments, not counting Savelli's Imperials.

		Reported Strength in			
Unit	Date	1635/36	1638	1640/42	Notes
Metternich IR	1620	6/600	--	8/785	ex-Comargo
Gotz IR	1620	10/1200	1392	10/688	ex-Gronsfeld
De Puech IR	1620	9/1000	985	8/623	ex-Alt-Tilly
Albert IR	1620	10/800	10/1000	8/658	ex-Jung-Tilly
Reinach IR	1620	13/800	10/1143	10/700	ex-Schmidt
Hasslang IR	1631	11/1300	--	8/574	ex-Fugger
Schnetter IR	1633	5/900	5/225	--	AKA Snetter.
Edlinstetten IR	1633	8/1000	--	8/658	ex-Ruepp.
Wartenburg CR	1632	10/350+150	--	--	New
Truckmuller ARK	1632	2/150+50	--	--	ex-Lohn
Limbach DR	1633	10/400+160	--	--	ex-Wahl
Neu-Werth DR	1634	6/350	--	--	ex-Gant
Kolb KUR	1634	9/600	--	8/495+234	ex-Binder
Harthausen CR	1634	6/300+150	*	--	New
Gotz KUR	1635	10/800+200	--	9/987	New
Meissenger CR	1635	5/218+72	--	--	New
Vehlen CR	1635	10/400+140	*	7/400	New
Redetti CR	1635	6/150+80	*	--	New

* - Metternich Arkebusier Regiment, Harthausen, Vehlen, and Redetti formed 1 squadron of 150.

Estimates of the Bavarian-Imperial army run between a low of 15,000 and a high of 19,000. Savelli's Imperials are set at 4000 to 7000, leaving Gotz's Bavarians at 10,000–12,000.

The Catholics deployed 11 battalions in 8 brigades and 26 squadrons of horse. Given the Bavarian 15 cavalry regiments (including 1 squadron) and 8 infantry regiments (1 very small), plus the Imperial 8 cavalry regiments and 4 infantry regiments, I assume that the larger cavalry regiments formed 2 squadrons each, the smaller 1. The 12 infantry regiments formed in "brigades" of about 1000, the 4 Imperials composing 2, the 8 Bavarians 6. Presumably, the smaller infantry regiment's were combined into single battalions, "brigades," probably De Puech & Schnetter in the van and Edlinstetten & Hasslang in the rear.

APPENDIX B: THE IMPERIAL ARMY

Gallas's army of 1636 was mustered in January 1637, that is, after the disastrous failure of his offensive.

Unit	Strength	Unit	Strength
Gallas IR	350	Piccolomini KUR	?
Alt-Wangler IR	200	Gotz KUR	?
Neu-Wangler IR	25	Wilhelm ARK	?
Seefeld IR	?	Croats	?
Becker IR	150	"other regiments"	?
Tiefenbach IR	300	Cavalry	9000
Baden IR	200		
Florence IR	200		
Grana IR	100		
Aldringer IR	300		
Kehraus IR	150		
"5 other IR"	2800		
Infantry	4425+		

To this some would add 4000 infantry and 2000 cavalry, for a total of 19,425+.

Savelli's contingent at Rheinfelden consisted of 1 infantry regiment and 2 cavalry regiments: Henderson Infantry Regiment, the Lamboy Cuirassiers (1632), and the Wallis Arkebusiers. Some would also place the Sperreuter Cavalry Regiment (300 horse) there. However, Lamboy and Sperreuter did not take part in the second battle. Wallis formed 2 squadrons, and Henderson 1 battalion. Unlike their Bavarian counterparts, Pappenheim, Wahl, and Gold, Henderson was able to fight at Wittenweier as well.

The identity of the Croat companies is unclear, but they were probably from Rejkovic or, less likely, the Corpes Cavalry Regiment. Except for Sperreuter, the individual strengths of Imperial units at both Rheinfelden and Wittenweier can only be estimated.

Savelli's contingent at Wittenweier is variously given as 4000, 5000–6000 and 7000. It consisted of 4 infantry regiments, 6 cavalry regiments, and 2 dragoon regiments.

Unit	Date	Notes
Grana IR	1627	AKA Caretto; ex-Alt-Aldringen; High German (10)
Henderson IR	1628	ex-Wangler; Low German (10)
Wallenstein IR	1629	Alt-Waldstein; Low German (10)
Neu-Enkefort IR	1635	New; Tyrolian (10)
Nicola KUR	1628	AKA Montard de Noyrel (5)
Lamboy KUR	1632	German (10), ex-ARK
Sperreuter KUR	1636	ex-Protestant; 300 strong
Seneschal KUR	1636	AKA Schonfel, Sonschal.
Weyer KUR	1636	Silesian (6); AKA Weyher
Metternich KUR	1636	Wurzburg; 5 KUR & 4 Drag coy
Salis ARK	1636	ex-Hopping; AKA Wallis
Gallas Dragoons	1634	German (10), Alt-Gallas
Kratz Dragoons	1623?	Absorbed into Gallas DR 1638

Only 1 company of Henderson was present, 2 of Grana, and 5 of Enkefort. Another force, the "Burgundian Recruits," took part; it is unclear whether these were some kind of ad hoc unit, possibly raised by Savelli, or just replacements for the others. Apparently, Wallenstein, Henderson, and Grana formed 1 "brigade," Enkefort and the "recruits" the other. A possible eighth cavalry regiment was the Wevin "Recruits." Wrede states that the Savelli and Solis infantry regiments and the Marsinay, MilliDraghi, and Beygott Croats were also present.

APPENDIX C: THE WEIMAR ARMY

The Weimar Army originated with the Swedish and Protestant German forces salvaged by Bernhard after Nordlingen, 15 cavalry regiments and 9 infantry regiments, plus the Rhinegrave's army, 6 cavalry regiments and 6 infantry regiments, plus another 12 infantry regiments in garrisons. These units were a polyglot crew to begin with, formed ad hoc from as many as 4 or 5 pre-battle regiments. Thus, the new Rosen Cavalry Regiment combined the survivors of both Rosen and Taupadel, the new Forbus Infantry Regiment combined the old Forbus, Haubald, Feldmeister, Wurmbrand, and Schneidwinds, and the new Schonbeck Infantry Regiment combined not only Bernhard Leib, Mitzlaff, and Zerotin, but even the Yellow Regiment. To this unit turbulence was added the loss of troops as garrisons surrendered and as the minor German princes accepted the Peace of Prague. Finally, several units marched north to join Baner. Some regiments disappeared, and others were given new colonels.

Given this situation, we can understand why much unit continuity was lost. We can identify certain ex-Swedish officers among the Weimarians, men like Bodendorf, Ohm, Caldenbach, Taupadel, Rosen, Kanoffsky, Schonbeck, Forbus, Schaffelitzky, and

Wurmbrand, but their regimental continuity cannot be taken for granted. The new Taupadel Cavalry Regiment was not connected to the original. Although the Schonbeck Infantry Regiment had been built around the Swedish Yellow Infantry Regiment, Gustavus's elite leib regiment, the new unit had no elite status and no connection with Sweden. There is a real break between the Gustavan and Weimarian armies.

Bernhard's Army —November–December 1634

Unit	Coy/Strength		Corps	Notes
Boullion CR	8/500	8/750	Bernhard	
Bodendorf CR	8/500	8/580	"	Weimarian
Ohm CR	8/500	8/690	"	Weimarian
Landgrave CR	5/400	5/480	"	Retired
Caldenbach CR	8/700	8/800	"	Weimarian
Rosen CR	4/300	4/460	"	Weimarian
Hoffkirch CR	8/400	8/650	"	Returned to Saxony?
Witzleben CR	5/500	5/550	"	
Plato CR	8/600	8/500	"	
Bruneck CR	7/500	7/560	"	To Baner
Wrangel CR	4/250	4/480	"	To Baner
Wachtmeister CR	4/250	4/400	"	To Baner
Wittenberg CR	4/250	4/450	"	To Baner
Beckermann CR	8/600	8/500	"	To Baner
Villefranche CR	4/200	4/150	"	
Forbus IR	8/800	8/650	"	AKA Forbes; Weimarian
Pfuhl IR	8/800	8/750	"	To Baner
Scots IR	8/800	8/940	"	"Green Brigade," to France
Schonbeck IR	9/600	9/760	"	Weimarian
Thurn IR	8/600	8/650	"	Retired
Hodiowa IR	7/600	8/580	"	Weimarian
Gortzke IR	8/500		"	To Baner
Nassau IR	8/400		"	Weimarian
Vitzthum IR	6/600	8/740	"	To Baner
Rhinegrave CR	12/800		Rhinegrave	Weimarian
Kanoffsky CR	8/400		"	Weimarian
Zillert CR	8/450		"	AKA Zillhard; Weimarian
Wurtemberg CR	8/350		"	Weimarian
Gassion CR	4/150		"	
Freyberg CR	5/300		"	
Wurtemberg IR	16/1600		"	Weimarian
Bernhold IR	8/540		"	AKA Bernolf; Weimarian
Rhinegrave IR	8/420		"	Weimarian
Kanoffsky IR	8/820		"	Weimarian
Schaffelitzky IR	6/460		"	Weimarian
Schmidtberg IR	8/500		"	To the French
Ramsay IR	2/230		Hanau Gar	Held out to Feb 13, 1638
Burgsdorf IR	8/580			
Hogendorf IR	8/950		Mainz Gar	To Baner?
Wittgenstein IR	8/680			To Baner?
Lilliesparre IR	8/650		Lahnstein	To Baner
Lolson IR	8/600		Dieburg	Weimarian
Quernheim IR	4/400		Benfeld	Weimarian
Hastfehr IR	8/500		Nuremberg	To Baner

Winckel IR	12/1200	Augsburg	"Blue Brigade," to Baner
Finn IR	8/400	Augsburg	To Baner
Wallenstein IR	8/800	Memmigen	Lost 1635
Schlammerdorf IR	8/800	Ulm	" "

On October 27, 1635, Bernhard signed an agreement with the French whereby he would receive 4,000,000 livres (=1,666,667 talers) per annum, 1,000,000 each quarter. In exchange, he was to maintain an army of 18,000; 12,000 foot and 6000 horse. He also received rank as a French marshal and the promise of a principality of his own in Alsace, if and when it was conquered.

In theory, Bernhard's army required 4,000,000 talers (=12,000,000 livres) a year, but the idea was that local kontributions and food would constitute two-thirds of their pay. This was a departure from Swedish practice, which set kontribution at one-half pay.

Neither side kept the agreement in full. Bernhard's army never reached the contract total or anything like it. The French claimed that garrisons didn't count, as they should be supported entirely by kontribution (there are numerous complaints about starving garrisons from this sort of policy, but it did work in quiet areas). There was disagreement as to whether the Weimarians were entitled to free bread, supplied by the French. In any case, of the 14,000,000 livres that he should have received between October 27, 1635 and July 9, 1639, he actually collected 5,110,000. This does not include the 300,000 that he was paid in early 1635, the 150,000 that he was granted for extra expenses in 1637, the 300,000 that he was given for raising costs, or the 200,000 livres per annum that he was paid as his personal salary. Redlich sets his total at 3,000,000 talers (=9,000,000 livres).

Units in the Weimarian army were organized as the Swedish regiments they had once been. Tactical evolution was similar to Baner's, that is, the abandonment of the tactical brigade, the use of infantry battalions 500–1000 strong, and the adoption of cavalry squadrons. Bernhard seems to have aimed at a cavalry regiment of 400–600 men in 2 squadrons. He used light regimental guns with his infantry battalions, but not the cavalry. Weimarian horse seemed to have been less "chargeworthy" than Swedes, and depth of formation may have increased after 1638. There was little difference between Werth's troops and Bernhard's; in fact, many of them were the same troops, according to the luck of battle.

Despite the ultra-Protestantism of Bernhard and some of his officers, the war in the south soon lost all extremist character. Even aside from the French, there were plenty of Catholics in Bernhard's army and even more Protestants with the Imperials. A level of "professionalism" similar to that associated with the 18th century evolved. Surrenders were accepted. Officer prisoners were exchanged or ransomed, while enlisted men cheerfully joined their captors' ranks. It is claimed that some fortresses retained their same garrisons throughout, casually surrendering, then merely switching officers to adhere to their new allegiance. This did not imply mildness, either to foe or to the civilian population.

We have some figures for strengths. In mid-1637, Rosen Cavalry Regiment mustered 500, and Potbus Cavalry Regiment, 400. In November, the 10 cavalry regiments totaled 5000, the 4 infantry regiments, 3000. In January 1638, there were 4000 horse in 10 cavalry regiments and 2000 foot in 2 infantry regiments. About the same time, 3 cavalry regiments mustered 1200. After Rheinfelden, the 10 cavalry regiments had 5200 (viz., 1200 prisoners); Schmidtberg Infantry Regiment had 1000. In December, the 3 infantry regiments Forbus, Hattstein, and Flersheim totaled 2317.

Bernhard had 14 guns at Rheinfelden, two demicannon (24 pdr), four 12 pdrs, and eight regimental guns (3 pdr). In May, he was using 4 siege guns, 12 field guns, and 7 lights. At Wittenweier, he had four 12 pdrs, 10 "heavy" guns, and 18 light guns. During the siege of Breisach (September 30, 1638), he listed four demicannon, six 12 pdrs, seven

6 pdrs, 14 regimental guns, two light mortars, and two heavy mortars.

Heilmann indicates that there were 10 cavalry regiments at 2nd Rheinfelden, Potbus, Wurtemberg, Nassau, Bodendorf, Rosen, Caldenbach, Ohm, Kanoffsky, Taupadel, and Wurtemberg (again). As Rhinegrave Cavalry Regiment was certainly there, between colonels, the second "Wurtemberg" may be Rhinegrave. Together they had about 4000, but the individual strengths are uncertain. The 400 in 2 squadrons is only an average. There were 2 infantry battalions, Forbus and Hattstein, about 2000 foot in all. However, as Schonbeck Infantry Regiment was at Laufenburg and Flersheim Infantry Regiment was available, it is possible that these were augmented by the other regiments.

In June 1638, Bernhard mustered 5200 cavalry, 6600 infantry, 660 dragoons, and 23 guns of his own, plus 2500 French under Guebriant, 1000 Scots and Irish under Leslie, and Schmidtberg's 1000 Germans in French pay. Turenne brought another 1900 French in July, so that at Wittenweier he had about 18,860 available of whom 10 battalions and 24 squadrons actually took part. Units certainly present include the Kanoffsky, Ohm, Taupadel, Rosen, Nassau, Rhinegrave, and Rotenhan cavalry regiments.

A muster list is available of March 22 (April 1), 1639 (reprinted in Droysen):

Cavalry			Infantry		
Bernhard Leib	1 Coy	100 Men	Bernhard Leib	1 Coy	300 Men
Rosen CR	8	588	Schonbeck IR	16	1734
Taupadel CR	8	427	Hodiowa IR	9	824
Nassau CR	8	568	Hattstein IR	12	1066
Ohm CR	8	504	Forbus IR	10	899
Muller CR	8	405	Flersheim IR	8	1036
Schon CR	8	515	Bernhold IR	9	808
Caldenbach CR	8	433	Moser IR	9	620
Kanoffsky CR	7	421	Scots	7	330
Witersheim CR	7	438	Wiederhold IR	12	1200
Rotenhan CR	7	328		93 Coy	8817 Men
Breisach Garrison	1	100	Month's Pay = 59,401 talers		
	79 Coy	4827 Men			
Month's Pay = 136,313 talers					
Artillery		264 Men	Handworkers for Artillery		40
Miners		50	Month's Pay = 554 talers		
Fireworkers		5			
Artillerymen		319 Men			

Month's Pay = 5106 talers
Cavalry, Infantry, and Dragoons receive 3 pays per year (587,132 talers), Staff, Artillerymen, and Drivers receive 12.

Note that the Quernheim, Kanoffsky, and Schmidtberg infantry regiments and Berg Cavalry Regiment do not appear, whereas Leslie's Scots and Wiederhold do. Bernhard's cavalry were organized in regiments of 8 companies totaling 500 horse. Some had a dragoon company in addition or in place of one of the cavalry companies. Six regiments served throughout the campaign: Rosen (occasionally referred to as Leib Cavalry Regiment), Taupadel, Ohm, Caldenbach, Nassau, and Kanoffsky. Of the other four, Bodendorf, killed at Rheinfelden, was replaced by Rotenhan; Rhinegrave Johann Phillip was also killed at Rheinfelden; his brother Johann Ludwig commanded at Wittenweier, then seems to have turned the regiment over to LtCol Schon; Witersheim took over the Wurtemberg Cavalry Regiment in July, and Muller succeeded Potbus early in 1639. There seems to have been an eleventh unit, the Berg Cavalry Regiment, under LtCol Johann von Rosen, brother of Reinhold von Rosen of the Rosen Cavalry Regiment.

The infantry regiments were, on paper, 12 companies totaling 1200 men. The Forbus, Hattstein, Schonbeck, Flersheim, and Hodiowa infantry regiments served throughout the campaign. Schaffelitzky Infantry Regiment seems to have garrisoned Basel throughout 1638. Most of Kanoffsky Regiment went into the Freiburg garrison in March, but at some point a rump battalion of 300 was split off as a new regiment under LtCol Moser. Quernheim Regiment in Benfeld and Wiederhold Regiment in Hohentwiel served as garrisons throughout. The Schmidtberg Infantry Regiment, although German, was considered a French unit, not part of the Weimar army. It joined Bernhard about the same time as Guebriant, in March.

APPENDIX D: THE FRENCH ARMY

At the time of the outbreak of war, the French army was formidable in size, but deficient in experience and especially in competent officers. Eventually, able generals such as Guebriant, Turenne, and Conde appeared, but the qualitative inferiority persisted throughout. German and other foreign mercenaries (Swiss, Scots, Irish) were in great demand in France, forming whole brigades—in Weimar's case, a whole army.

The French infantry closely imitated Swedish and Dutch practice, a 6- or 8-rank battalion, one-third pike, two-thirds shot. The matchlock arquebus was the weapon of choice. The regiment had a paper strength of 1200, 12 companies of 100 each, real strengths running 500–1000. For example: Rohan's 7 infantry regiments in 1635 totaled 8000; in the same year, 10 infantry regiments in Flanders mustered 5571 in June, 4470 in July: in 1638, Turenne's 2 infantry regiments mustered 1300, Leslie's 2 infantry regiments, 1000; in 1644, Conde's 9 infantry regiments totaled 5000–6000.

The French cavalry lagged somewhat in development. They still favored the old system of independent companies, grouped for battle into ad hoc squadrons, as opposed to proper regiments—although both systems were used. These companies ran 50–100 strong. They distinguished between "Gendarmes," fully armored cuirassiers; "Light Horse," (*chevaux leger*) corresponding to demicuirassiers or armored arkebusiers; carabinieres, that is, arkebusiers, and dragoons. In action, they formed rather solid squadrons of 200 to 400, up to 7-deep. French horse were not highly regarded until after Rocroi, 1643.

Like their Swedish mentors, the French used 3 pdr regimental guns to support the foot, but after 1643, a shift to heavier 4 and 8 pdrs is seen. At 2nd Nordlingen (1645), the weighty guns hampered the infantry advance.

As an example, Rohan's army of 1635–6:

Montausier IR	12 coy	Leib Coy (Roque-Cervier)
Frezeliere IR	9	3 Gendarme Coys (Montbrun, Joux,
Canisy IR	10	Coq-Fontaine)
Bies IR	9	Carabiniere Coy (Villette)
Serres IR	12	5 coy = 400 horse (both years)
Cerny IR	12	
Vandy IR	12	
76 coy = 8000 men in 1635		
5500 men in 1636		
Chamblay IR	20 coy = 1400 in 1636	
Lecques IR	12 coy = 840 " "	

French strategy 1635–48 was to disperse their efforts between four to six fronts, maintaining a constant pressure until the opposition cracked. This lack of concentration both minimized risk—there were always reserves available—and limited gain. The principal fronts were Flanders (north), Germany (east), Italy (southeast—the Alps, Savoy, and Milan), Languedoc-Rousillon-Catalonia (south—eastern Pyrenees, Mediterranean), and Gascony-Navarre (southwest—western Pyrenees, Biscay). In addition, Dutch and Swedish allies were subsidized.

In 1635, Chatillon and Breze defeated the Spanish in an action at Avesnes. Thereafter, everything went wrong. The Dutch were late for the rendezvous. The Spanish cut off the allies, rolling back their gains. The Dutch and French commanders quarreled, the French troops, starving and deserted by their leaders, dwindled to 8000; they had to be evacuated home by the Dutch fleet. La Force held Lorraine and made minor gains in Franche-Comte. Crequi and the duke of Savoy did as much in Italy. Rohan secured the Valtelline, beating off both Imperial and Spanish corps in the battles of Mazzo, Valfraela, and Morbegno. La Valette and Bernhard lost a little ground in Germany but rebuffed Gallas.

In 1636, the Hapsburgs planned a simultaneous attack from Flanders, Germany, and Spain into France. Unfortunately, the Spanish offensive had to be postponed until 1637. The other 2 achieved success at first. Gallas drove into Burgundy but was halted by Bernhard and the elder Conde at Dijon. The Flanders attack was delayed by the Cardinal-Infante (the victor of Nordlingen). He finally moved in August, 32,000 strong, Piccolomini acting as deputy and Werth leading the cavalry. They achieved surprising success, brushing aside the Army of Picardy under Soissons and capturing the three fortresses of La Capelle, Le Catelet, and Corbie August 4–15 (Richelieu subsequently executed the unfortunate commandants). The road to Paris was open! Werth reached Compiegne, where he won a cavalry action. However, the main body lagged behind, and the French improvised a new army (Louis XIII and his guards, Soissons's regulars, plus militia) with a paper strength of 35,000 foot and 15,000 horse. By the time that Piccolomini reached Compiegne, the French were too strong to attack. Unwillingly, the Hapsburgs retired; Corbie was retaken November 9. Piccolomini and Werth blamed each other for the failure. To some extent, the Cardinal-Infante was at fault for the delay, but the overextension was inherent in their very success. The campaign might have fared better had Gallas been more aggressive and the southern offensive on time; the whole plan was too hastily contrived. Nevertheless, the "Year of Corbie" briefly presented a chance to knock Richelieu out of the war; it was the greatest Hapsburg opportunity against the French and the greatest disappointment.

Farther south, Rohan and Crequi hoped to take Milan. Rohan took Fort Fuentes (May 30), while Crequi and Savoy defeated the Spanish field army at Tornavento (June 22). Unfortunately, the duke of Savoy had entered the war to profit himself, not to replace Spain with France as master of Italy. He refused to support an attack on Milan. In August, Rohan had to fall back into the Valtelline.

The year 1636 also saw the first peasant uprisings in France; these, caused by war taxation, were easily crushed by royal forces but continued to crop up until 1659.

In 1637, the delayed Spanish offensive from Catalonia was defeated by Schomberg. Bernhard overran the Franche-Comte. In Flanders, the Spanish were so occupied with the relief of Breda that the French under La Valette were able to gain some ground. On the other hand, an anti-French uprising in the Valtelline restored the pass to Hapsburg control—Richelieu's broken promises had alienated both factions in the region, Catholic and Protestant alike. Another setback came in Italy, where the allied dukes of Savoy and Mantua died. Savoy dissolved into civil war, dividing into French and Spanish factions.

In 1638, the French fielded five armies plus Bernhard: Chatillon in Flanders, La Force in Picardy, Crequi in Italy, Longueville in the Franche-Comte, and the elder Conde in Biscay. Bernhard and, to a lesser extent Longueville, were the only successes. In Savoy, Crequi was killed, and his successor, La Valette, was defeated in the action of Vercelli. Worst of all, Conde's offensive against Spain, intended to reach Madrid, was halted by the insignificant fortress of Fuenterrabia (September 7).

This pattern was largely repeated in 1639. The main French army in Flanders was destroyed by Piccolomini at the Battle of Thionville (July 17). Conde's new offensive in Rousillon made very slight progress. In Italy, Valette lost all of Savoy except Turin, but his successor, Harcourt, managed to salvage something by winning the action of the Route de Quiers. Moreover, by purchasing the Weimar Army, Richelieu secured Alsace and the upper Rhine.

French units serving with Bernhard in 1638 included the Batilly, Burgundy, Navarre, Normandy, Picardy, Vardy, Castelmain, Volunteer, German, Leslie Scot, and Irish infantry regiments, Vattronville Cavalry Regiment, and some cavalry companies under Guebriant and Turenne.

Guebriant's corps (2500) included 3 infantry and 2 cavalry regiments, Leslie had 1000 in 2 infantry regiments (Leslie Scots and Sinot Irish) and Turenne had 1300 foot in 2 infantry regiments and 600 horse in 3 cavalry regiments. The 5 French infantry regiments were Burgundy (Batilly), Navarre (Vardy), Normandy (Castelmoron), Picardie (Melun), and the Volunteers. The 5 cavalry regiments were Turenne, Guebriant, Vattronville, Tracy, and Du Hallier.

APPENDIX E: EMPEROR FERDINAND II

I have not had occasion to refer directly to the emperor in this history: he led no armies, fought no battles, planned no campaigns—in fact, he played about as little direct role in military operations as any "Supreme War Lord" could. It was very rare for him even to issue orders to his generals. It is one of the ironies of history that this most pacific of rulers should have presided over this most destructive of wars.

Over and over, Ferdinand appears in a passive or reactive role: the Bohemians rebel, he crushes them; the Palatine aids the rebels, he moves against him; the Danes strike, he strikes back, the Swedes invade, he opposes. He never acts directly; it is always his allies, Spain or Bavaria, or his generals, Bucquoy, Tilly, Wallenstein, who do the real fighting. This same passive stance is reflected in his dealings with allies and subordinates; when Bavaria, Saxony, Spain, or Wallenstein demanded payment for services, territory was found. When Spain demanded support against France, it was given. When Wallenstein wanted to dominate the Baltic, he was given a free hand—despite the risk of antagonizing Sweden. Similarly, when Tilly insisted on invading Saxony, the emperor gave "reluctant" permission.

It would be a mistake to imagine the emperor as a weakling or nonentity. The rewards that he so generously gave away were merely a part of the conquests made possible precisely by his allies and generals. Similarly, he might have been much less enthusiastic about Spanish policy if he had relied less on their financial subsidies, on the order of a third of his military budget. Nevertheless, his policy was unaggressive; he had no desire for war and little understanding of military matters. No one was more optimistic about the prospect of peace. This would have surprised his opponents, the extreme Protestants; of course they lacked modern perspective. To a considerable extent, they were victims of their own propaganda. Having painted a portrait of a power-mad bigot, they interpreted everything that he did in that light. It was an age of paranoia; this compares with Richelieu's fear of "Spanish plots" or Pym's obsession with "Catholic conspiracies." To some extent, these were self-fulfilling prophecies, each "defensive" move by one side fueling the fears of the other. Thus, when the emperor favored the Bohemian Catholics, it "proved" that he was planning to destroy the Protestants, so they revolted, which, in turn, "proved" that the Protestants were planning to overthrow the dynasty; when the emperor moved against the rebels, it again "proved" his evil intent, so the Elector Friedrich, Christian of Brunswick, Christian of Denmark, and Gustavus Adolphus, each in turn had to "stop" him. All the antagonists, needless to say, had their own dynastic and religious goals, and in the eyes of the other side, relatively modest ambitions became major threats to the balance of power.

Nevertheless, Emperor Ferdinand did make decisions that had major impacts on the course of the war: (1) diplomatic initiative of 1619-20—isolated the rebels, gained the support of Bavaria and Saxony; (2) Wallenstein's appointment as generalissimo, 1625; (3) support of Spain in Mantua, 1628; (4) the Edict of Restitution, 1629—alienated moderate Protestants; (5) dismissal of Wallenstein, 1630; (6) reappointment of Wallenstein, 1631; (7) removal of Wallenstein, 1634; (8) the Peace of Prague, 1635. Less important decisions were the failure to make peace in 1622 (Friedrich refused concessions); Wallenstein's Baltic plans, 1627-30 (he was unaware of Sweden's power); the rejection of Gustavus's peace terms 1630-32 (his demands were increasingly unreasonable); the break with Saxony in 1631 (Tilly claimed military necessity); the order to relieve Regensburg in 1633 (no lasting effect), and supporting Spain against France in 1636 (France was already attacking the Empire).

Ferdinand II, Hapsburg, Holy Roman Emperor
Born: 1578; Emperor: 1619; Died: 1637

NOTES

1. Although Stradling and Parrott do not think so, see R. A. Stradling, "Olivares and the Origins of the Franco-Spanish War 1627-35," in *English Historical Review*, 101 (1986), pp. 68-94; David Parrott, "The Causes of the Franco-Spanish War of 1635-59," in Jeremy Black, *The Origins of War in Early Modern Europe* (Atlantic Highlands, NJ: Humanities Press, 1987), pp. 72-111.

2. The Valtelline, nestled betwixt neutral Switzerland and neutral Venice, was the principal link between Spanish Milan and Vienna. As such, it was of great importance during the Bohemian War 1618-20, but less thereafter. Nevertheless, the Spanish saw it as a vital route to Flanders and expended some effort to keep it open. The French tried to cut it several times.

3. The Danes had received 716,666 talers. Under the Treaty of Barwalde, 1630, the French promised the Swedes 400,000 talers per annum; it was not paid in full.

4. It might seem to us that these attacks, with open fighting in Trier and Alsace, would already constitute a state of war, but 17th century governments were prepared to accept border skirmishes. The Hapsburgs were not, at this time, in a position to defend their more vulnerable holdings.

5. The Flanders army, of 20,000 foot and 6000 horse managed to lose 18,000 men for no gain! The Italian and Spanish fronts bogged down from the first. The Valtelline army, under the French Protestant Rohan, gained immediate success, only to be swept out in May 1637.

6. A council of war (October 15) had voted to engage the French directly, but Gallas overruled it. This timid decision marks the beginning of Gallas's military decline.

7. He had already been receiving a French pension and had been paid 300,000 livres (=100,000 talers). See Appendix C for details of treaty.

8. See Appendix D. For a dissenting view see Jonathan Israel, "Olivares, the Cardinal-Infante and Spain's Strategy in the Low Countries," in Richard Kagan and Geoffrey Parker, *Spain, Europe, and the Atlantic World* (Cambridge: Cambridge University Press, 1995), pp. 272-283.

9. Not to be confused with his son "The Great Conde."

10. Ridiculously described as 80,000!

11. February 15. See Appendix E.

12. There was already a Wurtemberg regiment in the Weimar Army, under a younger brother of the ruling duke. One can see why the Imperials might doubt Wurtemberg's

goodwill. Wiederhold proved a capable officer and triumphantly returned his command to the duke of Wurtemberg at war's end in 1648.

13. It was defended by 600 men and 22 guns under Rodel.

14. He was persona non grata in Paris after his failure in the Valtelline.

15. Wedgewood says *south* bank, but Heilmann, Droysen, and Noailles indicate north. It certainly appears that both actions took place on the same side of the Rhine.

16. Savelli escaped, but Werth was sent prisoner to Paris until 1642. In view of his later bungling, Savelli's escape was lucky for Bernhard. If it were possible, one would almost suspect he was *allowed* to escape!

17. See Chapter 4 for Gotz.

18. Gotz's report to Elector Maximilan, August 11, 1638, from Johann Heilmann, *Kriegsgeschichte von Bayern, Franken, Pfalz, und Schwaben, 1506–1651* (Munich: Cotta, 1868), vol. 2, p. 598.

19. The 7 cavalry regiments Rosen, Nassau, Ohm, Caldenbach, Potbus, Rotenhan and Witersheim; 400 musketeers under Schonbeck, 300 under Guebriant, three 6 pdrs, and four 3 pdrs = 4400.

20. The Muhlenschanze (Mill Fort), defended by Leslie's Scots.

21. The Hattstein and Schonbeck infantry regiments under Bernhard; Turenne with Batilly, the Volunteers, and Schmidtberg; Vardy IR and Castelmoron IR under Guebriant.

22. Taupadel was still a POW.

4

Torstensson's War, 1642–45: Second Breitenfeld and Jankow

The problem that faced Torstensson when he assumed command of the Swedish army was very different from that confronting Gustavus in 1631—or Napoleon in 1805 for that matter. He could not simply seek out and smash an inferior army, then overrun large, lightly defended areas. To win the war, he would instead have to force his way into the Imperial heartland, protected by a dense network of garrisons and fortresses backed up by a field army of great size and considerable defensive and skirmishing capability, tested by over two decades of continuous warfare. Frederick the Great would have understood.

As noted in Chapter 2, Baner's death in 1641 was followed by a general mutiny, not to mention dissension among the generals and severe political and financial crises. Torstensson, Baner's natural successor, was in Sweden at the time. Nevertheless, the Swedes bestirred themselves to join Guebriant's French in the siege of Wolfenbuttel. The idea was that an Allied success in Brunswick would persuade the dukes of Brunswick-Luneburg (Georg's successors) to remain allied.

Gallas having proven incompetent in 1638–39, Archduke Leopold Wilhelm and FM Piccolomini had replaced him in command of the Imperial Army and successfully warded off Baner's offensives of 1640–41. Now they resolved to take advantage of the Swedish disarray to relieve Wolfenbuttel. Guebriant succeeded in blocking them in the Action of Wolfenbuttel, June 29, 1641,[1] however the sullen Swedes deprived him of total victory. The fortress did surrender, but the subsequent defection of the Brunswick dukes more than nullified the whole campaign.

When Torstensson confronted his new army at Winsen, November 25, 1641, he was facing a disunited, distrustful, and disgruntled crew. But he had two trumps to play; he'd brought 180,000 talers to cover their arrears in pay and

8000 native Swedes to crush any dissidents. Discipline was restored within the week. He spent the next couple of months in winter quarters, first in Westphalia, then at Salzwedel in the middle Elbe.

The Imperials were already preparing their own war-winning operation. On January 28, 1642, the archduke and Piccolomini mustered the army at Eisleben; by February 5, they had secured the strategic crossing at Tangermunde-Stendal. They hoped to catch the Swedes still in disorder, cut them off from the Baltic, and defeat them decisively. Unfortunately for them, Torstensson had sent Konigsmarck's cavalry on a wide raid/reconnaissance southward; he discovered their advance. As the Imperials were stronger in cavalry than the Swedes but weaker in infantry, Torstensson moved to a fortified camp at Arendsee-Seestadt between Salzwedel and Werben. Naturally, he was unwilling to risk a battle while his horse were so inferior—both qualitatively and quantitatively—moreover, he was very sick (his condition always worsened during the winter). The Imperials found him strongly emplaced, with a marsh to his front and the Elbe covering his left. The archduke attempted to turn the defense by advancing up the east bank but found the area both devastated and snow-covered. His troops suffered greatly. The Imperials had to retire back to Eisleben in early March, the winter operation proving both costly and futile.

They busied themselves recovering from this fiasco and arguing about blame. They made no especial effort to prepare for attack—somehow they had formed the notion that Torstensson was a "defensive" general.

His orders from Stockholm were concerned with defense, but Torstensson himself had opposite ideas. The position that he had inherited from Baner was neither good nor bad. The Swedes had control of the Baltic coast, Pomerania and Mecklenburg, a foothold in Westphalia, and a scattering of strongholds to the south, Erfurt in Thuringia and Chemnitz in Saxony. They were in effective control of neutral Brandenburg. There were small independent corps in Silesia under Stalhansk and in Westphalia. However, the Imperials had taken advantage of the situation in 1641 to push Stalhansk back to Brandenburg.

The Austrian heartland could be attacked in three ways: the Danube, the Elbe, and the Oder. The Danube route, as attempted by Gustavus in 1632 and Wrangel in 1648 (not to mention Napoleon in 1805 and 1809), led through heavily defended Bavaria and the narrow Passau gap. The Elbe route, as used by Baner in 1639 and Konigsmarck in 1648 (it was Frederick the Great's preferred choice as well), required the occupation of pro-Imperial Saxony, then the conquest of Bohemia, specifically Prague. Unfortunately, as the events had shown, this was a very difficult undertaking. Prague was hard to capture but easy to lose; no foothold in north Bohemia could be maintained without it, but even with it in hand, the invaders would have to push through Imperial fortresses in southern Bohemia. Baner had found it impossible to subsist his army there for more than a few months.

The third route was up the Oder into Silesia, then south to Moravia, and thence to Vienna. This route had drawbacks too; Silesia was full of fortresses and not particularly well supplied. At least the Imperials could not simply dig in at a central "Prague" and defend, as happened to Baner, and hitherto untouched

Moravia had potential *re* forage.

Two other options, to link up with the French on the Rhine or a direct attack on the main Imperial army, Torstensson rejected out of hand. To win the war, he would have to strike at Austria itself.

Torstensson spent February and March preparing for his planned offensive, by training and the imposition of discipline, by gathering a stockpile of supplies, and by reconnaissance. The main Imperial forces lay in quarters in Saxony and Thuringia. Konigsmarck was dispatched with a raiding force to alarm them. Posing as the vanguard of the main Swedish army, he swept right through them westward, toward Quedlinburg, drawing their attention toward Westphalia. Meanwhile (April 5), Torstensson was actually moving eastward, crossing the Elbe, and proceeding along the route Bleckede-Belzig-Treuenbrietzen-Juterbogk to Luckau in northern Lusatia (April 16); it surrendered the next day. Then he proceeded to link up with Stalhansk at Sorau near Sagan (April 28). With 20,000 men they laid siege to Glogau, dominant fortress of north Silesia (May 1). It was a very strong place, defended by 1700 men and 20 guns, well supplied with food and powder.

Duke Franz Albrecht von Sax-Lauenburg[2] commanded the Imperial corps in Silesia; he had expelled Stalhansk the year before. Hearing of the invasion, he sent to the archduke for help and began gathering his own small army at Neisse. Konigsmarck, leading a raid south, discovered his approach. Now Torstensson, unwilling to waste his troops in storming so strong a fortress, had begun a formal siege. But when he was informed of Franz's advance, he ordered an immediate assault. Glogau fell May 4, with a loss of some 200 Swedes.

This enemy success seemed to demoralize the Imperial defense in the province. Franz waited inert, while Torstensson marched triumphantly through Steinau, Leubus, Paechwitz, Jauer, and Striegau, each town surrendering without resistance—Liegnitz, which did resist, was bypassed. His goal was the small fortress of Schweidnitz, the strategic link between Silesia and Bohemia.

When he heard that Schweidnitz was under siege, Franz moved to its relief with 7000 horse, 500 dragoons, and 4 guns, Swedes and Saxons. It may seem odd that he might move against so superior an army, but he must have hoped that his all-mounted force could harass the Swedes without direct contact or risking a general action.

On May 30, Piccolomini with a strong detachment from the main army had reached Trautenau, 30 miles southwest of Schweidnitz; he expected to join up with Franz—then at Breslau—by June 3. Franz had other plans. Moving from Breslau, he bumped into Konigsmarck's outriders. These drew him back onto a larger force under Torstensson.

Torstensson had detached most of his cavalry and 2 brigades of infantry, plus most of his guns, from the blockade to some hills east of the fort. Here he met Franz in the Action of Schweidnitz or Zobten Berg, May 31, 1642. He deployed two strong cavalry wings with a much weaker screen between, the infantry farther behind. Franz advanced in two wings, each in two echelons, personally leading the left. Thrusting into the weak screen, he assumed that he was routing a broken enemy—the right engaged the Swedish left. As Franz advanced, the wings enveloped his flanks, while the foot and guns in front opened fire. Franz was shot down, struck by 2 cannon balls, and the army dissolved. Many were captured as the wings closed; it was a Cannae in miniature. The Austro-Saxons lost over 4000 dead and wounded and 1200 prisoners, including Franz himself.[3] Swedish losses were trivial; Piccolomini pulled back, and Schweidnitz surrendered June 3.

Torstensson then divided his army into two forces. Lilliehook with 6000 foot, 2000 horse, and most of the guns was directed to capture the fortified town of Neisse. Torstensson himself with 8000 horse, 1500 musketeers, and some light guns seized Troppau and then moved south into Moravia. Olmutz, the provincial capital was a strong place with 50 cannon and plenty of supplies and munitions, but only 800 recruits in garrison. After a short siege (June 11–14), they were granted honors of war.[4] Torstensson levied a kontribution of 300,000 talers and placed 3000 men in garrison. Konigsmarck, Wittenberg, and Stalhansk led a series of vicious raids south and west, Moravia, Bohemia, and Austria. Consternation reigned in Vienna; after 20 years, the fighting had returned home.

The main Imperial Army, regrouped and reinforced, quickly assembled at Brunn, the archduke from Saxony, Piccolomini's detachment, Franz's 4000 survivors, and a corps from Hungary. By July 11, they had collected 8–9000 foot and 12,000–15,000 horse.

Torstensson was well aware that he was no match for such numbers. He decided to take advantage of their alarm by completing his conquest of Silesia. On June 6—the same day that Lilliehook took Neisse—he marched to secure the minor places of Kosel (June 20) and Oppeln (June 26). The reunited Swedes then moved against Brieg (June 30).

Brieg was small but important, and its commandant, Col. Morder, and his 900 men were determined not to yield easily. The Swedes were unable to quickly reduce the outworks, even though they knew that the Imperials were on the way.

Having gathered his forces, the archduke moved on Olmutz (July 16), where he left a blockading force of 5000. The main army, 20,000 strong, drove north for Brieg. A strong detachment of Swedish cavalry under Schlang tried to obstruct their advance, but was routed by the Imperial van, some 2000 horse under Montecuccoli (Action of Troppau, July 25, 1642). Torstensson realized that the siege could no longer be maintained—at the time he had only 11,000 effectives—so he hastily retired to Guhrau in northern Silesia.

Unwilling to cross the Oder in the teeth of the enemy, the archduke decided to lay siege to Glogau instead (August 10). Torstensson, meanwhile, dispatched Konigsmarck toward Saxony and Thuringia on a combined raiding and recruiting mission, while the main army established itself in the Krossen-Guben area. There the Swedes could forage freely while awaiting a reinforcement column of 4000 foot and 2000 horse under Wrangel and Axel Lillie. When Torstensson heard that they were approaching (September 3), he marched to Beuthen, near Glogau, in hopes of lifting the siege. Schlang revenged his earlier defeat by a cavalry skirmish between Neusaltz and Beuthen. Torstensson hoped that the Imperials would leave their entrenchments to give battle, but they cautiously declined. So he crossed the Oder (September 10) and advanced down the east bank, opposite the fortress. The Imperials considered giving battle, but this would require most of them crossing from the west bank, risking the army's being cut in half. Instead they raised the siege and fell back to Luben on the 12th.

The following maneuvers are not easy to understand. Even with Axel Lillie's arrival (September 19), the Swedes were still much outnumbered by the archduke. Nevertheless, Torstensson was sufficiently encouraged to advance aggressively. He crossed the river at Glogau (September 20) and pressed forward to Buntzlau (September 25). The archduke, unwilling to give battle without reinforcements of his own, fell back on Lowenberg. Torstensson moved faster, got there first, seized the town, and deployed for action atop some hills. The Imperials, finding themselves cut off, moved south into the mountains forming the Bohemian border. Torstensson marched west, than south, through the upper Neisse pass to an outflanking position at Friedland; the Imperials countered by digging in at Friedeburg. The Swedish advantage quickly dissolved. The archduke was too strongly emplaced to attack, and the superior Imperial light cavalry, Croats and Hussars, quickly depleted the mountainous district. Torstensson retired to Zittau, which small town he stormed, the archduke following at a safe distance. The advantage had shifted again; now the Swedes were on the defensive and very short of supplies. Torstensson sent orders to Konigsmarck to rejoin him with all the troops that he could collect, then abandoned the Zittau position (October 17) to move north and west through Lusatia to Saxony. Raiding and plundering the whole way, he crossed the Elbe at Torgau (October 24-25), and laid siege to the Saxon city of Leipzig (October 27). Konigsmarck arrived the same day, 70 companies of cavalry, 8 of infantry, and 12 of dragoons, largely drawn from the Swedish garrisons in Chemnitz and Erfurt. Equally important to Torstensson, he brought provisions looted from the Imperial districts around Magdeburg.

Torstensson pressed the siege energetically and had already achieved a breach by the 30th. However, he did not wish to risk destroying so rich a prize by ordering a general assault. The Saxon garrison resisted stubbornly, repelling his initial thrusts.

After he had left Zittau, the Imperials moved with Torstensson, paralleling him somewhat to the south and crossing the Elbe at Dresden on October 24. On the 31st, his scouts reported them approaching from the east, over 5000 horse under Puchheim. Torstensson took all 10,000 of his own cavalry to try and smash them, crossing the Mulde River near Wurzen. As it turned out, however, Puchheim was merely the vanguard, with 20,000 more close behind. Torstensson withdrew to the siege camp at Leipzig, then, the next day (November 1), assumed a blocking position east of the town. As the Imperial van came into sight, it occurred to him that his present deployment, with a hostile fortress and two rivers blocking his line of retreat, was a bad one, so he directed his troops to start "sliding" to the left, north and west, thus, "edging" out of that corner. Either deliberately, to deceive the archduke, or due to the difficulties of this awkward maneuver, this movement assumed the appearance of a disorderly retreat. The Imperials turned to the right to parallel him, still some miles away. By nightfall, the two armies had arrived at Breitenfeld.

After dark, the Imperials held a council of war. The enemy was retreating in disorder; should they force battle or not? Piccolomini said no. He held the fighting qualities of the Swedes in great, even exaggerated respect, and distrusted their apparent "disorder." It was, he argued, never safe to engage them, except with a real superiority in numbers. Much better to continue following them, using superior light cavalry to harass them and prevent them from capturing Leipzig or any other stronghold. This was not a war-winning strategy, but it would at least avoid defeat.

The Imperial army was full of officers who disliked Piccolomini ("Germans"), and these assumed a bellicose attitude. The Swedes, they alleged, were in full flight; there would never be a better opportunity. As for numbers, they had a 3-2 edge. Finally, if they did not finish Torstensson now, he would link up with Guebriant's French, at that time in Westphalia, only 100 miles away, and moving east. Their combined force would be too strong to stop.

The council entirely misjudged the situation. Torstensson was not in flight; in fact, he wasn't even trying to avoid battle. He simply wanted to fight in a less risky spot. Neither he nor Guebriant had any idea of linking up; Guebriant had gone as far from home as he meant to and would soon be retiring. Nevertheless, their arguments swayed the archduke; he overruled Piccolomini and ordered an attack. This did not necessarily imply a field battle: given the "beaten" attitude of the Swedes, he might merely maul their fleeing army, perhaps capture their guns and train.

THE COMMANDERS

Field Marshal Lennart Torstensson, Count of Ortola (1603-51), was the "golden boy" of Sweden's Golden Age. At fifteen he became a royal page to Gustavus Adolphus, he distinguished himself in the wars with Poland, he was sent to the Netherlands to complete his military education, and in 1629 he became the first colonel of Gustavus's experimental artillery regiment. After successful operations in Germany, Breitenfeld and the Lech, he was made general. All this changed after he was captured at the Alte Veste. When he was exchanged in 1633, he returned home bitterly disillusioned and broken in health, the king dead and the cause in ruins.

He acted as Baner's second-in-command 1635-40, taking part in the victories of Wittstock and Chemnitz, but his deteriorating health forced him to return to Sweden in 1641; for the same reason he was reluctant to accept the command on Baner's death. His contemporaries diagnosed his ailment as gout, but a kidney infection picked up in prison seems more likely. This disease caused him increasing pain and weakness and seriously hampered him, especially in 1645. Torstensson may have nursed a trace of hypochondria, exaggerating his condition, but his sufferings were real; unable to ride, he commanded his army from a litter.

As a general, Torstensson was an excellent tactician, an above average strategist, and arguably the best operational mind of the war. As compared to his royal mentor, he was less of an innovator but had a better grasp of command and, technically, of artillery employment. The best artilleryman of his day, he is called the "father of field artillery." A better general than Baner, he lacked that leader's knack for "small war"; he normally delegated such operations to Konigsmarck or Schlang. In contrast to Gustavus or Baner, he preferred a sound, cautious approach to strategy and logistics, although he combined this with a flair for rapid movement and surprise. It was said of him that while he never showed Baner's brilliance at escaping disaster, he also lacked his tendency toward getting himself so caught. Torstensson was, in 1642, the last of Gustavus's paladins, old Marshal Horn having retired, Oxenstierna assuming a purely civilian role, and the rest dead. Generally speaking, the men of the post-Gustavan generation were not the equals of their predecessors.

In character, Torstensson was a cynical, embittered man but not as malicious or quarrelsome as his friend, Baner. His harsh military discipline was unpopular with his men, but this was balanced by his leniency in matters of ravishing and plundering. Torstensson was ruthless in military matters, justifying any atrocity or cruelty by grounds of "*ratio belli*"—a favorite expression of his. The troops nicknamed him "*Blixten*," (Lightening) because of his predilection for surprise and rapid movement. On the plus side, he was (unlike Baner and Wrangel) personally honest.

Torstensson's disease worsening, he resigned command in late 1645. He survived, active in Swedish politics, until April 7, 1651.

General Count Johann von Konigsmarck (1600–63), a German Lutheran, served as a colonel under Gustavus, and was the only German advanced by Baner, rising to major general. He later fought unsuccessfully in Westphalia, notably at Lemgo. Torstensson entrusted him with several independent commands, in which he achieved considerable success, then promoted him to lieutenant general. Konigsmarck was a brilliant cavalry leader and an expert at mobile operations, raids, and "small war." His last great "raid" was the 1648 assault on Prague. He was a quarrelsome sort, falling out with the French marshal Conde and Torstensson's successor, Wrangel.

Konigsmarck continued in Swedish service after the war and took part in the war with Poland under Karl X.

Field Marshal Count Karl Gustav Wrangel (1613–76) was a scion of a Swedish military family; his father was a field marshal. Only a junior officer under Gustavus, he rose to major general under Baner and was the most important of the junta commanding in 1641. He fought well under Torstensson and commanded the fleet against Denmark, but his subsequent independent command, 1646–48, was lackluster. In character, Wrangel was arrogant, greedy, and dishonest. As a soldier, he was an able subordinate but not up to the standards of Gustavus's paladins.

Lieutenant General Torsten Stalhansk (1594–1644), as noted previously, was generally considered of common origin, although. Roberts believed that he was actually the son of a royal chancellor. In any case, he was outside the Swedish "charmed circle" and never achieved the advancement that his talents merited. A brigadier under Gustavus, he was favored by Baner, eventually being given the independent corps in Silesia. This was the height of his career; Torstensson did not regard him highly, preferring Konigsmarck, Wittenberg, and Wrangel.

Major General Erich Schlang AKA Slang (ca. 1600–42) was another of the post-Gustavan generation advanced by Baner. His moment of glory was the defense of Neunburg in 1641, where by sacrificing his rearguard force, he enabled Baner to escape Piccolomini's pursuit; thus, he was dubbed "the Swedish Leonidas." For the rest, his record was mixed, with successes in Westphalia and Neusaltz but a defeat at Troppau. He was better known for fearlessness than skill.

General Johann Lilliehook (ca. 1595–1642), a Swede, had never been one of Gustavus's inner circle, nor had he been favored by Baner; nevertheless, Oxenstierna made him Torstensson's second-in-command. A competent subordinate, he was, like Schlang, known for his bravery.

Major General Arvid Wittenberg, a Swede, had been Stalhansk's lieutenant colonel in the elite Finn cavalry. He was trusted by Torstensson and became his principal deputy. He proved a sound subordinate but not brilliant on his own.

Major General Axel Lillie had been one of Gustavus's leading colonels. Another competent subordinate, he never received independent command.

Major General Caspar Cornelius Mortaigne de Potelles, a Protestant Fleming, served under Gustavus in 1632 and benefited from the anti-German "purge" of 1635–37. He annoyed Wrangel (although not Torstensson apparently) by supporting the mutineers in 1641; thereafter he appointed himself "spokesman" for the soldiers. In 1647 he transferred from Swedish service to become commander-in-chief for allied Hesse-Cassel.

Archduke Leopold Wilhelm Hapsburg (1614–62) was a son of Emperor Ferdinand II and the younger brother of Ferdinand III. After Gallas had proven incompetent, 1638–39, he was an ideal compromise replacement; unfortunately, his first step was to fall under Gallas's influence. Given Piccolomini as mentor, he insisted on showing his "independence," usually at the worst times. Replaced after his failure in 1642, he was briefly recalled in 1645–46, then led a Spanish army to destruction at Lens in 1648.

The archduke was not devoid of military capability but had never received the proper training to bring it out; his good ideas were not balanced by experience. He and Piccolomini made a poor team: he refused to be a passive figurehead, like his brother at Nordlingen, but he lacked the natural genius of a Conde. He could not lead himself, but would not permit Piccolomini to do so either. The archduke's character was a mixture of good intentions, arrogance, and envy of his Imperial brother; defeat and disappointment left him bitter and vindictive.

Lieutenant General Prince Ottavio Piccolomini, Duke of Amalfi (1589–1656), had, after distinguishing himself at Nordlingen, led an Imperial corps to Flanders to assist the Spanish against the French, 1635–39. He achieved a number of successes there, most notably, the destruction of a French army at the Battle of Thionville, June 7, 1639. However, he felt himself hampered by his subordination to the Spanish prince, the Cardinal-Infante. So, when he was recalled to fill a similar post for the archduke, he had his doubts. These were borne out in practice.

Although the only competent senior officer available,[5] Piccolomini was repeatedly passed over for command in favor of such mediocrities as Gallas, the archduke, Hatzfeld, and Melander, apparently due to the intrigues of the "German" faction in Vienna.[6] After the fiasco with the archduke, he returned to Flanders, only to find that the war had been lost in his absence. He was recalled to Germany in 1648; too late to win the war, he nevertheless averted the worst. He subsequently played a prominent role in the demobilization process and final peace settlement.

Piccolomini was personally fearless, indomitable, possessed of limitless energy and resource, thoroughly loyal to the Hapsburg cause. As a soldier, he was a consummate professional, a brilliant leader, and excellent strategist. But behind his calm facade lay a streak of emotion that occasionally led him into misjudgments. Thus, he lacked the operational detachment that characterized Torstensson or Turenne. His attempts to enforce some semblance of discipline and his unconcealed disapproval of the more obviously incompetent made him disliked in the army. It has been well said of Piccolomini that while he invariably succeeded when on his own, his fate was to be constantly trying to retrieve the errors of others.

GWM Count Hans Christoph von Puchheim (1605–57) was from an influential Austrian military family. He achieved rapid promotion with very limited service on secondary fronts. His appointment to balance Piccolomini was a sop to the "Germans." His ineptitude at 2nd Breitenfeld was due as much to inexperience as incompetence. Family influence and that of the "German" faction saved him from punishment. He later rose to high military and civil rank.

FZM Baron Ernst Roland de Suys, a Walloon, had been a colonel in 1633 and played a vital role in suppressing the Wallenstein plot; to this he owed his subsequent promotion. He and his colleagues, the Gonzagas, Bruay, Borneval, Fernemont, Webel, and the heroic Nicola, were mostly experienced and competent, if unimaginative officers.

THE ARMIES

Imperial Army—Archduke & Piccolomini
Right Wing—H. Gonzaga: 32 squadrons
—1st Echelon—Bruay: 13 squadrons

UNIT	DATE	COY	SQD	NOTES
Mislik KUR	1632	8	2	German
Alt-Piccolomini KUR	1629	12	3	Low German
Bruay KUR	1625	7	2	German
Montecuccoli KUR	1634	6	2	German
Sperreuter KUR	1636	-	1	German
Neu-Piccolomini KUR	1632	10	2	German
La Coronna Traga	—	3?	1	

—2nd Echelon—Borneval: 11 squadrons

UNIT	DATE	COY	SQD	NOTES
Archduke Leib KUR	1641	8	1	Upper Austria
Piccolomini Leib	1636	4	1	German; mixed type
Spiegel KUR	1639	6	1	German
Luttke KUR	1641	—	2	Brandenburg
Wolframsdorf KUR	1640	8	1	Saxon
Capaun KUR	1638	10	1	Silesia

Alt-Nassau KUR	1635	10	2	Nassau-Dillenburg
Borneval KUR	1640	—	1	Silesia
Munster ARK	1639	6	1	Silesia

—Flankers: 8 squadrons of Croats & Cossacks

Center—Suys: 11 brigades, 8 squadrons & 46 guns
—Left Group—Fernemont & Webel: 5 brigades
—1st Echelon: 3 brigades

Caretto IR	1638	10	-	AKA Grana; German
Enkefort IR	1619	10	-	High German
Webel IR	1632	10	-	High German

—2nd Echelon: 2 brigades

Sax-Lauenburg IR	1641	—	-	German
Moncado IR	1641	—	-	German

—Right Group—C. Gonzaga: 6 brigades
—1st Echelon: 3 brigades

Suys IR	1631	12	-	Walloon
H. Gonzaga IR	1629	11	-	German
Ranfft IR	1618	10	-	High German

—2nd Echelon: 2 brigades

Archduke Leib IR	1619	10	-	Low German
Fernemont IR	1627	6	-	Low German
Wachenheim IR	1632	8	-	German

—Reserve—Suys: 8 squadrons
—1st Echelon: 4 squadrons

Nicola KUR	1628	10	1	Low German; 1 of 3 sqd
Novery KUR	1640	—	1	German
Grodetzky ARK	1639	6	1	Silesia
Gissenburg KUR	1630	8	1	Low German; ½ CR

—2nd Echelon: 4 squadrons

Desfurs KUR	1616	8	2	Spanish-German
Paconchay DR	1641	2	1	German
Gissenburg KUR	1630	8	1	Low German; ½ CR

Artillery: 46 guns

Left Wing—Puchheim: 31 squadrons
—1st Echelon—Nicola: 12 squadrons

Pompeji KUR	1639	—	1	German
Madlo ARK	1639	6	1	Silesia
L. Gonzaga KUR	1625	12	3	Bohemia
Vorhauer KUR	1641	—	1	Silesia
Wintz KUR	1631	10	1	German
Jung KUR	1629	5	1	Low German
Jung-Heister KUR	1632	10	1	Low German
Alt-Heister KUR	1632	8	1	Low German
Nicola KUR	1628	10	2	Low German; 2 of 3 sqd

—2nd Echelon—Schleinitz: 11 squadrons

Burksdorf KUR	1639	6	2	Brandenburg

Torstensson's War, 1642-45   115

Unit	Year	Coy	Sqd	Notes
Lammersdorf KUR	1634	8	1	German
Callenberk CR	1631	—	1	Saxon Leib CR #1
Warlowsky ARK	1639	6	1	Silesia
Knoche CR	1633	—	2	Saxon Leib CR #2
Gall a Burke DR	1633	10	1	German
Gallas DR	1634	—	1	German
Hanau CR	1631	—	1	Saxon CR #4
Schleinitz CR	1632	—	1	Saxon CR #6

—Flankers: 8 squadrons of Croats & Hussars
Total: 16,000 cav in 71 sqds; 10,000 inf in 10 brigades; 46 guns = 26,000

Swedish Army—Torstensson
Right Wing—24 squadrons, 13 detachments, 13 guns
—1st Echelon—Wittenberg: 14 squadrons, 13 detachments, 13 guns

UNIT	COY	SQD	NOTES
Torstensson Leib CR	8	3	German
Hesse CR	12	3	" Landgrave of Hesse Darmstadt
Duval CR	8	3	German
Hoking CR	8	3	"
Kinsky CR	8	2	"
Detachments	-	-	40 musketeers & 1 lt gun each

—2nd Echelon—Stalhansk: 10 squadrons

Derfflinger CR	8	3	German
Wittkopt CR	12	2	"
H. Wrangel CR	12	3	"
Polish CR	8	2	Poles

Center—Lilliehook: 11 brigades, 3 squadrons, 41 guns
—Left Group—K. G. Wrangel: 4 brigades
—1st Echelon: 2 brigades

| K. G. Wrangel IR | 16 | - | Mixed: Swedes & Germans |
| Mortaigne IR | 12 | - | German |

—2nd Echelon: 2 brigades

| Axel Lillie IR | 14 | - | Mixed: Swedes & Germans |
| Schlieben IR | 18 | - | German |

—Right Group—Mortaigne: 4 brigades
—1st Echelon: 2 brigades

| Lilliehook IR | 8 | - | German |
| Baner IR | 12 | - | " |

—2nd Echelon: 2 brigades

| Pfuhl IR | 8 | - | German |
| Jeschwitski IR | - | - | German? |

—3rd Echelon Reserve—Axel Lillie: 3 brigades, 3 squadrons

Maul IR	8	-	German
Plettenberg IR	8	-	"
Alt-Blau IR	12	-	" Gustavan veterans.
3 ad hoc sqd	?	3	mixed

Artillery: 18 heavy and 23 light guns

Left Wing—24 squadrons, 16 detachments, 16 guns
—1st Echelon—Schlang: 19 squadrons, 16 detachments, 16 guns

Stalhansk CR	12	3	Finn-German
Wittenberg CR	12	2	" "
Cratzenstein CR	6	2	German
Douglas CR	8	2	"
Billinghausen CR	12	2	"
Schulmann CR	8	2	"
Pfuhl CR	12	2	"
Seckendorf CR	8	2	"
Mitzlaff CR	8	2	"
Detachments	-	-	40 musketeers & 1 lt gun each

—2nd Echelon—Konigsmarck: 5 squadrons

Tideman CR	8	3	German
Lilliehook CR	8	2	"

Total: 10,000 cav in 51 sqds; 10,000 inf in 11 brigs+29 det; 70 guns = 20,000

THE BATTLE OF 2ND BREITENFELD, NOVEMBER 2, 1642

After dark on the 1st, both armies bivouacked in the open fields, already deployed for battle. The Swedes lay slightly in front of the two villages Breitenfeld and Lindenthal, the Imperials 2 miles southeast, between the villages Seehausen and Mockau. An important road, the Delitzsch-Leipzig and a fair sized woods, the Linkelwald, lay midway between the rival camps.

At dawn, both armies, still not quite in sight of each other, drew up in battle line. The Imperials then marched for an hour to the north and west, to roughly parallel to, and within 600 meters of, the main road. Piccolomini's plan, based on the council's decision, was to envelop Torstensson's left, forcing him either to give battle or to abandon his infantry and baggage to save the horse. Torstensson was quite willing to give battle; he therefore directed his right to swing forward, to bring his line directly opposite to theirs. This done, he advanced, sliding slightly to the left. A fold in the ground had hidden the Swedes from their opponents until they were almost at the road.

Fate, or the continuing strategic significance of Leipzig, had brought the Imperial and Swedish armies to the very field where, 11 years before, Gustavus Adolphus had won his greatest victory. The woods, the Linkelwald, which had been in Tilly's rear in the earlier battle, now bisected the archduke's deployment. Of course, at 1st Breitenfeld, they'd been facing north, against an advancing enemy, whereas now they were attacking an enemy to the south and west.

The Breitenfeld battlefield was a near-flat plain, open on both flanks, the opposing battlelines formed parallel to the Leipzig road. The only significant feature was the woods, the Linkelwald, set right in the middle of the Imperial center. A deep stream, the Ritschke, running west of the road, had already been crossed by the Swedish right before the battle started.

The moment that the Swedes appeared, the Imperial guns roared as one—according to legend, they were using chainshot. In any case, their first salvo rattled the Swedes, balls tearing into their ranks. Torstensson and the young Palsgrave[7] both lost their mounts. But it was folly to try to outshoot Torstensson! He countered by maneuver, moving and firing his guns and forcing his enemy to do the same. The Imperial fire became ragged and trailed off.

Both armies were deployed in linear fashion, a center and two wings, in two echelons with a reserve. Because of the woods, both Piccolomini and Torstensson divided their centers into two divisions or groups, on the right and left sides of the woods. Piccolomini's right extended beyond the Swedish left; Torstensson's right also extended beyond the Imperial left, but this was less obvious because of the 8 squadrons of light cavalry acting as flankers. Although the Imperials had a good edge in raw numbers, 26,000 to 20,000, no fewer than 16 squadrons were Croats, Hussars, and Cossacks, light cavalry of dubious worth in a pitched battle, 4 squadrons were arkebusiers, and 3 more dragoons; the real odds were more like 21,000 to 20,000. The Swedish cavalry wings were evenly balanced, but the Imperials weighted their right, both in quality and in quantity. The archduke and Piccolomini were there, with the striking wing, while Torstensson stationed himself in the center rear, where he could monitor the battle as a whole. He assigned as field word, "Hjalp, Herre Jesus!" (Help us, Lord Jesus!).[8]

The Swedes crossed the road, the armies facing off at 500 meters. Cannon shots were exchanged while Torstensson's wings regrouped and reformed. Wittenberg and Stalhansk had become somewhat disordered crossing the Ritschke. Schlang, on the other hand, was nervous. He could see that the Imperial line extended beyond and around his flank. He extended his own line, pulling at least 2 squadrons, Seckendorf Cavalry Regiment, out of the 2nd echelon to lengthen the first. The archduke paraded along the Imperial line, exhorting the men to courage and conduct. Torstensson rode[9] dramatically before his center and gave the signal, "In God's name, let everyone go forward against the enemy." When he saw them in motion, Piccolomini began his own countercharge. It was about 10:00 A.M.

The Swedes left the heavy guns behind, but rolled the 3 pdrs with them. The Imperial foot advanced very slowly, pushing their guns between the battalions. At 80 meters, both lines halted and began blasting away with musketry and grapeshot. Lilliehook, at the head of his men, was one of the first hit. Mortally wounded by a musket ball, he had his men set him down by some bushes to "watch the battle."

On the wings, however, the fighting had already come to cold steel. Wittenberg advanced at a near charge, leaving his supporting musketeers behind. For the Imperials in front of him, everything went wrong. Through unbelievable ineptitude, Puchheim had still not finished placing his squadrons in line. When the Swedes galloped toward them, they were disordered and "wrong-footed." The flanking irregulars justified their reputation for unreliability by dissolving en masse. Puchheim had made the mistake of placing an arkebusier regiment, Madlo's, in the 1st echelon. After letting off a few shots at long range, they too broke into rout. This indiscipline spread to the whole front line, Pompeji, Gonzaga, and Alt-Heister, all breaking before contact with the enemy onslaught. The 2nd echelon, mostly Saxons, fled without striking a blow. Aside from a few knots of diehards—Vorhauer suffered heavily—the entire wing had collapsed.

Col. Nicola rose to the occasion, through sheer determination managing to hold together 2 or 3 squadrons, his own regiment and Jung-Heister. These stubborn few threw back Wittenberg's first assault.

Wittenberg now had problems of his own. Some of his men had disappeared in pursuit of the broken Imperials, others had been repelled by Nicola, and the rest were milling around in confusion. All were disordered. Stalhansk came up with the 2nd echelon, some of whom pinned Nicola with a second attack, while the rest protected Wittenberg as he reformed. Nicola continued to stand. Suys, commanding the Imperial reserve, moved to his support with 8 squadrons.

Wittenberg and Stalhansk, meanwhile, began their third assault—not a charge, but a deliberate, controlled advance supported by 520 musketeers. Nicola and other officers were shot down. Imperial resistance was cut to pieces. Wittenberg and Stalhansk were ready to finish them when Torstensson appeared. He directed that Stalhansk, with about 7 squadrons, should finish dealing with the Imperial left; Wittenberg should prepare another 10 to intervene on the other wing; a couple would assault the Imperial center, supporting the foot, and Torstensson himself would hold the remaining 4 or 5 in reserve. Stalhansk drove the Imperials back in bloody rout upon Suys's reinforcing element, which in its turn dissolved without a fight. He continued pursuing Puchheim's defeated force for 10 miles.

On the Imperial right, however, the result was opposite. It seems that Schlang, like Gustavus at 1st Breitenfeld, relied on his supporting musketeers to repel the attack. He allowed the advancing Imperials to get too close before he started his own counter-charge. Piccolomini enveloped the open left wing, crumbling the Swedish line. It collapsed; Schlang was killed, and the musketeers massacred.

Some of the horse panicked and fled the field, Croats on their heels. But most of them were simply "bounced," falling back on Konigsmarck's echelon, 200 meters behind. Unlike the Saxons, these, although only 5 squadrons strong, fulfilled their role of covering and supporting the defeated front line.

In the center, the infantry had been fighting a battle of their own, apart from the cavalry. The 1st echelon brigades had continued firing, musket and cannon both, until the musketeers had exhausted their ammunition; about half an hour for 12 shots each. Then the aggressive Swedes threw in their 2nd echelon in a headlong, "Gustavan" charge straight upon the defenders. The Imperials countered with their own reserve, and it came to an old-fashioned melee, "push of pike and butts of muskets." The fight split into two separate struggles on each side of the woods, Mortaigne against Fernemont and Webel to the south, Wrangel against Gonzaga to the north. To the south, the Swedes had the edge; the Imperials were discouraged by the rout of their horse, and a couple of Swedish squadrons wandered in as support. Mortaigne shoved the Imperials back to their original position at to the Linkelwald.

The left group under Wrangel, on the other hand, had precisely matching disadvantages. Gonzaga's counterattack threw him back sharply, and the guns accompanying the assault were overrun and turned against their owners. Mortaigne, supported by Axel Lillie, disengaged from the retiring Imperial left group and swung to cover Wrangel. Gonzaga's advance was halted and pushed a little back, with the recapture of some of the guns. Both sides improvised a new line and exchanged fire for another hour, say 11:30 to 12:30.

At the end of the first phase, around 11:00, the initiative on the Imperial right rested with Piccolomini. He still had his 2nd echelon, 11 squadrons strong and entirely intact. He had several options: he could throw them upon the Swedish left and finish them off, he could swing them against the infantry in the center, or he could turn them south to restore the situation on his left. He did none of these, instead holding them in reserve. Why? Was he unaware of Puchheim's defeat (he certainly couldn't see it from where he was)? Was he too caught up with beating Schlang? Was it a judgment call? Or was the archduke the culprit? In any case, the moment was lost.

While the Imperials hesitated, Konigsmarck, assisted by the Palsgrave, had reassembled Schlang's remnants and his own people into a coherent defense, just in time to withstand Piccolomini's follow-up. The Swedes were beaten and outnumbered, but Bruay's edge had been blunted dealing with Schlang. The irregulars, of course, were off in pursuit of the broken Swedes. A grinding match developed, the Swedes being slowly pushed back. Individual squadrons from the Imperial 2nd echelon were drawn forward to help maintain the pressure.

Some commanders in Torstensson's position would have reinforced Konigsmarck with their reserve. What he actually did, as noted earlier, was to ride over to his victorious right and take control. Stalhansk would harry the beaten Imperials from field, while Wittenberg would move around and behind the Imperial foot and the Linkelwald, then attack the Imperial right. Sometime after 11:30, they appeared in Piccolomini's rear. Borneval and the 2nd echelon turned to ward them off. Wittenberg's 10 squadrons fell upon them in an all-out charge. They shattered like glass. Caught between two hostile forces, the Imperial cavalry sought to save themselves by flight. In this extremity, the archduke and Piccolomini managed to hold together a few regiments as a rearguard, their Leib regiments, Alt- and Neu-Piccolomini, Mislik, Borneval, Luttke, about 6 squadrons in all, plus a few scattered heroes from routed units. These suffered terrible losses trying to hold back the combined forces of Wittenberg and Konigsmarck. Many of the pursuing Swedes simply bypassed them for easier prey. They did, however, draw the attention of the Swedish leaders long enough for Gonzaga's brigade to make its escape, if not unbloodied, at least reasonably intact.

The Fernemont-Webel group was not so lucky. Pinned by Mortaigne against the Linkelwald, there was no escape for them. The final phase began around 12:30 as the whole of the Swedish infantry launched their attack. The Imperial foot defended themselves desperately, obstinately, as a storm of fire tore into them. The Swedes advanced, taking the last of the artillery and pushing the remnant back into the woods itself. There they stood, refusing to surrender, only a few yards from the site of Tilly's last stand in 1631. Repeatedly the Swedes came on, and repeatedly they threw them back. Finally, Torstensson sent forward the 7 squadrons he'd kept in reserve; this sealed their fate. Many fell, the rest yielded. By 1:30, the battle (although not the pursuit) was over.

Map 4.1
The Battle of 2nd Breitenfeld, November 2, 1642

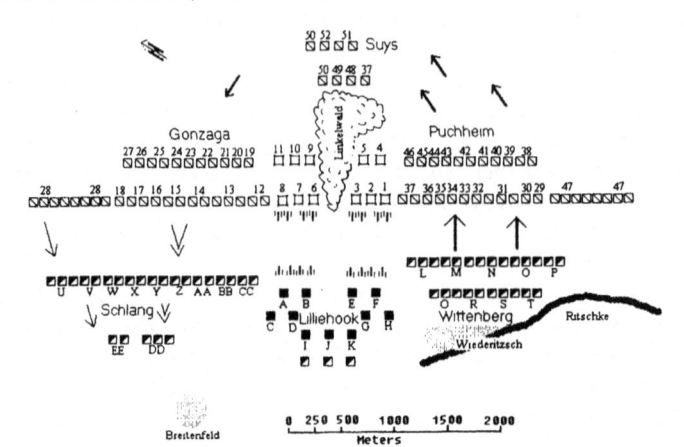

Imperials (Archduke)
1 - Caretto
2 - Enkefort
3 - Webel
4 - Sax-Lauenburg
5 - Moncado
6 - Suys
7 - Gonzaga
8 - Ranfft
9 - Archduke Leib
10 - Fernemont
11 - Wachenheim

12 - Mislik
13 - Alt-Piccolomini
14 - Bruay
15 - Montecuccoli
16 - Sperreuter
17 - Neu-Piccolomini
18 - La Coronna Traga
19 - Archduke Leib
20 - Piccolomini Leib
21 - Spiegel
22 - Luttke
23 - Wolframsdorf
24 - Capaun
25 - Alt-Nassau
26 - Borneval
27 - Munster
28 - Croats & Cossacks

29 - Pompeji
30 - Madlo
31 - L. Gonzaga
32 - Vorhauer
33 - Wintz
34 - Jung
35 - Jung-Heister
36 - Alt-Heister
37 - Nicola
38 - Burksdorf
39 - Lammersdorf
40 - Callenberk
41 - Warlowsky
42 - Knoche
43 - Gall a Burke
44 - Gallas
45 - Hanau
46 - Schleinitz
47 - Croats & Hussars

48 - Novery
49 - Grodetzky
50 - Gissenburg
51 - Desfurs
52 - Paconchay

Swedes (Torstensson)
A - Wrangel
B - Mortaigne
C - Axel Lillie
D - Schlieben
E - Lilliehook
F - Baner
G - Pfuhl
H - Jeschwitski
I - Maul
J - Plettenberg
K - Alt-Blau
L - Torstensson
M - Hesse
N - Duval
O - Hoking
P - Kinsky
Q - Derfflinger
R - Wittkopt
S - Wrangel
T - Polish
U - Stalhansk
V - Wittenberg
W - Cratzenstein
X - Douglas
Y - Billinghausen
Z - Schulmann
AA - Pfuhl
BB - Seckendorf
CC - Mitzlaff
DD - Tideman
EE - Lilliehook

2nd Breitenfeld was one of the most even, most hotly contested, and most bloody battles of the war. The Imperials lost almost 10,000, 4000–5000 dead and wounded, plus 5000 captured. This included many officers and some 15 regimental commanders. All 46 guns were lost, as well as 50 ammunition wagons and such of the train as had not been left in Dresden, 116 infantry ensigns, and 69 cavalry cornets. The victors suffered almost as much as the vanquished, 2000 dead and as many seriously wounded. Among the dead were Lilliehook, Schlang, and 3 colonels; Col. Gustav Baner, son of the field marshal, had been captured; Stalhansk was lightly wounded.

SIGNIFICANCE OF 2nd BREITENFELD

2nd Breitenfeld marked a number of "lasts." It was the last "big" battle of the war, the last in which both sides exceeded 20,000. Equally noteworthy, these were, aside from the 1650 Saxons, entirely composed of men in Swedish or Imperial service, not combined forces with French, Hessians, Bavarians, or Spanish. It was the last battle of the war in which the classic "push of pike" was significant. It was the last fought in Saxony. It marked a new and final stage in the conflict; if 1st Breitenfeld had established Swedish military predominance, if Nordlingen had called it into question, then 2nd Breitenfeld reestablished it.

More interesting from an operational standpoint is the "form" of the battle. Most of the battles of the war may be described as "attack-defend" with one side definitely on the offensive, and the other mainly fending it off. This was for sound strategic reasons. No commander of the period would attack an enemy without what he considered favorable odds. A Tilly might be more optimistic than a Bucquoy or a Cordoba in estimating the odds, a Gustavus more optimistic than a Tilly, and a Conde or Bernhard more optimistic than Gustavus, but the same principle applied. Whatever their other shortcomings, the professional commanders of the period were quite capable of evaluating the relative strengths of rival armies. If a weaker leader found himself forced to fight, either because the enemy was too close, as at 1st Breitenfeld or Lutzen; or because retreat was endangered, as at Stadtlohn or Lutter; or because a vital area had to be defended, as at White Mountain or 2nd Nordlingen; or simply because he judged the position strong enough to resist, as at Wimpfen or Freiburg, he would assume as strong a defensive position as he could find and offer the enemy the option of attack. The enemy might simply decline, the most common result. He might attempt a probe, as at Rakonitz or Werben. He might hover around the area, harassing with raids and actions, as at Brieg. Or he might judge the position weak enough to attack. As a general rule, such judgments were correct; the only outright failures of attack are 1st Nordlingen and Freiburg—some would add Dessau Bridge.

But at 2nd Breitenfeld, both armies were attacking. While this was common enough in some periods, it was rare in the Thirty Years War. The only other example is Oldendorf, an example of patently bad judgment, in a very similar strategic situation. Now, although Piccolomini did not regard the Imperial superiority as enough to justify battle, he did think it enough to deter Torstensson from attack. Clearly, Torstensson considered the barest margin enough. In fact, the course of the battle indicates that both sides were virtually equal.

However, the major significance of 2nd Breitenfeld lies in the fact that it was the first true linear battle, the first example of a style of warfare that would dominate Europe for a century and a half. It did not appear out of nowhere, of course. We may trace its origins to Maurice of Nassau, while the battles of 1st Breitenfeld, Lutzen, and Oldendorf represent a transitional phase. By 1642, the development was fully grown and inevitable.

In the space of four years, three strikingly parallel battles took place, 2nd Breitenfeld in 1642, Rocroi in 1643, and Naseby in 1645. In these may be seen the basic features of linear warfare, not as a Dutch or Swedish experiment, but already implemented by six entirely different armies and tactical systems. As has been pointed out, most recently by Parrott,[10] linear warfare was characterized by a marked increase in infantry defensive capacity through the emphasis on static firepower and the use of supporting reserve lines. This was accompanied by a relative decrease in offensive capability due to shallower formations and the declining employment of the pike. Given the relative invulnerability of the infantry center, linear battles tended to be resolved on the cavalry wings.[11]

Of less scholarly interest but equal tactical importance was the shift from large, relatively independent, pike-based columns to a multiplicity of small, *interdependent* units, thin, shallow battalions, with a parallel shift from solid cavalry regiments to squadrons. Tilly's tercios were 2000 strong, 80 wide and 25 deep; his cavalry 500–1000 strong and 10-deep. A linear battalion, ca. 1700, was 500 strong, a squadron 165, both 3-deep. Torstensson's battalion was 800, 6-deep; Piccolomini's 1000, 10-deep. Their squadrons were, respectively, 200, 3-deep, and 225, 4- or 5-deep. At the same time that the units shrank, and their frontages grew, the formerly quite wide intervals between units dwindled to mere maneuver gaps.[12] It was no longer possible for lines to pass between each other. The massed echelons became single elements. The days when single battalions could reverse the outcome of battles, such as at Wimpfen or Lutter, were over.

THE 1643 CAMPAIGN

To the disappointment of the more enthusiastic Swedes, Torstensson failed to "exploit" his victory in a large-scale "Gustavan" offensive. His army was victorious, but battered and winter was upon them. He contented himself with renewing the siege of Leipzig. Konigsmarck was dispatched to Westphalia, the 2000 wounded were consigned to hospital in Halle, while the bulk of the cavalry, those not needed to cover the besieging force, went into quarters at Zeitz. Reinforced by many of the captured Imperials, Torstensson was now stronger than he had been before the battle. There was no chance for relief. Nevertheless, the Saxon defenders, Schleinitz and Trandorf, put up a creditable defense; Leipzig did not surrender until December 7. Torstensson placed the stronghold under Axel Lillie and levied a kontribution of 150,000 talers, 30,000 in cash, the balance in kind. The prolonged siege had had an unfavorable side effect, in that most of the Imperial defectors took the opportunity to desert. Nevertheless, the loss of his second largest town was a crippling blow to the elector of Saxony.

Torstensson spent most of December at a strategy summit with the French Marshal Guebriant; in his absence Wittenberg secured the much-disputed stronghold of Chemnitz (December 29). Upon returning, Torstensson resolved to finish off Saxony, then invade Bohemia. His target was the fortress of Freiburg between Chemnitz and Dresden, held by 1200 Saxons under LtCol Schweinitz. In early January, he advanced on it with 8 brigades of foot, 1000 horse, 100 guns, and five mortars. The Saxons fought heroically. Although large breaches were made with guns and mines, a major storm by the Alt-Blau and White brigades was repelled with over 400 lost (January 13).

After the Breitenfeld defeat, the archduke had returned to Vienna, leaving Piccolomini to reform the army at Rakonitz, which he did so effectively that by February he had 14,000 men available to relieve Freiburg. Upon their approach Torstensson had to lift the siege (February 27); he went into winter quarters at Elsterwerda east of Torgau (March 13). This was a considerable setback, as Freiburg had been on the point of surrender. The unsuccessful siege cost the Swedes 2000 men to the Saxon 200. Upon his return to Bohemia, however, Piccolomini was advised that not he, but Gallas, had been appointed to overall command (March 27); he therefore left Imperial service for that of Spain.

Torstensson broke quarters March 25 and moved east with his main body while Konigsmarck was detached west. In late April, he entered Bohemia from Lusatia. Gallas guessed, correctly, that he was making for Moravia, so he assumed a strong blocking position at Koniggratz. Gallas's force was too strong for Torstensson to assault directly. Gallas's plan was to confine the Swedes by blocking the crossings of the Elbe. It failed; Torstensson feinted toward Brandeis, then while Gallas was distracted, crossed at Melnik, north of Prague. He narrowly skirted that fortress, to rush east, reaching Moravia via Zwittau. Arriving triumphantly at Olmutz, he resupplied the Swedish garrisons and set about expanding the occupied area, taking the minor places of Kremsier (June 26) and Tobitschau (July 3). Outmaneuvered but not defeated, Gallas followed to Brunn. Gallas had no intention of risking battle; instead he adopted a strong defensive position at Kojetin, while using his superior light cavalry, especially Croats, to harass and hamper Swedish operations. In a particularly humiliating skirmish, 3 of Torstensson's best cavalry regiments[13] were ambushed by 2 Imperial companies, for the loss of 180 officers and men. Despite increasing pressure, Torstensson held on into September, raiding up to the outskirts of Brunn and hoping for support from Transylvania.

A small force under Konigsmarck had been sent west before Torstensson invaded Bohemia. After a very successful raid into Franconia, he was able to increase his group to 3000. He spent July and August operating against the Saxons near Magdeburg, but in September he was abruptly summoned to the Baltic.

As a diversion against Torstensson, Gallas had formed some 4000 men under GWM Krockow and dispatched them via Brandenburg to Pomerania (August

10-30). With the support of friendly Poles, he quickly overran Kolberg, Treptow, and Kammin. Gallas sent a reinforcement of 1500 more horse under Puchheim,[14] but Torstensson ambushed them near Troppau for the loss of 900. Puchheim decided to rejoin Gallas instead.

Unfortunately for Gallas, Krockow proved remarkably inept. He antagonized his subordinates so badly that there was an officer mutiny; the enlisted men simply deserted. When Konigsmarck arrived (September 20), he quickly retook the lost ground; Krockow had only 1200 men left to oppose him. He fell back to the safety of "neutral" Poland.

Back in Moravia, Torstensson realized that his campaign had failed. The Transylvanians had not appeared, and any reinforcements that he might have hoped for had been diverted to deal with Krockow. Gallas's attritional strategy had succeeded: the Swedes had not taken any important fortresses, and they had, Torstensson admitted, lost more men than if they'd fought a field battle. Moravia was devastated, "laid in ruins." In October, he fell back into Silesia, Gallas and Gotz following at a safe distance.

Gallas had good reason to be satisfied. Although he had not held Torstensson at the Elbe, he had turned him back, with loss, at no risk to the Imperial cause. This was Gallas's last success.

Torstensson briefly besieged Jagerndorf before retiring into northern Silesia. After a futile protest to the Poles regarding Krockow, Konigsmarck moved south to Krossen. The news from other fronts was mixed: a Spanish army had been defeated at Rocroi, but a French army destroyed at Tuttlingen.

THE 1644 CAMPAIGN

Torstensson had cut short his siege of Jagerndorf (October 1643), less because of Gallas's proximity than orders received from Sweden. The regent, Oxenstierna, directed him to abandon operations against Austria and move northward for the invasion of Denmark. It was part of a larger plan: Torstensson would strike into Jutland from the south, while old Marshal Horn (dragged out of retirement) would overrun the northern districts of Norway and Skane with the home army. The Swedish fleet, under Fleming, would secure the Baltic and ferry the victorious armies to the islands. It was a propitious time to settle accounts with Denmark, which had been covertly pro-Imperial and anti-Swedish since 1st Breitenfeld. The aged King Christian IV was bankrupt, his army virtually nonexistent, and his authority ebbing. He had so alienated his Estates that they preferred being overrun to voting taxes for defense. Only the fleet was ready for action.

Torstensson did not agree with Oxenstierna's design. He feared that in his absence the Imperials would retake his hard won footholds in Silesia, Moravia, and Saxony. Nevertheless, he had no choice but to obey. On November 13, he began his northwestern march—he had first placed his strongholds in a position of defense, those too weak to stand alone being evacuated, and had (falsely) announced his objective as Pomerania. This seemed likely enough to both armies. Gallas wrote the emperor that the barren coasts of Pomerania would be unsuitable for a winter campaign; he would concentrate on Silesia until spring.

Torstensson did not advise his officers of the real objective until reaching Havelberg (December 16).

The invasion of Denmark began with Torstensson's arrival at Oldesloe in Holstein. Poor food, hard marching, and wintry weather had reduced him to less than 12,000 effectives, all hard-bitten veterans. The fortress of Christianspreis, guarding Kiel, fell to his storm (December 26); ruthlessly, he put the whole garrison to the sword. With Kiel, he gained a large store of munitions, food, and money; moreover, the "frightfulness" shown then and later by the Swedes demoralized the Danish defenders. Fortresses raised at great expense by King Christian yielded without show of resistance, Rendsburg, Tonning, and others. Only Gluckstadt and the tiny outwork of Krempe chose to hold out. A Col. Buchwald with 1600 horse and some militia attempted a stand at Kolding; they were overrun January 20, 1644. Thereafter, Jutland lay at Sweden's feet.

However, the main objective was not Jutland itself but the offshore islands specifically, Fyen. Torstensson left a small blockading force to watch Gluckstadt while massing his main body at the "Little Belt," the narrow channel separating Jutland and Fyen. The Danes had assembled a defense force for the island, based on the fort of Middelfart. The fleet, which was supposed to carry the Swedes across, had not yet left port—it was still winter, of course. The rapid conquest of Jutland had thrown off the invaders' timetable. Impatient as always, Torstensson gathered some 80 boats to cross on his own. His first attempt (February 9) ended in disaster and the loss of 1000 men; the second (March 20) was intercepted by Danish warships with the loss of 300 men and most of the boats. So Torstensson resolved to wait for the promised sailing of the Swedish fleet in May.

Events seemed to be turning against the Swedes. Although abandoned by his nobles, old King Christian had managed to collect 15,000 men by late March— mostly raw recruits but able to fire a musket.[15] Further, he had assumed personal command of the fleet. After a successful start, Horn's offensive in Skane had run out of steam. The initiative was lost.

Christian's defensive strategy was similar to that he had employed against Tilly in 1627–28. Using the Gluckstadt complex as both foothold and base, he launched a series of harassing raids against Torstensson, some by land, others via amphibious landings. He stirred the peasantry into irregular resistance. Torstensson replied with harsh repression; any armed peasant was denied quarter. Nevertheless, the whole position was rendered doubtful as the Swedish "conquerors" had to fortify their camps against raiders and partisans. As if this were not enough, Hatzfeld, the Imperial commander in Westphalia, was operating against Torstensson's strategic rear in Holstein. Expected assistance from Holland had not materialized. Only a naval victory could give Oxenstierna his quick victory.

It was not to be. On July 11, the rival fleets met in the Battle of Kolberger Heide; the Swedes were defeated and driven into Kiel. The Danes began an active blockade, inflicting considerable damage on the entrapped fleet, including the loss of its commander, Admiral Fleming.[16] Of even greater impact on the situation was the arrival of Gallas with the main Imperial army (July 29).

Gallas's appearance in Holstein came as a considerable surprise to the

Swedish command. Oxenstierna had persuaded himself that the Imperials would not risk anything for such a doubtful ally as Denmark. Even when their movements had become unmistakable, he believed that they were proceeding against Pomerania (like Krockow the in 1643). At one point he was considering stripping troops from Torstensson to reinforce the Pomeranian garrisons.

He was almost right. Gallas had not wished to follow Torstensson northward[17] but was given a direct order from the emperor. Even then, he drew out his preparations and delayed as long as possible; although he broke quarters in late March, he did not begin the operation until June. Gallas mustered some 13,000 men,[18] and soon after his arrival at Oldesloe he was joined by another 3000 Danes from Gluckstadt. Operations and detachments had reduced Torstensson to 5000–6000. The Danes' hope of annihilating the Swedish invaders and reversing the outcome of their war seemed within Gallas's grasp.

Torstensson responded with the most successful display of stomach strategy of the war. His first step was to devastate the land south and east of the Eider ("scorched earth"), then dig in behind that river in the area Tonning-Friedrichstadt. Gallas advanced into the barren zone, then bumped into Torstensson's defenses. Paralyzed by indecision, Gallas could not bring himself either to attack or to withdraw; he wasted a month probing the Swedish outposts while his army starved. The horse were ruined for lack of forage.

Torstensson watched and waited,until the arrival of reinforcements under H. Wrangel enabled him to go over to the offensive. Crossing the Eider at Rendsburg, he tried to fix Gallas's attention at Bardesholm while his cavalry turned his left at Nortorf and Neumunster, then struck into his rear at Segeberg. Like a man awakening from a daze, Gallas hastily fell back out of the trap. Torstensson occupied Oldesloe, intending to establish communications with the friendly port of Lubeck to his east, while H. Wrangel re-secured Jutland and Holstein from the Danish resistance. Gallas advanced on Oldesloe, but when the Swedes offered battle, he raised fortifications. The initiative had definitely passed. After attempting to "shadow" the Swedes, as he had done so successfully the year before, Gallas implemented a new strategy, to defend the line of the Elbe. If he could keep the Swedes north of the river, he might yet salvage the campaign.

The Danes, thoroughly disillusioned, returned to Gluckstadt. A part of the Swedish forces continued operations against Denmark after Gallas's retreat. The arrival of a pro-Swedish fleet from Holland and subsequent destruction of their navy at the Battle of Femern (October 23, 1644) forced the Danes to accept humiliating terms of peace.

Gallas's new plan began successfully enough by blocking an attempted crossing at Domitz. Torstensson, who was too sick to effectively command, lost several weeks gathering bridging materials.

While Gallas and Torstensson had been dueling on the Eider, Konigsmarck had been active farther south. Torstensson had given him 7 cavalry regiments and a few dragoons, which, when combined with some Hessian allies, briefly threatened Westphalia, then Saxony (January through March). Next he returned to Westphalia, drawing off any support that Hatzfeld might have given Gallas

(May–July). Before leaving for Denmark, Gallas had left detachments to deal with the abandoned Swedish garrisons in the south. The most formidable of these corps was a combined Imperial-Saxon force under Enkefort, which laid siege to Chemnitz (August 9). Konigsmarck was unable to preserve Chemnitz or Luckau, but he did save Erfurt and Leipzig and retook Torgau and Halberstadt as well. By late September, he and Enkefort seemed to have balanced each other.

Gallas, meanwhile, had lost faith in his Elbe plan; the defense could not be maintained against a serious attack. Instead, he would fall back into friendly territory and establish a fortified camp, just as he had in 1643. He therefore retired to Bernburg, just south of Magdeburg (September 8).

Torstensson had had time to consider his failure the year before and had come up with a solution. The moment that he heard that Gallas had abandoned the river line, he forced himself from his sickbed, driving the army in hot pursuit. By September 16, he was assaulting Gallas's outposts.

The Bernburg position was on a defensible hill, dug in, and well provided with artillery. Despite the losses suffered on the Eider, Gallas was fully capable of repelling any direct attack. Torstensson had a more ingenious scheme in mind. He established a ring of strongpoints, Eisleben, Halberstadt, Kalbe, Aschersleben, Munschen-Nienburg, and Mansfeld, around the Imperial encampment. Each fort had a garrison and a squadron of cavalry. From these positions the Swedes patrolled and devastated the area around Bernburg hill. If the Imperials struck back, the cavalry simply fell back into their supporting strongpoint, which could hold out for relief from the main army. This system could only work against inferior horse, but Gallas's people had been ruined in Denmark. Many were now on foot, and the condition of the rest was poor. The Imperial commander watched, uncomprehending and inert. By the time that Konigsmarck arrived,[19] the web was complete.

Once all foraging was cut off, the Imperials began to starve. With a last flicker of his former ability, Gallas countered Torstensson with a gambit of his own; 1500 of his best troops staged a major probe toward Eisleben. While the Swedes were swallowing this bait, the main army broke out of the web and reached Magdeburg to the north. The sick, the baggage, munitions, and all the cannon had to be left behind, but the army was saved. The Saxon troops in Magdeburg provided supplies and reinforcements.

Gallas had not exactly distinguished himself up to this point, but now his incompetence reached its height. He held the army immobile at Magdeburg while Torstensson patiently reestablished his encirclement. The arrival of a Hessian corps brought the Swedes up to 5000 foot and 7000 horse, while Gallas had less than 10,000 in all, many of them no longer battleworthy. Generals Bruay and Enkefort, having lost all faith in Gallas, decided to stage their own escape. Gathering the 3000–4000 cavalry still fit, they slipped out on the night of November 21–22, heading for Wittenberg, some 50 miles east. Konigsmarck, with a mixed force of horse and musketeers, caught and destroyed them just short of the town. Bruay got clear with 200–300, but Enkefort and 1500 were captured.

The entrapped army suffered terribly from hunger; the last of the horses died or were killed for food. Gallas lapsed into complete drunkenness, with bouts lasting days at a time. Desertion was rife. Before the army could finish destroying itself, the late autumn rains caused the Elbe to rise, sweeping away the Swedes' pontoon bridges. While the enemy army was thus, temporarily divided, Gallas and his remnants moved out. Torstensson harried their escape, taking 1000 prisoners, but 3000 reached Wittenberg.

The wits in Vienna revived Gallas's old nickname of "Army-Wrecker"; this was the third army that he'd managed to ruin. In fact, the campaign of 1644 may well have been the worst Imperial disaster of the war, the main field army, 20,000 strong, reduced to 3000 and those a demoralized rabble. This strategic success by Torstensson was more decisive than any battle. Austria was, for the moment, defenseless.

Torstensson was determined to force Elector Johann Georg to the peace table and to this end devoted the rest of 1644 to the devastation of Saxony—like Baner and Wallenstein before him. The stubborn elector, who did not understand just how serious Gallas's defeat was, only pretended to negotiate.

Overall, 1644 was a bad year for the Imperials. In addition to the defeat of Denmark and the destruction of Gallas, the French had made gains on the Rhine.[20] The detachments in Saxony, Moravia, and Silesia had achieved little. Only Gotz's army in Hungary could claim success, having driven back an invasion from pro-Swedish Transylvania.

THE 1645 CAMPAIGN

Torstensson's army enjoyed a brief respite from late December to early January, during which they were reequipped, clothed, and armed for the new year. Their commander's fertile mind had engendered a plan to win the war, "to strike the Imperials in the heart of their power and so force them to yield." Three columns would simultaneously strike toward Vienna, the Swedes through Bohemia, the French through Bavaria, and the Transylvanians through Hungary. At the same time, the Protestant resistance in Upper Austria would rise in armed revolt. In the past similar offensives had failed due to poor coordination between the allied armies; when the Hapsburgs found themselves under heavy pressure on one front, they simply drew reinforcements from less endangered areas. By striking from all sides at once, Torstensson hoped to eliminate that option.

Hatzfeld, the new Imperial lieutenant general, found that his problem was not so much to assume command of an army as to build one practically from scratch. His situation was worse than Wallenstein's in 1632. The new field army was assembled from disparate corps: Gallas's remnants, a detachment from Hatzfeld's own Westphalia army, Gotz's Hungarian command, a brigade of Saxon horse, and various regiments collected from Bohemia and Silesia. All told, these came to less than 12,500. Hatzfeld wished to concentrate the detachments opposing the allies in Silesia, Moravia, and Hungary as well, but the Imperial War Council refused to leave those areas completely defenseless. Realizing that the army as it stood was completely inadequate, the Imperials persuaded Bavaria to lend Hatzfeld a corps of 5000 veterans under Werth, making them, in numbers at least, roughly a match for Torstensson.[21] Needless to say, this hastily collected and polyglot crew was no substitute for a properly trained, organized and coordinated force; only Hatzfeld's Westphalians were fully reliable. Gotz was insubordinate, Gallas's people were demoralized, and Werth regarded himself as the leader of an independent contingent. Hatzfeld had neither the time nor the charisma to weld these elements into an effective team.

Torstensson, whose sickness was worsening daily, was determined to begin operations as soon as possible, while he was still able to command. The total Swedish field forces in mid-January 1645 came to 28,794, including 4500 men under Wrangel, watching the Danes. As before, Konigsmarck would command a separate detachment 9000 strong, to operate in the area Saxony-Westphalia. With the main body, 6500 foot and 9000 horse, Torstensson would "force the enemy to peace." An unseasonable thaw and the resultant mud immobilized his army through the first half of January 1645, but a detachment of 1000 horse and 300 musketeers under MajGen Goldstein defeated some arkebusiers and Croats and secured the Erzgebirge Pass.

By the 19th, the ground had frozen, so Torstensson was able to move. The weather was still a factor; the guns and baggage had to be drawn through the snow on sledges. The Erzgebirge operation had been a ruse, the real advance was via the pass at Pressnitz (January 24). The Imperial outposts on the lower Eger River, Saaz, Komotau, and Laun, fell without resistance; only in Brux did Hatzfeld's people hold out.

Hatzfeld had expected an attack, but not so soon. His army, concentrated at Pilsen, was adequate in numbers but weak in artillery, infantry, and equipment. As already noted, this winter offensive had deprived him of the time that he needed to weld his troops into a coherent body. Hatzfeld was, moreover, under pressure from both above and below on his own side. He had earlier deployed Werth with 1000 horse to the west of Pilsen, while Gotz with 2000 lay near Prague. At this point the Imperial War Council directed that he concentrate all forces and that when the Swedes, as anticipated, entered Bohemia, he should at once engage them in battle.[22] Gotz, insubordinate as always, was reluctant to give up his independent command and even delayed informing Hatzfeld of the Swedes' passage of the Pressnitz. The Imperials were unable to agree on a strategy. Hatzfeld believed, correctly, that Torstensson was en route for Olmutz, but he didn't know whether he meant to move east and cross the lower Moldau near Prague or to move south, passing west of Pilsen. If he opted for the former course, Prague might be lost. The best that he could figure out was to try and cover both possibilities, but Prague had priority.

Incapacitated by a relapse, Torstensson had not been able to join his troops until January 31. Another thaw, combined with flooding, paralyzed his advance for several weeks. He spent the time scouting Hatzfeld's dispositions. Apparently, he had not yet decided himself which route to take. He determined that although Hatzfeld's main body was to the west, at Pilsen, his reactions were focused on Prague. On February 18, the Swedes crossed the Eger and in a week's march bypassed the Imperials to the west, passing within 10 miles of Pilsen. Hatzfeld didn't dare interfere; if the Swedish force turned out to be a feint or raiding party, he would uncover Prague. Once he realized that it was in fact the main body, he maneuvered to head him off. The key point was Horazdiowitz, a crossing on the middle Wottawa River.

Hatzfeld reached the town after dark on the 25th, a critical 12 hours ahead of Torstensson. His plan was to defend the far bank, blocking the Swedes from crossing. The Wottawa is not a major obstacle, but yet another thaw had broken the ice and swelled it to flood; it could be forded only at a few crossings, Horazdiowitz, Strakonitz, and Pisek. Hatzfeld had secured them and prepared his army for a fight. Both Werth and Gotz had finally rejoined, so he was at full strength. As encouragement, Hatzfeld advised the troops that the Virgin Mary had appeared to him[23] and promised victory. He issued a simple battlecry, "Strike and Win!"

When he found the Imperials so well deployed, Torstensson hesitated. After a futile exchange of cannon fire, the Swedes settled in for the night. Finding the Imperial position proof against both attack and bombardment, Torstensson resolved to draw them into the open, then destroy them in a pitched battle, where superior mobility and firepower would outweigh superior numbers. The following day, the 27th, he conducted a feigned retreat, but Hatzfeld was not fooled. On February 28, Torstensson threatened the Moldau, and on March 1, he formed to offer battle at Pisek crossing. In both cases, Hatzfeld sat tight and strengthened his defenses.

Hatzfeld had been directed by the War Council not to let the Swedes across the Moldau, which was in line with his own ideas. At this time, he had effectively pinned Torstensson between the Moldau, the Wottawa, the western mountains, and the fortress of Pilsen, but his success was dependent on the unseasonably warm weather. Once the thaw broke, the rivers would freeze over, and much of their value as obstacles would be lost.

Torstensson's feelings, of course, were precisely the opposite. While the mildness of the winter alleviated the sufferings of his troops, the mud and swollen rivers had repeatedly frustrated his operations. On the night of March 1, he summoned an unexpected council of war and informed his surprised colonels that the army would cross the Moldau in the morning. The train, he explained, had been sent off during the day, while the army held the Imperials' attention. When the enemy awoke on March 2, they found that the Swedes had vanished.

Hatzfeld's first thought was that his strategy had succeeded; deprived of forage and unable to advance, the Swedes had returned to Saxony. Still cautious, he sent scouts north to reestablish contact.

Of course, Torstensson was actually at Altsattel on the Moldau, taking his army across the river. The ice was strong enough to bear the infantry, but the cavalry and artillery had to ford the freezing water. By the time that Hatzfeld learned the truth, the Swedish outriders were 20 miles east of the river. The Imperial commander was in a dilemma: he had to stop the enemy advance, but, given his inferior infantry and artillery, he didn't dare meet them on even terms. Gotz and his supporters argued that superiority in cavalry would counterbalance their deficiencies. They also reminded him of the emperor's orders to keep the enemy west of the river.

Hatzfeld decided that the best solution was to somehow get in front of Torstensson and occupy a defensible blocking position. In a determined forced march, he covered 50 miles in 2 days, along the route Horazdiowitz-Pisek-Muhlhausen-Tabor. Resting in Tabor (March 4), he received the good news that he had succeeded; the Swedes lay well to his northwest.

After crossing the Moldau, Torstensson had advanced at a surprisingly leisurely pace, both to allow the troops to recover from the rigors of the crossing and to avoid disorder in the unfamiliar, hostile territory. Hatzfeld was able to march north on the 5th and establish a defensive position at in the hills around the village of Jankow (Jankau, Jankowitz).[24] Torstensson was not aware that he'd been cut off until his vanguard cavalry bumped into 400 Bavarian horse. This sharp little skirmish alerted both armies to the other's presence.

Hatzfeld was not entirely happy. His army was not in good spirits. Gotz's faction was increasingly insubordinate. Worse, the rank and file were feeling "let down" after the emotional high of February 26 and had not recovered from their sufferings during the forced march. Discipline had suffered; there had been nasty outbreaks of plundering at Tabor. Nevertheless, he had outmaneuvered Torstensson and now occupied a good defensive position.

Torstensson directed his units to camp for the night in battle formation; they would attack the next morning.

THE COMMANDERS

Field Marshal Graf Melchior von Hatzfeld (1593–1658), as noted in Chapter 2, served successfully under Wallenstein and Gallas prior to his defeat at Wittstock; he did well in the secondary Westphalian theater 1638–44. A competent strategist and organizer, he proved an unsuccessful battlefield commander. Although a Hessian Lutheran, he lacked the rabid anti-Italianism of most "Germans." Hatzfeld's relatively mild character left him unable to deal with forceful types like Gotz.

Field Marshal Count Johann von Götz (1599–1645), a Luneburg Lutheran, began his military career under Mansfeld (1621) but switched to the Imperials after Fleurus, rising to colonel by 1626. He was made GWM by Wallenstein (1632) but avoided the purge of pro-Wallenstein officers in 1634. Given command of the Silesian front, he mismanaged it so badly as to be court-martialed for incompetence and possible treason. He therefore switched to Bavarian service in 1636 and was made field marshal and supreme commander. He did well in Westphalia (1638), but his failure to relieve Breisach (1639)[25] led to another court-martial. He switched back to the Imperial army in 1640 and immediately became a leading general. In 1641 he conducted the Imperial-Saxon siege of Gorlitz, in 1643 he was Gallas's second-in-command, and in 1642 and 1644 he commanded in Hungary against the Transylvanians, all successfully.

Personally, Gotz was aggressive, abrasive, arrogant, obstinate, and insubordinate, incapable of cooperating with equals or superiors, but he got along well with subordinates. He was a leading member of the "German" faction and a bitter enemy to Italians like Savelli and Piccolomini; this did not prohibit his quarreling with fellow German Hatzfeld. Gotz had an exaggerated idea of his own abilities and asserted that all the other Imperial and Bavarian generals were unfit. As a general, Gotz was recklessly brave and possessed considerable leadership ability and charisma, but between repeated bad luck and unsound judgment, he suffered more than his share of defeats. Hatzfeld's scapegoating has so blackened his reputation that his successes have been overlooked.

GWM Tomas Pompeji, despite his name, was closely associated with Gotz, having served under him in Hungary.

Werth and Ruischenberg were the senior Bavarian commanders, dealt with in detail in Chapters 3 and 6.

FM Suys, Lt FM Bruay, and GWM Trauditsch were all good, experienced subordinates. LtFM Henrich von Mercy was another scion of that military family.

Torstensson and his principal subordinates, Wittenberg, Mortaigne, Douglas, and Goldstein, had all been at 2nd Breitenfeld. The newly promoted major generals, Douglas (a Scot) and Goldstein (a German), had been veteran colonels.

THE ARMIES

Imperial Army—Hatzfeld (see Appendix D)
Right Wing—Werth: 23 squadrons
—1st Echelon—Werth: 12 squadrons

UNIT	DATE	COY	SQD	NOTES
Lapierre KUR	1635	9	2	Bavarian
Alt-Kolb KUR	1634	8	2	"
Fleckenstein KUR	1620	8	2	"
Gayling KUR	1620	9	3	"
Alt-Werth ARK	1621	9	2	"
Sporck ARK	1638	10	1	" losses from skirmish.

—1st Echelon Reserve—Trauditsch: 3 squadrons

Trauditsch KUR	1632	10	2	IMP; German
Pompeji KUR	1639	—	1	IMP; German; 1 of 3 sqd

—2nd Echelon—H. Mercy: 8 squadrons

Jung-Nassau KUR	1639	10	2	IMP; German
Waldeck KUR	1632	10	2	IMP "
Beck KUR	1633	9	2	IMP "
Hatzfeld KUR	1625	7	2	IMP "

—Flankers: Croats

Center—Suys: 6 battalions, 6 squadrons & 26 guns
—1st Echelon—Suys: 6 battalions & 26 guns

Zuniga Brigade	—	—	1 bn	IMP; 1000 mixed inf
Zaradetzky Brig	—	—	1 bn	IMP; 1000 mixed inf
Suys Brigade	—	—	1 bn	IMP; 1000 mixed inf
Holz Brigade	1620	—	1 bn	Bavarian; 650 mixed inf
Ruischenberg Brig	1620	—	1 bn	" 700 mixed inf
Gil de Haas Brig	1644	—	1 bn	" 650 mixed inf

Artillery: 4 x 12 pdr, 2 x 6 pdr, 20 x 3 pdr

Torstensson's War, 1642-45

—2nd Echelon—Callenberk: 6 squadrons

Unit	Year		Sqd	Notes
Callenberk CR	1631	—	2	Saxon; Leib #1
Hanau CR	1631	—	1	Saxon; CR #4
Schleinitz CR	1632	—	1	Saxon; CR #6
Gersdorff CR	1633	—	1	Saxon; Leib #2
Rukert CR	1642	—	1	Saxon: ex-Jung-Schleinitz

Left Wing—Gotz: 21 squadrons
—1st Echelon—Bruay & Bassompierre: 12 squadrons

Unit	Year	Coy	Sqd	Notes
Pallavicini KUR	1641	8	3	IMP; Aus; AKA Pallavicini-Sforza
Hennet KUR	1631	5	2	IMP; German
Neu-Piccolomini K	1632	10	3	IMP; Ger; AKA Jung-Piccolomini
Piccolomini KUR	1629	12	3	IMP; LG; AKA Alt-Piccolomini
Pompeji KUR	1639	—	1	IMP; German; 1 of 3 sqd

—2nd Echelon—Pompeji: 9 squadrons

Unit	Year	Coy	Sqd	Notes
Tapp KUR	1640	—	1	IMP; Silesian
Bruay KUR	1625	7	2	IMP; German
Gonzaga KUR	1625	12	3	IMP; Bohemian
Salm KUR	1636	—	2	IMP; Bohemian
Pompeji KUR	1639	—	1	IMP; German; 1 of 3 sqd

—Flankers: Dragoons
Total: 10,500 cav in 50 sqd; 5000 inf in 6 brg; 500 Croat/drag; 26 guns = 16,000

Swedish Army—Torstensson (see Appendix E)
Right Wing—Wittenberg: 24 squadrons, 12 detachments, 12 guns
—1st Echelon—Wittenberg: 13 squadrons, 12 detachments, 12 guns

UNIT	COY	SQD	NOTES
Fritzlaw CR	8	2	350; German
Raabe CR	4	1	200 "
Margrave CR	8	2	300 " Baden-Durlach
Karl Gustav CR	8	2	300; Kurland; AKA Palsgrave CR
Jordan CR	8	2	300; Livonia
Wittenberg CR	8	2	400; German
Torstensson Leib CR	8	2	600 "
Detachments	-	12	480; 40 musketeers & 1 lt gun each

—2nd Echelon—Goldstein: 11 squadrons

Unit	Coy	Sqd	Notes
Wittkopt CR	8	2	300; German
Rochow CR	8	2	350 "
Axel Lillie CR	8	1	220 "
Galbrecht CR	8	2	300 "
Goldstein CR	8	2	300 "
Derfflinger CR	8	2	330 "

Center—Mortaigne: 8 battalions & 37 guns
—1st Echelon: 6 battalions & 33 guns

Unit	Coy	Sqd	Notes
Wolckmar IR	12	1 bn	676; German; 2x 3 pdr
Paikull & Seestedt IRs	16	1 bn	955 " 3x 3 pdr
Mortaigne IR	12	1 bn	670 " 2x 3 pdr
Wrangel & Linde IRs	16	1 bn	810 " 3x 3 pdr
Torstensson Leib IR	12	1 bn	776 " Alt-Blau; 2x 3 pdr

Ribbing & Stalarm IRs	6	1 bn	500; Swedes; 2x 3 pdr
Artillery:	8 x 24 pdr, 10 x 12 pdr		

—2nd Echelon: 2 battalions & 5 guns

Lewenhaupt&Jordan IRs	16	1 bn	985; German; 3x 3 pdr
Axel Lillie & Koppy IRs	16	1 bn	763 " 2x 3 pdr

Left Wing—Douglas: 23 squadrons, 11 detachments, 11 guns

—1st Echelon—Douglas: 12 squadrons, 11 detachments, 11 guns

Landgrave CR	12	3	500; German; Hesse-Darmstadt
Horn CR	8	2	300 "
Hammerstein CR	8	2	300 "
Douglas CR	8	2	300 "
D'Avangour CR	8	1	250 "
Tideman CR	8	2	360 "
Detachments		11	440; 40 musketeers & 1 lt gun each

—2nd Echelon: 11 squadrons

Muller CR	8	2	400; German.
U. Pentz CR	8	1	250 "
Reuschel CR	8	2	250 "
Butler CR	8	1	150 "
Riesengrun CR	8	2	200 "
Dannenberg CR	8	1	270 "
Reichart CR	8	2	350 "

Total: 47 squadrons; 8 brigades; 23 detachments; 60 guns = 16,017

THE BATTLE OF JANKOW, MARCH 6, 1645

Late on the afternoon of the 5th, Torstensson had his litter dragged to the top of Hill 554, so that he could get an overview of the battlefield that he was unable to examine personally. The position occupied by Hatzfeld was a strong one. The ground was broken with hills and woods, so that there was little open ground and extremely limited fields of fire. This not only countered the superior Swedish artillery, but deprived their cavalry of the space needed for charging. The broken ground would hamper the movement of their infantry as well, and particularly the regimental guns. The Imperial front was further covered by a freezing stream, the Jankowa. Finally, the right flank was protected by steep ground and thick woods; it would be difficult to envelop.

The left flank, on the other hand, was much more open; it lacked the protection of the Jankowa, and it was dominated by high ground thrusting west of the Imperial line, the Kapellhojden, Chapel Hill. Despite the apparent weakness to the south, Torstensson drew up his army on the Svarta Bergen, Black Mountain, rather north than directly opposite the Imperial position.

Before 5:00 A.M. on the 6th, Hatzfeld was disturbed by the sounds of movement to his right. He had deployed his army in the groupings in which he'd found them, Werth's Bavarians on his right, backed up by his own Westphalians, Gotz on the left, the Saxons in reserve, with the infantry center divided between Imperials on the left and Bavarians on the right. As noted before, he lacked confidence in most of them, officers and men alike, and many of them felt the same about him. Hearing the noise that the Swedes were making, he concluded that Torstensson was up to something, but was he retreating, trying to turn the right flank, or moving toward the unreliable left wing? Hatzfeld ordered both Gotz and Werth to send out reconnaissance parties.

The evening before, after deploying the army and surveying the field, Torstensson had summoned his full council of war, generals and colonels both. He spoke frankly. The Swedish infantry were weak, the enemy position was strong, and battle in such bitter cold would be a chancy, dangerous proposition. However, having failed to outmarch the Imperials, they had no choice but to outfight them. The operation would begin before dawn. The threat to Hatzfeld's right was merely a feint; the real assault would be to the south, around Chapel Hill. The field sign would be "Hjalp Jesus!"

By 6:00 A.M., the Swedes were on the move. They deployed in 3 columns of march, the infantry forming the easternmost, closest to the enemy; next were Wittenberg's horse, with the heavy artillery, baggage, and train forming the third, westernmost column. Goldstein's brigade acted as vanguard, while Douglas, bringing up the rear, was not only reserve and rearguard, but also engaged in misdirecting the Imperial attention by continuing the feigned threat to the north. He was sufficiently convincing that Hatzfeld decided to conduct a personal reconnaissance, thus, effectively leaving his army without overall direction for a critical couple of hours. This was not the first time that Hatzfeld's "up-front" style of command had caused difficulties: by personally leading the counterattack at Wittstock, he had left the army virtually leaderless.

The next stage of the battle hinges on a question of interpretation. Before leaving on his reconnaissance, Hatzfeld had directed Gotz to occupy Chapel Hill. But did he mean merely to establish a forward outpost, as he later implied, or did he want Gotz to advance the whole left wing to that exposed position? Gotz seems to have believed the latter. Anyway, Gotz sent his dragoons to occupy Chapel Hill with orders to hold it until the main body arrived. The movement of the wing itself was delayed. The moment that Goldstein's vanguard came into view, around dawn, a bit after 7:30, the dragoons fled en masse, abandoning the hill to the enemy.

The news of the Swedish advance came as a surprise to Gotz, as he had assumed that they would be deterred by the defensive strength of the Imperial line. Nevertheless, he immediately resolved to counterattack and retake the hill. Was he unwilling to admit to Hatzfeld that the hill that he'd reported as safely occupied had been lost? Was he simply trying to occupy the position to which he thought he'd been ordered? Or was the aggressive marshal seizing the opportunity to force the offensive upon his "overly cautious" superior? In any case, the Imperial left was in motion before 8:00.

At the same time, over on the right, Hatzfeld had discerned Torstensson's real purpose. He at once returned to the army, intending to prepare the left wing for the approaching blow. However, when he reached the wing, around 8:15, he found only the 2nd echelon, and that advancing westward. Surprised, he demanded of Pompeji what was going on. Pompeji replied "without proper respect" that it was being "done on Gotz's orders and would undoubtedly serve the Imperial advantage."[26] Without another word, Hatzfeld rode to find Gotz.

Map 4.2
The Battle of Jankow, March 6, 1645

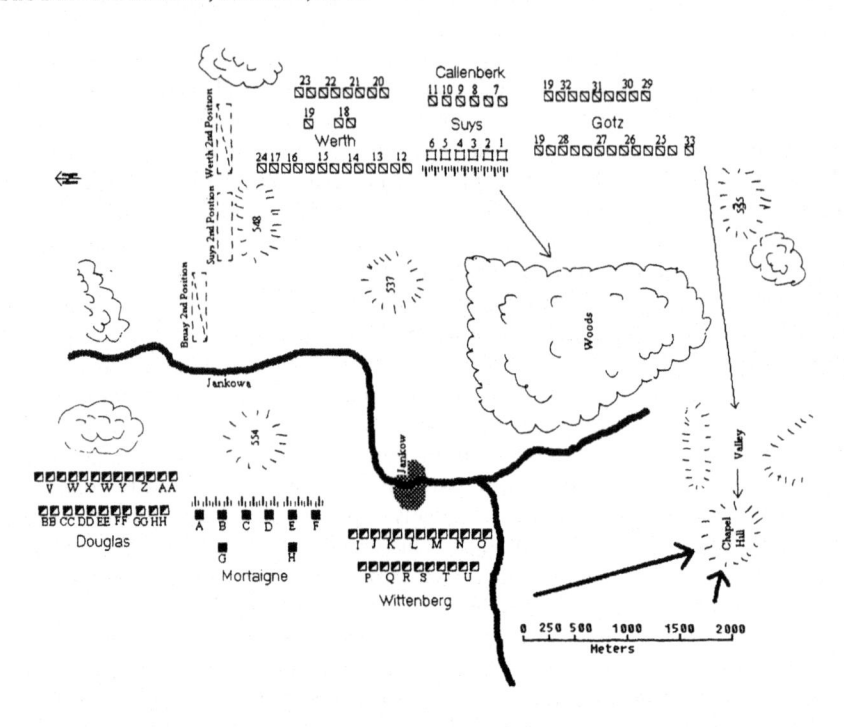

Imperials (Hatzfeld)
1 - Zuniga
2 - Zaradetzky
3 - Suys
4 - Holz
5 - Ruischenberg
6 - Gil de Haas
7 - Callenberk
8 - Hanau
9 - Schleinitz
10 - Gersdorff
11 - Rukert
12 - Lapierre
13 - Alt-Kolb
14 - Fleckenstein
15 - Gayling
16 - Alt-Werth
17 - Sporck
18 - Trauditsch
19 - Pompeji
20 - Jung-Nassau
21 - Waldeck
22 - Beck
23 - Hatzfeld
24 - Croats
25 - Pallavicini
26 - Hennet
27 - Neu-Piccolomini
28 - Piccolomini
29 - Tapp
30 - Bruay
31 - Gonzaga
32 - Salm
33 - Dragoons

Swedes (Torstensson)
A - Wolckmar
B - Paikul
C - Mortaigne
D - Wrangel
E - Torstensson
F - Ribbing
G - Lewenhaupt
H - Axel Lillie
I - Fritzlaw
J - Raabe
K - Margrave
L - Karl Gustav
M - Jordan
N - Wittenberg
O - Torstensson
P - Wittkopt
Q - Rochow
R - Axel Lillie
S - Galbrecht
T - Goldstein
U - Derfflinger
V - Landgrave
W - Horn
X - Hammerstein
Y - Douglas
Z - D'Avangour
AA - Tideman
BB - Muller
CC - Pentz
DD - Reuschel
EE - Butler
FF - Riesengrun
GG - Dannenberg
HH - Reichart

With criminal carelessness, Gotz had neglected to scout out the terrain in front of him, both when he first occupied his position and again before beginning his advance. The Swedes, in sharp contrast, had already established a defensive line, the cavalry at Chapel Hill supported by the infantry detachments with 12 light guns and their dragoons in occupation of a forward outpost, the village of Wlckowitz. The infantry of the 1st column was coming up more slowly.

Gotz's horse blundered awkwardly through the unfamiliar terrain. The exact route and order are unclear; accounts speak of "thick woods," hills, and "steep ravines." Their confusion was alleviated only by the visibility of their goal, Chapel Hill. Nevertheless, they made good time and by 8:15 were in the valley southwest of Nosakow. This was not good terrain for Gotz's attack, being low ground dominated by Chapel Hill itself and too narrow for more than a couple of squadrons to deploy, with woods and hills to the south, more woods, hills, and a frozen lake to the north. With total determination, Gotz shoved his troopers forward, his units meeting the enemy piecemeal, disordered squadrons trailing each other in an improvised column.

At the same time that Gotz's lead elements engaged the Swedes, around 8:30, Hatzfeld appeared to demand an explanation. They quarreled; Gotz threatened to resign. Hatzfeld started to ride off in a huff, at which Gotz backed down. They agreed that as the wing was already committed, the attack should continue, and Hatzfeld left to bring up support from the right and center.[27]

The attack on Chapel Hill was a nightmare for the Imperials. Coming up in bits and pieces, they were torn apart by Swedish musketry and artillery, while the dragoons in Wlckowitz hampered their efforts to deploy to the north. Gotz's only foot were the very dragoons who had earlier failed to defend the hill; they proved equally useless now. Gotz stubbornly refused to retreat, holding his troops in the killing ground through sheer force of personality. It was Wittenweier all over again, but mere courage could not stop Swedish firepower. At last, struck by 2 bullets, Gotz fell; Imperials resistance dissolved. By 9:00, it was finished. Wittenberg dispatched some horse to harry the broken enemy from the valley.

It is difficult to avoid the conclusion that Hatzfeld must have realized the hopelessness of the operation, that he should have countermanded it at once, and that he backed down from a confrontation with Gotz. Gotz's obstinacy on this occasion bordered on the suicidal; had he retired in good order upon determining the enemy's strength, the wing could have been salvaged. Always stubborn, he preferred a hopeless battle to the humiliation of admitting failure. The feud between the two generals had ruined both.

As the Swedes pursued the remnants of Gotz's wing, they encountered a fresh body of Imperials, the infantry of the center under Suys. They had arrived too late to support Gotz, as Hatzfeld had intended, so he formed them into a defensive line in the "thick woods" between Wlckowitz and Nosakow. The main body of the Swedish foot under Mortaigne had already occupied the Chapel Hill area, relieving the musketeer and dragoon detachments; they now placed the Imperials in the woods under fire. Suys was at a disadvantage replying. He and

Hatzfeld succeeded in deploying the infantry in good order, but dragging the artillery—even the light 3 pdrs—through the snow-clad woods had proven disastrous. No less than 9 guns and nearly all the ammunition remained stuck in the brush and had to be abandoned. Under pressure from the Swedish artillery, Suys pulled back behind the sheltering trees.

Mortaigne had already extended his right to secure Hill 535 on Suys's southern flank. Now the Swedish brigades advanced to engage the Imperial foot headon. The attack resolved as a set of disjointed clashes in and around the "thick woods," which close terrain nullified the Swedes' advantage in musketry and artillery. The Mortaigne and Seestedt Brigades pressed ahead and to the north of the others, only to be counterattacked and overrun by cavalry guarding the Imperial right, several Bavarian and one Saxon squadrons. The 2 units were badly cut up; Seestedt was killed, and 13 ensigns were taken. The fire of some Swedish regimental guns emplaced in the woods persuaded Werth to pull back, allowing the beaten foot to reform.

The more important part of this action occurred farther south. The main body of the Swedish foot pushed entirely through the "thick woods" to find the Imperials formed in line in front of Nosakow village and south to Hill 535. A prolonged firefight ensued. At the same time, Torstensson had regrouped Wittenberg's brigade and sent it southward, intending to envelop the Imperial left. Hatzfeld, spotting their maneuver, placed himself at the head of his remaining cavalry, Werth, Mercy, the Saxons, plus some of the left rallied by Bruay. They assumed a covering position southeast of Suys. Wittenberg engaged them at once, gaining an initial advantage as Bruay's demoralized squadrons gave way. The pressure of Mortaigne's foot on the left and Wittenberg's horse on the right bent the Imperial line into a half moon. Wittenberg's supporting musketeer/gun detachments occupied a linking position between him and Mortaigne; their fire contributed to the misery of the Imperial foot. Nevertheless, they and the horse continued to hold out for perhaps another hour. It seems likely that if Torstensson had committed Douglas's fresh squadrons, then in reserve at Chapel Hill, it would have proven decisive. Hatzfeld, seeing the way things were going, disengaged and fell back (around 11:30), his retreat ably covered by Werth.

Some of Wittenberg's troopers made an unexpected capture, the 9 guns and ammo wagons earlier abandoned by Suys. Although the Swedes had pushed back their opponents, they had not shattered them.

By noon, the two armies had broken contact. Despite disorder from traversing broken terrain and their scrambling fight, the Swedes reformed quickly, a testament to their excellent discipline. They expected to be ordered in pursuit; Wittenberg's veterans bragged of chasing Hatzfeld right back into Prague. Torstensson thought otherwise. The Imperials were safely beaten; the road to Olmutz was clear. A reckless pursuit through the broken terrain would risk ambush. He decided to let Hatzfeld escape without further molestation. He directed the army to form a defensive line, facing north and east, between the villages of Jankow and Radmeritz. The Swedish regiments formed in their original brigades and alignments, just as they had begun at dawn. The battery of heavy artillery was repositioned atop Hill 537, while the baggage and train were placed south and west of Radmeritz, not far from the "thick woods."

Hatzfeld, however, was unaware of Torstensson's intent. The Imperial leader conceded the battle as lost, but he believed that the Swedes were too close for him to withdraw safely. He would assume a defensible position, hold out until sunset, then retire under cover of darkness. The spot that he selected was a large, shallow valley running between the Jankowa and the village of Hrin; he also occupied Hill 548 to the south, between the valley and the Swedes. Hatzfeld hoped that the depressed terrain would provide cover from the superior enemy artillery—not only had he lost 9 of 26 guns, but the remaining ones had only a few rounds left. The valley slope was additionally strengthened by a 2-to-4-foot wall running along the length of the valley, east to west, on a ledge partway down the slope. Hatzfeld hoped that if the Swedes charged down into the valley, the wall would throw them, especially the horse, into disorder. Hill 548, a lightly wooded hillock, was to act as a shield. The Imperial battleline faced that of Torstensson about 2½ kilometers to the south. Between the intervening trees and the depression, it was concealed from Swedish observation and fire.

Like the Swedes, the Imperials had regrouped with commendable speed and discipline. Hatzfeld's new formation was:

Right Wing (Bruay): Gotz's remnants reinforced by Zuniga's brigade of foot;
Center: The other 5 infantry brigades, the artillery and the Saxon cavalry;
Left Wing: Werth's Bavarians.

Hatzfeld's intention in transposing the wings was that Wittenberg's veterans should be opposed by Werth's relatively intact command; necessarily, Gotz's demoralized survivors were left facing Douglas's fresh forces.

Hatzfeld was at Hrin, conferring with Werth, when, a bit after 1:00 P.M., the outpost at 548 raised the alarm. Scouts had informed Torstensson that the retreating Imperials had left behind a strong body of musketeers digging in on a small hill. Torstensson had himself carried forward for a personal look, then resolved to bag this rearguard. He dispatched 400 musketeers and 10 regimental guns[28] to the assault. Cautiously, the Imperial detachment fell back on the main line with no attempt at resistance.

Hatzfeld arrived on the right just as the musketeers streamed into the valley. He rebuked Bruay for allowing the outpost to fall to such a small force, directed him to retake it, then returned to Hrin. Bruay and Suys immediately organized a massive counterattack, all 6 battalions of foot supported by Bruay's cavalry. This was not what Hatzfeld had intended (he explained later); a small detachment was to secure the hill while the main forces remained safe in their defensive positions.[29] In any case, Bruay's attack achieved initial success, routing the musketeers, taking the hill, and capturing all 10 guns.

It was now clear to Torstensson that Hatzfeld had not, in fact, left the field. Immediately, he ordered Douglas and Mortaigne to begin a major assault, Wittenberg to stand ready. Primary fire support would be provided by the battery on Hill 537.

This battery came as an unpleasant surprise to the Imperials—they had simply not considered that the guns that had battered them from Chapel Hill around

10:00 could be relimbered, moved the 3-4 miles in question, and then deployed in such a short time. Some call this the decisive stroke of the battle, "the first operation mobile use of heavy artillery." This is exaggerated; the guns were valuable, not decisive, and heavy guns had been moved in battle before. If a gun could be used at all, it could be prolonged and fired. Nevertheless, Torstensson was introducing a new degree of artillery employment, one that would not be imitated for 100 years. Presumably, during the earlier firefight, he had kept the transport close behind the line, instead of sending it back to the train. They could start to limber the guns immediately after Suys fell back behind the "thick woods" thus, when the Imperials retired, they were ready to advance.

The cannonfire tore great holes through Suys's deep ranks; the Imperials, Torstensson gloated, had not so much as a single gun to reply with. Douglas's 1st echelon fell on Bruay, and the shaky Imperials recoiled from contact, "bounced," taking refuge behind the pikes of Zuniga's brigade. Douglas gathered 3 squadrons[30] and led them in a full tilt headon charge against Zuniga. The Imperial foot greeted him with a massed volley, but when they saw that he was not stopping, the brigade dissolved into a panicked mob. Douglas cut them to pieces, overthrowing the whole wing. Bruay was struck down and, "their horse took off as if the Devil were behind them."[31]

Mortaigne had been less successful. Despite losses, Suys's infantry repelled him; they stood, commented a Swedish observer, "as unyielding as a stone wall."[32]

Farther to the east, things were otherwise.

When he realized that his right and center were heavily engaged, Hatzfeld gave Werth permission to advance as well. Moving with great speed and skill, the Bavarians caught Wittenberg by surprise, his troops disordered and at the halt. The Swedish officers fought heroically; Wittenberg and Goldstein were wounded, and in the Kurland Cavalry Regiment every officer was either killed or wounded.[33] It was not enough. Werth drove them back in disorder and with heavy loss. The supporting musketeers retired into Radmeritz where they continued to resist, firing from inside houses and behind walls. All their guns, however, were lost.[34] Werth pressed the advance south and west: it seemed that he would envelop the Swedish right, salvaging the battle. Unfortunately, he now stumbled into the Swedes' baggage train. Brave but undisciplined, the Bavarians could not resist the temptation to loot. It was a prize worth taking; the plunder of half of Germany, collected over 10 years. The victors also captured the women of the Swedish army, including Torstensson's own wife!

A group of 5 squadrons[35] did not join the looting but continued southwest, as far as the "thick woods." Wittenberg, Goldstein, and the Palsgrave used the breathing space that Werth had so generously given them to regroup and reform their battered troopers. This took some time (say 2:30–3:00), but Werth showed no signs of interfering. Fortunately, the 2nd echelon was still fairly intact. The moment that they were ready, the Swedes counterattacked. Now the Bavarians were the ones surprised. They scattered with whatever treasure they could carry. The wives were liberated, and Werth barely escaped capture himself.

Up to this point, Callenberk's Saxons had been supporting the Imperial foot.

When he saw that both wings had collapsed, he decided to pull out, abandoning Suys to his fate.

Immediately afterward, just too late, Mercy's 5 squadrons appeared in Mortaigne's rear. The 2 reserve brigades[36] held them off with muskets and guns until some squadrons from Douglas's wing[37] came over and drove them off.

Now the final stage began, as the Imperial infantry, abandoned by their horse, made a desperate last stand. The Swedes, says Chemnitz, engulfed them "in a half moon of horse, foot, and guns." By 4:00, it was done. The Swedes harried their beaten opponents for miles; Hatzfeld, deserted and alone, was captured by 2 corporals.

The victory had not been cheap. The Swedes lost almost 2000 dead—including Colonels Seestedt and Reuschel—and as many too badly wounded to fight. Among the wounded were Wittenberg, Goldstein, Colonels Muller and Pentz, and 4 lieutenant colonels. Every officer of the Alt-Blau Infantry was either killed or wounded.

The Imperials lost, in all, about 5000 horse and virtually all the foot. Among the dead were Gotz, Bruay, and Colonels Waldeck and Piccolomini. The Swedes took all 26 guns, 34 ensigns, 48 cornets, and some 4450 prisoners.[38] Among the captured were Hatzfeld, Mercy, Trauditsch, Zuniga, Zaradetzky, Sporck, and 7 other colonels. Torstensson remarked that the prisoners would more than fill up his losses. Considering its hasty improvisation, the Imperial army, especially the infantry, showed a remarkable degree of fighting spirit. However, the battle starkly illustrated every flaw in the Imperial command: Hatzfeld's ineptitude, Gotz's obstinacy, Werth's fecklessness, Bruay's lack of judgment, Pompeji's stupidity, and, above all, the lack of communication between them. Hatzfeld's strategy had been sound, if unenterprising; for 2 months he had blocked Torstensson's every move. But in action he seemed to lose his grip, repeatedly hurrying to the wrong place, issuing confusing "misunderstood" orders, letting Gotz and the others drag him into disadvantageous positions, and, always, blaming everyone but himself for everything that went wrong.

Torstensson, on the other hand, was as cunning as ever: both clever and imaginative. His initial maneuvers would have won the battle even without Gotz's bungling, his redeployment of the heavy battery was a military first, and his rapid exploitation of the Imperial errors converted an ordinary victory into the destruction of an army. However, at several points, notably during the second phase around Nosakow and, later, when Wittenberg was defeated and the flank endangered, he seems to lack the smooth operational control demonstrated at 2nd Breitenfeld. He was doubtlessly greatly hampered by his inability to ride and exercise personal command.

MARCH ON VIENNA AND THE SIEGE OF BRUNN

The Imperial army being effectively destroyed, Torstensson was able to continue his march, capturing Tabor, Neuhaus, Iglau, and Znaim without difficulty. In view of the improved situation, he decided not to detour to Olmutz at all but to press on directly to Vienna. By March 25, he was at Krems, less than 50 miles upriver from the Hapsburg capital. At this point several weaknesses had become clear.

Torstensson's fundamental strategy had hinged on a combined offensive by himself, Turenne, and Rakoczy, but his decision to launch a winter campaign had upset the plan for simultaneous action. Turenne did not break camp until March 24,[39] while the Transylvanians had not even begun their preparations until they heard about Jankow. Thus, Torstensson was over a month ahead of his allies. Further, the lack of forage in the late winter had weakened his cavalry; the horses sickened, many died. Worst of all, Torstensson's health suffered a major relapse. After Jankow, he was running on sheer determination.

The destruction of their hard-built army caused consternation and panic in the Imperial cabinet. Desperation decisions were made. The Imperial family fled to Graz. Torstensson's earlier victims, Gallas and the archduke, were recalled to command. Gallas, at Prague, was to reassemble Hatzfeld's wreckage into a fighting force, while the archduke, at Vienna, was directed to build a fresh army from scratch. In this emergency he was given full powers and a free hand.

Torstensson garrisoned Krems and advanced down both banks of the Danube as far as Kornenburg, a day's march from Vienna. Here he hesitated. He had less than 16,000 effectives. The industrious archduke had drawn reserves from Moravia, Silesia, and Hungary plus recruits from Italy and Inner Austria; 5000 Viennese were armed. Finally, Gallas slipped by the Swedes with the reformed field army. By April 29, there were over 30,000 Imperials in and around the city. This assemblage was of mixed quality but adequate to defend a fixed position.

Torstensson had several options: he could encircle them, as he had in 1644, he could try to draw them into the open, or he could lay waste the countryside around them. But the French and Transylvanians were full of promises, talking about reinforcements of 30,000 men, "nearby," to arrive "soon." He decided to postpone the attack on Vienna until Rakoczy arrived. In preparation for this operation, he established a fortified bridgehead at Graveneck-Kornenburg based on an earthwork that he named "Wolfsschanze" (Fort Wolf). Then, as the Transylvanians still failed to appear, he decided to use the time to capture Brunn, the chief Imperial stronghold left in Moravia. Leaving a detachment at Fort Wolf, he began the siege on May 4.

This was the most fatal decision that Torstensson ever made; he remarked later that he'd give 400,000 talers not to have gone to Brunn.

De Souches, the Imperial commandant of Brunn, was a rara avis even for the polyglot Imperial Army. He was a French Huguenot and had begun his military career fighting Louis XIII at La Rochelle; later joining the Swedish Army, he served under Gustavus and Baner. In 1642, as a colonel, he was "insulted" by Stalhansk, so he challenged that general to a duel. Stalhansk replied that it was against regulations to challenge a superior officer, so he resigned his commission. When Stalhansk still refused to fight, Souches resolved to continue the feud by joining the Imperials. Eccentric, irascible, and capable, he later became governor of Moravia and a member of the Imperial cabinet.

Had Torstensson marched to Brunn straight from Iglau, he would have found neglected defenses and a minimal garrison. But Souches had used the intervening month to gather provisions and prepare the walls. The town's fortifications were strong, if antiquated, dominated by a citadel on a steep hill. Through recruiting and the formation of a militia, Souches increased his defenders from 300 to 1500.

Torstensson hoped to bluff Brunn into a quick surrender, as he had Olmutz in 1642. Souches was informed that if he refused terms, he would be treated as a "deserter" from the Protestant army. When his threats were rejected, Torstensson had to settle down to a formal siege, for which he was unprepared both logistically and numerically.

The siege began slowly. Even after drawing more troops from Olmutz, Torstensson was short of reliable infantry, heavy siege guns, and ammunition. Food supplies were little better. Worse, Torstensson himself lacked the drive and energy that he'd shown at Glogau and Leipzig. Souches was proving an able opponent, determined and resourceful, totally unmoved by stratagem or bluff. On May 11, Transylvanian FM Bakos-Gabor met MajGen Douglas at Tyrnau, 3 weeks march sourtheast. He informed the Swedes that his own contingent[40] was merely the vanguard of Prince Rakoczy's main army, 30,000 men and 100 guns. Torstensson decided to await their arrival.

This was the last good news for the Swedes. Word arrived that Turenne's army had been destroyed at Marienthal,[41] the French would not arrive soon, or ever. The archduke and Gallas started showing signs of life, raiding with Croats as far as the siege works. On June 3, a powerful Imperial detachment invested Fort Wolf. Torstensson sent Wittenberg to relieve it with 3000 Swedes and 2000 hussars. En route, well before contacting the enemy, the Transylvanians mutinied, claiming that they had not been paid enough to fight. Before their grievances could be met, the fort fell (June 9).

The archduke now began harassing Torstensson in earnest. He offered 50 talers a head for any soldier who wished to switch sides. Men deserted in droves, starting with the Jankow prisoners. Plague broke out. Finally, on July 19, Rakoczy's son Sigismund arrived with 7000 hussars and 9 heavy guns. Rakoczy's main body was 50 miles southeast. It was now clear to Torstensson that the vaunted Transylvanian army was nearly all light cavalry, of limited value in siege or battle. Shocked by the mismanagement of the siege, Sigismund's report to his father was equally disillusioned. Nevertheless, the Swedish commander was unwilling to concede failure. On July 24, the Imperial army established a fortified camp on the March River, between Vienna and Brunn. Their tactics were similar to those employed by Gallas in 1643. It was decided that only a *coup-de-main* could salvage the situation. At 5:00 A.M., August 15, Torstensson conducted a general storm, continuing it until 6:00 P.M.—long after any hope of success had disappeared. Souches repelled every thrust with heavy casualties. Torstensson stubbornly prolonged his attacks in the vain hope of exhausting Brunn's ammunition. But on the 18th, the Transylvanians decamped; Torstensson lifted the siege the following day.

The "Defense of Brunn" was to be remembered as one of the epic stands of the Imperial Army; it was Torstensson's worst defeat. Between Souches, disease, and desertion, the allies lost 8000 men; the Imperials counted 200 dead and 150 wounded.

Although Torstensson was sick and disheartened, he was not yet beaten. After again drawing on his garrisons, he mustered 6000 infantry and 8000 cavalry (not all horsed) to the archduke's 20,000 foot and 10,000 horse. He determined to renew his offensive, marching to Mistelbach in northern Austria (August 28). His plan was to combine his army, Rakoczy's, and that of Konigsmarck for a final assault on Vienna itself. The archduke fell back on the line of the Danube. On September 10, the Swedes advanced to Stockerau near Kornenburg, some 16 miles from Vienna. The archduke and Gallas stood on the defensive, covering the capital and blocking the river crossings. No attack was possible. The treacherous Rakoczy signed a separate peace.[42] News of a French victory over Bavaria[43] did not compensate for shortages of food and fodder. On September 25, Torstensson ended the campaign. After safely garrisoning his conquests, Krems, Kornenburg, Iglau, Falkenstein, Nikolsburg, Ravensburg, and, of course, Olmutz, he left for Jaromeritz in northwestern Bohemia.

The Swedes would not get so close to Vienna again.

Konigsmarck's corps had scored some successes on its own. From February through April, he gained ground in Westphalia, whose Imperials had been weakened by Hatzfeld's departure. After briefly operating with Turenne,[44] he joined Axel Lillie in Saxony. Elector Johann Georg had been demoralized by the disaster of Jankow and was now willing to sign a separate peace with Sweden. Saxony was out of the war.[45] Konigsmarck then marched to reinforce Torstensson but did not arrive in time to take part in the later Vienna operation.

Torstensson's physical condition had deteriorated to such an extent that he was no longer able to exercise command. On December 23, he handed the army over to FM Karl Gustav Wrangel.

Historians condemn Torstensson's campaigns as indecisive and pointless; in fact they compare favorably with the grandiose triumphs of Gustavus. In 4 years, Torstensson destroyed three major armies, knocked Denmark and Saxony out of the war, and extended Swedish control from a Baltic foothold deep into the Hapsburg heartland. More than any other individual, Torstensson is responsible for Sweden's ultimate victory in the Thirty Years War.

SOURCES

The principle sources for Torstensson's operations are Swedish, Tingsten's *Baner och Torstensson* (1932) and the army historical section study, *Slaget vid Jankow* (1945), supplemented by Mankell, Wrede, Heilmann, and *Theatrum*. Bjorlin (1914) is worth a glance. There is also the (obsolete) De Peyster English biography of Torstensson (1855).

APPENDIX A: THE IMPERIAL ARMY AT 2ND BREITENFELD

This chart is derived from *Theatrum Europeum*, Wrede, and Tingsten. Unfortunately, they are not in complete agreement, and there are anomalies and uncertainties in all three.

Unit	Date	Coy	Nation	Notes
Piccolomini Leib	1636	4	German	Mixed KUR, ARK & DR coys
Ranfft IR	1618	10	H Ger	ex-Alt-Breuner
Archduke Leib IR	1619	10	L Ger	ex-Collato; LtCol Gustav cmd, KIA
Enkefort IR	1619	10	H Ger	ex-Schaumburg; Hv Loss *

Torstensson's War, 1642-45

Unit	Year	#	Origin	Notes
Zuniga IR	1625	10	Bohem	ex-Colloredo; Lt Col Villani cmd
Fernemont IR	1627	6	L Ger	ex-Farensbach; LtCol KIA *
Henderson IR	1628	10	L Ger	ex-Wangler; LtCol Steinkeller cmd
Reich IR	1629	10	L Ger	ex-Waldstein; Lt Col Rabein cmd *
H. Gonzaga IR	1629	11	German	ex-Zweyer; Lt Col Hauser cmd.
Soye IR	1629	10	Bohem	ex-Ander Waldstein; Lt Col Amon
Bourre IR	1631	12	HG/Bo	ex-Illow; Lt Col Averdank cmd
Suys IR	1631	12	Walln	
Webel IR	1632	10	H Ger	*
Borri IR	1632	10	German	ex-Funk; Lt Col Bourre cmd
Wachenheim IR	1632	8	German	ex-Schlick
Grana IR	1638	10	German	ex-Mora; Lt Col Pestaluzzi cmd *
Moncado IR	1641		German	
Sax-Lauenburg IR	1641		German	Lt Col Rohrscheid cmd *
Schleinitz IR	1631	8	Saxon	Saxon IR #5; ex-Loser IR #3
Desfurs KUR	1616	8	Sp-Ger	ex-Marradas; Hv loss *
Bruay KUR	1625	7	German	ex-Alt-Saxon; Lt Col & Major KIA
L. Gonzaga KUR	1625	12	Bohem	Major Khauts cmd & KIA
Nicola KUR	1628	10	L Ger	ex-Hydrou-Mayence; Col KIA *
Jung KUR	1629	5	L Ger	ex-Schaffgotsche; LtCol captured *
Alt-Piccolomini KUR	1629	12	L Ger	Lt Col Graff cmd, KIA
Gissenburg KUR	1630	8	L Ger	ex-Bonninghausen
Wintz KUR	1631	10	German	Wintz KIA *
Neu-Piccolomini KUR	1632	10	German	Lt Col Bechamp cmd, KIA
Alt-Heister KUR	1632	8	L Ger	ex-Bonninghsn; LtCol Stahl cmd *
Jung-Heister KUR	1632	10	L Ger	ex-Bonninghsn; Heister cap-died
Mislik KUR	1632	8	German	ex-Trcka
Montecuccoli KUR	1634	6	German	ex-Trappl; LtCol Lannoy cmd, cap
Lammersdorf KUR	1634	8	German	AKA Krafft; LtCol Desfurs
Alt-Nassau KUR	1635	10	L Ger	Nassau-Dillenburg; LtCol Urias c
Sperreuter KUR	1636		German	ex-Protestant; Lt Col Walter cmd
Capaun KUR	1638	10	Silesia	AKA Kapoun; Capaun wnd & cap
Burksdorf KUR	1639	6	Brandb	ex-Brandnbg; Lt Col Quitzau cmd*
Pompeji KUR	1639		German	
Spiegel KUR	1639	6	German	Lt Col Lutzelburg cmd
Borneval KUR	1640		Silesia	AKA D'Arlin; ex-De Waghi.
Wolframsdorf KUR	1640	8	Saxon	ex-Saxon CR #17 *
Novery KUR	1640		German	*
Vorhauer KUR	1641		Silesia	Vorhauer wnd & cap; Hv Losses
Archduke Leib KUR	1641	8	UpAust	Lt Col Pallavicini cmd, wnd
Luttke KUR	1641		Brandb	ex-Sax-Lauenburg Leib
KUR Free Coys	—	3	German	
Munster ARK	1639	6	Silesia	Munster KIA *
Grodetzky ARK	1639	6	Silesia	*
Warlowsky ARK	1639	6	Silesia	*
Madlo ARK	1639	6	Silesia	Unit disgraced, Madlo executed *
Gall a Burke DR	1633	10	German	Lt Col Stephanson cmd
Gallas DR	1634		German	Lt Col Ablmont cmd
Pachonay DR	1641	2	German	
Foldvary Croats	1631	10	Croat	ex-Corpes; Major KIA
Marcovich Croats	1641	8	Croat	Lt Col Jankovich cmd
Palffy Hussars	1641	10	Magyar	*

Unit	Year	Coy	Nation	Notes
Esterhazy Hussars	1641	30	Magyar	Some possibly present *
Nouskowsky CR	1640	10	Pole	Cossack–Imp 1640-43; Col KIA
Herlikowsky CR	1640	10	Pole	Cossacks-Imperial 1640–43
Callenberk CR	1631		Saxon	Saxon Leib CR #1; ex-Taube C #3
Hanau CR	1631		Saxon	Saxon CR #4; ex-Bindauf CR #2
Schleinitz CR	1632		Saxon	Saxon CR #6; ex-Anhalt CR #6
Knoche CR	1633		Saxon	Saxon Leib CR #2; ex-Taube #14

*- Unit destroyed or disbanded

Alt-Nassau KUR appears in *Theatrum* but not Wrede, Zuniga, Henderson, Reich, Bourre, Borri, Soye, Jung, Novery, Grodetzky, Pachonay, and the free companies appear in Wrede but not *Theatrum*. Schleinitz and Hanau appear only in Saxon sources. *Theatrum* gives the only location details, but seems to have confused the different Leib units, and is probably incomplete; it gives the right 1st echelon 13 squadrons, the 2nd, 10; the left 1st, 11; the 2nd, 9, and the reserve 7. Tingsten makes it 13; 11–13; 12–15; 11, and 8. All agree that there were 6 Croat squadrons and 8 Hussar, but they are uncertain which were on the right and which the left, and the location of the Poles is unknown. The composition of the squadron called " La Coronna Traga " (Spanish: "The Crowning Envelopers") is unknown, possibly the free companies.

Tingsten sets the Imperials at 10,000 foot and 16,000 horse in 10 battalions and 69–74 squadrons. Kalterborn estimated 25,000–27,000, but Mankell only 18,000–19,000. Each battalion averaged 1000, each squadron about 225. The Saxon contingent is set at 450 foot and 1200 horse. The "missing" IRs were doubtless grouped with the smaller IRs to bring them up to strength, Reich possibly with Webel, Schleinitz with Moncado; Zuniga, Henderson, Bourre, Borri, and Soye on the right. Most likely the right hand battalions were stronger than the left and the 1st echelon battalions stronger than those in the 2nd.

ARK regiments had been declining in popularity since Lutzen and Nordlingen, but in 1639 4 new ones were raised in Silesia. Their poor performance at 2nd Breitenfeld finally doomed the concept; all were broken up as KUR replacements. Technically, they should have been used in skirmishes, not pitched battles, but even there they were being superseded by Croats and Hussars.

The Imperials had 46 guns, "mostly" of "large" caliber (viz., 6 pdr and up), as opposed to the Swedes with their preponderance in 3 pdrs. Estimate 20–25 of 8, 12, and 14 pdrs, a few 24 pdr demicannon, the rest 3–6 pdr lights.

APPENDIX B: THE SWEDISH ARMY AT 2ND BREITENFELD

This chart is derived from *Theatrum Europeum*, Mankell, and Tingsten, who are in essential, if not complete agreement. Unfortunately, the nearest muster, in early 1643, is not very useful.

Unit	Coy	1643	Nation	Notes
Alt-Blau IR	12	600	German	"Gustavan" veterans; Torstensson Leib
Pfuhl IR	8	—	"	
Mortaigne IR	12	600	"	
Schlieben IR	18	—	"	
Lilliehook IR	8	—	"	
K. G. Wrangel IR	4	616	Swede	Dalkarna Regt
K. G. Wrangel IR	12	400	German	
Axel Lillie IR	2	482	Swede	East Gothland Regt
Axel Lillie IR	8	—	German	
Plettenberg IR	8	400	"	
Baner IR	12	626	"	
Maul IR	8	—	"	

Jeschwitski IR	?	—	"?	
Torstensson CR	8	370	"	Leib; 3 sqd
Landgrave CR	12	—	"	Hesse-Darmstadt; 3 sqd
Duval CR	8	104	"	3 sqd
Hoking CR	8	83	"	AKA Hocking; 3 sqd
Kinsky CR	8	—	"	2 sqd
Derfflinger CR	8	161	"	3 sqd
Wittkopt CR	12	97	"	2 sqd
H. Wrangel CR	12	—	"	3 sqd
Poles CR	8	—	"	2 sqd; from Silesia
Stalhansk CR	8	200	"	3 sqd
Stalhansk CR	4	452	Finn	3 sqd ; Nyland Regt
Wittenberg CR	4	303	"	2 sqd; Abo Regt
Wittenberg CR	8	275	German	2 sqd
Cratzenstein CR	6	242	"	2 sqd
Douglas CR	8	133	"	2 sqd
Billinghausen CR	12	180	"	2 sqd
Schulmann CR	8	593	"	2 sqd
Pfuhl CR	12	—	"	2 sqd
Seckendorf CR	8	216	"	2 sqd
Mitzlaff CR	8	—	"	2 sqd
Tideman CR	8	150	"	3 sqd
Lilliehook	8	—	"	2 sqd
Detachments	-	—	-	3 sqd

The 10,000 cavalry were divided into 51 squadrons averaging some 200 each. The 3 reserve squadrons were made up of detachments from the other regiments and were doubtlessly the smallest and weakest. The size of the regiments can only be roughly estimated from the number of squadrons.

The 10,000 infantry were deployed in 11 brigades and 29 (?) detachments of 40 musketeers each, thus, 800 men per brigade and 1160 musketeers supporting the cavalry. The brigade designations refer only to the chief regiment; therefore, any other units included are unknown. Probable units present were:

Kyle IR	8	728	Swede	Uppland Regt	to Schieben?
E. Stenbock IR	4	509	"	Westmanland Regt	to Axel Lillie?
G. Stenbock IR	4	400	"	Smaland	To Axel Lillie?
Ratkie IR	4	200	German		to Alt-Blau?
E. Hansson IR	8	400	"		to Lilliehook?
Bibau IR	8	—	"		
Daniel IR	8	400	"		
Ermis IR	8?	—	"	Erfurt garrison	

Any dragoons would have been with the musketeer detachments.

The artillery came to 70 guns, of which at least 18 were "heavy"—12 and 24 pdrs. The rest were 3 pdr regimental guns. In all, therefore: 20,000 men and 70 guns.

The musketeer detachments do not appear in *Theatrum Europeum*, but are emphasized in Montecuccoli's evaluation of the defeat. These detachments were probably similar to those at Jankow and thus much smaller than those at Breitenfeld and Lutzen. Even so, they ate up 20% of Torstensson's foot—keeping in mind that he had, relatively speaking, much more cavalry to support and much less infantry than the king.

Theatrum indicates some guns among the horse, presumably 3 pdrs with the musketeers.

APPENDIX C: SCHWEIDNITZ, MAY 31, 1642

The Austro-Saxon army of Duke Franz Albrecht von Sax-Lauenburg at the Action of Schweidnitz or Zobten Berg is set at 7000 cavalry, 500 dragoons, and 4 guns, from the following regiments:

Wintz, Jung-Heister, Burksdorf, Gall a Burke, Vernier, Montecuccoli, Capaun, Borneval, Sax-Lauenburg (=Luttke), and L. Gonzaga KUR plus 1 free coy.

Grodetzky and Warlowsky ARK.
1 free coy of dragoons.
Sax-Lauenburg Leib IR.
Saxon cavalry regiments Callenberk, Knoche, Hanau, and Schleinitz.

Units possibly present include the Wachenheim Infantry Regiment and the Saxon Schleinitz Infantry Regiment.

The 4 Saxon cavalry regiments mustered 2060, the 12 Imperial about 5000. In the battle, Montecuccoli's LtCol commanding and Jung-Heister won commendations, while Gall a Burke KUR was practically destroyed. The Imperials, a bit unfairly, blamed the Saxons for the defeat. Of the total loss of 5200—2000 dead, 2000 wounded, and 1200 prisoners—the Saxons suffered 600. Franz also lost 40 flags and 4 guns. Torstensson hoped to send Franz to Sweden for trial, but he died on June 5, of wounds received.

Note that most of the survivors ended up in Puchheim's wing at 2nd Breitenfeld.

Torstensson's O.B. is uncertain, but lists for December 18, 1641 and September 9, 1642 survive:

December	September
Leib CR (3 sqd)	Torstensson (2 sqd))
Wittenberg CR (2	Wittenberg (2)
J. Wrangel CR (3)	J. Wrangel (2)
Finns (1)	Wittenberg Finns (1)
Livonia CR (1)	Livonia (1)
Kurland CR (2)	
Grubbe CR (1)	
Mortaigne & Haake CRs (1)	
Derfflinger CR (2)	Derfflinger (2)
Munchhausen CR (2)	
Duke Friedrich CR (1)	Duke Franz Henrich (1)
Duval CR (1)	
Pfuhl CR (2)	
Hoditz CR (2)	
Konigsmarck CR (2)	
Birkenfeld CR (1)	
Cratzenstein CR (1)	Cratzenstein (1)
Ruckwald CR (1)	
Witzleben CR (2)	Wittkopt (1)
Fritzlaw CR (1	Fritzlaw (1)
Kinsky CR (1)	Kinsky (1)
Hoking CR (1)	Hoking (1)
Behr CR (1)	
Schlang CR (1)	Schlang (1)
Smaland CR	
Lilliehook CR	Lilliehook (1)
Stalhansk CR	Stalhansk Finns (2)
Schulmann CR	Schulmann (2)
Dewitz CR	Dewitz (1)

Torstensson's War, 1642-45

Wrangel CR	H. Wrangel (2)
Wurzburg CR	Wurzburg (1)
Seidelitz CR	
Trotz CR	Trotz (1)
Axel Lillie CR	Axel Lillie (1)
Riesengrun CR	Bock & Riesengrun (1)
Schirenhausen CR	
Poles	Poles (1)
	Billinghausen (2)
	Douglas (1)
	Tideman (1)
	Baner's East Gothland (1)
	Horn (1)
	Muller (2)
	Landgrave Hesse (2)
	K. G. Wrangel (1)
	unknown (1)
	Total: 45 sqd = 8000 cav

(Note that CRs have fewer sqds than in November)

Ribbing IR (1 brigade)	Ribbing & Forbes (1 brigade)
Kagge & Thomasson IRs (1)	Kagge, Horn & Wittenberg (1)
Tuwe Bremen IR (1)	
Stenbock, Dorkel & Dorning (1)	Stenbock, Stenbock & Axel Lillie (1)
Leib IR (1)	Alt-Blau & Radike (1)
Neuwad & K. G. Wrangel IRs (1)	K. G. Wrangel (Swede & Ger) (1)
Bibau, Pfuhl & Ruth IRs (1)	Bibau & Daniel (1)
E. Hansson & Plettenberg IRs (1)	
Wittenberg, Goltz & Osterling (1)	
Wust & Cratzenstein IRs (1)	
Scheudorf IR (1)	
Stenbock Swede IR	
Metstacke Finn IR	
N. Kagge IR	
Lilliehook IR	Lilliehook & E. Hansson (1)
Axel Lillie IR	Axel Lillie (Swede) & Plettenberg (1)
Thurn IR	Burtz & Thurn (1)
Konigsmarck IR	
Wancke IR	
Dyouju IR	
Radike IR	
Guns IR	
Lilliesparre IR	
Stalhansk DR	
	Kyle & Schlieben (1)
	Fleming & Cunningham (1)
	Mortaigne & Paikull (1)
	Stalarm & Maul (1)
	13 brig = 6500 inf

(Torstensson used only 2 brigades at Schweidnitz; approximately 2000 men)

APPENDIX D: THE IMPERIAL ARMY AT JANKOW
Chart derived from *Slaget*, Wrede, and Tingsten; strengths are from late 1644.

Unit	Date	Coy	Nation	Str	Corps	Notes
Baden IR	1618	10	High Ger	299	Gallas	IMP; ex-Alt-Saxon
Colloredo IR	1619	10	Low Ger	760	Gallas	IMP; ex-Collato
Hunoldstein IR	1619	12	Low Ger	553	Gallas	IMP;AKARiedesel
Gallas IR	1626	10	Low Ger	—	Gallas	IMP; ex-Pallant
Knoring IR	1628	10	Low Ger	—	Hatzfeld	IMP; ex-Wangler
Reich IR	1629	11	German	781	Gallas	IMP; ex-Zweyer
Henderson IR	1629	10	Bohemia	477	Hatzfeld	IMP; ex-Waldstein
Mercy IR	1630	10	High Ger	173	Gotz	IMP; ex-Hardeck
Fernemont IR	1631	12	Walloon	—	Gallas	IMP; ex-Suys
Enkefort IR	1632	10	German	496	Gallas	IMP; ex-Funk
Wachenheim IR	1632	8	German	—	Gotz	IMP; ex-Schlick
Sparr IR	1636	10	German	296	Hatzfeld	IMP; ex-Hatzfeld
Bunau IR	1637	10	Cologne	—	Hatzfeld	IMP
Conti IR	1639	10	German	114	Gallas	IMP;ex-GildeHaas
Fernberger IR	1642	—	High Ger	—	Gotz	IMP; Lowr Austria
Schifer IR	1642	10	German	170	Gallas	IMP
Ferraris IR	1643	—	Italian	—	Gotz	IMP
L.B.Waldstein IR	1643	—	Moravia	—	Moravia	IMP
Ruischenberg IR	1620	10	Bavaria	837	Bavaria	ex-Anholt
Mercy IR	1620	10	"	827	"	ex-Herliberg
Holz IR	1620	8	"	998	"	ex-Mortaigne
Cobb IR	1620	8	"	748	"	ex-Bauer
Winterscheid IR	1621	9	"	701	"	ex-Springen
Fugger IR	1632	8	"	733	"	ex-Ruepp
Gil de Haas IR	1644	10	"	2000	"	

18 IMP IR = 3000 men = 3 "brigades." 7 BAV IR = 2000 men = 3 "brigades."

The IMP brigades were probably Suys, Zaradetzky, and Zuniga; the BAV possibly Ruischenberg, Holz, and Gil de Haas.

Hatzfeld KUR	1625	7	German	—	Hatzfeld	IMP; ex-NeuSaxon
Bruay KUR	1625	7	German	525	Bohemia	IMP; ex-Alt-Saxon
Gonzaga KUR	1625	12	Bohemia	—	Gotz	IMP; ex-Lamotte
Lannoy KUR	1627	5	German	674	Bohemia	IMP; ex-Bernstein
Stahl KUR	1628	6	German	—	Gotz	IMP;exJColloredo
Gissenburg KUR	1630	8	Low Ger	444	Bohemia	IMP;exBonninghn
Hennet KUR	1631	5	German	—	Gotz	IMP; ex-Vehlen
Vernier KUR	1631	8	German	520	Silesia	IMP; ex-NeuTrcka
Trauditsch KUR	1632	10	German	490	Bohemia	IMP; exHasenburg
Piccolomini KUR	1629	12	Low Ger	—	Gotz	IMP; AltPiccolom
Neu-Piccolomini	1632	10	German	—	Gotz	IMP;JungPiccolom
Waldeck KUR	1632	10	German	—	Hatzfeld	IMP; ex-Westfalen
Beck KUR	1633	9	German	—	Hatzfeld	IMP
Lammersdorf KU	1634	8	German	414	Gallas	IMP; ex-S.Piccolo
Mercy KUR	1634	—	German	—	Hatzfeld	IMP
Alt-Nassau KUR	1635	10	Low Ger	293	Bohemia	IMP
Salm KUR	1636	—	Bohemia	—	Bohemia	IMP; ex-Hanensee
Velradt KUR	1636	—	German	378	Silesia	IMP; AKAMeutter
Walter KUR	1636	—	German	320	Gallas	IMP; ex-Sperreuter
Knigge KUR	1637	4	German	426	Hatzfeld	IMP;Bodelschwing

Torstensson's War, 1642-45

Unit	Date	Coy	Nation	Str	Province	Notes
Konigsegg KUR	1637	—	Westphl	608	Hatzfeld	IMP; ex-Ohr
Pompeji KUR	1639	—	German	—	Gotz	IMP
Jung-Nassau KU	1639	10	German	—	Hatzfeld	IMP; Wiedemann
Tapp KUR	1640	—	Silesia	—	Bohemia	IMP; ex-de Waghi
Pallavicini KUR	1641	8	Upr Aus	—	Gotz	IMP; ex-Archduke
Luttke KUR	1641	—	Brndnbg	480	Silesia	IMP; exSaxLauenb
Kolowrat KUR	1642	—	German	—	Gotz	IMP
Gotz KUR	1643	—	German	514	Silesia	IMP
Bassompierre KU	1643	—	German	311	Silesia	IMP
Marcovich Croats	1641	8	Croat	—	Gallas	IMP
Callenberk CR	1631	—	Saxon	—	Saxony	Saxon; Leib #1
Hanau CR	1631	—	Saxon	—	"	" CR #4
Schleinitz CR	1632	—	Saxon	—	"	" CR #6
Gersdorff CR	1633	—	Saxon	—	"	"Leib#2;exKnoche
Rukert CR	1642	—	Saxon	—	"	" ex-Jng-Schleinitz
Fleckenstein KU	1620	8	Bavaria	671	Bavaria	Bav; ex-Erwitte
Gayling KUR	1620	9	Bavaria	872	"	" ex-Cratz
Alt-Kolb KUR	1634	8	Bavaria	732	"	" ex-Binder
Lapierre KUR	163	9	Bavaria	918	"	" ex-Gotz
Alt-Werth ARK	1621	9	Bavaria	886	"	" ex-Eynatten
Cosalky ARK	1634	9	Bavaria	689	"	"ex-Neuenheim
Sporck ARK	1638	10	Bavaria	1153	"	"

29 IMP KUR = 6100 horse = 32 sqd; 5 SAX CR = 1400 horse = 6 sqd; 7 BAV CR = 3000 horse = 12 sqd; 500 dragoons & Croats

Smaller regiments such as Lannoy, Stahl, Gissenburg, Vernier, Lammersdorf, Mercy, Velradt, Walter, Knigge, Konigsegg, Luttke, Kolowrat, Gotz, Bassompierre, and Cosalky seem to have been absorbed into mixed squadrons.

The identities of the Imperial dragoons are uncertain. Moreover, it is possible that 1 or 2 additional Croat regiments took part. Likely units were:

Unit	Date	Coy	Nation	Str	Province	Notes
Gallas Dragoon	1634	2	German	—	Bohemia	IMP
Paconchay DR	1641	2	German	—	Bohemia	IMP
Masslehner DR	1643	—	Hungary	300	Bohemia	IMP
Mislik Dragoons	1644	1	German	—	Gallas	IMP; free coy
Schoh DR	1638	6	Bavaria	857	Bavaria	Bav; ex-Nussbaum
Palffy Croats	1631	10	Croat	—	Bohemia	IMP; ex-Corpes
Zrinyi Croats	1642	8	Croat	800	Bohemia	IMP

The Imperial field artillery had been seriously depleted by 2nd Breitenfeld and Bernburg. Hatzfeld had only 26 guns available: 4 x 12 pdr, 2 x 6 pdr, 20 x 3 pdr. Total: 5000 infantry; 11,000 cavalry; 26 Guns = 16,000 Men &

APPENDIX E: THE SWEDISH ARMY AT JANKOW

Chart derived from *Slaget*, Mankell, and Tingsten.

Unit	Coy	Str	Nation	Notes
Ribbing IR	2	500	Swede	West Gothland; 1 bn w. Stalarm
Stalarm IR	4			Bjornborg; 1 bn w. Ribbing
Torstensson Leib	12	776	German	Alt-Blau
K. G. Wrangel IR	8	383	"	1 bn w. Linde
Linde IR	8	427	"	1 bn w. Wrangel
Mortaigne IR	12	670	"	
Paikull IR	8	342	"	1 bn w. Seestedt

Seestedt IR	8	613	"	1 bn w. Paikull	
Wolckmar IR	12	676	"		
Axel Lillie IR	8	434	"	1 bn w. Koppy	
Koppy IR	8	329	"	1 bn w. Axel Lillie	
G.Lewenhaupt IR	8	323	"	1 bn w. Jordan	
Jordan IR	8	662	"	1 bn w. Lewenhaupt	
8 brigades (total)		5215			
23 detachments		920		40 each	
		6135 infantry			
Karl Gustav CR	8	300	Kurland	Palsgrave; 2 sqd	
Jordan CR	8	300	Livonia	2 sqd	
Torstensson Leib	8	600	German	2 sqd	
Wittenberg CR	8	400	"	2 sqd	
Margrave CR	8	300	"	Baden-Durlach; 2 sqd	
Raabe CR	4	200	"	1 sqd	
Fritzlaw CR	8	350	"	2 sqd	
Derfflinger CR	8	330	"	2 sqd	
Goldstein CR	8	300	"	2 sqd	
Galbrecht CR	8	300	"	2 sqd	
Rochow CR	8	350	"	2 sqd	
Axel Lillie CR	8	220	"	1 sqd.	
Wittkopt CR	8	300	"	2 sqd	
Landgrave CR	12	500	"	Hesse-Darmstadt; 3 sqd	
Horn CR	8	300	"	2 sqd	
Hammerstein CR	8	300	"	2 sqd	
Douglas CR	8	300	"	2 sqd	
D'Avangour CR	8	250	"	1 sqd	
Tideman CR	8	360	"	2 sqd	
Muller CR	8	400	"	2 sqd	
U. Pentz CR	8	250	"	1 sqd	
Reuschel CR	8	250	"	2 sqd	
Butler CR	8	150	"	1 sqd	
Riesengrun CR	8	200	"	2 sqd	
Dannenberg CR	8	270	"	1 sqd	
Reichart CR	8	350	"	2 sqd	
26 CR (total)		8130 Cavalry		47 sqd	
Pegau Dragoons	5	340	German		
Goldstein DR	1	60	"		

Guns: 4 demicannon (24 pdr), 4 culverins (24 pdr), 4 demiculverins (12 pdr), 6 quarter cannon (12 pdr), 6 "sixteenth" cannon (3 pdr), and 36 regimental guns (3 pdr) = 60 total. Note that while the ball weights were standardized, 24, 12, and 3 pdrs, the gun types were not. They were manned by 383 gunners in 4 companies, supported by a train of 69.

The following figures, from Torstensson's own notes, included only enlisted men; there were over 900 officers as well:
      6135 Infantry
      8130 Cavalry
      400 Dragoons
      452 Gunners
      +900 officers = 16,017 Men & 60 Guns

Swedish Forces in Germany, January 11, 1645

	Torstensson	Wrangel	Konigsmarck
Inf	6135	880	3950 (550 recruits)
Cav	8130	2820	3750
Drag	400	650	330
Total:	14,665	4350	8030

27,045 + 1749 officers = 28,794

Garrisons:

West Pomerania (Stralsund, Greifswald, Wolgast, Anklam, Demmin)	3003
East Pomerania (Stettin, Greiffenhagen, Wollin, Damm, Kolberg, Landsberg, Dreisen)	3566
Mecklenburg (Wismar, Domitz, Bleckede, Plau)	1457
Holstein & Mark (Friedrichsort & Gardelegen)	778
Silesia (Glogau & Trachenberg)	980
Moravia (Olmutz, Neustadt, Eulenburg)	1830?
Saxony (Leipzig & Mansfeld)	1193
Thuringia (Erfurt)	860
Westphalia (Minden & Nienburg)	2064
Halberstadt Bishopric (Halberstadt Oschersleben, Osterwieck, Querfurt)	520
Total:	16,251

Grand Total: 45,045

APPENDIX F: THE "GERMAN" FACTION

The officer corps of the Austrian Hapsburgs was, and long remained, a remarkable collection representing nearly every nationality in Europe, Germans of every variety, Poles, Spaniards, Italians, Czechs, Frenchmen, Magyars, Croats, Walloons, Danes, English, Scots, and Irish. Despite the regime's avowed Catholicism, there were plenty of Lutherans and even a few Calvinists as well. Up until Wallenstein's second generalate, 1631–4, this heterogeneous group had been able to operate in unity, if not harmony. When Wallenstein fell, he dragged down many Germans with him, Illow, Schaffgotsche, the Sax-Lauenburgs, one of the Badens, and so on. Wallenstein's fall had been chiefly engineered by "Walschen" officers, that is, Italian- and French-speakers. These counter-conspirators were Marradas, a Spaniard; Piccolomini, an Italian; Aldringer, a Lorrainer; Onate, the Spanish ambassador, and Maximilian of Bavaria, the sole German. Piccolomini had acted out of loyalty and in good faith, but when the subsequent examination of Wallenstein's papers failed to bear out his assertions (even at that stage, the generalissimo had been shrewd enough not to put anything incriminating in writing!), Ferdinand II began to have doubts about whether the charges had been warranted. A clique of German officers, many of them, like Gotz, over-promoted by Wallenstein, coalesced. These were motivated by professional envy as well as regionalism. Note that this "German" clique included both Catholics and Protestants, Austrians, High Germans, Rhinelanders, Low Germans, and even non-Germans like the Scot Leslie.

During Wallenstein's command, he had been bitterly opposed by the "Anti-Spanish" courtiers attached to the king of Hungary. These rejected the broader implications of the Spain-Austria dynastic link, favoring a self-interested, purely German policy for the Empire. After 1634, the "Anti-Spanish" courtiers allied themselves with the "German" officers. As the king of Hungary gained increasing power after 1634 (cumulating with his accession as Ferdinand III in 1637), this faction gained predominance.

The Germans, such as Gotz and Schlick, conducted a continuous campaign against the "Walschen," questioning their loyalty, their competence, and their courage. Italians, particularly those close to Piccolomini, were held responsible for every defeat.

Montecuccoli was blamed for Hofkirchen's blundering at Brandeis, while Piccolomini and Pallavicini were made the scapegoats for 2nd Breitenfeld. These tactics cleared the German Puchheim; Piccolomini was unable to defend himself without exposing the archduke's ineptitude.

Of course, some of the "Walschen," such as Savelli and Marrazino, really were unfit. However, as the "Germans" were increasing able to veto appointments, the supreme command was reserved to Germans (Hatzfeld and Melander), the archduke (as a Hapsburg, "above" politics), and Gallas (although an Italian, not connected with Wallenstein's fall).

This "Walschen-German" split was not duplicated in the almost equally polyglot Bavarian Army.

NOTES

1. See Chapter 6, Appendix G.
2. The man who had abandoned Gustavus at Lutzen.
3. The Swedes, who blamed him for Gustavus's death, hoped to put him on trial, but he shortly thereafter died of his wounds.
4. The inept commandant, Col Miniati, was court-martialed in Vienna.
5. Counting Mercy as Bavarian rather than Imperial.
6. See Appendix F.
7. Later King Karl Gustav X of Sweden.
8. Gustavus and Baner had always used "Gott mit uns!"
9. It must have been one of his good days.
10. See Parrott, "Strategy and Tactics in the Thirty Years' War," in Clifford J. Rogers, *The Military Revolution Debate* (Boulder, CO: Westview, 1995), pp. 227-52.
11. This was a tendency, not a hard-and-fast rule. Able tacticians like Luxembourg, Marlborough, or Frederick could get around it; also there were plenty of fights where a weaker infantry was simply battered into retreat.
12. The "narrowing of the gaps" was partially due to improved training and drill; less clumsy units could be deployed more closely. However, the old units had been able to operate independently, whereas under the new system, battalions were merely components of a solid line.
13. Dewitz, Werner, and Douglas, under Col. Dewitz. Dewitz was court-martialed for his ineptitude.
14. Cleared from his behavior at 2nd Breitenfeld.
15. The Danish king had abolished the pike!
16. He was succeeded by K. G. Wrangel, who later succeeded Torstensson.
17. Perhaps he remembered the Baltic from 1638.
18. 4000 infantry, 8000+ cavalry, 600 Croats, and 2 dragoon regiments, exclusive of later reinforcements.
19. He joined Torstensson at Halberstadt, October 1, with 800 foot and 9 cavalry regiments.
20. See Chapter 6.
21. See Appendix D for breakdown.
22. Prince Lobkowitz, Vice President of the War Council, came in person to "confer" with Hatzfeld. Torstensson had the advantage here; as his superior, Oxenstierna, was in Sweden, he granted his commander carte blanche in strategy.
23. Although he was himself a Lutheran!
24. The baggage train was left at Tabor.
25. See Chapter 3.

26. Svensk Försvarsstaben. Krigshistoriska avdelningen, *Slaget vid Jankow, 1645–24/2* (Stockholm: Generalstabens, 1945), p. 88.
27. Accounts of their conference derive entirely from Hatzfeld's official report, which was sharply critical of Gotz.
28. Probably 10 musket detachments from Douglas's wing.
29. Bruay, like Gotz, was killed and unable to contradict the survivor. Hatzfeld showed a remarkable talent for being in the wrong place at critical moments.
30. Possibly Pentz and Muller cavalry regiments.
31. *Slaget vid Jankow,* p. 100.
32. From Quartermaster Marderfelt's account; see *Slaget.*
33. Except for the colonel, Palsgrave Karl Gustav.
34. *Slaget* suggests that these guns were a secondary battery of heavies, but it is more likely that they were the 3 pdrs attached to Wittenberg.
35. Possibly Mercy's brigade.
36. Probably Axel Lillie and Lewenhaupt.
37. Possibly the Reichart, Dannenberg, and Riesengrun regiments.
38. Including 238 officers, 138 NCOs, 66 artillerymen, and about 4000 rank and file.
39. Even that was very early for a French army.
40. 1200 musketeers and 6000 hussars.
41. See Chapter 6.
42. Supposedly on orders from the Ottoman sultan.
43. 2nd Nordlingen, see Chapter 6.
44. See Chapter 6.
45. August 27, 1645. The Saxons were permitted to attach a small cavalry brigade to the Imperial army.

5

The Battle of Rocroi: The War in Flanders and France

The Flanders War of 1621–59 stood at the confluence of three larger wars, the Eighty Years War between Spain and the Netherlands, the Thirty Years War in Germany, and the Franco-Spanish War of 1635–59. The theater was Spanish Flanders, which in 1621 was almost twice as large as modern Belgium and included Luxemburg and parts of Holland, Germany, and northern France. Spanish rule depended on the support of the majority Walloons, French speaking and thoroughly Catholic. While the Walloons formed the largest individual component of the heterogeneous Spanish army, the minority Flemings, ethnically and linguistically related to the Protestants of the Netherlands, were employed in naval and secondary roles.

In 1560, both Flanders and the Netherlands were under Spanish overlordship, but in 1566, the Protestant minority began its attempts to take over the country.[1] The Spanish responded in kind, and open warfare resulted. Leadership of the revolt soon passed to the extremist Calvinists. As the fighting dragged on, a split developed between the north, where the rebels established an independent government, the United Provinces of the Netherlands based on Holland, and the south, centered in Brussels, where Spanish-Catholic rule prevailed. The war became a sort of institution, with the first European professional armies locked in seemingly endless fighting, the struggle itself constituting a school for modern warfare. Many of the ideas and leaders of the earlier Thirty Years War derived from the Netherlands war.

In 1609, both sides had fought to a standstill; however, they were too far apart to reach peace. A compromise, the "Twelve Years Truce" (1609–21), suspended the actual fighting, but both sides remained poised to resume operations, and there were the usual "Cold War" crises, maneuvers, and flare-ups. Despite the signed peace, the Dutch continued an aggressive colonial policy at the expense of Spain and Portugal.[2] Both Spain and Holland chose to intervene in the outbreak of the Thirty Years War in Germany, and in this early test, the Spanish emerged the winners. Nevertheless, the king of Spain attempted to convert the truce into a permanent peace settlement; the two states were unable to reach agreement.

This Flanders War of 1621-48 was less a continuation of the original Dutch War of Independence than a sequel; it may be compared to the War of 1812 in America. The Spanish had no intention of reconquering the north, but they had specific war goals: (1) to assure the safety of the colonies under threat; (2) to obtain a symbolic or formal recognition of Spain's legal suzerainty over the Dutch; (3) to guarantee a degree of tolerance for the Catholic minority in Holland, and (4) to end the Dutch blockade of the port of Antwerp. Dutch goals were more nebulous, but they certainly wished to expand at Spain's expense, both in Europe and overseas; to force Spain to recognize their total independence, and to keep Antwerp closed.

THE SPANISH-DUTCH WAR 1621-35

The Flanders War was essentially a war of sieges, with no field battles at all. This was deliberate strategy. Despite their reputation as the best-trained and most efficient army in Europe, the Dutch were never willing to risk a field battle with the Spanish on any but the most lopsided of odds.[3] This was to prove a sound strategy. Both Flanders and Holland were so densely fortified that no mere field victory, however decisive, could do more than permit the victor to carry on more sieges. Throughout the war, both sides employed upward of 30,000 men in garrison. In 1639, the Spanish maintained no fewer than 208 permanent garrisons, consuming 33,399 men.[4] Equally, the Dutch must have maintained over 100. Only a couple of dozen of these were "superfortresses" comparable to the later Vauban type. Towns like Breda, 's-Hertogenbosch, Antwerp, Maastricht, Julich, were fortress-complexes with strong garrisons of 1000-5000, protected by numerous outworks and a ring of subsidiary sub-forts. The capture of such a place ranked with a major victory in the field. Even taking a medium-sized place, defended by 300-600 men and a few outworks, was an important gain. Finally there were very minor places with garrisons as small as 10 men, but even these could delay an enemy movement.

The Spanish-Dutch War divides neatly into two phases: the Spanish offensive of 1621-25 and the Dutch offensive of 1626-34. The normal pattern was for active operations to run from May to October (an ongoing siege would normally be extended through the winter). The larger, better-financed army would assume the offensive for the year—both sides were generally aware of the other's effective strength—while the weaker force would attempt to hamper it by defensive positions, raids, and diversions. Both sides purchased much of their food from contractors, and barge transport was generally available, so the logistical situation was better than in Germany. Unlike the savagery of the Dutch War of Independence, both Spanish and Dutch commanders tried to fight a "gentleman's war," with scrupulous regard for the laws of war and as much protection as possible for noncombatants. The devastation so common in the

German war was uncommon. Both sides thought of it as a war for limited objectives, in which each operation was a part of the ongoing negotiations. In these regards, the emphasis on siegecraft, the use of magazine supply, and the civilized conduct of operations, the Flanders war appears as a direct ancestor of the linear war period.

Although the Dutch leadership had sabotaged the Spanish peace initiatives, Maurice's government was at a military disadvantage in 1621. The Spanish army under the leadership of the famous Spinola was superior in size and quality. Spinola's strategy would be affected by the military geography involved.

The "front line" between the opponents ran roughly along the "great river barrier," the lines of the Maas and the Rhine. During the truce, both sides had given some attention to outflanking the river defenses. The Spanish expanded their two isolated forts in the north, Grol and Oldenzaal, by fortifying the area around Lingen in Germany. The Dutch developed a similar salient up the Rhine in the area Rheidt-Papenmutz-Julich. In the Geldern area, Dutch and Spanish forts were intermingled. Also, the Dutch possessed the Breda salient and the mouth of the Scheldt as well.

Spinola believed that the war with Holland was essentially unwinnable and that the best course would be to inflict such defeats on the enemy as to induce them to agree to a more favorable peace. His political masters, Philip IV and Olivares, would not have disagreed. However, Olivares favored using the Lingen-Grol area to outflank the Dutch line and overrun a supposedly soft underbelly, thus scoring a quick win at the negotiation table. Spinola instead opted for the less risky, but less promising, approach of pinching off the exposed Dutch salients. Spinola was very aware of the quality of the Dutch army and the need to cover Flanders from counterattack, and his response was one of great, one might say excessive, caution.

Operations began in August 1621—the Spanish were forced to withdraw most of the army from the German Rhineland, where they had been supporting the Imperials. Spinola and his Walloon lieutenant, Bergh, overran Rheidt, cutting off Julich. Then Bergh encircled that town with 8000 men while Spinola and the main army obstructed Maurice's attempts at relief. Julich was a very strong place, held by 3500 of Maurice's best men, but a 5-month blockade starved them into surrender.

In 1622, Spinola, perhaps encouraged by the success at Julich, attempted something more ambitious, the capture of Bergen-op-Zoom. This strong town was the major Dutch stronghold against Antwerp; it was also a port, which, given Dutch naval superiority, meant it could not be starved out like Julich. Everything went wrong for Spinola. His initial approach alerted Maurice, who reinforced the town. Attempts to cut off seaborne communication failed. Supplies broke down, and the besiegers starved. He could not, despite repeated assaults and heavy casualties, penetrate the outer defenses. Finally, a German relieving force under Mansfeld and Brunswick defeated the covering force under his Spanish lieutenant, Cordoba, and forced him to lift the siege.[5] The Spanish lost 5000 men in the siege and another 4000 deserters. The capture of the minor places of Goch, Papenmutz, and Steenbergen was no compensation for this disaster, especially as Steenbergen could not be held while Bergen remained Dutch.

Spinola wasted 1623 rebuilding his field force from this failure. Neither side attempted anything of importance. In 1624, Spinola resumed the offensive. First Bergh led a successful diversionary attack against the eastern sector, taking Cleves and Gennep without difficulty. A more aggressive commander would have tried for the main Dutch base in the area, Grave, but Bergh hesitated. Nevertheless, Spinola had a free hand for his main operation, the capture of Breda. Spinola determined that this time nothing would go wrong. He employed the starvation tactic that had proven so successful at Julich; it was less a siege than a blockade. The Dutch in turn tried to cut off Spinola's supplies; it was remarked that the besieged ate better than the besiegers. Although the Spanish ran short, they got by. The siege lasted 9 months, well into 1625. Maurice died on April 23, 1625, to be succeeded as Dutch leader by his younger brother, Frederick Henry (Frederik Hendrik). The new stadtholder attempted to force Spinola's line of circumvallation but was beaten off with 200 dead (May 15, 1625). Supplies exhausted and without hope of relief, Breda had no choice but surrender. Spinola's near-bloodless capture of the strongest fortress in Holland was hailed throughout Europe as proof that Spain's former invincibility was still valid.

This was to be Spinola's last triumph. Back in Spain, Olivares had grown dissatisfied. He had hoped for a quick win over the Dutch, yet after four years peace seemed as far off as ever. The expense of the offensive was beggaring the kingdom. Olivares's fertile mind had devised an alternative strategy that seemed to guarantee victory at a bargain rate. Holland's power rested not in its land possessions, like other nations, but in its seaborne commerce. The land army in Flanders would assume a defensive posture (*guerra defensiva*), while the war was won at sea. A squadron of commerce raiders and privateers would wage *guerre de course* against the Dutch in their own waters, while the regular navy cut their trade with the Mediterranean and strangled their colonies.[6] Reasoning from the defensive strength of the Dutch 1621–25, Olivares considered that it would be possible to reduce the Flanders army to 48,000,[7] saving 600,000 ducats a year. Spinola disagreed, arguing for a minimum of 70,000,[8] but he was overruled.

On the Dutch side, the situation was entirely opposite. The Dutch Republic was a representative oligarchy characterized by local autonomy, particularism, and deliberation. It combined the decisiveness of democracy with the flexibility of monarchy. But it had an unrivaled ability to finance and an innate knack of rising to the occasion in an emergency. The Dutch legislature, the States General, was splintered into a number of factions—they can't be called parties—representing the views of the oligarchies of each of the seven provinces. There were rabid anti-Spanish warmongers and Catholic sympathizers hoping for peace. The merchant classes were divided between those who wanted a return to normal trading conditions and those who hoped to expand into the Spanish-Portuguese colonies. The religious feud between the Gomarist and Arminian religious factions[9] continued to divide the government. Finally, there were local interests trying to use the war to benefit their own provinces.

At the outbreak of war, the Dutch increased their standing army from 30,000 to 48,090. The cost of these forces was divided among the provinces according to a complicated formula, Holland province being responsible for over half (24,710). It was always an option for a province to simply refuse to pay, so the stadtholder could not increase the army size above what was politically possible. It was common for operations to be delayed while the States argued funding. Maurice had personally alienated so many political interests that he could not persuade the legislature to approve more funds. With his death, followed by the crisis at Breda, the States began to take a more reasonable attitude. Also, Frederick Henry showed a talent for political maneuver and intrigue that his brother had lacked. The years 1626–29 were characterized by steady growth in army funding.

The Dutch offensive began on a very small scale. In August 1626, being aware of the Spanish inertia, Frederick Henry dispatched a force of 7000 to assault Oldenzaal. The Spanish, diminished in numbers and poorly deployed—the Spanish "ring" of fortresses, on exterior lines, was well sited for offensive warfare but difficult to defend—were unable to relieve the position. The garrison yielded after a mere 10 days' bombardment. Encouraged by this success, Frederick Henry determined on something more ambitious in 1627.

Although Frederick Henry did not fight battles, he was able to devise a strategic offensive that nullified the Spanish defense. Under his system, the Spanish covering force would be outmaneuvered or drawn off from the target fortress long enough for his army to invest it. Powerful lines of circumvallation would not only cut off the town from the outside but also protect the besieging force from any Spanish attempt at relief. If the lines were sufficiently strong, the Spanish would be unable to penetrate.[10] Under their protection, the real siege would be conducted.

The campaigns of Frederick Henry represent the apogee of the scientific siegecraft of the Spanish-Dutch school.[11] A typical siege followed a certain pattern. First, the main line of circumvallation would be dug, at extreme cannon range from the fortress (1000–1500 yards). This primary line would be raised as quickly as possible, using soldiers, sappers, and civilian labor; it would face both inside, to keep in the garrison, and outside, to ward off relief.[12] Next supplies would be stored, some by transport, others purchased locally. The siege proper would begin with the erection of one to three redoubts at extreme musket range (250–300 yards). Approach trenches would be opened, snaking toward the fortress. Approaches were supposed to be angled or curved to reduce the danger of enfilade. Smaller redoubts could be raised along the approach line and/or the trenches could be widened laterally as a marshaling point for assault troops. The number of lines of approach would be a factor of the resources available: the more lines of approach, the greater the pressure on the defenders, but too many would diffuse the besieger's attack power.

Batteries of cannon and demicannon would be placed in the main redoubts, but their primary mission was covering fire. They would attempt to silence the defending guns and suppress their musketeers, rather than actually breach the walls. It seems that the (mostly earthwork) Low Country fortresses were more resistant to gunfire than the (mainly masonry) fortresses of Germany or France. A secondary artillery mission was "bombardment," that is, firing into the town to cause casualties, start fires, and generally terrorize the populace.

The outlying sconces, ravelins, and fortlets would be reduced individually or stormed. Often the garrison would abandon a work as it was rendered untenable.

As the approach trenches neared the glacis and covered way, the covering fire would no longer be enough. Sappers and miners, receiving special pay under contract, would take over the digging. Inadequately protected by gabions, these specialists would sap into the glacis, relying on supporting infantry to clear the covered way.

Once the saps have reached the glacis and the covered way has been opened, mining becomes possible. A chamber is dug under the wall and filled with gunpowder. Finally, the mine is exploded, breaching the wall. The earthwork walls of Holland and Flanders seem to have been more vulnerable to mines than stonework ones. Minor breaches might be penetrated by small raiding parties, but a large one was the signal to prepare a grand assault. The defenders invariably surrendered at this point (if not earlier). Garrisons were normally granted "honors of war" and free passage back to their own side, but sometimes the defeated had to pay ransom.

During the course of the operation, the enemy might attempt to interfere by attacking the lines from the outside, cutting off supplies, making a diversionary attack, or trying to run supplies and reinforcements into the town. The garrison might sally against the approach trenches and batteries, improvise new works inside the breaches, or dig countermines and rob the mines of their powder.

It was rare for a siege to be resolved by starvation, as at Julich and Breda. Sometimes a fort might run out of powder, but most sieges were resolved by a surrender after a major breach. Surrenders such as Oldenzaal in 1626 or Venlo in 1632 were held in contempt because they resulted from a mere bombardment, before the wall was actually breached.

In 1627, Frederick Henry descended on Grol, the most important of the Spanish "flanking" fortresses, catching it undermanned. The Spanish managed to assemble a strong relief column, but by the time they reached the town, the lines of circumvallation were complete. The relief commander, Bergh, made some more or less halfhearted assaults on the lines, then gave up and abandoned Grol to its fate. The garrison yielded few days later (August 19, 1627). Spinola, realizing that the situation was strategically hopeless and that his reputation would be ruined, went to Madrid to lobby in person for a more realistic policy. As Cordoba had been transferred to Italy,[13] command devolved on Bergh, whose defeatism had forfeited the support of his Spanish and Italian subordinates.

The Dutch adopted an unnecessarily cautious defensive strategy in 1628. King Christian of Denmark had been thoroughly defeated in Germany, and it seemed possible that Wallenstein and Tilly would invade in support of Spain. This did not mean that Spain's troubles were over. A Dutch raiding fleet off Cuba captured the annual New World convoy (Battle of Matanzas Bay, September 8, 1628), which not only cost Spain millions in direct revenues but threw the country into a recession.

Spain entered 1629 at a marked disadvantage. The kingdom was financially crippled, and such resources as were available had been allotted to Mantua. The Dutch, by way of contrast, had raised their army to a new peak of 77,193. The Grol and Oldenzaal salients had been eliminated, and the German threat seemed less. The objective was s'Hertogenbosch (Den Bosch, Bois-le-Duc), perhaps the fourth most important city in Flanders.

This important place was protected by 3 lesser forts: Heesch blocked the approach route, while Eindhoven and Boxtel maintained communications to the south and west. These places were garrisoned by 800 men. In addition, the town proper was surrounded by marsh. The marshes were protected by 2 sub-forts, Greater St. Anthony and St. Isabella. St. Anthony was almost a fortress in itself, with hornworks, demilune, glacis, and ditch; it was connected to the main enceinte by a third fortlet, Little St. Anthony. The 3 sub-forts required 1000 men. The main wall was equally strong, especially the Pettebeer redoubt.

The Spanish were somewhat aware of the threat to s'Hertogenbosch, but they lacked the funds to bring it to full strength. In any case, Frederick Henry misdirected their attention with diversionary raids in the Wesel and Lingen areas. His striking force, 28,000 strong,[14] was assembling at the fortress center of Schenkenschans. He crossed the Maas on April 29 and overran Heesch on the 30th. By May 1, s'Hertogenbosch was surrounded.

The town was commanded by Baron Grabendonk, who, although a Walloon, was very attached to the Spanish cause. When the Dutch appeared, he had only 2800 men in all, but he succeeded in raising enough volunteers in the town to bring the main garrison up to 2000, exclusive of militia. Funds were very short, but there were plenty of muskets and powder. He was determined to hold out as long as possible; Brussels had promised him relief.

The Dutch lines of circumvallation were completed by May 8, and Boxtel had fallen. The bombardment began on the 13th. These lines were called the strongest ever seen and were the more impressive in that much of their length had to be constructed on "galleries" through the marsh. The siege became a tourist attraction, with visitors from all over Protestant Europe.

Frederick Henry determined to reduce all 3 sub-forts before approaching the main defenses. By May 23, his saps had reached St. Anthony and mined the demilune, but the strong place repelled an assault with loss. This led to a change in approach: the Dutch spent June sapping around Isabella and Anthony, to cut them off from the town proper.

The Spanish relieving army under Bergh, 25,000 strong,[15] finally materialized on July 1, a good 2 months after the siege began. Bergh drove the Dutch out of Boxtel and tried to reopen communications with the town. For his part, Grabendonk made an unsuccessful sally on the 4th. Bergh spent several weeks trying to assist the town, but in vain. As the Dutch held the river, with its barge traffic, he could not even interfere with their supply lines. The only way in was directly through the lines of circumvallation. Reluctantly, he attempted to force the lines, but was beaten off with loss (July 17).

With admirable sangfroid, Frederick Henry had simply carried on operations as if Bergh were not even there. The Dutch saps having reached the Little Fort, Grabendonk had to evacuate Greater St. Anthony or risk the men there being cut off when the Little Fort fell (July 17–18). St. Isabella had to be abandoned about the same time. By this time, the Dutch were within 25 yards of the main wall.

Bergh realized the futility of his operations, so he decided to try to relieve s'Hertogenbosch by diversion. He left Boxtel, crossed the river barrier at Wesel, and moved into Dutch territory (July 22). Shortly thereafter, an Imperial corps of 10,000–20,000 under Ernesto Montecuccoli arrived to support Bergh's operation.[16] Both columns pressed into the Dutch rear in August. Bergh's probes were repulsed, but Montecuccoli captured the town of Amersfoort (August 13), whose feeble defense and premature surrender sent shock waves throughout the whole Republic. Montecuccoli then proposed a joint attack on the important city of Utrecht, but Bergh deemed it too risky.

Despite this critical situation, Frederick Henry still refused to be budged from his siegeworks. The Dutch homeland would see to its own defense. The Dutch rose to the challenge: militia were mobilized, garrison troops fielded, new units raised, and sailors armed, bringing the available manpower to its wartime peak of 128,877. Bergh's caution becomes understandable, if not excusable.

The Spanish operation collapsed as quickly as it had materialized. On August 19, the Dutch commander of Emmerich (one of the forts supporting Schenkenschans and Grave) assembled a strike force of 1000 and attempted a *coup-de-main* against Bergh's base at Wesel. He found the town defenses in neglect and the garrison unpaid and demoralized. The Spanish-Italian cadre, about 100 strong, resisted but were cut down, while over 1000 Germans surrendered or fled. Much of Bergh's material, including 50 cannon, was lost. Montecuccoli abandoned Amersfoort, while Bergh pulled back to safety.

This fiasco cost Bergh whatever credit he had left; Spanish opinion now ran that he was not merely an incompetent coward but actually pro-Dutch.

Back at s'Hertogenbosch, the Dutch exploded their first mine on August 4. This was followed by repeated mines, minor breaches, and skirmishes. With equal stubbornness, the defenders made several sallies, with mixed results. Finally, on September 10, the last mine created a major breach in the main wall, and Dutch troops actually entered the town. It was over; negotiations were opened, and, on September 17, the garrison marched out under honors of war.[17]

This epic siege, perhaps the hardest fought of the war, was the first of the five great blows that destroyed the "Spanish System." At a stroke, Spain had lost all the credit from Spinola's earlier victories, moreover, it had been demonstrated that they could not defend Flanders from Protestant attack. Walloon confidence in the regime plummeted. *Guerra defensiva* had failed.

The Dutch followed up their victory by overrunning the Spanish outposts in the Wesel area, pushing almost as far as Düsseldorf. But, as often happened in the Dutch Republic, effort and success were immediately followed by parsimony and complacency. The States General decided to reduce the army to below its 1628 level. No major operations were attempted, giving Spain a breathing space to recover. Cordoba was offered the command but flatly refused. Even Olivares had to admit that defending Flanders would require men and money. Fortunately, the Mantuan War was being wound up. Nevertheless, retrenchment was required. In July 1630, the Spanish handed over most of their German forts, including Lingen, to the emperor and the Catholic League. Only Rheinberg, now their chief stronghold on the Rhine, was retained. Also, forces were withdrawn from their garrisons in the Lower Palatinate.

In 1631, Frederick Henry persuaded the States General to finance an attack on the city of Bruges. In early June, his force had penetrated the outer defenses and had begun the siege when Santa Cruz, the new Spanish commander, suddenly appeared in his rear. The threat to their supply line made the States' deputies break off the siege, against Frederick Henry's will. This failure was balanced by the subsequent Dutch destruction of an important Spanish riverine convoy, the so-called Battle of the Slaak.

In Fall–Winter 1631, King Gustavus Adolphus of Sweden destroyed the main Imperial field army and overran most of Germany. The minute Spanish force in the Palatinate could not arrest this unstoppable advance. Although this did not directly affect this theater—the Catholic allies managed to retain most of the area adjoining the Low Countries—it did sever the only land link between Spain and Flanders.[18] Fortunately, an increasingly porous Dutch blockade had made use of the sea route practicable. But this was another strain on the already overtasked Spanish navy. Also, it had become necessary to divert resources to support the Imperials. If these problems were not enough, Bergh, the resentful former commander, had organized a Walloon conspiracy to foment a revolt, oust Spain, and join the Dutch.

The Dutch offensive of 1632 was launched on four fronts: Bergh and his associates went into open revolt, the Dutch Republic issued a "manifesto" guaranteeing full rights to Catholics,[19] 8000 Dutch under Willem threatened Antwerp, and Frederick Henry marched up the Maas with 30,000 men. With only 14,000 at his disposal, of whom 5000 were diverted to Antwerp, Santa Cruz could only watch as the Dutch gobbled up the minor forts of Venlo, Roermond, Straelen, and Sittard before laying siege to the fortress of Maastricht (June 8). The situation seemed on the verge of collapse, a grimmer replay of 1629. Willem's small force took 4 forts in the Antwerp-Hulst area. In this extremity, the Spanish were forced not only to withdraw Cordoba's corps from Germany but to bribe Pappenheim[20] to bring 8000 Germans as well. The three armies together were barely equal to Frederick Henry's force, but nevertheless they assaulted his lines of circumvallation (August 17). The result was predictable: Santa Cruz had to fall back, Pappenheim returned to Germany, and Maastricht surrendered (August 23). As a sequel, the stronghold of Limburg fell almost without resistance (September 5).

Spanish prestige lay in ruins. The usually pessimistic States General advised Frederick Henry to march directly on Brussels and proclaim the reunification of the Netherlands. It seemed as though the regime would simply collapse.

It would be going too far to say that in this extremity the Walloons rallied to their king, but they didn't rise in revolt either. They stood back, waiting to see what would happen. Frederick Henry blinked. Too accustomed to the Flanders style of warfare, the patient reduction of a fort or two a year, he was (exactly the opposite of Gustavus Adolphus) unable to exploit this "missed opportunity of 1632." He cautiously consolidated his gains, waiting for his army to recover from the strain of the siege. The critical moment passed; the Spanish were never in such danger again.

In 1633, Frederick Henry captured the strong fortress of Rheinberg, but the smaller Spanish forces, aggressive and well led, were able to restrict his gains. Some minor places changed hands on both sides. More importantly, a major Spanish army was being assembled in Milan under King Philip's younger brother, the Cardinal-Infante. In 1634, this army marched up through Germany, helped the Imperials shatter the Swedes at the Battle of Nordlingen (September 6), then arrived safely in Flanders before winter. Frederick Henry, now on the defensive, had wasted the year preserving Maastricht from a Spanish siege. The arrival of the Cardinal-Infante was intended to mark the beginning of a new *guerra offensiva* and Spanish victory. It was not to be. In an oddly medieval ceremony, a French herald "threw down the gauntlet" to Spain (May 21, 1635). Having failed to defeat one enemy, the Spanish would now face two.

Table 5.1
Spanish-Dutch War, 1621–34

Year	Army (1000s)s Spain	Dutch	Major Siege	Days	Attacker	Def	Note
1621	60	48	Julich	130	8,000	3500	Starved
1622	50	48	Bergen-op-Zoom	78	20,600	??	Failed
1623	60	48					
1624	70	48	Breda	275	22,840	3500	Starved
1625	70	55					
1626	54	55	Oldenzaal	10	7,000	1500	Guns
1627	54	58	Grol	30	28,000	900	Mined
1628	50	71				??	
1629		77*	's-Hertogenbosch	140	28,000	3000	Mined
1631		75	Bruges		30,000	??	Failed
1632		75	Maastricht	77	30,000	1400	Mined
1633	65	70	Rheinberg	25	25,000		Mined

Spanish figures include local forces; Dutch do not.
* Briefly increased to 128,877 during emergency.

THE FRANCO-SPANISH WAR, 1635–42

Spain's strategic problem in 1635 was straightforward: it had a strong enough army to deal with either the French or the Dutch but not both at the same time. So, whichever one it struck at, the other would gain the initiative. The French were a very different sort of opponent from the Dutch, in that they were at once more aggressive and less professional. They were willing, even eager, to meet the Spanish in the field, and they were not good at sieges. They were not at all interested in the Spanish-Dutch concept of sparing the civilians; their plundering and violence were considered wanton even by German standards. The Spanish were aware that dealing with a less siege-oriented enemy would require changes in their force structure (more cavalry); they also knew that cavalry was proving increasingly important in the German war. But their mindset retained its infantry orientation. On the other hand, the French Army as a whole was slow to adapt to the "Swedish" style of warfare; their preferred model was the Dutch.

The Franco-Dutch plan for 1635 was to link up their two armies, of 30,000 each, for a joint strike at the enemy center—the French were indulging hopes of a quick win. The Cardinal-Infante tried to upset their scheme with a preemptive strike at the Dutch, but it failed. The French smashed a Spanish blocking force at the Action of Avesnes (May 22), pressed into Flanders, and joined the Dutch at Maastricht (June 1). The Dutch were disappointed to find the French so much weaker than had been agreed. The allies fell on the weak place of Tirlemont, which yielded easily. To the shock of the Dutch, the French brutally sacked the town; their behavior now and later did much to shore up Walloon support for the Spanish regime. Overconfident in the allied numbers (50,000), the French insisted on laying siege to the strong fortress-town of Louvain. Unfortunately for them, it was defended by Grabendonk, the hero of 's-Hertogenbosch, and 4000 men. Between the too-large army and Spanish interference with their own supplies, the Dutch could only watch as the French melted away in desertion. The approach of an Imperial corps under Piccolomini persuaded even the stubborn French to break off the siege (July 4). Frederick Henry pulled the much-depleted force back to a more modest objective, the capture of Geldern, but even this was preempted. A raiding force of 1300 Spanish from the Geldern garrison surprised and captured the "invincible" Dutch base of Schenkenschans (July 26). The Cardinal-Infante and Piccolomini, with 40,000 men, pushed into the Maas area, occupying Cleves, Goch, Helmond, Eindhoven, and several other places; Frederick Henry was, of course, unwilling to risk a battle. The 8000 surviving French had to be shipped home by the Dutch navy. The first year of the new war had gone well for Spain.

Table 5.2
Attrition of the French Army in Flanders, 1635[2]

	Infantry	Cavalry	Total
Paper Strength	28,000	6,000	34,000
May (actual)	22,000	4,500	26,500
Mid-June	13,000	4,000	17,000
September*	8,000	2,000	10,000

* This figure includes reinforcements received in July.

The initiative for 1636 rested with Spain. The original plan was to assume the defensive vis-à-vis France, while using Schenkenschans to assault Holland. The Dutch, however, had taken the loss of their fortress as another crisis and mobilized a major force to retake it (April 30, 1636). Cleves and other forts were retaken at the same time. Fortunately, the spring operations had exhausted Dutch military funding for the year, so Frederick Henry had to assume the defensive. This freed the Spanish to strike at France. As an Imperial army under Gallas was attacking Burgundy, and a third army was supposed to advance from Spain itself, this may have been intended as a coordinated attempt to knock France out of the war at a blow. A combined army of Spanish under the Cardinal-Infante, Imperials under Piccolomini, and Bavarians under Werth, 32,000 strong, marched into France in August. The French army, now under Soissons, still mustered a risible 10,000; Soissons was understandably reluctant to risk battle. In a remarkable display of cowardice and incompetence, the border forts of La Capelle and Le Catelet surrendered without a fight, while a third fortress, Corbie, held out only 10 days (August 15). Werth led his cavalry as far as Compiegne, and it seemed possible that Paris would be attacked. Like Frederick Henry in 1632, the Cardinal-Infante was hesitant to exploit this unanticipated success. Keeping their heads amid the panic, King Louis and Richelieu augmented Soissons's handful with recruits and militia to a (paper) total of 50,000. At the same time, Frederick Henry, with a pathetic 13,000, made a threatening gesture to the north. The Cardinal-Infante abandoned the offensive and, with it, his chance to win the war. After the Spanish withdrew, the French retook Corbie (November 9) and the other forts.

After the drama of 1635 and 1636, 1637 represented a return to siegework as usual. Frederick Henry besieged Breda (3500) with 18,000 men; the Cardinal-Infante attempted to relieve it with 17,000. Unable to break the lines of circumvallation, the Spaniard tried to divert the Dutch by taking Venlo and Roermond. Frederick Henry, of course, refused to be diverted. Before the Spanish could proceed against a more important target, 20,000 French laid siege to Landrecies and had to be driven off, diverting him in turn. Breda surrendered October 7.

The year 1638 saw the Spanish on the defensive, forced to parry blows from both opponents. The Dutch intended to besiege Antwerp, their most ambitious project yet. Frederick Henry dispatched a vanguard, 6000 of his best men under Willem, to seize 3 of the protecting sub-forts. In the Action of Kallo (June), the Dutch detachment was shattered and the whole offensive was aborted. Kallo was the largest action of the whole Spanish-Dutch War. As an encore, the Cardinal-Infante defeated the French at St Omer (July 16). Moreover, Piccolomini had returned with an Imperial army and overran some Dutch outposts in Cleves. Frederick Henry desperately attempted to restore the situation—the Dutch seem to have been better off without the French!—by capturing Geldern. In a very unusual success, the Cardinal-Infante and Piccolomini succeeded in breaking his lines of circumvallation, forcing the Dutch to retire with a loss of 1000 men.

In 1639, the French scored their first success since Avesnes, capturing the minor fortlet of Hesdin. Unfortunately, this was counterbalanced by the near-destruction of a second French army at the Battle of Thionville (June 7). Between Piccolomini's activity and the inaction of the French, Frederick Henry failed to capture both Hulst and Geldern. However, the significant event of the year occurred at sea, the Dutch destruction of the main Spanish fleet at the Battle of the Downs (October 21, 1639).[22] This disaster, from which the Spanish navy never recovered, was the second great blow to the Spanish monarchy.

The year 1640 passed quietly in Flanders. The French captured Arras after a 2-month siege, but even though the Spanish were tied up in Artois, Frederick Henry's attacks on Bruges and Hulst were repelled by local garrisons. Unfortunately for Spain, the same was not true elsewhere. Annoyed by war taxes and the presence of an army, the province of Catalonia, on the French border, revolted against the Spanish Crown. Showing an unusual degree of ineptitude, the local Spanish commander managed to lose control to the rebel horde.[23] Encouraged by the Catalan success, the Portuguese followed suit. These were not mere peasant uprisings, as were so common in France, but the formal secession of entire nations from the ramshackle Spanish monarchy. France sent aid to Catalonia, and the Dutch to Portugal.[24] The Olivares regime was doomed; thereafter, reconquering the lost provinces would have a higher priority than the war with France. These revolts were the third and fourth blows to the Spanish system, each blow heavier than the one before.

In late 1640, a vigorous debate broke out in the States General over the conduct of the war. Frederick Henry argued that the Spanish setbacks had brought victory within his grasp. The peace faction, now assuming a major role, felt the opposite. Frederick Henry had accomplished nothing since 1637 to justify further increases in war taxation.[25] The victory of the Downs and the revolts in Iberia made the Spanish that much less threatening. Finally, it was not in the interests of the Dutch Republic to exchange familiar Spain for an aggressive France as ruler of Flanders. Frederick Henry managed to put together a compromise, but his control of the state was weakening. His field army for 1641 numbered a mere 19,500; nevertheless, he captured Gennep (1500). Although distracted by the death of the Cardinal-Infante, the Spanish defeated the French again, in the action of Marfee (July 6).

Spain's new governor, Melo, started 1642 badly, with the defeat of Kempton[26] (January 17). The Dutch and French agreed to another joint operation, this one directed against the stubborn Spanish fortress of Geldern. However, Melo was able to retake the fortress of Lens, then to smash a combined French corps at the action of Honnecourt (May 26). The disappointed Dutch broke off their preparations. At the end of 1642, it seemed that Spain's position in Flanders was as strong as ever.

Table 5.3
Franco-Spanish War, 1635–42

Year	Major Action	Type	Won	Lost	Notes
1635	Avesnes	Action	France	Spain	Failed siege of Louvain
1636	Corbie	Siege	Spain	France	Schenkenshans (Dutch)
1637	Breda	Siege	Dutch	Spain	
1638	Kallo	Action	Spain	Dutch	St Omer
1639	Thionville	Battle	Spain	France	Hesdin
1640	Arras	Siege	France	Spain	
1641	Marfee	Action	Spain	France	Gennep
1642	Honnecourt	Action	Spain	France	Kempton

THE 1643 CAMPAIGN

The initiative in 1643 rested with Spain. The Spanish were aware that the French were in disarray after their defeat at Honnecourt, that Cardinal Richelieu was dead, and that King Louis XIII was dying. More prudent elements suggested leaving them alone and concentrating on the Dutch. Melo did not agree. The fact that the French were vulnerable made them the ideal target. If they could be hit hard enough at this time, they would surely sue for peace. Melo's position was a reasonable one.

The conduct of operations lay with the German Beck, commanding the Imperial contingent (Piccolomini had returned to Germany). Melo had chosen him as chief military adviser above his Spanish and Walloon officers. History has not been generous to Beck, but he seems to have been a competent, if unimaginative, officer, a good adjutant for the mercurial Melo. The Spanish field army was divided into five corps:

Corps	Commander	Composition	Location
Main Army	Alburquerque	12 IR (6 Spn, 3 Ital, 3 Walloon)	Artois
Walloons	Bucquoy	24 cav coy & 4 IR	Hainault
Army of Alsace	Isenburg	5 Ger IR, 6 CR, 1 Croat, Fr Sqd	Meuse-Sambre
Imperials	Beck	5000–6000 men (mixed)	Luxemburg
Observation	Cantelmo	10,000–15,000	Dutch Border

Melo proposed to assemble the first four elements, some 27,000–28,000 men, and invade France itself, starting with the border fort of Rocroi (or Rocroy). The Spanish army was in excellent condition, although a bit weak in cavalry. Isenburg's vanguard crossed the Sambre River on May 10.

Aware of the need to safeguard his supply lines, Melo detached some 4000 men[27] under Beck to occupy the nearby (22 miles) castle of Chateau-Regnault on the Meuse. Rocroi was a small place, but strong enough, held by a garrison of 1000 and 400 militia. The town was under blockade by May 12, the lines of circumvallation were opened on the 15th, the battery established on the 16th, and the outer demilune taken on the 17th. On May 18, Melo's outposts reported the approach of a French army of relief.

The dying Louis XIII and his new minister, Cardinal Mazarin, had entrusted the principal French army to the untried Conde. It had been intended that the experienced and cautious l'Hopital act as military adviser, but the young prince instead preferred the company of the firebrands Gassion and Sirot. Upon reaching the vicinity of Rocroi, the French commanders were confronted by an awkward choice of strategies. Rocroi lay on an open plain surrounded by forests, marshes, and broken ground. To reach this plain and lift the siege, it would be necessary to traverse narrow defiles and ground unsuited to the numerous French cavalry. Also, news had just arrived of the death of the king. With the accession of a child and an uncertain regency, France could not afford a disaster. Cautious old l'Hopital thought the area better adapted to skirmishing than open battle. He suggested that, rather than attacking directly, they should bypass the obstructions and cut the Spanish supplies. This could have worked—in fact, many historians argue it was the sounder plan—although that was precisely what Beck's corps was supposed to prevent.[28] Gassion, supported by Persan and Sirot, argued for the dangerous, direct approach, and Conde decided in his favor.

The defile march put the French at some risk, as a smaller Spanish force could easily have blocked them and cut them up in skirmishes. It is uncertain whether Melo was informed too late of their arrival (indicating carelessness) or whether he deliberately allowed them through (indicating overconfidence). Melo may have been pleased to see them; loss of a major battle would hurt the French more than loss of a small fort. By allowing them onto the battlefield, Melo

The Battle of Rocroi

raised the stakes; instead of repelling Conde in a skirmish, he would destroy his army. The defile to the French rear would hinder their escape.

In any case, the French shoved aside the 50 Croats outposted there, passed the narrows safely, and deployed onto the field, late in the afternoon of May 18. Melo sent an urgent message to Beck, instructing him to come at once, as he would be needed in the morning. For the moment, the veteran Fontaine was directed to place the army into line of battle. A small force under Suarez was left to guard the camp and watch Rocroi.

The prideful La Ferte, resentful of Conde's favor of Gassion, decided to drive off Suarez and lift the siege on his own. Elements of the German cavalry under de Vera pushed him back in a sharp skirmish.

Conde drew up his army for battle, reviewed them just before dark, then went to his tent to sleep.[29] Melo, full of nervous energy, spent the night prowling along his battle line, trying to encourage his officers and men. Beck was expected at dawn.

Unknown to Melo, Beck was not coming. He had received the message after dark, so he decided to let the men sleep and set off in the morning. The phlegmatic German, knowing how excitable Melo was, does not seem to have taken the message as seriously as he should have.

THE COMMANDERS

Louis II de Bourbon, Duke of Enghien, Prince of Condé (1621–86) was a "Prince of the Blood," fourth in line for the throne of France. From his youth, he had been regarded as a prodigy. At the age of 22, with negligible experience, this young prince was made commander of the main army opposing the Spanish in Flanders, where he displayed the skill and aggressiveness that were to win him fame as "the Great Conde." Conde was the most prominent member of the rebel faction during the Fronde and, after the failure of that rebellion, assumed command of the Spanish in Flanders, but in both capacities he was defeated by his rival, Turenne (Battle of the Dunes, June 14, 1658). Pardoned by King Louis XIV, Conde was to win his final victory for France, Senef (August 11, 1674).

In character, Conde was arrogant and quarrelsome, as impetuous in his personal dealings as in battle. He soon acquired a reputation as a man who could win battles, but not campaigns. He seems to have mellowed somewhat after his restoration to royal favor. His private life was rendered unhappy by a forced marriage to Richelieu's niece.

Louis did not succeed his father as prince of Conde until 1646, so 19th century histories referred to him as "Enghien" at Rocroi, Freiburg, and 2nd Nordlingen, but "Conde" thereafter.

Marshal Francois de l'Hôpital, Count of Rosnay (1583–1666) had put in a pedestrian performance during the 1630s in Lorraine and Champagne. He was regarded in Paris as a reliable officer. Mazarin's plan had been for l'Hopital to act as Conde's military mentor and de facto commander, but the prince preferred the advice of the fiery Gassion. L'Hopital was rewarded for his services at Rocroi with a marshal's baton, but he nevertheless retired from the army.

Marshal Count Jean de Gassion (1607–47), a French Huguenot, was one of the most experienced officers in the French Army, having served with Gustavus Adolphus and Bernhard in the early 1630s. He joined the French Army in 1636, but although his military expertise was valued, his Protestantism was not. This lack of court favor hampered his career, and even after Rocroi it was with reluctance that he was given his baton. His short career as a marshal was spent in crushing peasant uprisings and in operations against the Spanish; he was killed campaigning in Flanders. Wholly devoted to warfare, he was as impetuous and quarrelsome as his student, Conde.

Marshal Henri de Saint-Nectaire, Duke of la Ferté (AKA Senneterre) (d. 1683) was a throwback to the medieval French nobility. An arrogant, insubordinate hothead, this often-wounded duke possessed plenty of personal courage and little military acumen. La Ferte was later made marshal, possibly for loyalty to the Crown during the Fronde, and his bungling greatly assisted both the rebels and the Spanish.

Colonel Claude de Létouf, Baron of Sirot (1606–1652), like Gassion, was an unusually experienced officer; his prewar service had been with both the Dutch and the Swedes. He spent the later 1630s with the French army in Italy. Sirot had a reputation as an aggressive and effective leader of cavalry, but as senior colonel he was relegated to the reserve. Sirot left one of the few eyewitness accounts of the battle.

Captain-General Francisco de Melo, Marques of Tordelaguna (1597–1651), a protégé of Olivares, was one of the few Portuguese to remain loyal to Spain after 1640. Although lacking in both military and administrative experience, he was appointed to succeed the Cardinal-Infante as governor-general of Flanders, and his victory at Honnecourt seemed to promise a successful term of office. After his return to Madrid, he was restored to royal favor and served in the cabinet 1646–51, also acting as royal military adviser.

General Francisco Fernandez de la Cueva, Duke of Alburquerque (1619–76), scion of a very prominent noble house, had arrived in Flanders in 1640 and had served as a tercio commander before being promoted to general of cavalry. He seems to have been competent, but no more.

Maestro de Campo General Count Paulo Bernard de Fontaine (ca. 1575–1643), a poor gentleman from the minor province of Franche Comte, rose by long and faithful service to the titled nobility and third in command of the Army of Flanders (an extreme example of the opportunities for advancement in the heterogeneous Spanish Army). Unfortunately, the exploits that won him the admiration of his fellow soldiers have mostly fallen into obscurity.

Count Ernst von Isenburg (AKA Ysenburg, Issembourg) (ca. 1590–1664), from the Catholic branch of a prominent German (not Fleming) military family, fought for Spain from 1619. Although he was always in Spanish service, many of his German troops were ex-Imperials.

Alvaro de Melo, the artillery commander, was the governor's younger brother.

THE ARMIES

There is some dispute on the size of these forces, particularly the Spanish. The French army is set at 20,000 to 23,000, the Spanish at 19,000 to 28,000.

The Battle of Rocroi

Map 5.1
The Battle of Rocroi, May 19, 1643

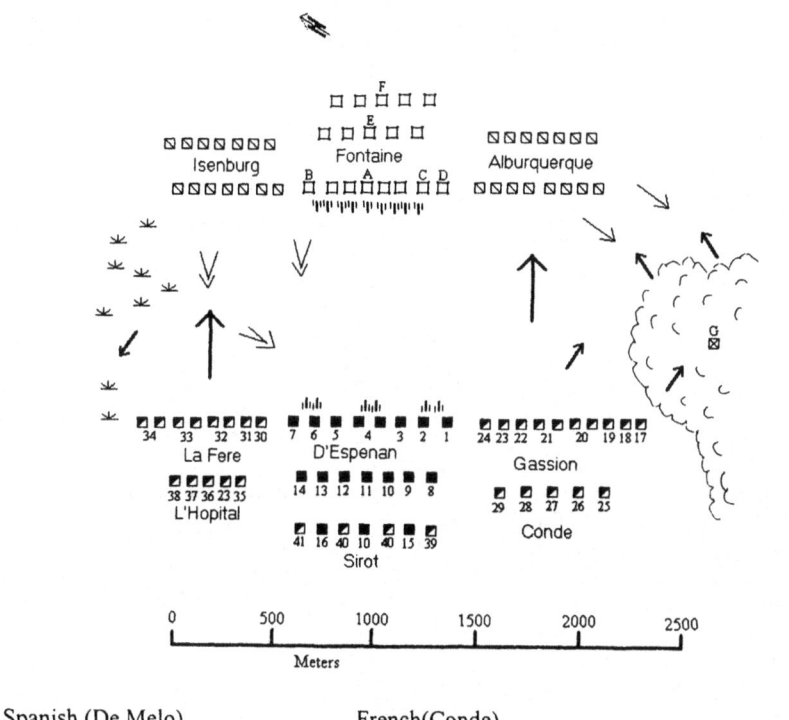

Spanish (De Melo)
A - Spanish Tercios
B - Visconti
C - Burgundians
D - Strozzi
E - Walloon Bns
F - German Bns
G - Musketeers (ambush)

French (Conde)
1 - Picardie
2 - La Marine
3 - Persan
4 - Molodin
5 - Biscarras-
6 - Rambures
7 - Piedmont
8 - La Pree
9 - Vidame
10 - Watteville
11 - Ecossais
12 - Roll
13 - Breze
14 - Guiche
15 - Harcourt-
16 - Royeaux

17 - Gardes
18 - Raab
19 - Chacks
20 - Royal

21 - Mestre de Camp
22 - Lenoncourt
23 - Coislin
24 - Sully
25 - Roquelaure
26 - Menneville
27 - Sillart
28 - Leschelle
29 - Vamberg
30 - La Claviere
31 - Beauvau
32 - La Ferte
33 - Guiche
34 - Fusiliers
35 - Netaf
36 - Marolles
37 - Heudicourt
38 - Harcourt
39 - Sirot
40 - Gendarmes
41 - Chaost

Spanish Army of Flanders—Francisco de Melo (see Appendix A)
Right Wing—Isenburg: 2800 cav in 14 sqd.

UNITS	COY	EST STR	NOTES
3 German CRs	30	1200	6 sqd of 200 each
Free Coys	5	200	1 sqd

Right Wing—2nd Echelon

UNITS	COY	EST STR	NOTES
3 German CRs	30	1200	6 sqd of 200 ea
Croat CR	10	200	1 sqd

Center—1st Echelon—Fontaine: 12,000 inf in 8 bns & 30 guns.

UNITS	ESTSTR	NOTES
Visconti Bn	1500	Italian: Visconti & Delli Ponti IRs
Velandia IR	1250	Spanish "old" tercio
Villalva	1250	Spanish "old" tercio
Mercador	1250	Spanish "old" tercio
Garcies	1750	Spanish tercio
Castelvi	1500	Spanish-Burgundian tercio
Burgundian Bn	1500	Gramont & St Amour IRs
Strozzi IR	2000	Italian
Alvaro de Melo	18 guns	10 siege guns remained in the camp

Center—2nd Echelon—2500 inf in 5 bn

Prince de Ligny	500	Walloons
Ribaucourt	500	
Granges	500	
Meghen	500	
Bassigny	500	

Center—3rd Echelon—2500 inf in 5 bn

D'Ambise	500	Germans
Montecuccoli	500	
Frangipani	500	
Rittburg	500	
?	500	

Right Wing—Alburquerque: 2250 cav in 15 sqd & 1000 inf

UNITS	COY	EST STR	NOTES
Walloon CRs	16	1200	8 sqd of 150 ea
Forlorn Hope	-	1000	"ambush"

Right Wing—2nd Echelon

UNITS	COY	EST STR	NOTES
Walloon CRs	14	1050	7 sqd of 150 ea

Total: 18,000 inf in 18 bn; 5050 cav in 29 sqd; 18 guns = 23,050

French Army—Conde (See Appendix B)
Right Wing—D'Enghien: 17 sqd
1st Echelon—Gassion): 10 sqd + musketeers

UNITS	DATE	NOTES
Gardes		Conde's Personal Guard; 1 coy; 200?
Raab Croats		1 Sqd
Chacks Croats		1 sqd
Royal CR		2 sqd
Mestre de Camp General CR	1635	Gassion?; 2 sqd; 9 coy

Lenoncourt CR	1636–38	1 sqd; 9 coy
Coislin CR	1636–38	1 of 2 sqd; 9 coy
Sully CR		1 sqd
Forlorn Hope		300(?) musketeers from Picardie IR

2nd Echelon—Conde: 5 sqd

Roquelaure CR		1 sqd
Menneville CR		"
Sillart CR	1634?	" Zillard? German
Leschelle CR	1635	" Liege; 9 coy
Vamberg CR		" foreign (German?)

Center—D'Espenan: 15 bns & 12 guns
1st Echelon: 8 bn

Picardie IR	1569	
La Marine IR	1635	
Persan IR	1636	Col wnded
Molodin IR	1635	Swiss; 2 bn
Biscarras-Bourdonne IR	1635	Biscarras, 1635; Bourgogne, 1635
Rambures IR	1627	AKA Bearn IR
Piedmont IR	1569	
La Barre		12 guns (4–8 pdr)

2nd Echelon—La Valliere: 7 bn

La Pree-Vervins IR	1632–43	Vervins, 1632; La Pree 1643
Vidame IR	1622	
Watteville IR	1639	1 of 2 bn; Swiss
Ecossais	1635	Scots
Roll IR	1641	Swiss; 20 coy
Breze-Langeron IR	1627–28	Breze, 1627; Langeron, 1628
Guiche-Bussy IR	1627–29	Guiche, 1629; Bussy-Rabutin, 1627

Left Wing—L'Hopital: 13 sqd
1st Echelon—La Ferte: 8 sqd

La Claviere CR		
Beauvau CR	1635?	Liege; col wnded
La Ferte CR	1636–38	2 sqd; La Ferte wnded; 9 coy
Guiche CR	1635	2 sqd; 9 coy
Fusiliers a cheval CR	1636–38	2 sqd ex Richilieu; 9 coy

2nd Echelon—L'Hopital: 5 sqd

Netaf CR		Foreign
Coislin CR	1636–38	1 of 2 sqd
Marolles CR	1634?	
Heudicourt CR		
Harcourt CR	1635	Lorraine

Reserve—Sirot: 4 sqd & 3 bn

Sirot CR	1635	Hungarian; as chevaux leger; 9 coy
Harcourt-Aubeterre-Gesvres	1634–39	Harcourt, 34; Aubeterre, 35; Gesvres, 39
Gendarmes		1 sqd of 3 coys; 200–300
Watteville IR	1639	1 of 2 bn; Swiss

Gendarmes		1 sqd of 3 coys (Queen's Coy); 200–300
Royeaux Bn	1642	8 "royal" coys
Chaost CR		

Total: 14,400 inf in 18 bn; 6400 cav in 32 sqd; 12 guns = 20,800

DEPLOYMENT

The plain southwest of Rocroi measures 2500 meters across, of which the infantry on each side occupied the 1000 meters in the center, the cavalry wings 600–750 meters on each side. The French left (to the north) rested on a marsh; their right, on a woods. Conde's center consisted of two echelons of infantry, deployed in standard checkerboard intervals, followed by a small reserve of both horse and foot. The 2nd echelon was 250 yards (300 paces) behind the 1st and the reserve 335 yards (400 paces) behind the 2nd echelon. The 1st echelon consisted of Conde's 8 largest and most reliable battalions, formed 85 men wide and 10 ranks deep.[30] The right wing, under Conde himself, was in two echelons of 10 and 5 squadrons, Gassion leading the 1st and Conde the 2nd. The left wing, under l'Hopital, consisted of a 1st echelon of 8 squadrons under La Ferte and a 2nd echelon of 5 squadrons under l'Hopital.[31] The squadrons averaged about 200 and were probably 35 files by 6 ranks.[32] All 12 guns were placed in front of the infantry.

The Spanish line, to the east, was almost a mirror image of the French, with two cavalry wings in two echelons each and an infantry center of three echelons. There was about 1000 yards (900 meters) separation between the two battlelines. Isenburg commanded the right wing, of German cavalry, and Alburquerque the Walloons on the left. The center consisted of 5 Spanish tercios, 1 Burgundian, and 2 Italian. Visconti was on the far right, followed by Velandia, then the other 4 Spaniards, then the Burgundians, with Strozzi on the far left.[33] The 1st echelon tercios were organized in the traditional Spanish "double battalion," 70–80 men wide by 20–25 deep. The small battalions in the 2nd and 3rd echelons may have been formed in the newer Imperial style, 50 wide by 10-deep. The 18 field guns in front of the tercios probably averaged heavier than their French counterparts. Fontaine was old and sick and had to be carried in a chair, nevertheless he took his place at the head of his tercios. While his courage was not in doubt, the Spanish center might have benefited from a more active leader.

Isenburg's Germans seem to have been formed in the Imperial style, 200-man squadrons, 50 wide and 4 deep. The Walloons were probably supposed to be the same as the French, 200 sabers, 35 wide, 6-deep, but since they had only 150 men per squadron, they may have been shallower.

The Spanish also had a forlorn hope of up to 1000 men, which they slipped into the woods on Alburquerque's left. Presumably, they hoped this "ambush" would swing the balance against the superior French cavalry.

THE BATTLE OF ROCROI, MAY 19, 1643

Around 3:00 A.M., a Spanish deserter warned Conde and Gassion of the ambush, adding that Beck was on his way with 5000–6000 men. Conde decided that Melo must be defeated before his reinforcements arrived. The French army was awakened and set in order, while a strong forlorn was sent into the woods;

they caught the ambush group still asleep and wiped them out.

The French guns started firing around 4:00, the Spanish replying at once. It was too early for visibility though. Melo was somewhat lost without Beck. He decided to stay on the defensive line until the German finally arrived. After encouraging his officers with an emotional speech, "We want to live and die for our King!"[34] he drifted over to join Isenburg, effectively delegating direction to his wing commanders.

The battle began around 5:00 with a simultaneous attack by both French cavalry wings. Having first disorganized his line by moving through soft ground near the marsh, La Ferte began his charge too fast and too soon, swarming toward Isenburg in a confused mass. Isenburg advanced at a slow trot, keeping his men controlled and together. Superior order defeated impetus; the French fell into rout, and La Ferte, charging bravely, was wounded and taken prisoner. The Germans threw the broken 1st echelon back onto their reserve. L'Hopital tried to counterattack, but he too was wounded and his echelon defeated. L'Hopital and the Marolles Regiment fled into the woods west of the marsh; the rest of the wing left the field altogether.

Having achieved this success, Isenburg wheeled his wing—less elements of the 1st echelon that had scattered in pursuit or had gone after the French baggage[35]—against the French infantry line. At the same time, Visconti, supported by Velandia, advanced in support. Piedmont and Rambures were pushed back, La Barre was killed, and some of the French guns were captured. It seemed to many that the French had lost the battle by 6:00 A.M.

As was so often the case, the result on the other wing was entirely opposite. Gassion and 7 squadrons of the 1st echelon rode through the woods captured earlier and made to envelop Alburquerque's left. Alburquerque moved his front to push them back—they were probably disordered from moving through the woods—but turning his flank to Conde in the process. Conde advanced at a brisk, controlled trot with the remaining 8 squadrons.[36] Alburquerque, in turn, threw in his 2nd echelon. The musketeers in the woods and Picardie added their fire to Conde's attack. Strozzi and the Burgundians in their turn began to press Picardie. After fierce resistance, the Walloons were overwhelmed and dissolved into rout, Alburquerque among them. Strozzi seems to have broken as well.

Those two hotheads, Conde and Gassion, calmly reorganized their cavalry and divided it into two groups. Gassion, with the smaller force, would pursue the Walloons and prevent them from reforming. If he encountered Beck, he would delay his arrival as long as possible. Conde, with the bulk of the cavalry, would defeat the Spanish center and right. The moment that his force was ready, Conde swung behind the Spanish line and struck the flanks of the Walloon and German infantry in the 2nd and 3rd echelons. These units did not put up much of a fight but fell apart at his first onset. It seems likely that they had too many musketeers and not enough pike to stand up to cavalry.

When we compare the quick collapse of these 10 battalions with the brave stands of Schmidt at Wimpfen, Gronsfeld at Lutter, and Holstein at Breitenfeld, it becomes apparent that the new linear style of warfare had its disadvantages. The old tercios could stand as individuals and, without the support of other units, rebuff any number of cavalry. The interdependent linear battalions could not; once the line was outflanked, the whole echelon was lost.

Back to the north, the victorious Isenburg, supported by Visconti and Velandia, had pushed back the French infantry; it seemed as though they, too, would break. It was perhaps a mistake for him to have directed his efforts against the French front echelon, rather than the rearward elements like Conde. Also, Fontaine should have thrown the other 4 Spanish tercios forward, as well as Velandia. In any case, the chance was lost. Sirot, with the reserve, including 800 cavalry, moved to Isenburg's right and halted his advance. Then La Valliere advanced with the French 2nd echelon. The courage of the 2 tercios was equaled by that of Picardie, La Marine, the Swiss, and the Scots. Vivero, with a few Walloons from Alburquerque's broken wing, came up to join Isenburg. Nevertheless, a little ground was lost, and the French retook several of the guns that they had lost earlier. The final outcome hung in the balance, to be decided by the slightest effort in either direction.

Conde had ridden through the Spanish 2nd and 3rd echelons without stopping, then bypassed their 1st echelon to the north, emerging in Isenburg's rear. At about the same time, l'Hopital, with Marolles Cavalry Regiment and parts of his other units, emerged from the woods to strike the German right. The Germans put up a fight, but the situation was hopeless. Isenburg was wounded but managed to get away; Rittburg was struck down and captured. Savary attempted in vain to rally the broken wing.

Melo made his way to the Visconti battalion saying, "Here I wish to die with the Italian gentlemen!" Visconti replied reassuringly, "We are all prepared to die in the service of the king."[37] But the 2 forward tercios were now exposed to overwhelming numbers on all sides. The Italians were cut to pieces and the Spaniards were broken; Velandia, Visconti, and delli Ponti were all killed.

Back in the main line, Fontaine, seeing the way things were going, formed his remaining 5 tercios into a sort of square. He would have done better to have disengaged and left the field, but he probably didn't have a full grasp of the situation on his wings. Also, he may still have hoped that Beck would arrive and salvage the situation. In any case the Spanish had, between 6:00 and 8:00 A.M., lost the battle.

Conde was also thinking of Beck. As quickly as he could, he set his forces in order to take out the Spanish square. The Spanish position was not quite as hopeless as it appeared. The 4 tercios were practically fresh, whereas all of the French were more or less battered. They still had all 18 of their guns, and they had been augmented by the most stubborn elements of the cavalry and the 13 broken battalions.

Conde gave orders to prepare a coordinated attack but did not wait for them to be carried out. As soon as an attack line had been improvised, he fell upon the Spanish front. This group consisted of Picardie, La Marine, the Scots, the 5 Swiss battalions, Piedmont, Rambures, and his own right wing cavalry. Three times they attacked, and three times they were repelled by the gallant Spanish. Old Fontaine, in his chair, was shot and killed in the first repulse.

While this was going on, Suarez and the camp guard tried to slip away with the baggage and siege guns. A squadron of French cavalry spotted them and cut them to pieces, taking the whole train. This minor incident was later exaggerated into a defeat of Beck's column by Gassion; actually Beck was still 20 miles away and entirely unaware of what was happening.

Around 9:30, the French were preparing their fourth assault. This time everything was ready. The French had dragged up some of their guns to support the infantry attack on the square's west face (or front). Sirot's reserve had marched to face the square's south (or left). Gassion's people had returned from the pursuit to report no sign of Beck, they took the east face (or rear). L'Hopital had the north face (or right), and Conde was between l'Hopital and Gassion. The Spanish were completely surrounded and almost out of ammunition; their effectives came to about 8000. Mercador, as acting commander, signaled to Conde for a parley. Unfortunately, when Conde rode forward to speak to him, some of the Spanish mistook his escort for another attack and opened fire. Conde was unhurt, but this launched the fourth attack. The enraged French burst into the Spanish, what was called *furia francese,* and simply overwhelmed them. Little quarter would have been given had Conde not personally averted the threatened massacre.[38] Nevertheless, by 10:00, the square had ceased to exist; there remained only prisoners and the dead, still lying in formation like the veterans they were. Spain had died hard but died nevertheless.

In all, the Spanish lost upwards of 5000 dead and as many captured (mostly from the square), plus 28 guns, 170 ensigns, 60 cornets, and all their baggage, including the army pay chest. The French dead came to 2000.

ROCROI CHRONOLGY

May 18, 5:00 P.M.	French arrival
May 19, 3:00 A.M.	Discovery of the ambush
4:00 A.M.	Artillery open up; destruction of the ambush
5:00 A.M.	French cavalry attack
5–6:00 A.M.	Defeat of both left wings
6–8:00 A.M.	Defeat of Isenburg
8–10:00 A.M.	Destruction of the Spanish square
May 20, 6:30 A.M.	Spanish survivors meet Beck

AFTERMATH

Beck had marched a leisurely 17 miles on the 19th, and spent the night in the village of Philippeville, 5 miles east of Rocroi. Between 6:00 and 7:00 the next morning, Melo, Alburquerque, Isenburg, and others reached the place. Having served in the Imperial Army, Beck was well used to disasters. He pragmatically gathered up as many of the survivors as he could, then fell back 18 miles to the fort of Marienbourg.

Beck was able to regroup 1600 Spanish, 1700 Italians, and 1200 others, for 4500 infantry of the original 18,000—1960 of them were wounded. About 4000 of 5000 cavalry survived. Although the Walloon and German infantry had not suffered heavily in dead, many of their officers were lost. The men had scattered, and the units ceased to exist.

The heaviest loss was the destruction of the Spanish tercios, or rather their myth. Since the battles of Cerignola (1503) and Pavia (1525), the Spanish tercios had enjoyed a reputation for unstoppable courage and invincibility that at once intimidated their opponents and encouraged the men themselves. They had, in fact, a few setbacks over the years, but these were tacitly lost in the parade of victories. Finally they suffered a defeat, a destruction so total that it could not be ignored. Rocroi was the fifth and last of the disasters that destroyed the Spanish system. It was also the worst. Fortresses might be recaptured, rebellions crushed, ships replaced, but a century-old tradition, once lost, is gone forever.

Twelve years after Breitenfeld, the Spanish finally abandoned the tercio. Hereafter, the Spanish army would fight in Dutch-style battalions, like the French. The new methods do not seem to have suited them, though, and the Spanish Army went into a sharp decline.

FOLLOWUP

Although Rocroi was as serious a defeat as Breitenfeld or Nordlingen, its strategic consequences were much less. Having achieved the relief of Rocroi, Conde decided to lay siege to the much-disputed fortress of Thionville. Thionville was a strong, modern fortification, but its normal garrison was only 800. Having expected something of the sort, Beck waited until Conde revealed his objective, then threw another 2000 men into the place. As a result, Thionville was able to hold out for 56 days (June 16–Aungust 10). The season being almost over, Conde broke off operations and returned to France.

Frederick Henry had some idea of exploiting the situation, but Beck combined the surviving troops with Cantelmo's corps of observation and demonstrated so fiercely that the Dutch were bluffed into backing down.

THE WAR IN FLANDERS, 1644–48

King Philip and his councilors realized that after a Rocroi there was no longer any hope of victory. The Imperial alliance was tacitly discontinued; Spain no longer had any money or men to spare. All remaining resources would be concentrated in Spain itself, against Catalonia and Portugal. Peace would be made with the Dutch on any terms that could be obtained. Until peace could be made, Flanders would have to fend for itself.

The Army of Flanders had lost its best men, its reputation, and its funding, but it retained its professionalism. That and the remaining "superfortresses" were the only defense against the allies. They proved sufficient. There was no collapse such as had nearly occurred in 1632.

In 1644, Conde was diverted to Germany to assist Turenne,[39] while a new French force under the incompetent duke of Orleans,[40] undertook the offensive. At the same time, Frederick Henry conducted his last great siege, the capture of Sas van Gent, near Ghent (July 27–September 5). Melo, Beck, and Isenburg were able to keep him from attacking Antwerp or Ghent. Orleans took advantage of their distraction to capture the fortress of Gravelines.

In 1645, Frederick Henry and his war party came under political attack for their refusal to accept the Spanish peace initiative. Nevertheless, he was able to finance the siege of Ghent. Ghent proved too strong to take, but, as it turned out, it was merely a feint. The real target, Hulst, was surprised, and its 5 protecting sub-forts fell almost without resistance. The demoralized garrison surrendered (November 4) after less than a month's siege. On the other front, Orleans captured the medium-size fortress of Mardyck near Dunkirk. In an interesting display of professionalism, the Spanish waited until the French had retired into winter quarters and surprised the place, reversing the French gains of the year.

In 1646, Frederick Henry was able to take the offensive only because of the dispatch of a French corps of 6000 to assist him. Nevertheless, three separate attacks on Antwerp were rebuffed by the Spanish field force. The Dutch then besieged the weak fort of Venlo, but it resisted so unexpectedly that they broke off the operation. To the south, Conde had, to his chagrin, been subordinated to Orleans. After capturing Courtrai and recapturing Mardyck, Orleans lost interest and returned to Paris. Conde took advantage of his absence to undertake the siege of Dunkirk (September 19–October 11). As Dunkirk was the chief base of the Flanders navy, its conquest was the most important success since Rocroi.

The years 1647–48 saw a major realignment of the situation. The peace party came to power in Holland and discontinued the war. The Spanish-Dutch War was officially ended with the Treaty of Munster (January 1648). It represented defeat for Spain, but the situation elsewhere was so critical that King Philip could only be grateful to have ended one war at least. At the same time, the Archduke Leopold, from Germany, had been appointed governor-general; his tenure saw a brief reinvigoration of the Spanish cause. The French, although under the aggressive Gassion, lost ground in 1647.[22]

Table 5.4
Selected Sieges 1635–48

Year		Days	Attacker	Defender	Note
1635	Louvain	15	50,000 FrDt	4000 Sp	Failed
1636	Schenkenschans	40	30,000 Dt	1500 Sp	900 Sp killed
1637	Breda	129	18,000 Dt	3500 Sp	1900 Sp killed
1637	Landrecies	7	20,000 Fr	?? Sp	
1643	Thionville	56	21,000 Fr	2800 Sp	Mined
1644	Sas van Gent	40	20,000 Dt	?? Sp	Mined
1646	Dunkirk	35	30,000 Fr	3000 Sp	Plus 5000 militia
1647	Landrecies	21	16,000 Fr	1600 Sp	

In 1648, Conde resumed command in Flanders, opposed by the archduke and Beck. He captured Ypres, only to lose Courtrai.[23] Then the Spanish-German force laid siege to Lens. In the last great battle of the war, Conde shattered their army and retook both Lens and Furnes (Battle of Lens, August 20). Events were to render this victory irrelevant. The Peace of Westphalia was to end the war in Germany, while the outbreak of civil war in France, the War of the Fronde, gave Spain a chance to recover. The Franco-Spanish War was to drag on to 1659, and Conde would soon be commanding the army that he had destroyed.

SOURCES

The indispensable work on the Army of Flanders is Parker, *The Army of*

Flanders and the Spanish Road 1567–1659 (1972); unfortunately, everything after 1609 is treated only in passing. An excellent, if general, account of the Spanish-Dutch War as a whole is Israel, *The Dutch Republic and the Hispanic World* (1982). Rocroi itself tends to be treated as a drama rather than military history. There are many brief English accounts in "Famous Battle" collections, but they are of little or no value. The best French account is D'Aumale (1886); Canovas del Castillo (1888), the best Spanish. Perkins (1902) has an interesting passage about the primary sources. The modern French treatment in Barbe (1977) is fairly detailed, but the section on the Spanish contains too many errors.

APPENDIX A: THE SPANISH ARMY AT ROCROI

The Spanish infantry was organized into regiments, traditionally known as tercios; these units claimed corporate descent from the invincible tercios of the early 16th century and from the original Army of Flanders of 1567. After the reorganization of 1636, Spanish, Italian, Burgundian, and Irish tercios had the same organization. In theory at least, a tercio consisted of 12 companies, each of 200 men: 11 officers, 65 armored pike, 34 unarmored pike, 30 musketeers, and 60 arquebusiers. A Walloon company was slightly different: 11 officers, 47 armored pike, and 142 muskets. Germans fought in regiments organized like those of Austria and Bavaria.

Traditionally, the Spanish cavalry had no administrative grouping above the company level, the loose companies fighting in temporary squadrons on an ad hoc basis. In 1642, under Dutch and Swedish influence, they were reorganized into regiments, apparently of 6 companies of 100 horse each. By this time the Flanders horse was predominantly Walloon, but Spanish and Italian officers remained common.

The Army of Flanders was a most heterogeneous force, drawing recruits from Spain, Portugal, Italy, Franche Comte (=Burgundy), England, Ireland, Germany, and Flanders itself. Spanish foot were the elite of the army, followed closely by the Italians. The Burgundians and Irish were also highly regarded. The Walloons, most numerous of the contingents, had a reputation for unreliability, and their performance was spotty. It was a 17th century truism that men fought best farthest from home, so the same Walloons who were despised in Flanders were valued in Germany and constituted an elite in Spain itself. Most of these units were recruited from subjects of the Most Catholic King. The Germans were the only true mercenaries in the army, and even they were drawn from Catholic Germans and Hapsburg allies. Nevertheless, the German performance in Flanders was generally disappointing. Spanish policy was to rely on the Spaniards and Italians, while the more numerous Germans and Walloons were, as much as possible, relegated to garrisons and supports.

The Spanish at Rocroi have been variously estimated from 28,000 (by Conde) to 20,000 (by the Spanish). There is some basis to both figures:

	French Figures	Spanish Figures	Estimate
Infantry	18,000	18,000	18,000
Walloon Cavalry	2,000	2,000	2,000
German Cavalry	3,000	—	3,000
Beck Detachment	5,000	—	
Total	28,000	20,000	23,000

The French were in error in assuming that Beck took part in the battle.

The strengths of the individual units can only be approximated. Spanish reports state that 3400 Spaniards were killed, 2000 captured, and 1600 escaped, for a total of 7000 men in 5 battalions. As there were 12,000 men in the 1st echelon, this indicates 5000 men in the 2 Italian and 1 Burgundian battalions, probably 3000–4000 Italians and 1000–2000

Burgundians. The 2nd and 3rd echelons totaled 5000 Walloons and Germans. The composition of the 1000 men in the ambush is unknown—Spanish accounts do not mention them—but picked Walloons with Spanish cadre seems probable.

The 12,000 in the 1st echelon seems fairly solid, as does the 2000 Walloon cavalry, but the 5000 reserve infantry and 3000 German cavalry may have been derived from a rough estimate of units: 10 battalions of 500 and 14 squadrons of 200. The "1000 musketeers" in the ambush was strictly a French guesstimate.

Units	Notes
Velandia IR	Spanish "old" tercio; col KIA
Villalva IR	Spanish "old" tercio; col KIA
Mercador IR	Spanish "old" tercio; ex-Alburquerque; col captured
Garcies IR	Spanish tercio; col captured
Castelvi IR	Spanish-Burgundian tercio; col captured
Strozzi IR	Italian tercio
Visconti IR	Italian tercio; col KIA
Delli Ponti IR	Italian tercio; col KIA
Gramont IR	Burgundian tercio
St Amour IR	Burgundian tercio
D'Ambise IR	German; Walloon col; col captured
Montecuccoli IR	German; not Raimondo Montecuccoli; col captured
Frangipani IR	German
Rittburg IR	" AKA Riedburg, Ritburg; col captured
?	" Isenburg Leib?
Prince de Ligny IR	Walloon tercios
Ribaucourt IR	"
Granges IR	"
Meghen IR	"
Bassigny IR	"

As regards the cavalry, we know that Melo had 105 companies in all, with 6 German regiments, 1 Croat, a squadron of free companies, and 5 or 6 Walloon regiments. Alburquerque's 2000 Walloons were divided into 15 squadrons. Isenburg's wing was divided into 14. Assuming that the German and Croat regiments numbered the standard 10 companies, and allowing 5 free companies, this leaves 30 for the Walloons. It is tempting to suggest that the Walloons had 5 regiments of 6 companies each, and that each divided into 3 squadrons of 2 companies each. The German regiments probably formed 2 squadrons each; the free companies and Croats, 1 each.

Only one of Isenburg's regiments is positively identified, the Rittburg Cuirassiers. This may or may not be the same unit as the Imperial regiment of 1631-36. Possible regiments are Savary, de Vera, Donquel, and Isenburg Leib.

Three of the Walloon squadrons were led by Alburquerque and his lieutenant generals Vivero and Villamor. Possibles include the Burgy and Padilla regiments.

APPENDIX B: THE FRENCH ARMY AT ROCROI

By 1643, the French Army had evolved somewhat from 1634, but the changes were not uniform nor in a single direction.

French infantry regiments were divided into four classes: the "Vieux" (old), the "petit vieux" (little old), common regiments, and foreign regiments. The Vieux were the 7 regiments that dated before 1587; they were permanent standing units, considered an elite, and were larger than ordinary regiments. A common regiment numbered 12 companies of 100 men each; they were temporary organizations intended for short-term wartime service and might be raised and disbanded as needed. These were normally raised by nobleman-owners as a "gift" to the king, and were much the same as the military enterpriser regiments in Germany. The "petit vieux" were temporary regiments that had been made permanent; this advance in status was symbolized by the grant of a special ensign, the *drapeau*. Foreign regiments were ranked between the temporaries and the petit vieux; the most valued were the Swiss, the Scots, and the Irish, followed by the Germans. Other foreign units were Italians, Lorrainers, Poles, Walloons, Corsicans, Grisons, Catalans, and Liegeois (the cavalry also numbered Hungarians and Croats).

French infantry regiments were generally understrength, especially the temporary units. These were often only 720 strong when raised, what contemporaries called "12 for 20." Many were broken up in their first year of service, the men being used to fill out more valuable units. In battle it might be necessary to combine 2 or 3 regiments to form 1 battalion. There was always a high degree of turnover in regiments, but quite a few achieved petit vieux status and permanency.

Foreign units might be quite large—this was especially true of the Swiss—or no better than temporary regiments.

Table 5.5
French Infantry Regiments 1635–48

	Disbanded 1635–47	Lasted to 1648	Total Raised
Pre-1618	2	19	N/A
1618–34	42	40	200*
1635	48	18	66
1636	40	13	53
1637	13	4	17
1638	10	6	16
1639	7	1	8
1640	16	3	19
1641	3	7	10
1642	5	2	7
1643	3	6	9
1644	6	12	18
1645	4	10	14
1646	3	17	20
1647	0	15	15
1648	0	8	8

* including 118 IRs disbanded prior to 1635.

Prior to the declaration of war, the French cavalry were organized in individual companies, similar to Spanish practice. This was to remain true of the 9 guard companies and the gendarmes, but the line cavalry, what the French called *Cavalerie Legere* or chevaux leger ("Light Cavalry"; actually they were "light" only by comparison with the gendarmes), were formed into 12 regiments (of 7 companies each), plus a carabin regiment, in May 1635. Eleven more regiments were added by September, exclusive of the 16 (?) Weimar regiments. By 1638, they had been reorganized into 36 regiments, each of 8 companies of light cavalry and 1 of carabins (for skirmishing). There were an additional 25 foreign regiments, including the Weimarians. The turnover in cavalry regiments was noticeably less than with the infantry. In battle, these regiments were expected to provide 2 or 3 squadrons of 200 sabers each.

The gendarme companies remained "free"; they seem to have been a sort of hobby for

The Battle of Rocroi

their aristocratic owner-captains, and their organizations varied. The better companies numbered 100 men or more, most of them about 50, so there were 2–4 companies to a squadron. Then there were "garde" companies. These were not part of the royal guard but were personal escort units for French generals, similar to the leib units of the German war. They seem to have run 100–200 strong and might form a squadron on their own or combine with gendarmes. There were at least some cases where a commander had a light regiment, gendarme company, and garde all grouped together at the same battle. Finally, the French had (at least until 1642) an elite cavalry company called *La Cornette Blanche* (the White Cornet), again 100–200 strong.

Turenne's Army of Germany was largely ex-Weimarian and heavily influenced by the Swedish system, whereas the armies on the Flanders front were still following Dutch practices as late as Rocroi. Most of the French seem to have retained the 10-deep infantry battalion until about 1647 and switched to 8 thereafter, dropping to 6 during the 1650s. Although fusils early became popular in the French Army, the depth of formation reduced their efficacy.

Like the Dutch and the Spanish, the French tried to supply bread to their troops by contract, but, between poor financial practices, sloppy administration, and difficulties of transport, the results were much less effective. Once outside their borders, and often enough within, the French had to rely on local supply, by kontribution and plundering.

The French at Rocroi have been estimated from 20,000 (by Conde) to 22,000 (by the Spanish), to 23,000 (by D'Aumale). It seems to be a matter of Conde rounding down his numbers and the Spanish rounding them up: 14,000–15,000 foot and 6000–7000 horse.

Units	Date	Notes
Gardes		Conde's Personal Guard; 1 coy; 200?
Royal CR		2 sqd; did well
Mestre de Camp General CR	1635	Gassion?; 2 sqd; 9 coy
Guiche CR	1635	2 sqd; 9 coy
Marolles CR	1634?	Associated with Lenoncourt? Did well
La Ferte-St Nectaire CR	1636–38	2 sqd; La Ferte wnded; 9 coy
Lenoncourt CR	1636–38	9 coy
Coislin CR	1636–38	2 sqd; 9 coy
Sully CR		
Roquelaure CR		
Menneville CR		
Chaost CR		
La Claviere CR		
Heudicourt CR		
Leschelle CR	1635	Liege; 9 coy
Beauvau CR	1635?	Liege; col wnded
Harcourt CR	1635	Lorraine
Sirot CR	1635	Hungarian; 9 coy
Sillart CR	1634?	Zillard? German, ex-Weimar? Did well
Vamberg CR		Foreign (German?); did well
Netaf CR		Foreign
Raab CR		Croat; did well
Chacks CR		Croat
Fusiliers a cheval CR	1636–38	2 sqd; ex Richilieu DR; 9 coy
Gendarmes		2 sqd; 6 coys; Queen's Coy was elite
Picardie IR	1569	Vieux; did well
Piedmont IR	1569	Vieux

La Marine IR	1635	Petit vieux, later vieux
Rambures IR	1627	AKA Bearn IR ; petit vieux
Ecossais	1635	Scots Guards (junior)
Molodin IR	1635	2 bn; Swiss (Soleure); did well
Watteville IR	1639	2 bn; Swiss (Berne)
Roll IR	1641	Swiss (Soleure); 20 coy
Persan IR	1636	Col wnded
Biscarras IR	1635	
Bourdonne IR	1635?	Bourgogne?
Vidame IR	1622	
Vervins IR	1632	
La Pree IR	1643	Did well
Breze IR	1627	
Langeron IR	1627	
Bussy IR	1627	Bussy-Rabutin
Guiche IR	1629	
Aubeterre IR	1635	
Gesvres IR	1639	
Harcourt IR	1634?	
Royeaux Bn	1642	Bn formed from 8 of 30 royal coys

12 guns under La Barre

APPENDIX C: THE DUTCH WAR EFFORT

The Spanish-Dutch War was not merely a secondary theater of the Thirty Years War but a fiercely waged conflict in its own right. In a sense, it was the first world war. While the main armies maneuvered in Flanders, the privateers of Dunkirk ravaged both Dutch commerce and the vital fisheries. Lesser forces were fighting in the Mediterranean and the Caribbean, Africa, India, the Philippines, and Brazil. Such remote potentates as the emperor of China, the shogun of Japan, and the kings of Ceylon and Kongo were drawn into the conflict. The Dutch navy, although the best in the world, was overburdened by its mission; in addition to supporting the army and blockading the Flemish coast, it had to protect the fisheries and supply escorts to the far-flung trade convoys. It became necessary for mercantile and provincial interests to supplement the regular forces with hired ships and privateers. The overseas war was conducted by the semipublic trading monopolies, the East India Company operating in the India-Ceylon-China-Japan-Philippines area, while the West India Company attacked Spain and Portugal in the Caribbean, Brazil, West Africa, and Angola.

The Dutch Army was a supreme triumph of practicality over system. At a time where every nation was modernizing, standardizing organization, and rationalizing finance, the much-admired Dutch were doing precisely the opposite, with great success. There was no attempt at standardizing units; rather, their size differed according to nationality, the status of the officer commanding, and the financial situation. An infantry regiment might have 4 companies or 19, with company sizes of 50, 60, 70, 80, 90, 100, 200, or 250 men. Cavalry regiments ran 3-10 companies, of 70, 85, 100, 150, or 250 sabers. Note that companies varied within regiments, so the colonel's company might be 150-200 strong, while the juniormost mustered 70 or so. Whatever the size of the regiment, in battle it would be divided into 2 or 3 battalions of 550 each—200 pike, 300 musketeers, and 50 arquebusiers for the forlorn, the formation 50 wide and 10-deep. Of course, this varied too. At the Battle of Nieuport (July 2, 1600), the largest battalion had 750 men, the smallest 250. Cavalry fought in squadrons of 300, 50 wide by 6-deep.[43]

It is theorized that the Dutch used firelocks on a large scale, issuing snaphances during the mid-1620s and fusils by 1640. While it is certainly true that the Dutch were the first power to adopt the flintlock as the standard infantry weapon, the exact chronology of this transition is uncertain. The degree of Swedish influence accepted by Frederick Henry is equally unclear. It is known that ex-Swedish officers served in the Dutch Army after 1632. A diagram of 1650 shows Dutch battalions drawn up only 6-deep and supported by light 3 pdrs. On the other hand, as late as 1642, the English referred to 10-deep "Dutch brigades," as opposed to 6-deep "Swedish" ones. Note that the deep formations largely nullified the rate of fire advantage of the firelock.

The Dutch were hailed throughout Europe as the best paymasters in Europe; however, this refers to reliability rather than scale. A Dutch infantryman earned about 60–70 florins per annum, as opposed to 72 for a Swede, 90 for a Walloon, and 108 for an Imperial. Moreover, the Dutchman was subject to deductions for food and equipment. However, he actually received his pay, regularly and in cash, which was more than any other army could boast. This was not achieved by a well-organized central system of finance. Rather, the Dutch divided the army, by regiments and companies, among the seven provinces of the republic, and each provincial government was individually responsible for paying its own share. It sometimes became necessary for the States General to nag a province to do its assigned part.[44] If a province point blank refused to agree to an increase, it could delay operations. On the plus side, as Dutch troops were mustered and paid every 10 days, fraud was reduced and they always knew exactly how many men were available.

Dutch war expenditure ran from a low of 13,000,000 guilders a year (in the early 1620s) to a peak of about 20,000,000. As a guilder was about 60% of a florin, this came to 8–12 million florins or 5–8 million talers. This expenditure was divided into regular items and special expenditures, the latter of which had to be re-authorized annually.

Model Dutch Budget 1621–47	Guilders	Forces
1st Regular Bill (1621–47)	9,441,010.75	48,153
2nd Regular Bill (1626–47)	1,097,067	7,000
3rd Regular Bill (1627–47)	639,000	3,000
6000 Waardgelders	200,000	(6,000)
Gieten van Geschut	50,000	
The Navy	2,000,000	40+ warships
West India Company	600,000	
Emden Garrison (1627–47)	62,000	
Interest on Loans (1629–48)	200,000	

Annual Expenditures	Guilders
Logistics (army supply)	100,000–600,000
The field laager (fortified camp)	500,000–3,000,000
Fortifications	200,000–600,000
50 coys of 150 men (1629–48)	900,000
Rouillac & Mountjoy Cavalry (1628–33)	84,300
Other Troops	72,000–2,000,000
Subsidies to Germany, Denmark, Sweden	100,000–600,000
Extraordinary Expenses	approx. 200,000

Logistics and lagger expenses varied according to the size of the army and the difficulty of the year's operations (siege). The "50 companies of 1628" were a sore point with the Holland taxpayers, who, on occasion, reduced them in size (from 150 to 100) and tried to shift them to the "commonality" budget (reducing the funds available for operations). The "other troops" were raised for specific operations on a temporary basis, including the crises of 1629 and 1636 and the hire of Mansfeld and Brunswick in 1622. They also included garrisons of fortresses captured or built after 1622.

The Dutch paid out subsidies to various Protestants in the German War, 920,000 guilders to the Bohemians 1618–20; 1,340,000 to Christian of Denmark 1625–29; 30,000 to Stralsund in 1629; 750,000 to Gustavus Adolphus 1631–33, plus varying sums (up to 150,000 a year) to Friedrich of the Palatinate 1621–32. In addition, they supplied troops and arms, at varying terms.[26] These subsidies dried up after 1634. The French subsidized the Dutch 1630–47 to the tune of 23.3 million livres (about 11 million guilders). After 1640, the Dutch began to subsidize the Portuguese secessionists, also providing a contingent of troops and naval support.

Table 5.6
French Subsidies 1630–47 (millions of livres)

Years	Per Annum	Total
1630–33	1	4
1634–35	2.3	4.6
1636	1.5	1.5
1637–47	1.2	13.2
1630–47		23.3

APPENDIX D: THE GARRISONS OF THE NETHERLANDS

Spanish lists of December 1626 and March 1628[27] give the fixed garrisons and their strengths thus:

Province	Fortress	Dec 1626	Feb 1628	1628 Plan
Flanders Province	Hulst & area	600	884	1,500
	Dunkirk		704	(1,000)
	Damme	1,000	481	
	Sas van Gent	600	500	600
	Bruges-Ghent canal	1,400	481	400
	Bruges	"	99	"
	Dendermonde		355	
	Blankenberge canal		318	
	Mardijk (Mardyck)		317	
	Nieuport		319	
	Cadzant forts		280	
	Aalst		220	
	Blankenberge		172	
	Ostend	1,000	166	800
	Passendale		134	
	Veurne		113	
	Minor places		182	
	Total:	(6,000)	5,750	
Brabant	Breda & area (taken 1625)	2,000	4,067	2,500
	's-Hertogenbosch	1,500	2,730	2,500
	Zandvliet-Antwerp	600	3,518	2,360
	Total:	(3,962)	10,315	
Netherlands	Grol (lost 1627)*	1,500		
	Oldenzaal (lost 1626)	(1,500)		
Maas	Maastricht		1,000	
	Roermond	400	506	
	Venlo		94	

Walloonia	Total: Cambrai		1,600 558	
Germany	Wesel	2,500	3,077	2,750
	Rheinberg	800	1,695	1,800
	Lingen	2,000	1,353	2,200
	Orsoy		434	
	Lippstadt		696	
	Dusseldorf	600	581	200
	Geldern	400	400	400
	Julich (taken 1622)		397	
	Papenmutz		270	
	Duren		186	
	Minor places		2,016	
	Total:		11,105	
Grand Total:		(31,046)	29,328	

* Grol was defended by 900 men in 1627.

Garrison sizes differed from year to year, sometimes sharply. As this list indicates, there were only a few strong places with garrisons of 1000 or more. The average fortress ran 300–600. In addition to the regular army, the Spanish possessed locally paid forces of 12,000–16,000 (Walloons), mostly employed in garrisons and defenses. Some areas possessed unpaid militias as well. Away from the battlefront, even such important towns as Brussels, Louvain, Lille, and Arras were relegated to locals. After 1635, there were two fronts, and the garrison requirements rose to 44,000 by 1637 (excluding locals).

A Dutch list of 1607[47] gives an idea of their later defenses:

Province	Fortress	Coys	Garrison
Holland	Heusden	8	1,000
	Geertruidenberg	7	800
Brabant	Breda	26	3,000
	Grave	23	2,700
	Bergen-op-Zoom	19	2,300
	Willemstad	7	900
	Lillo	4	550
Gelderland	Doesburg	22	2,600
	Nijmegen	21	2,500
	Zutphen	16	2,000
	Bredevoort	14	1,700
Flanders	Sluys	16	2,000
	Aardenburg	12	1,500
Overijssel	Deventer	?	?
	Steenwijk	4	550
Drenthe	Coevorden	12	1,600
Groningen	Delfzijl	?	?
Wedde	Bourtange	6	800
	Bellingwolde	3	400
Moers	Moers	3	400
Cleves	Schenkenschans	4	550

Like the Spanish, the Dutch delegated defense of important rear area town, including Amsterdam, Utrecht, and Flushing, to local forces and part-time soldiers (*waardgelders*).

Noteworthy wartime garrisons included:
Julich 1621–22   3000–4000 men
Papenmutz 1622   500 men

Breda 1624–25	3500 men
Amsterdam 1628	800 militia
Amersfoort 1629	7 coys
Venlo 1637	1200 men

APPENDIX E: MINOR ACTIONS

Action of Avesnes (Avein), May 22, 1635

A French army of 22,000 foot and 4500 horse under the incompetent Marshal Chatillon and Richilieu's brother-in-law Breze encountered a Spanish force of 14,000–16,000 under the inept Prince Thomas of Savoy near Avesnes on the France-Flanders border. Thomas's corps was supposed to be a blocking/delaying force, but he allowed them to be drawn into a fight in the open with Chatillon's much bigger army. The Spanish were routed with the loss of 4000.

Action of Kallo (Calloo), June 1638

A Dutch army of 6000 Scots, Germans, and Dutchmen under Prince Willem of Nassau, a cousin of Frederick Henry, was dispatched ahead of the main army to capture 3 Scheldt bank fortlets near Antwerp. The Antwerp garrison, under Governor de Silva, counterattacked, forced their way through the protecting dykes, and surprised Willem in a night attack, near the fort of Kallo. The Spanish loss was 284 killed and 822 wounded; the Dutch lost several hundred dead, 2500 captured, several dozen cannon, and 81 barges. This was the worst Dutch defeat of the war.

Siege of St Omer (Saint-Omer), May 24–July 16, 1638

A French army overestimated at 30,000 under Chatillon engaged 20,000 Spanish and Germans defending this medieval town. As usual, Chatillon got the worst of it. After losing 4000 men, the French were forced to retreat.

Battle of Thionville, June 7, 1639

A French army of 8000 foot and 2600 horse under the Marquis de Feuquieres was besieging the fortress of Thionville, when Piccolomini appeared at the head of 14,000 Spanish and Germans. Despite the unfavorable terrain, Feuquieres proudly refused to retreat. In the subsequent battle, the superior Spanish artillery and infantry proved decisive, despite the courage of the French Navarre IR and their cavalry. Feuquieres was killed, and most of his infantry were captured for less than a thousand Spanish casualties.

Action of Marfee (La Marfée), July 6, 1641

The Count of Soissons, former commander of the French army in Flanders, attempted to organize a rising against the Richelieu regime. A Spanish-German army under the always incompetent Lamboy advanced to support him, but was blocked near Sedan by a French force under the equally incompetent Chatillon. Both armies were in the 10,000–12,000 range; the French included the Queen's Gendarme Coy, the Duke of Orleans Gendarme Coy, and Piedmont IR. Chatillon launched a head-on attack against higher ground but was beaten off and driven from the field. However, Soissons had been killed in the fighting, and the revolt collapsed.

Action of Kempton, January 17, 1642

Lamboy with a Spanish-Westphalian army of perhaps 10,000 engaged a similarly sized French-Weimar-Hessian force under the able Guebriant at Kempton, west of Cologne. Lamboy should probably have waited for the arrival of reinforcements under his Imperial colleague Hatzfeld; however, he did assume a strong defensive position. Guebriant

The Battle of Rocroi

pinned his front with infantry, then turned both of his flanks with his superior cavalry. Lamboy lost 2500 killed and 4000 captured as well as 120 flags and all his guns.

Action of Honnecourt, May 26, 1642

A strong Spanish army under Melo and Beck recaptured the fortress of Lens, then laid siege to nearby La Bassee. Marshal Harcourt, commanding the French army in Picardy, and Marshal Guiche, commander of Champagne, agreed to relieve the town. Advised of their approach, Melo took 10,000 men to intercept them, catching them at the abbey of Honnecourt on the Escault River.

Melo deployed in two wings:

Right Wing—Velada: 3 Bns & Spanish-Italian Cavalry

Units	Notes
Alburquerque IR	Spanish "old" tercio; later Mercador
Avila IR	Spanish "old" tercio
Mercador Forlorn	Spanish; 1000 musketeers
Vivero	Cavalry

Left Wing—Beck: 9 IRs & Walloon Cavalry

Velandia IR	Spanish "old" tercio
Villalva IR	Spanish "old" tercio
Castelvi IR	Spanish-Burgundian tercio
Strozzi IR	Italian tercio
Guasco IR	Italian "old" tercio
Delli Ponti IR	Italian tercio
Prince de Ligny IR	Walloon tercios
? IR	" "
Bucquoy	Walloon Cavalry (several regiments)
Padilla KUR	Walloons

Total: 8000 infantry; 2000 cavalry; ? guns = 10,000

The French mustered 7000 infantry, 3000 cavalry, and 10 guns, including the Piedmont IR, the Dauphin Gendarme Coy, and the elite Cornet Blanche. The French also divided into two wings, the right, under Guiche, facing Beck, and the left, under Harcourt, facing Velada. The French position was fairly strong. Their right rested on the river itself and was protected by the abbey and a light woods. The left was open but on higher ground and shielded by 2 earthworks in front of the main line.

Melo put his larger force under Beck, possibly fearing that the superior French cavalry would turn his right. The opposite occurred; after a brisk fight in which Mercador's musketeers proved invaluable, Velada and Vivero turned the French left. The Avila and Alburquerque tercios were repelled at first but carried the works in their second assault. At about the same time, Beck's group penetrated the woods and hit Guiche. The 3 Italian tercios spearheaded the attack, followed closely by the Spanish. The Walloon cavalry traversed the woods without difficulty. Guiche was pushed out of Honnecourt at about the same time Avila and Alburquerque broke through Harcourt. The French abandoned the field, losing 1200 dead, 3000 captured, all 10 guns, and "many" flags. Total Spanish loss was set at 400.

Battle of Lens, August 20, 1648

Archduke Leopold and Beck were so strongly positioned on high ground that Conde (rather uncharacteristically) decided that they were too strong to attack. He drew up his army and staged a formal retreat in the presence of the enemy. Beck, leading some Lorrainer horse and Croats, harried his rearguard cavalry and gained the advantage. He then sent to the archduke to join him in mauling the fleeing French.

This was exactly as Conde had planned it. Once he had drawn the archduke onto the plain, his army suddenly reformed into line of battle. It is interesting that the stolid and professional Beck was so thoroughly deceived. In the ensuing fight, Gramont's charge shattered the Spanish right. Conde was halted on their left, but Erlach's reserve gave him the victory. While Conde and Ligniville were struggling, Erlach enveloped the open Spanish left and turned the flank. In the center the Spanish infantry had been more successful. 4 of the French 1st echelon battalions recoiled from contact, leaving the French Guard and Scots Guard on their own. The Bonifaz and Bentivoglio battalions overwhelmed the French Guards in a "revenge for Rocroi." Nevertheless, with both wings routed, the Spanish found themselves in the same position as Fontaine at Rocroi. This time there was no heroic last stand but only a battlefield capitulation.

French Army—Conde
Right Wing—Conde: 17 cavalry sqds
1st Echelon—Conde: 9 sqd
   Conde Garde, Orleans Garde (2), La Melleraye, St Simon, Bussy, Streif (Ger), Harcourt, Beaujeu,
2nd Echelon—8 sqd
   Chappes (2), Ravenel, Coudray, Salbrick, Vidame, Villiette (2)
Center—Chatillon: 12 infantry bns & 6 sqds
1st Echelon—7 bns
   Picardie-Orleans, Erlach (Ger)-Perrault, Scot, French (2), and Swiss Guards; Persan IR
Cavalry— 12 coys=6 sqds (King's, Queen's, Conde, Longueville, Conti, Conde, and
   Orleans gendarme coys; Orleans and Enghien chevaux leger coys)
2nd Echelon—5 bns
   La Reine,* Erlach (Fr)-Razilly, Mazarin (It), Conti, Conde IRs
Left Wing—Gramont: 16 cavalry sqds
—Gramont: 9 sqd
   Gramont-La Ferte Gardes, Carabins, Mazarin (2), Gramont (2), La Ferte (2), Beins (2)
2nd Echelon—La Ferte: 7 sqd
   Roquelaure, Gesvre, Lillebonne, Noitlieu (2), Meille, Chemerault
Reserve—Erlach: 6 cavalry sqds
   Erlach (2), Ruvigny (2), Sirot (2)
Total: 16,000 men in 12 bn, 45 sqd & 18 guns
* La Reine was reinforced by elements of the Rokeby (Eng) IR and the La Bassee garrison.

Spanish Army—Archduke
Right Wing—Bucquoy: 27 coys of Walloon cavalry in 2 echelons
Center—Beck: 16 infantry bns & 15 cavalry sqds (
1st Echelon—10 inf bns (3 Lorrainer, 2 Walloon, 2 Irish, 1 German, 1 Italian, 1 "new"
   Spanish) & 13 cav sqds
2nd Echelon—6 inf bns (3 "old" Spanish, 3 mixed) & 2 cav sqds
Left Wing— Ligniville: 20 "large" sqds of Lorrainer cavalry in 2 echelons
Total: 18,000 men in 16 bn, 62 (?) sqds & 38 guns
Units present included the the Bonifaz and Bentivoglio IRs and the Bucquoy and Savary CRs. Possibles include Ligny, Bar, Bargue, Broce, Solis, and Morphis (Right); Beck, Toleac, Dario, Moroy, Hove, Chastein, Treucoeur, Touenin, Silly, Blonqurt (Blankhart?), Verdusan, Gondrecourt, Clinchan, Doumarest, Loues, and St Amour (Center), and Ligniville, Auton, Luneville, Mentauban, Salm, Castelet, Aigre, Valentin, Fauge, and Loues (Left).

The French were probably in battalions of 600–700 formed 8-deep and squadrons of about 200, 4- or 5-deep. The Spanish were probably using a version of the Imperial system, with battalions of 500–600 formed 10-deep, and squadrons of 100–200, 4- or 5-

deep. It would seem that Beck put too much of his cavalry in the center and not enough on the right. D'Aumale says that Beck's 13 center squadrons were in 4 groups in intervals between battalions along the 1st echelon line, rather than behind the foot or alternating, squadron-battalion-squadron. Had the archduke intended to fight a battle, he would have waited for the return of 4 or 5 cavalry regiments that had been detached to forage.

The French lost 1500 in all; the Spanish 3000 dead and 5000 captured, plus 100 flags and all 38 guns. Beck was among the prisoners and died of his wounds. The archduke has been criticized for abandoning his men to save himself.

Aug 20, 5:00 A.M.	French retire; skirmish
6:30 A.M.	Archduke advances
8:00 A.M.	Armies assume line of battle
8:30 A.M.	French cavalry attack
9:00 A.M.	Fighting in the center begins
11:30 A.M.	Spanish surrender

APPENDIX F: THE FRANCO-SPANISH WAR

The period 1640–43 saw the combatants evenly matched, the Spanish holding the edge on the Flanders front, the French gaining ground in Italy (Battle of Casale, April 29, 1640; actions of Turin, July 11, 1640, and Ivree, March 23, 1641). Internal revolts hampered both sides, but the protonationalist revolutions in Portugal and Catalonia were much more dangerous than the anti-taxation peasant uprisings in France. In 1642, the French took advantage of Spain's internal troubles to overrun Rousillon and intervene in Catalonia, winning the battles of Montjuich (January 26) and Lerida (October 7).

In 1643, the disaster of Rocroi effectively severed the Hapsburg coalition. The Spanish discontinued their financial support of Austria—they no longer had anything to spare. Ferdinand III, on his side, abandoned hope of victory and began the negotiations that would, in five years, end the war—separate negotiations that did not include Spain.

The deaths of Cardinal Richelieu (December 4, 1642) and King Louis XIII (May 15, 1643) did not immediately hamper French progress; the unpopular Cardinal Mazarin proved an adequate replacement for both.

The "decisive" victory did not bring about a rapid Spanish collapse; if anything, they redoubled their determination. The French at last secured the much-disputed fortress of Thionville, but progress in 1644 was negligible; Conde was called away from Flanders to help Turenne. The Catalonian and Italian fronts also bogged down, and this stalemate continued into 1645.

APPENDIX G: FLANDERS LEVIES, 1619–22

The Spanish levied the following units, mostly in Flanders, for service in Bohemia, Germany, and against the Dutch:[48]

Unit	Date	Coy	Str	Notes
Bucquoy IR	1619	15	3000	Walloon
Hennin IR	1619	15	3000	"
Gauchier CR	1619	10	1000	"; cuirassier
Wallenstein CR	1619	10	1000	"; cuirassier
Nassau IR	1619	10	3000	German
D'Epinoy CR	1620	5	500	3 KUR & 2 ARK coy; Walloon
Nassau CR	1620	5	500	3 KUR & 2 ARK coy "
Isenburg CR	1620	5	500	3 KUR & 2 ARK coy "
Free Coys (KUR)	1620	2	400	Walloon
Free Coys (KUR)	1620	11	1100	"
Free Coys (ARK)	1620	6	600	"

Free Coys (ARK)	1620	2	200	Burgundian
Free Coys (KUR)	1620	3	600	"
Gulzin IR	1620	15	1796	Walloon
Aershot IR	1620	12	3600	Low German
Bauer IR	1620	8	2500	German
Balanzon IR	1620	?	—	Burgundian
Balanzon CR	1621	5	500	4 KUR & 1 ARK; Walloon-German
Free Coys (KUR)	1621	9	1000	Walloon-German
Free Coys (LtCav)	1621	2	250	Walloon
Free Coys (ARK)	1621	7	700	"
Wingard IR	1621	12	—	"
Fontaine IR	1621	12?	—	Mixed?
Hennin IR	1621	15		Walloon; reformed from 1619 IR
Free Coys (Inf)	1621	39	11,583	Low German
Balanzon IR	1621	15	—	Burgundian
Free Coys (KUR)	1622	8	800	Walloon
Free Coys (ARK)	1622	2	200	"
Free Coys (Inf)	1622	14	4200	Low German
Balanzon IR	1622	1?	—	Liege
Beauvoir IR	1622	12	—	Burgundian
Cordoba IR	1567	16	1400	Spanish; "Naples" Tercio
Spinelli IR	1619	31	7000	Neapolitan; Brigata Spinelli
Campolattaro IR	1619	—	7000	Neapolitan; "Capua" Tercio
Verdugo IR	1617	15	3000	Walln; raised for Montesferrat War

The Spinelli and Campolattaro Irs were both raised in Naples in 1619; Spinelli was sent to Austria, and Campolattaro to Spinola. In 1622, Spinelli was split, half staying in Austria and half being sent west, where they were eventually reunited with Campolattaro.

NOTES

1. The impact on confessional relations and European politics was pivotal.

2. Spain and Portugal had been united under a single monarch, although the kingdoms remained constitutionally and administratively separate.

3. Possibly because of the disappointing outcome of the Battle of Nieuport (July 2, 1600). Despite all their supposed advantages, this engagement with a slightly smaller Spanish army resulted in the most marginal of victories. Apparently, the superior elan and cohesion of the Spanish counterbalanced the Dutch training and efficiency.

4. Geoffrey Parker, *The Army of Flanders and the Spanish Road 1567–1659* (Cambridge: Cambridge University Press, 1972), pp. 11–12; Jonathan I. Israel, *The Dutch Republic and the Hispanic World, 1606–1161* (Oxford; Clarendon Press, 1982), pp. 96–97. See Appendix H. Note that these figures do not include places held by local militias.

5. The Battle of Fleurus, August 29, 1622; see Guthrie, *Battles*, pp. 100–101.

6. This plan is the linear ancestor of the *guerre de course* of Louis XIV against England and Holland, the Continental System of Napoleon against Britain, and the German U-boat campaigns of the World Wars. In Olivares's case, the commerce raiders proved quite successful but were not, of themselves, enough to win the war. The regular navy was barely able to hold its own.

7. 20,000 infantry, 4000 cavalry, and 20,000–24,000 in garrisons, exclusive of militia.

8. 30,000 infantry, 5000 cavalry, and 35,000 in garrison.

9. These were rival Calvinist schools; the Catholic and Lutheran minorities were officially excluded from the government.

10. Such lines had been used before, notably, in Spinola's blockade of Breda.

11. Soon to be superseded by the Vauban school. See Olaf van Nimwegen, "Maurits van Nassau and Siege Warfare (1590–1597)," in Marco van der Hoeven (ed.), *Exercise of Arms, Warfare in the Netherlands, 1568–1648* (Leiden: Brill, 1997), pp. 113–31.

12. Some dub the inner face the "contravallation" and the outer the circumvallation.

13. As governor of Milan, he started the Mantua War in 1627.

14. 262 infantry coys, 76 cavalry coys, and over 100 guns and mortars of all types.

15. 20,000 infantry, 5000 cavalry, and 60(!) guns.

16. These Germans did *not* observe the Spanish-Dutch arrangements for sparing civilians; their casual looting made a terrifying impression on the Dutch.

17. They numbered 1800 men in 22 coys, plus 200 sick. The garrison had lost over a thousand men in all, and the Dutch about the same.

18. The "Spanish Road," or rather roads, ran via Genoa from Spain's holdings in Italy through Switzerland, Savoy, or the Valtelline into southern Germany, down the Rhine to the Cologne area. With the Rhine Palatinate and most of Swabia in Swedish hands, transit of reinforcements became extremely risky.

19. These promises were not kept.

20. Pappenheim, acting for the Catholic League, had organized an independent army in Westphalia; see Guthrie, *Battles*, pp. 233–39.

21. David Parrott, "Strategy and Tactics in the Thirty Years' War," Rogers, *The Military Revolution Debate*, p. 243.

22. See W. P. Guthrie, "Naval Actions of the Thirty Years War," *The Mariner's Mirror* 87/ 3 (August 2001), pp. 266–273.

23. After the arrival of French aid, he was actually driven out of the province (Battle of Montjuich, January 26, 1641).

24. The Dutch did not find it necessary to suspend their attacks on Portugal's overseas colonies, so Holland and Portugal found themselves allies against Spain in Europe but still at war in Brazil and India.

25. The financial strain of the war, which had already begun to tear Spain apart, was felt by the Dutch and French as well.

26. Not his fault but a gain for the French.

27. 3160 infantry and "some" cavalry; Beck's detachment included the veteran Spanish tercio of Avila, the Walloon commander Bucquoy, and the Spanish cavalry regiment of Fuensaldana.

28. This approach later proved necessary at Freiburg, see Chapter 6.

29. Or "pretended to sleep." Antonio Canovas del Castillo, *Estudios del reinado de Felipe IV* vol. 2 (Madrid, 1888), p. 177.

30. There is some dispute about the state of French tactical organization at this point, some arguing that the French were still using the 10-rank-deep battalion, some that they had adopted the Swedish 6-deep formation, and others opting for 8 ranks. Similarly, the cavalry might be 3, 4, 5, or 6-deep; see Lynn, *Giant of the Grand Siècle*, pp. 477–78, 496–98. However, the known frontage at Rocroi excludes the use of the shallow Swedish formations. A letter of Conde, written after the battle, states that each French battalion plus intervals had a frontage of 170 "paces," indicating a rank 85 men wide; see Henri D'Aumale, *Histoire des Princes de Condé pendant les XVIe et XXVIIe Siècles*, vol. 4 (Paris: Calmann Lévy, 1886), pp. 489–90. Of course, the smaller battalions would have had to thin their depth to maintain this frontage.

31. It was a bit unusual for the wing commanders to lead the 2nd echelons.

32. One would expect a squadron of 200 to be 50 wide and 4-deep, but, unless the intervals were much smaller than usual, this cannot have been the case.

33. Probably. We know that the 5 Spanish were in the center, that Visconti was on the right, and that Velandia was next to him, but the location of the other 2 battalions is disputed.
34. Canovas, *Estudios*, p. 179.
35. Probably the Croats.
36. His lesser impetus, as compared to a Swedish charge, may have contributed to prolonging this fight.
37. D'Aumale, *Histoire*, p. 108.
38. The Spanish never forgot his generosity, and Conde became a hero to them.
39. See Chapter 6.
40. Uncle of the child-king Louis XIV.
41. Turenne's Germans mutinied when ordered to Flanders.
42. In an "unprofessional" display, the commander at Courtrai had brought so many men to the siege of Ypres that his own fort was left undefended.
43. An "ideal" infantry regiment had a colonel's company of 150 and 8 others of 120 for 1110 men in 2 battalions. An "ideal" cavalry regiment had 4 companies of 100 in a single squadron. It is unclear if *any* units followed this model exactly.
44. Israel, *The Dutch Republic and the Hispanic World*, p. 150.
45. The Dutch contributed 4 or 5 regiments to the Bohemian army. For arms deals, see Hans Vogel, "Arms Production and Exports in the Dutch Republic, 1600–1650," in Hoeven, *Exercise*, pp. 201–209.
46. Jonathan I. Israel, *The Dutch Republic, Its Rise, Greatness, and Fall 1477–1806* (Oxford: Clarendon Press, 1995), p. 498; Israel, *The Dutch Republic and the Hispanic World*, pp. 163–64.
47. Israel, *The Dutch Republic, Its Rise, Greatness, and Fall*, p. 498.
48. Louis de Haynin du Cornet, *Histoire Gènèrale des Guerres de Savoie, du Bohême, du Palatinat, & des Pays-Bas, 1616–27* (Brussels: Société de l'Histoire de Belgique, 1868), vol 1, pp. 106–110, 227–236, vol 2, pp. 79–123.

6

Mercy and Turenne: The Battles of Freiburg and Second Nordlingen

As a result of the operations of 1639, the war in Germany split into two major theaters: the Northeastern or Swedish front, which was principally the concern of Vienna, and the Southwestern or French front, which was primarily directed by Bavaria. Westphalia was, after 1635, a secondary front, consisting mostly of local forces under joint command, while Spanish operations in Flanders also had a real impact on the German situation. There are, of course, numerous examples of cross-front intervention by the various allies. Nevertheless, during 1639-45, the emperor concentrated on the Swedes, and Bavaria on the French.

The Bavarians and, to a lesser extent, their allies of the former Catholic League, had enjoyed a remarkable recovery from the devastation that they had suffered 1631-35. By 1640, an army of 20,000-30,000[1] had been restored, and it remained at that strength up to the end of the war.

After Richelieu's purchase of the Weimar Army, French general Guebriant assumed command on the Rhine. His new "Army of Germany" consisted of two separate corps, the old Weimar army under Taupadel, Erlach, and Rosen, and an expanded French contingent. Guebriant's position was unenviable; the Weimar colonels quarreled incessantly, with him and with each other, splitting into bitter factions at the least excuse. In addition, to his left flank, the French commanders against Spanish Flanders compiled a dismal record to 1643. Finally, his allies, the Swedes and the Hessians, repeatedly demanded assistance. Nevertheless, he managed to make some headway during his short command.

By the time that the army was safely bought and the quarrelsome colonels pacified, 1639 was already past. The following year, 1640, was similarly wasted in a futile attempt to cooperate with Baner's offensive.[2] In 1641, Guebriant marched northeast to Wolfenbuttel (in Westphalia) for a major combination of French, Swedish, and Hessian armies. Unfortunately, the Swedes were still in a state of confusion following Baner's death earlier that year. The allies were able to repel a threatening Imperial army,[3] but the sullenness of the Swedish troops prevented any real gain.

During the period 1635–40, the otherwise inert Imperial commanders in Westphalia had managed to overrun most of the territory of Hesse-Cassel; that minuscule state still maintained an army of 10,000, partly on French subsidies, and partly on the possession of a few scattered garrisons with the resultant ability to levy kontributions. Guebriant's plan for 1642 was based on the surviving Hessian strongholds. He would drive not east, but north into the Cologne area and re-establish the Hessian position in Westphalia. His offensive was opposed by Hatzfeld,[4] now Imperial commander in Westphalia, and Lamboy,[5] leading the local Catholic forces (viz., Cologne). In the action of Kempton (Jan 17, 1642), Lamboy engaged the combined forces of Guebriant and the Hessians without waiting for Hatzfeld. It proved an unmitigated disaster—Lamboy was captured with 19 colonels, 120 flags, 4000 men, plus all his artillery and baggage; another 2500 were killed. This neat little victory won Guebriant his marshal's baton; it also enabled him to capture several strongpoints (for Hesse) in Julich and the lower Rhine.

Guebriant's operations in 1643 were largely nullified by the ineptitude of his superior, the elder Conde. Resuming independent command in August, he moved against Rottweil in southern Wurtemberg, near the upper Danube. This small place was quickly taken (November 7–17), but Guebriant himself was mortally wounded. The commander of the French contingent, the Danish veteran Rantzau, assumed command of both corps, taking up winter quarters at nearby Tuttlingen. Unfortunately, Rantzau, while brave enough, was not only incompetent but disliked and despised by the Weimarian colonels.

The Imperial commanders were not idle while this was happening. Gotz had been succeeded by the overcautious Wahl, but after Guebriant took Rottweil, his principal subordinates, Mercy and Werth, combined their forces with those of Charles of Lorraine and Hatzfeld for a joint attack on Rantzau. It was not a battle but an ambush and surprise attack, a "beating up quarters" operation on an army scale. Werth and Mercy were both experts in this sort of action.

At dawn, November 24, 1643, Werth took a special task force[6] against the French position. Surprise was complete; they achieved such immediate and overwhelming success that Mercy and Hatzfeld converted it into an all out assault, throwing in the rest of their men. It seems that the Weimar colonels had deliberately defied Rantzau's authority; the defenders were in complete disorder. Some fled, some were cut to pieces, others defended themselves only to be surrounded and forced to surrender en masse. The fighting lasted a day and a half as each scattered group of Frenchmen was cut off and isolated. By the end of the 25th, the victors boasted 7000 prisoners, including 8 generals, 9 colonels, 10 guns, and the baggage; another 4000 were dead or wounded. The infantry were almost entirely destroyed, and whole regiments simply ceased to exist. The Weimarian army never recovered from this disaster.

Unfortunately for the Imperials, this success was more than counterbalanced by the French victory of Rocroi (May 19, 1643), which destroyed the Spanish army of Flanders.⁷ Nevertheless, the initiative in Germany now rested with Bavaria. The victorious Mercy was appointed to the supreme command, while Turenne received the unenviable task of restoring Guebriant's army and holding onto the Rhine.

Mercy's 1644 offensive was initially directed against French strongholds in Swabia. He began operations April 15 by besieging Überlingen on the northern Bodensee, held by 1300 French under Courval. Courval capitulated May 12, having lost 700 men to Mercy's 400. Then the Bavarians, still over 19,000 strong, moved on Hohentwiel, which was still commanded by the cunning Wiederhold (May 15). The place successfully repelled all assaults, so Mercy resolved to reduce it through starvation.

Turenne, meanwhile, had his own problems. Financial support from Paris was—as usual—lacking, pay was in arrears, and, at one point, the garrison of Breisach actually mutinied. It was feared that they would sell out to Bavaria. The mutiny was quickly settled, but the affair had drawn Mercy's attention to the possibility of undoing Bernhard's conquest of the Breisgau.

Turenne's eye was on Hohentwiel. Although Mercy outnumbered him almost 2-1, he decided to advance, crossing the Rhine (June 1) in 3 divisions, and to move on Donaueschingen, a village some 15-20 miles northeast of Hohentwiel. The main column, under Turenne himself, crossed at Huningen and moved along the upper Rhine, via Rheinfelden and Sackingen, then north to St. Blasien (June 3). Seven cavalry regiments under Rosen crossed farther north, at Breisach. The third corps, the artillery train plus an infantry guard, followed in Rosen's wake.

Advancing rapidly—they were all mounted, of course—via Freiburg and St. Margen, Rosen reached the hamlet of Hufingen, near Donaueschingen, on the 3rd. A Bavarian cavalry squadron under Mercy's brother was outposted there. They mistook Rosen's force for a reconnaissance. A sharp skirmish developed, in which only the intervention of Wolf Dragoon Regiment saved the Bavarian from capture. As it was, Mercy lost 400, killed, wounded, and captured, plus 7 cornets and 900 horses.

Turenne joined Rosen June 4, by which time Mercy was aware of his presence and preparing to deal with him. The French immediately—the same day—retired, falling back through Freiburg to Breisach and over the Rhine to Alsace again. Turenne gained considerable—one might say excessive—credit for this bold march, but it did not alter the relative power of the armies.

Mercy, meanwhile, had wearied of Hohentwiel. On June 20, he left 1000 men to blockade it, while the main army moved west. On the 26th, he laid siege to Freiburg, 1500 foot and 150 horse under Kanoffsky. Kanoffsky did his best, but the town was too weak to hold out for long. On July 29, he and his surviving forces[8] were granted honors of war.

Turenne could only watch helplessly. He was not idle; he had established a fortified camp, Batzenberg, some 4 miles west of Freiburg, and from there dispatched cavalry to harass the siege operations. A series of skirmishes resulted. On July 7, Taupadel ambushed a party of Bavarian horse, capturing many. On the 13th, Kurnreuter Cavalry Regiment was sharply defeated by

Rosen, losing 700–800. On the 27th, some 4000 horse skirmished against the Bavarian position. This was, however, a last gesture. Turenne had already abandoned the Batzenberg position and retired. Despite these efforts, which did not show Werth to advantage, the French still had only 10,000 men, whereas Mercy mustered almost 20,000. As things stood, even Breisach was not secure. Mercy seemed on the verge of undoing all the reverses of 1638. Fortunately for the cause of France, Conde's corps, operating against the Spanish, had been freed up by Rocroi. Richelieu's successor, Cardinal Mazarin, directed Conde to join Turenne and assume overall command. Conde set off at once (July 20) and covered the 68-mile march from Metz to Breisach in 13 days, joining him on August 2. With his usual impetuosity, Conde moved against Mercy the very same day.

THE COMMANDERS

Louis II de Bourbon, Duke of Enghien, Prince of Condé (1621–86) was a "Prince of the Blood," fourth in line for the throne of France. At the age of 22, he was made commander of the main army opposing the Spanish in Flanders, where he immediately won the historic battle of Rocroi.

Although only a middling strategist, Conde had considerable operational ability, an instinctive talent for grasping a situation, and instant reactions. This was counterbalanced by an aggressive and reckless temperament, impatient of caution and restraint. The German campaigns do not show him at his best.

Henri de la D'Auvergne, Viscount of Turenne (1611–75) was the younger brother of the duke of Boullion, one of the most powerful French nobles, but not in favor at court. Unlike his brother, Turenne clung to his family's traditional Protestantism, thus, he was doubly out of royal favor. At a very young age Turenne had already resolved on a military career, so he joined the Dutch army at 14, serving five years (1625–30). Upon his return to France in 1630, he was immediately made a colonel—experienced officers, particularly nobles, were rare—and he took part in the early campaigns against the Spanish under Schomberg, La Force, and La Valette. In 1634, he captured the small fortress of La Motte and was promoted to marechal de camp (major general). He distinguished himself by the defense of Mauberge against the Cardinal-Infante in 1637 and served under Bernhard and Guebriant in 1638. In 1639–41, he assisted Harcourt in the successful Savoy campaign. In 1643, he was promoted to marshal and given Guebriant's old command in Germany.

Turenne was arguably the best military mind of his age and a pivotal figure in the transition between the Thirty Years War and post-1660 linear warfare. While he lacked Conde's elan, he was thoroughly expert in both tactics and the operational and far superior in strategy and maneuver. However, he did not reach his military peak until the 1650s. By comparison with Conde, he was cautious and miserly of his manpower, unwilling to waste men. Despite their differences in temperament, Conde and Turenne cooperated well, the even-tempered Turenne unresentful of his less seasoned superior.

Major General Reinhold von Rosen (1600–67), of a noble Livonia house, served under Gustavus and Bernhard. He was one of the directors named in

Bernhard's will and accompanied the Weimar army into French service. His blundering 1643–45 does not indicate much competence. In 1647, the cavalry under his command mutinied and deserted en masse for Swedish service. He was blamed, court-martialed, and imprisoned but later released and restored to royal favor. His brother Johann and cousin Volmar were also Weimar colonels.

Field Marshal Baron Franz von Mercy (1598–1645), a Lorrainer, made his start in the army of his own ruler, Duke Charles. He quickly acquired substantial rank among the Catholic allies, becoming an Imperial colonel in 1633, a Bavarian colonel in 1638, and GZM of Lorraine the same year. Mercy is an interesting example of rank held in three armies at once. After Tuttlingen, in 1643, he was promoted to Bavarian field marshal and commander of the field army. Mercy was a very able officer but hampered by logistical, financial, and organizational constraints.

The whole Mercy family was involved in the war, Franz's brother Kaspar serving under him both at Tuttlingen and Freiburg, while the younger Henrich and Leopold were Imperial colonels.

Field Marshal Jan de Werth (1591–1652) acted as Mercy's chief of cavalry at both Freiburg and Second Nordlingen. Entirely successful in this limited role, he lacked capacity for wider responsibilities. He was made field marshal in 1646 but switched to Imperial service in 1647 after the failure of the plot to defect with the Bavarian army.

General-Feldzeugmeister Johann von Ruischenberg (d. 1648), Mercy's chief of infantry at Freiburg, was strictly a third-rater of limited experience; his career had been spent mainly in the secondary Westphalian theater. He was promoted to field marshal in 1648.

Field Marshal Count Gottfried von Geleen (ca. 1600–57), was an old League officer and one of the last of the Walloons recruited by Tilly in 1620. He had considerable experience under Tilly, Anholt, Pappenheim, and Gronsfeld and had taken part in the battles of Breitenfeld and Oldendorf. In 1645, he was in Imperial service and commanded the corps sent to aid Mercy. Although, like Gallas and Gronsfeld, early singled out for advancement, he never quite lived up to this promise. A competent subordinate, he failed to excel on his own.

THE ARMIES
Bavarian Army—Mercy

UNIT	DATE	COY	STR JAN	EST	NOTES
K. Mercy KUR	1620	8	?	825	ex-Erwitte, Horst
Gayling KUR	1620	9	?	950	ex-Kratz, Cronberg, Keller
Alt-Kolb KUR	1634	8–10	?	925	ex-Binder
Lapierre KUR	1635	9	?	950	ex-Gotz
Alt-Werth ARK	1621	8–9	?	925	ex-Eynatten, Salis
Cosalky ARK	1634	9	?	700	ex-Lohn, Truckmuller
Sporck ARK	1638	10	?	1175	New
Wolf Dragoons	1638	6	?	900	New
Kurnreuter DR	1644?	—	?	850	New?
9 CR			9713	8200	cavalry (1600 on foot)
Ruischenberg IR	1620	11	917	800	ex-Anholt, Geleen

Unit	Year		EstStr		Notes
Holz IR	1620	8	977	750	ex-Mortaigne, Comargo
F. Mercy IR	1620	10	1031	950	ex-Herliberg, Gronsfeld
Miehr IR	1620	9	951	900	ex-Bauer, Alt-Tilly, De Buich
Rouyer IR	1620	8	862	750	ex-Haimhausen, Albert
Enschering IR	1620	10	929	600	ex-Schmidt, Reinach
Winterscheid IR	1621	8	850	750	ex-Springen, Pappenheim
Wahl IR	1624	6	705	500	ex-Erwitte, Gallas
Hasslang IR	1631	8	741	550	ex-Fugger
Fugger IR	1632	8	900	800	ex-Ruepp, Eblinstetten
Gold IR	1638	8	1064	950	New
11 IR			9927	8300 infantry	

Artillery (Vehlen): 4 demicannon (24 pdr), 5 demiculverins (12 pdr), 8 falcons (5 pdr), 3 falconets (3 pdr), and 3 mortars

TOTAL: 8300 infantry; 8200 cavalry; 20 guns = 16,500

Also present was the Freiburg garrison: 300 foot from Enschering and 40 horse from Cosalky.

Werth, assisted by Kaspar Mercy, commanded the cavalry, Ruischenberg the infantry.

Army of France—Conde & Gramont

UNIT	ESTSTR	NOTES
Enghien IR	800	French; D'Espenan Brigade
Persan IR	800	French; D'Espenan Brigade
Mazarin IR	800	French; Tournon Brigade
Conti IR	800	French; Tournon Brigade
Le Havre IR	800	French; Marsin Brigade
Bussy IR	800	French; Marsin Brigade
Guiche IR	400	French
Desmartes IR	400	French
Fabert IR	400	French
9 IR		6000 infantry
Enghien Garde	200	French; Leib
Gendarmes Coys	600	French
Cheveau Legers CRs	3400	French
		4000 cavalry
Artillery:	2 demicannon & 15 falconets	

Army of Germany—Turenne

Unit	EstStr	Notes
Hattstein IR	500	Weimar; German Brigade
Bernhold IR	500	Weimar; German Brigade
Schmidtberg IR	500	German: German Brigade
Du Tot IR	600	French; 1st Brigade
Aubeterre IR	600	French; 1st Brigade
La Couronne IR	600	French; 2nd Brigade
Montausin-Melun IR	600	French; 2nd Brigade
Mezieres IR	600	French; 3rd Brigade
Mazarin IR	500	Italian; 3rd Brigade
9 IR	5000 infantry	
Turenne CR	400	French-German
Guebriant CR	250	French
Tracy CR	300	French

Alt-Rosen CR	400	Weimar (German)
Taupadel CR	400	Weimar (German)
Erlach CR	400	Weimar (German)
Kanoffsky CR	350	Weimar (German)
Fleckenstein CR	350	Weimar (German)
Baden CR	400	Weimar (German)
Witgenstein CR	350	Weimar (German)
Russwurm CR	350	Weimar (German)
Neu-Rosen CR	350	Weimar (German)
Scharfenstein CR	350	Weimar (German)
Berg CR	350	Weimar (German)
14 CR	5000 cavalry	
Artillery:	6 demicannon & 14 falconets	

TOTAL: 11,000 infantry; 9000 cavalry; 37 guns = 20,000

DEFENSIVE DEPLOYMENT

Although Mercy's army had begun the campaign with 19,640 men, between sieges, detachments (Hohentwiel), skirmishes, and normal attrition, it had dwindled considerably by August. The cavalry was in particularly poor condition; of a nominal 9713 horse, only 6600 were fully serviceable, with 1600 dismounted.[9] The 8300 infantry, on the other hand, were in quite good shape. With this in mind, Mercy decided to conduct an infantry defense based on earthworks, not unlike the Imperial position at Nordlingen. The ground was favorable to this tactic. Freiburg stands in a large valley dominated by surrounding hills and narrow river valleys, streambeds, and gorges. Mercy's scheme was based on a large hill called the Schonberg, several miles south of Freiburg. The defense line ran north-south, facing west, incorporating the siege works earlier dug against Kanoffsky. Freiburg itself would cover the northern flank. Running west of the town was a small river, the Dreisam. A line of obstacles—cheveaux-de-frise, palisades, and the like—running from the village of Haslach to the Dreisam secured the right. Then came the main encampment, earthworks strengthened with redoubts, between Haslach and the Schonberg. There was only a narrow gap, perhaps a mile wide, between the camp face and a thick wood, the Mooswald. Thus, any French movement along this front would expose their flank to attack.

The Schonberg itself was a steep, wooded, almost impassable hill. Mercy placed a small sconce on the northern slope (St. Wolfgang's Chapel), a much larger work, the Sternschanze ("star-sconce"), higher up, and two redoubts farther south, on the Bohl, overlooking the valley village of Ebringen. The Sternschanze was manned by Enschering Infantry Regiment and 5 small guns; the others by musketeers from Holz, Wahl, and Hasslang infantry regiments. The Sternschanze and redoubts were additionally protected by a row of more obstacles, set near the top of their slope. Behind, in support, the balance of Holz, Wahl, Hasslang, and Winterscheid infantry regiments were under GWM Ruischenberg. The east flank of this position was covered by the thickly wooded Schonberg peak.

A narrow pass, the Bannstein, ran between the Schonberg and the dense Black Forest to the east. Mercy blocked this pass with 5 thick ranks of obstacles manned by musketeers from Rouyer Infantry Regiment. The rest of Rouyer waited behind in support at Morzhausen village. A small party was posted at the Schonberg peak to signal the separated wings of what was happening on the other side.

The balance of the army, 5 infantry regiments, 9 cavalry regiments, and 15 guns, lay in reserve in the main encampment.

FRENCH ATTACK, AUGUST 3, 1644

At the council of war, Turenne argued that the Bavarian defenses were too strong to assault head-on. Instead, Mercy could be drawn out of position by maneuver. The French could march north, west of Freiburg, to the Glotter River valley, cross that river at Denzlingen, then move east toward St. Peter and occupy that valley northeast of Freiburg. They would then stand across the Bavarian line of communications, giving Mercy the choice of retreat or starvation. As he retired, he could be mauled by the superior French cavalry. This plan was supported by Gramont and Erlach.

Conde, however, disagreed. The Bavarian position, he believed, could be overwhelmed frontally. He directed Turenne to personally reconnoiter the defenses.

Obeying, the marshal discovered the Bannstein Pass on the Bavarian left. Conde then overruled the council and ordered a frontal attack. This was not sheer bullheadedness on his part; the year before, at Rocroi, he had similarly overruled a cautious council and gained that vital victory.

Conde would assault the Bohl redoubts directly with his French infantry, while Turenne with the "German" foot would simultaneously force their way up the Bannstein. The bulk of the cavalry stood at Conde's left to cover the flank; the rest would accompany the infantry reserves.

Turenne had to make a considerable detour to get into position, but Conde insisted that the assault go forward on the 3rd. Therefore, both attacks were set for 5:00 P.M., only about 3 hours before sunset—Conde was so confident of a rapid success.

On the hour, Conde and Gramont began their attack. The most vulnerable point was the southern redoubt, as the work itself masked supporting fire from the other redoubt or the guns in the Sternschanz. The main attack force would consist of the 3 brigades D'Espenan, Tournon, and Marsin, some 4800 men. D'Espenan would conduct the first assault on the southeastern face—a 300-meter front—while Tournon lay to his left, and Marsin behind Tournon. Farther back, at the start line, the village Ebringen, remained the other 3 battalions plus the Enghien Cavalry Regiment. The balance of Conde's horse, under Marechal de Camp Palluau, covered the open left flank. Some heavy guns were posted on a slope behind as support; the rest of the guns remained in camp.

The French advanced with remarkable courage and *furia*, up the Bohl from Ebringen, but Mercy had fortified the position well. After climbing the hill, they had to cross a 4-foot wall, then penetrate the ranked obstacles, all under the killing fire of musketeers from Holz and Wahl infantry regiments (Hasslang Infantry Regiment was farther north). The men of both battalions had fallen into disorder penetrating the obstacles—those that got through at all. They tried to regroup, caught in a 150-meter-wide killing ground between the redoubts and the obstacles; they failed. Their nerve gave way; they retired back through the obstacles and down the hill.

Conde immediately ordered a second attack. This time D'Espenan's assault would be supported by Tournon, D'Espenan advancing again against the southeastern front while Tournon struck the southwestern. The Bavarians greeted them as warmly as before; nevertheless, the fresh battalions of Tournon succeeded in reaching the killing ground. D'Espenan's battered units, Enghien and Persan infantry regiments, did not. They dissolved under the heavy fire, many of them taking shelter in the woods to the east, the lower slopes of the Schonberg. The rout of their friends to the right disheartened Tournon's people; they wavered for a while, under enemy fire, then drifted back to safety.

Conde, who had watched the assault repulsed, was unwilling to accept defeat. He put himself at the head of the Conti Infantry Regiment to personally lead a third attack; Gramont and his other generals followed his heroic example. More prosaically, he also ordered Marsin's reserve into action.

His new plan was to overwhelm the Bohl defenses with maximum power. Tournon would again strike the southwest with Marsin following close behind in support. The rest, 3 battalions and Enghien Cavalry Regiment, would act as reserve. The remnants of D'Espenan would attempt to distract the Bavarians with musketry. Conti Infantry Regiment, under Conde himself, would assault the southern redoubt, while Mazarin (Fr.) Infantry Regiment hit the northern.

Conde's third offensive was headed by a musketeer screen penetrating the obstacles, the assault columns following. They closed quickly, suffering but not as badly as the first two times. Mazarin was hard hit, as the garrison of the northern redoubt was still fairly fresh, and the Bavarians had turned the 5 guns in the Sternschanze against them. On the other hand, the men in the southern redoubt were tiring and running low on ammunition—an oversight on the Bavarians' part. Conti Infantry Regiment reached their target. At this point, the French enjoyed a stroke of unexpected good luck. A party of diehards from Persan Infantry Regiment had regrouped in the woods and now made their way around the Bavarian flank to take the southern redoubt from behind. Surprised and outnumbered, it fell. The Bohl position was lost.

Turenne's fight had actually begun before Conde's, at about 4:15. The Bannstein Pass was not heavily manned, but the obstacles were dense, the route narrow, and both pass and surrounding slopes wooded. Turenne's advance was led by a vanguard of 1000 musketeers under Roqueserviere, followed by the veterans of the German Brigade, the first and second brigades plus some cavalry trailing uselessly behind. The outposts sent word to Mercy of the French approach. He reacted immediately, mustering a strong force, the Fugger, Gold, Miehr, and Mercy infantry regiments, plus 2 cavalry squadrons, then moved to block Turenne personally. Apparently, he regarded this flanking threat as a greater danger than Conde's frontal assault. When he arrived, he found that Roqueserviere had already ejected Rouyer from the defenses. A sharp counterattack pushed them back in their turn, and Mercy regained the woods.

Map 6.1
The Battles at Freiburg, August 3–5, 1644

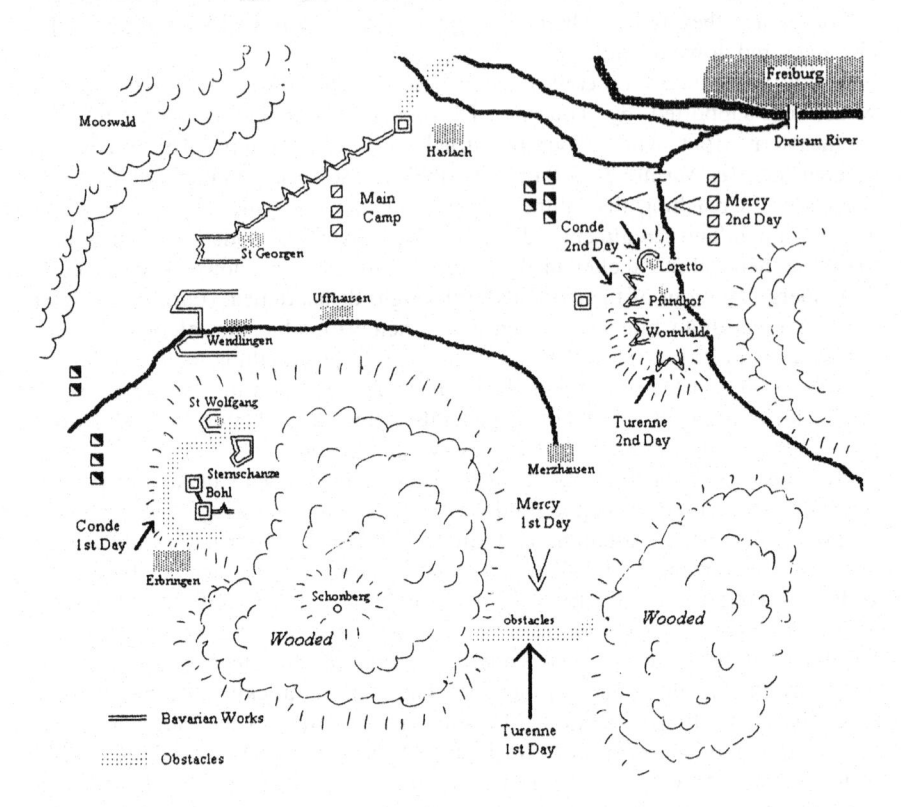

Rouyer Infantry Regiment returned to the fray.

Turenne found himself in an unenviable situation. His vanguard was repulsed, the enemy blocked his way, and his army was strung out in a long, awkward column. Moreover, it was now 5:00, and Conde was expecting his support in the combined attack. Turenne directed the now leaderless van—Roqueserviere had been wounded—to move right and left as flank guards, while the German Brigade units, Bernhold, Hattstein, and Schmidtberg infantry regiments, hastily formed into line and advanced. The attack on the pass degenerated into a bloody deadlock in favor of the Bavarians. In that close, blind fight, Turenne could not use his reserves, his cavalry, or even his artillery. Mercy took 2 ensigns and a number of prisoners; Hattstein and Miehr were killed.

While Mercy was so engaged, Conde had led his men to victory on the Bohl. Only his personal bravery and example, his "elan," had enabled Conde to bring them up the hill a third time. Ruischenberg had been left in charge on this wing while Mercy dealt with Turenne. Seeing Conde's renewed advance, he had mustered some 2550 men, the Wahl, Winterscheid, Holz, and Hasslang infantry regiments, onto the Schonberg. However, he had failed to reinforce the redoubts and, after the southern one fell to the French, he decided not to attempt a counterattack. After a little skirmishing, he contented himself with falling back in good order, evacuating the remaining redoubt and the Sternschanze but preserving the guns.

Conde had originally intended to drive through the redoubts, over the Sternschanz, into the camp itself, but between his troops' battered condition and Ruischenberg's defiant posture, he merely occupied the Schonberg. It was dark by this time, and it had started raining, rendering a bad situation miserable.

Fighting on Mercy and Turenne's wing dragged on until 4:00 A.M. When Mercy was advised of the collapse of the Bohl defense, he disengaged from Turenne and directed the army to fall back under cover of darkness.

The first day of the Battle of Freiburg ended with the French in possession of the field, but the losses definitely favored the Bavarians. Conde had lost 1000–1200 men, mostly from the heroic Persan and Enghien infantry regiments, to Ruischenberg's 600–700. Turenne had lost fully 1500–1600, while Mercy conceded only 400, for a French total of 2500–2800 to Bavaria's 1000–1100.

INTERMISSION, AUGUST 4, 1644

The French spent the next day, August 4, recovering from their ordeal of the 3rd and preparing for a renewed offensive. Conde occupied Mercy's former camp at Uffhausen, while Turenne quartered at Merzhausen. Both sides were too exhausted for more than a little skirmishing.

It would appear that the flaw in Mercy's original position was the separation between the two avenues of attack, the western Schonberg (Bohl) and the Bannstein valley. Mercy could not personally command at both points, and the loss of either would compromise the defense. As things worked out, Ruischenberg was clearly unequal to the task; the loss of the Bohl redoubts owed much to his inadequacy. However, had Mercy opted to face Conde himself and send Ruischenberg against Turenne, the flanking force might easily have turned the whole position, even cut off the army.

Mercy's new defensive line avoided this flaw. He improvised it on the 4th, while the French were recovering. At any given time, one-third of the Bavarians were resting, a third watching the French, the remaining third digging the new works. The defense was based on the Loretto ridge, south of Freiburg. Two major earthworks were raised, one on the north end, the Loretto Hill, around the chapel of Loretto, the other on the southern end, the Gipfel hill, near the hamlet of Wonnhalde. Ten guns were emplaced at Loretto, and 7 at Wonnhalde. Three sconces, with 1 falconet each, lay between, one on Wonnhalde's northwest flank; one south and west of Loretto, the Loretto Hof; and one midway on the saddle between the hills, west of the mill called Pfurdthof. The Gipfel was the steeper hill, so the Wonnhalde was protected by an extra-steep approach, while Loretto was shielded by another line of Mercy's favorite obstacles. All 5 works were well manned with trusty infantry.

The southeastern flank of the line was covered by thick woods, the Black Forest, with some cavalry east of Wonnhalde. An attempt to squeeze through the gap between the plateau and the woods would be exposed to fire from the Wonnhalde work and blocked by the cavalry. However, a potential weakness marred the Wonnhalde defense: the Becher Wood, a collection of small evergreens, stretched up to the foot of the Gipfel, providing cover for an advance from Merzhausen.

The northern flank was covered by Freiburg itself. An envelopment there would be raked from both sides, Loretto and Freiburg. The bulk of the cavalry lay here, just west of the village of Adelhausen. The infantry was divided between the Loretto plateau works, a reserve to the east of that hill, and Adelhausen. Mercy himself made his headquarters there. In this tighter position, he could maintain personal control throughout the battle.

SECOND ACT, AUGUST 5, 1644

Turenne was as well aware as anyone that a frontal attack on an equal-sized enemy so strongly emplaced would be a very hazardous undertaking. Conde, however, believed that the Bavarians had been mauled on the 3rd, that Mercy's withdrawal was virtually a rout, and that the preparations on the Loretto ridge were fraudulent, part bluff, part rear guard for a strategic retreat. If the assault was not pressed at once, the Bavarians would escape unmolested. This was a complete misreading of the situation, possibly inspired by Ruischenberg's sluggishness on the Bohl.

The three marshals, Conde, Turenne, and Gramont, agreed that the Wonnhalde was the key to the Bavarian position. Once the higher peak was in French hands, Loretto Hill would be untenable and the defense turned. The Becher Wood would provide cover for the assault. Nevertheless, the defenses were too strong for a simple attack.

Conde's plan was to tie down Mercy's reserves with diversionary attacks before the main assault overwhelmed the Wonnhalde. His Army of France, at Uffhausen, would conduct the diversions, while the Army of Germany delivered the decisive blow. The French infantry were placed under D'Espenan—despite his ineptitude on the 3rd—9 infantry regiments massed in a single column 2 battalions wide. With them were 15 falconets, and 2 companies of gendarmes followed in support. Behind D'Espenan, as a rearguard under Marechal de Camp De Chouppes, waited Mazarin (It.) Infantry Regiment and Alt-Rosen Cavalry Regiment, both borrowed from Turenne. The bulk of the French cavalry and all the rest of Conde's horse plus 8 cavalry regiments from Turenne stood on D'Espenan's left, the northern flank, under Gramont, Palluau, Marsin, and Rosen. Thus, Gramont had about 7000 horse, D'Espenan some 5000 foot and 200 horse, and Chouppes not quite 1000 in all. Conde's 2 demicannon were posted in support to D'Espenan's right rear.

On the right, Turenne's infantry was similarly formed in column. They were led by a vanguard, a forlorn hope of 1000 musketeers and 4 falconets under Marechal de Camp L'Eschelle. Marechal de Camp D'Aumont commanded the main column, 2 battalions wide. The first brigade formed the first rank, the second the second, and the third consisted of Mezieres Infantry Regiment and the remnants of the German brigade. Four cavalry regiments under Taupadel protected the right and rear. The remaining artillery was posted in support, 6 demicannon in battery near the place called Jesuitenschloss and 10 falconets a bit north and east of there, on the hill called Buck.

Turenne had, in all, less than 3000 foot and 2000 horse.

D'Espenan was to open the battle with a head-on assault on Loretto. While his lead battalions were so engaged, 2 infantry regiments[10] would leave the main column to launch a feint against the 2 sconces Loretto Hof and Pfurdthof. Once Mercy's attention was engaged, L'Eschelle would secure the Becher Wood and approaches to Wonnhalde, at which D'Aumont would conduct the main assault. This plan has some oddities—8000 foot storming 7300 entrenched on a ridge, a "main assault" of 2800 men, with "supporting" attacks and feints totaling 5000, and the key role entrusted to the dubious D'Espenan. Nevertheless, it offered a chance of success, provided that proper coordination was maintained between the widely separated columns.

August 5 dawned a beautiful summer day, to Conde's encouragement. The French were on the move by 7:00, D'Espenan and Gramont from Uffhausen, Turenne from Merzhausen. By 8:00, they were formed and ready to advance. Conde and Turenne, who had stationed themselves on Buck Hill, were about to order D'Espenan to begin, when word arrived of a suspicious Bavarian movement on the far right, south of Wonnhalde. A counterattack from that quarter would ruin the whole scheme. Ordering that nothing be done until their return, both commanders rode off to the right to see for themselves—this seems incredible in retrospect, but personal reconnaissance was a vital part of warfare well into the 19th century. The army was left leaderless—Gramont was out on the left—but a Bavarian attack was unlikely.

When D'Espenan had deployed his column, he'd expected to move immediately, so he was quite close to the Bavarian defenses. A tiny entrenchment west of the main works was held by a party of dragoons. These, seeing the French within range, started harassing D'Espenan's front line with arkebus fire. Annoyed, he directed a battalion to take the earthwork. Mercy responded by reinforcing the outpost, D'Espenan reinforced his battalion, some guns joined in, and soon a lively firefight had developed. L'Eschelles, hearing the shooting, assumed that the battle had begun and started forward. When he realized what had happened, D'Espenan tried to repair matters by launching his assault and the feint against the sconces. By the time the commanders returned to the battlefield, they found everything had started without them, and all their careful planning had gone up in smoke.

By 8:00, L'Eschelle and his musketeers had secured the Becher Wood, but D'Aumont, with his formed units, was having trouble keeping up. He had still not arrived when L'Eschelle heard the "signal." That officer was, of course, out of communication with both D'Espenan and D'Aumont. He decided to go forward without waiting for D'Aumont. The musketeers swarmed up the steep slopes under a rain of Bavarian fire. As they neared the defenses, L'Eschelle was struck down. The vanguard dissolved,[11] the musketeers fleeing singly and in small groups. D'Aumont tried to restore the situation by leading forward his first brigade. Du Tot and Aubeterre infantry regiments advanced bravely through the broken vanguard. However, a deadly storm of musket and cannon fire brought them to a standstill. Then the Bavarians went on the offensive, meaning to shove D'Aumont right back down the hill.

At this point, Conde arrived on the field. Seeing D'Aumont's predicament, he assumed personal command of the second brigade[12] and led them in an improvised counterattack on the Bavarian flank. At this, the Bavarians hastily withdrew back into the Wonnhalde earthwork.

Ever optimistic, Conde saw this as an opportunity to regain the initiative. He had already sent Tournon to rally L'Eschelle's musketeers. Now he directed both brigades and the forlorn to resume the planned assault. The defensive fire was murderous; Conde's own saddle was hit, and most of his staff wounded. The infantry wavered—first brigade and the musketeers were already shaken. Men began breaking away, trying to shelter under the slopes from the terrible fire. The plight of the wounded was piteous. A Bavarian counterattack at this point would be ruinous.

Fortunately, Turenne had taken command of Taupadel's cavalry brigade and now led them against the Loretto Hof sconce, already under attack by 2 battalions (the "feint"). This threat to the center drew Mercy's attention, allowing Conde and D'Espenan to disengage (noon).

The combined assault had been a complete failure, with grossly lopsided losses: 1100 French of all sorts to 300 Bavarian dead and wounded.

Characteristically, Conde refused to admit defeat—even though his original assumptions were fairly solidly disproven. He now proposed to achieve with 7000 (to 7000 Bavarians) what he had failed to do with 8000 plus. Even he could see that Turenne's people were not going to take the Wonnhalde, so he improvised a new scheme based on D'Espenan's column. Victory would be won by a head-on assault on Loretto Hill; Turenne's battered crew would merely secure the southern wing and try to draw off as many Bavarians as possible.

The new assault began around 3:00 P.M. Basically, it was the same formation as before. D'Espenan's column stood 2 battalions wide and 5-deep. The remnants of Persan (on the left) and Enghien (on the right) infantry regiments would lead,[13] then, respectively, Conti and Mazarin (Fr.), then Le Havre and Guiche, Bussy and Desmarets, with Fabert Infantry Regiment last. The rearguard, Mazarin (It.) Infantry Regiment and Alt-Rosen Cavalry Regiment waited in support. However, a 400-musket forlorn hope under De Mauvilly had been formed as a vanguard. Also in support were the 15 light guns and 2 cavalry brigades. The first, on the left, consisted of 2000 Gendarmes and Leib cavalry under Marsin; they had been borrowed from Gramont. On the right was Taupadel with 2 of his 4 regiments, the Turenne and Tracy cavalry regiments. Some of the horsemen were dismounted as heavy shock troops. All 6 demicannon were placed to support the attack. In all, the assault group totaled over 8000 horse and foot.

This new plan shows elements of desperation: a previously disregarded target, attacked by already beaten troops, under D'Espenan with two blunders to his credit already.

Mercy, on Loretto Hill, could see the French forming up, so he posted his infantry reserves close behind.

Although the northern slope was not as steep as that of the Gipfel, De Mauvilly found it difficult going. The hill was given over to vineyards, which, unlike the Becher Wood, gave little cover but did obstruct the movement of the attacking French. Further, log obstacles crowned the top. The entire advance was under fire by musketeers and the 10 guns. No sooner had De Mauvilly set foot on the hill then he was shot and killed, which did little for his men's cohesion.

Close behind followed the lead battalions Persan and Enghien. Despite slopes, vines, and defensive fire, they forced their way to the peak but failed to pass the obstacles. The already weakened units wilted under fire, then dissolved into retreat. Obstinately, Conde sent in his second wave, Conti and Mazarin infantry regiments, and after them the third, but each assault suffered the fate of the first, reaching the obstacles only to be stopped and driven back. But Conde had one trick left. He threw in Marsin's horse; they stormed up the north slope of Loretto Hill. Simultaneously, the fourth wave, Bussy and Desmarets infantry regiments, struck from the west. The dismounted cavalry were formidable stormtroopers with their body armor, pistols, and swords. Hit from two sides, the Bavarians wavered and gave ground; the French penetrated the ranked obstacles and overran the outer defenses. Mercy, however, countered with his own horse. GWM Kaspar Mercy led a counterattack of both dragoon regiments and the Werth Arkebusier Regiment. These crossed the Holderle Bach and took Marsin's group in the flank. A confused and bloody struggle resulted between two masses of cavalry, some mounted, some on foot; some hand to hand, others firing pistol, carbine, and arkebus at pointblank range. Kaspar Mercy was struck down in the melee. De Gramont brought his division forward; Werth mirrored the movement with his, but no major collision took place. The Bavarian strike had already brought the French advance to a standstill. As a last effort, Conde ordered in the last battalion, Fabert Infantry Regiment, plus the rearguard, Mazarin (It.) Infantry Regiment and Alt-Rosen Cavalry Regiment. The last attack was a combination of formed foot, mounted and dismounted cavalry, and bits of wreckage from the preceding assaults.

Both sides showed great courage; the French "performed marvels of bravery." Great clouds of gun smoke had turned afternoon into night, lit only by muzzle flashes. Mercy threw in his last reserves. The French forced their way up to the Bavarian battery; one ensign planted his banner on the breastwork itself. This was their high-water mark. The ensign was killed, and the attackers receded.

It but remained for Conde and Turenne to cover the retreat of their defeated foot. This task fell to Marsin's gendarmes and Taupadel's 2 regiments. They moved aggressively, blocking any Bavarian pursuit, driving, sword in hand, up to the earthworks themselves. From 5:00 to nightfall, the horse held the line and protected the defeated infantry.

The French offensive lay in ruins, 2000 dead and as many more wounded, an incredible figure. Mercy admitted to 1100 lost in all, mostly wounded. Among these were 3 French generals and Mercy's brother.

EPILOGUE: ST. PETER'S VALLEY

The French had suffered 7000–8000 casualties in 3 days' fighting, the Bavarians 2500.[14] Having lost the advantage in numbers, Conde was willing to reconsider the earlier proposal of Turenne and Erlach.

Conde's first thought after the disaster of the 5th was that Mercy would use his new superiority, 14,000 to 12,500, to crush the demoralized French. He and Turenne spent the 6th entrenching the camp at Uffhausen against the anticipated assault. It never materialized. While Conde was no doubt judging what *he* would do, Mercy was a very different sort of general. He would never attack 8000 good cavalry in the open with 6000 inferior horse, whatever the condition of the infantry.[15] Also his own army had suffered heavily and needed to rest and recover.

Conde's second thought had been to restore the balance. He and Turenne sent to all the nearby fortresses, strongholds, and outposts, Breisach, Alsace, the Upper Rhine, and even the Franche Comte, stripping their garrisons to skeletons so as to fill up the main army. Within 24 hours, 5000–6000 men were marching for Uffhausen—Mercy's superiority in numbers proved short-lived.

The Bavarian line of communications ran north and east of Freiburg through the Eschbach or St. Peter valley to Villingen, then Rottweil and points east— Swabia and Bavaria. The plan was to move north, west of Freiburg, to the Glotter valley, then east along the Glotter to St. Peter. Mercy knew Conde was still dangerous, but he judged that attempting to retire in the face of a superior cavalry would be riskier than holding on. Here, he would block further offensive moves by Conde. He believed that the French would move into Baden next and had some idea of paralleling their march. It would be necessary to avoid contact, of course.

Mercy felt his inferiority in numbers keenly and was concerned to concentrate his available forces. This may account for his relative lack of precautions. Although he was somewhat aware of the weakness of the St. Peter valley, he contented himself with placing small garrisons in the St. Peter Abbey and

Waldkirch Castle, raising a small sconce on high ground guarding the route east, and stationing a single company of dragoons there as a patrol. The Glotter was completely unguarded.

The French had completed their preparations by August 8 and were on the move early on the 9th. The Weimar cavalry under Rosen formed the vanguard, followed by Turenne and his "German" foot, then the Army of France infantry under D'Espenan, and lastly the French horse under Palluau. As rough going was expected along the Glotter, the artillery and train had been sent back to Breisach. Still expecting a Bavarian counterstroke, Conde accompanied Palluau to protect the rear.

The French moved north out of Uffhausen toward Haslach, along Mercy's abandoned obstacles to the Dreisam, crossing at Betzenhausen. They pressed north to the Glotter, which Rosen reached around noon. They then spent the whole afternoon establishing a camp at Denzlingen. This waste of half a day is difficult to explain.

Mercy had watched the French departure from Loretto, assuming that they were giving up on Freiburg. But at noon, he received a report that they were at Denzlingen and about to advance through the Glotter valley. He realized instantly that there was no time to lose. It was a race for the St. Peter pass, and if his route was shorter and more direct, Conde had a head start.

Mercy's march was thus: Col. Gayling[16] with the cuirassier and dragoon regiments formed the vanguard, then came the foot under Ruischenberg, next the artillery and baggage trains, Werth and the 3 arkebusier regiments bringing up the rear as rearguard. Mercy wasted no time—he fully intended to march through the night. Gayling reached St. Peter Abbey around 4:00 P.M. The main body of infantry slowed in the dark, and didn't get there until about dawn on the 10th, the train and rearguard still far behind.

On the evening of August 9, Conde was informed that the Bavarians had broken camp and were marching east. He at once ordered Rosen to take his 8 best squadrons, to ride through the Glotter valley in that night, and cut off Mercy in the St. Peter. After they'd left, Conde and Turenne set the rest of their army in motion. No more time would be wasted, but too much had been lost already. Even more was lost in traversing the awkward, obstacle-filled Glotter route. It was already daylight when Rosen reached the high, narrow passage between the upper Glotter and the St. Peter. Here he saw that the mass of the Bavarian foot were already east of the abbey plateau that dominated the center of the valley—and that the train was still well south. Mercy, informed of Rosen's approach, established his headquarters at the abbey.

Rosen divided his force into 3 groups; 1 regiment would fall upon the baggage wagons, Rosen himself with 5 more would attack the marching infantry, and the remaining 2 would stay behind as a rearguard and reserve.

The first squadron succeeded; they overran the baggage and fell to plundering it, halting the escape of the train, which was still south of the St. Peter plateau.

Rosen and the main group moved north around the plateau, then east to assail the Bavarian foot. Mercy had halted them and formed them into a defensive line. Rosen's 1st echelon was received by such a powerful volley that they were reduced to wreckage. Undaunted, he threw in his 2nd echelon. Again the foot stood firm, and, at just the right moment, Gayling's cuirassiers caught Rosen in the left flank as he was repelled. The Weimarians dissolved, losing 3 cornets and sweeping away their own reserve in their flight. Mercy ordered the cuirassiers to pursue the broken foe; to his fury, they declined.[17]

Rosen had attempted to carry out his orders, but he might have accomplished more had he let the foot go and concentrated on the train and rearguard.

At this point, Werth arrived with the arkebusier regiments and "persuaded" the last of Rosen's squadrons to leave. He conferred with Mercy; the Bavarian cavalry was in poor spirits, and they could see Turenne at the pass with 6 cavalry regiments and 9 infantry regiments. They resolved to save the army, even though it meant abandoning most of the baggage and 3 guns.[18]

Conde pressed Mercy as far as the sconce on the high ground east of the abbey, then broke off the pursuit. Without artillery, he had no way of reducing the tiny place. The Bavarians had escaped. By midnight, Mercy was in Villingen, a march of over 40 miles.

Conde spent August 11 capturing the cut-off garrison in the castle and looting the abandoned baggage. On the 12th, he retired to Denzlingen, consigning the abbey to fire as a precaution.

Conde wished to retake Freiburg, but Turenne dissuaded him. So weak a place was hardly worth the effort; also operations had devastated the whole area with resultant supply difficulties. Instead they should capture the Rhine fortress of Philippsburg. They opened the siege on August 25, and the place surrendered on September 12.

Mercy had somewhat paralleled their march, assuming a defensive position at Neckarsulm near Heilbronn, some 30 miles east of the French. The two marshals decided not to try conclusions with him again but spent the remainder of 1644 in siegework.

FREIBURG CHRONOLOGY: 1644

Apr 15–May 12	Siege of Uberlingen	Aug 3	1st Freiburg
June 3	Action of Hufingen	Aug 5	2nd Freiburg
June 26–July 29	Siege of Freiburg	Aug 10	Action of St. Peter
Aug 2	Conde-Turenne Link Up	Aug 25–Sept 12	Philippsburg

MARIENTHAL-MERGENTHEIM, MAY 5, 1645

After the capture of Philippsburg, Conde and Turenne quickly overran Worms, Oppenheim, Mainz, and Landau. In October, Conde returned to Paris, and Turenne went into winter quarters. Early in 1645, Turenne received word that Mercy had been forced to send a third or more of his army to support the Imperials against the Swedes.

The rumor was true; Werth, Ruischenberg, and 5000–8000 men had been detached to help repel Torstensson's Jankow offensive.[19] Mercy made no secret of his situation; if anything, he advertised it. Clearly, his weakened army would be no match for a determined offensive.

Turenne broke quarters on March 24, crossing the Rhine at Spires with 10,500 men and 10 guns. Mercy, with 6000–7000, could only retire into Swabia. After looting his way through the Stuttgart-Heilbronn area, Turenne took Rothenburg in April. He seemed on the verge of overrunning the whole Bamberg-Wurzburg area. Mercy appeared helpless. Advancing north, Turenne entered a district of small, scattered villages called Marienthal, between Rothenburg and Wurzburg. There he found it impossible to subsist his army[20]; it would either have to break up or retire.

This was what Mercy had been counting on.

Mercy's apparent defeatism had actually been a cunning display of stomach strategy. He had exaggerated his own helplessness, precisely in hopes of luring Turenne to his destruction. What Turenne had heard was true enough but misleading. While he was advancing through nearly undefended territory, Mercy had been regrouping. The return of Werth (April 20) brought him up to 13,384. He was now ready.

While Turenne was hesitating in Marienthal, he received word that Mercy had abandoned the field and split his army up among the fortresses. This report was wholly false, deliberately circulated by Mercy. It is unclear whether Mercy had actually planned to draw him into Marienthal, but he certainly took advantage of it.

Fooled but still cautious, Turenne split his cavalry among the surrounding villages—it was that or starvation—but kept all the artillery and most of the infantry near his headquarters at Mergentheim. Instinct seemed to be warning him that something was wrong. Uneasily, he sent cavalry patrols in Mercy's direction. On May 4, one reported that Mercy was approaching; he had, in fact, camped for the night only a mile east of Turenne's outposts, in battle formation.

Turenne burst into desperate activity, summoning his scattered horse, dispatching Rosen with 2 cavalry regiments to stall the Bavarian approach, setting his foot and his guns in motion. As Mercy was so close, with a superior cavalry, he decided to fight a defensive action. Any other choice would mean sacrificing baggage, guns, and most of the foot. He selected for the purpose a bottleneck position midway between his headquarters—the castle of Mergentheim in the Marienthal—and Mercy's encampment at Bettenfeld village. The site was bounded by the Tauber River on the north, the Jaxt on the south, with woods (suitable for infantry) between.

When Rosen arrived, he found that there were two woods, a large one almost blocking the passage and a smaller one farther west. In another of his misjudgments, Rosen allowed the Bavarians to occupy the larger wood. Turenne's defensive line would have to be based on the smaller one.

Turenne would begin the action with 6000 men, 3000 foot in 5 battalions and 3000 horse in 9 squadrons. The guns had not come up in time. He divided his force into two wings. The right wing, under Rosen, was composed of all 5 battalions and was positioned in the smaller woods—this was a relatively open woodlot, but the trees would help protect them from enemy cavalry. The left wing, under Turenne himself, had 5 squadrons of horse. Each wing had a second echelon of 2 more squadrons.

Mercy had about twice Turenne's strength, roughly equally divided between horse and foot, plus 9 light guns. The infantry formed 10 battalions; the horse,

30 squadrons.[21] The battle line was in two echelons, the infantry in the center, 25 squadrons divided between the wings. The guns were in 3 batteries of 3 guns each, set before the center. Three more squadrons under Col. Kolb—his own regiment, in fact—were placed behind the second echelon center as a reserve. The remaining 2 squadrons remained with the baggage train at Bartenstein. Mercy commanded the center himself, and Werth had the left wing.

The two commanders had opposite intentions for the action. Turenne hoped to hold the Bavarian left with his passive right, while he shattered their right with his horse. To this end, he placed 5 of his 9 squadrons, over 1500 sabers, in his striking echelon, with 2 more in support. As the Bavarian right, about 2000 men in two echelons, was comparatively weak, he had some chance of success.

Mercy, on the other hand, regarded Turenne's open right flank as a weak point. He would pin Rosen's foot with his own, while Werth enveloped the wing.

The Bavarians opened the action by raking the French, specifically the infantry in the woods, with grapeshot from their guns. The French bore it bravely enough. Then they moved into contact. Rosen greeted the advancing enemy with a single great volley. At the same time, Turenne launched his counterstroke. It succeeded; the Bavarian 1st echelon broke and threw the 2nd echelon into disorder, the French capturing 12 cornets and overrunning the right battery. On the other flank, things were less promising. Mercy's foot endured the volley and returned it with interest. When they realized that their flank was being attacked, Rosen's battalions simply dissolved—no doubt they had been weakened by the cannonade. The support squadrons fled without striking a blow. Werth immediately fell on Turenne's wing; at the same time, Kolb charged his front. The beaten right wing, seeing the reversal of fortune, returned to the fray, and Turenne found his squadrons disintegrating around him. In the confusion, Turenne himself was attacked by several horsemen. At this point, fortune turned again. Three French cavalry regiments, Tracy, Beauveau, and Duras, arrived; too late for the battle, they were in time to cover the retreat.

Turenne set himself at the head of these regiments. He ordered Beauveau Cavalry Regiment to take the beaten horse across the Tauber while he and the other 2 acted as rearguard. Thinking ahead, he ordered the remaining infantry—those that didn't make it to the battlefield—to retire to Philippsburg, while the cavalry was to make for Hesse-Cassel. His idea was that joining the Hessians, instead of fleeing back into France, would discourage Mercy from pursuit or attempting to recapture the Rhine strongholds. Once they were across the Tauber, the worst was over.

The French losses were horrific. The infantry had ceased to exist; the cavalry also suffered heavily. Mercy captured 2700 men, including Generals Rosen, Schmidtberg, Passage, and La Motte, 6 guns, 32 ensigns, 27 cornets, and the whole baggage train. Imperial units all over the region helped harry the French retreat. In all, Turenne lost 3000 foot, 1400 horse, and 10 guns.

This striking little victory—the last important success achieved by the Imperial side—was based on Mercy's mastery of stomach strategy and his ability to mislead Turenne's informants. Turenne, who always learned from his defeats, was thereafter known for his careful logistical planning and became a leading advocate of the magazine system and regular lines of supply.

THE ALLERHEIM CAMPAIGN

Turenne reached Cassel May 18, where he was joined by the Hessian army, 6000 men under Geiso. He quickly regrouped the remnants of his own army, putting together 3500 cavalry and 1500 infantry. When they were joined by 4000 Swedes under Konigsmarck (May 29), they were considerably stronger than Turenne had been before his defeat. Unfortunately, Mazarin had lost faith in Turenne; he ordered that no offensive operations be attempted until Conde arrived to take charge. This cost the allies the whole of June.

Conde arrived on July 1 with the 7000 men of his Army of France. Having arrived, he wasted no more time, but moved at once. Wimpfen fell to the allies July 8. Unfortunately, Conde, in a disagreement about plans, insulted the allied commanders. Konigsmarck separated from the army to rejoin the main Swedish armies in the east. Geiso did not have that option—Hesse-Cassel was in no position to quarrel with France—so he accepted the apologies offered by Turenne.

Mercy, meanwhile, had attempted to capture the Hessian stronghold of Kirchheim (800 men under Uffeln) but retired at Turenne's approach. When Conde arrived, Mercy fell back from Gelnhausen to Aschaffenburg and then to Amorbach, when he received a valuable reinforcement, 4500 Austrians under FM Geleen (July 4). He now had 16,000–17,000 to Conde's 21,000–23,000. The next day, the 5th, both sides raced to Heilbronn; Conde won. Mercy could only watch as Wimpfen fell, July 8–10.

On July 10, Mercy retired to Hall, while Conde drove into the Rothenburg-Marienthal area. Because they suspected the locals of having assisted Mercy in his earlier destruction of Turenne, the French behaved with more than usual brutality there. Rothenburg surrendered after a short siege (July 18). Conde then continued east, Mercy paralleling his march, toward the towns of Nordlingen and Dinkelsbuhl. Mercy threw 600 men into the latter place and reinforced the Nordlingen garrison with another 300, while he himself took up a strong position at Durrwang. Conde was frustrated by this hovering, which interfered with his siegework, so on August 1 he moved directly against the Bavarian army. Unfortunately, Mercy had chosen a very inaccessible, broken position, blocked by marsh and water. The most that Conde could accomplish was a little skirmishing, costing the armies a few hundred men each.

Conde briefly besieged Dinkelsbuhl, but that tiny place defied him, and he could not bring sufficient pressure to bear with Mercy's main body so close, so he switched to Nordlingen. Mercy, of course, followed and took up another defensive position, this time immediately north and east of the town.

This position, while not as formidable as those at Freiburg or Durrwang, was strong enough. It was located in the area between the Wernitz River to the north and the Eger to the south, covering both flanks. The line itself stretched a bit over 1000 yards, between two hills, the Weinberg to the north, by the Wernitz, and Castle Allerheim to the south, above the Eger. These hills were fairly steep on their west sides, facing the French, but had a shallower decline between, forming a small valley or cup. In the low point of this valley lay Allerheim village. Mercy placed troops in the castle, the village, and in the buildings on the Weinberg; as usual, he strengthened these sites with extensive entrenchments. Allerheim village was especially fortified; works were raised in front, beside, and behind, and the better-built houses were converted into improvised forts. He drew up his army based on these defenses. His main infantry and cavalry reserve were placed in the center behind the village; his cavalry wings were drawn up in two echelons, the right, under Geleen, between the village and the Weinberg; the left, under Werth, between the village and the castle.

Unlike Turenne, Conde did not learn from his setbacks; he had chosen to regard Freiburg as a victory and saw no reason why the same "successful" tactics should not be used again here. He drew up his army in two wings and a center, each of three echelons, the left under Turenne, the right under Gramont, and the center under Marsin. The whole Hessian army, 6000 men strong, formed Turenne's third echelon.

THE ARMIES
Bavarian-Imperial Army—Mercy
Center—Mercy & Ruischenberg: 7100 infantry, 1167 cavalry & 9 guns
—Allerheim Village: 3450 infantry & 6 guns

UNIT	DATE	COY	EST STR	NOTES
Ruischenberg IR	1620	10	600	Bavarian
De Puech IR	1631	8	500	Bav; ex-Hasslang
Gil de Haas IR	1644	10	1150	Bav; 2 bn
Gallas IR	1626	10	400	IMP; German
Fernemont IR	1631	10	400	IMP; Walloon
Mercy IR	1633	4	200	IMP; Low Ger; 1 bn w Waldstein
Waldstein IR	1643	—	200	IMP; Bohemian; det; 1 bn w Mercy
Artillery:	1 battery of 6 guns			

—1st Echelon: 3650 infantry & 3 guns

Mercy IR	1620	10	600	Bav
Cobb IR	1620	8	550	Bav; ex-Miehr
Rouyer IR	1620	8	600	Bav
Gold IR	1638	8	700	Bav
Bournonville IR	1636	10	400	IMP; Polish
Halir IR	??	?	400	IMP?
Govo IR	??	?	400	IMP?
Artillery:	1 battery of 3 guns			

—2nd Echelon: 1167 cavalry

Free Companies	—	5	400	Bav; 2 sqd
Jung-Kolb ARK	1634	8	400	Bav; 2 sqd
Salis CR	1644	5	200	Bav; 1 of 3 sqd
Gil de Haas	—	-	200	IMP; 1 sqd

Right Wing—Geleen: 800 infantry, 3100 cavalry & 12 guns
—Weinberg: 800 infantry & 5 guns

Mandelslohe IR	1630	10	400	IMP; Low German; ex-Holk

Mercy and Turenne

Plettenberg IR	1644	10	400	IMP;-German
Artillery:	1 battery of 5 guns			

—1st Echelon: 2100 cavalry & 7 guns

Alt-Kolb KUR	1634	8	400	Bav; 2 of 3 sqd
Cosalky ARK	1634	9	400	Bav; 2 sqd
Gayling KUR	1620	9	400	Bav; 2 of 3 sqd
Beck KUR	1634	-	400	IMP; 2 of 3 sqd. AKA Hillin
Holstein KUR	1642	-	400	IMP; 2 of 3 sqd
Croats	1641	-	100	IMP; 1 sqd
Artillery:	2 batteries, 1 of 4 guns, 1 of 3			

—2nd Echelon: 1000 cavalry

Alt-Kolb KUR	1634	-	200	Bav; 3rd sqd
Stahl KUR	1628	5	400	IMP-Bav; 2 sqd
Gayling KUR	1620	-	200	Bav; 3rd sqd
Beck KUR	1628	-	100	IMP; 3rd sqd
Holstein KUR	1642	-	100	IMP; 3rd sqd

Left Wing—Werth: 950 infantry, 3000 cavalry & 7 guns
—Castle: 950 infantry & 3 guns

Winterscheid IR	1621	9	500	Bav
Marimont IR	1624	9	450	Bav; ex-Wahl
Artillery:	1 battery of 3 guns			

—1st Echelon: 1600 cavalry & 4 guns

Alt-Werth ARK	1621	9	400	Bav; 2 of 3 sqd
Fleckenstein KR	1620	8	400	Bav; ex-Mercy; 2 of 3 sqd
Sporck ARK	1638	10	400	Bav; 2 of 4 sqd
Lapierre KUR	1635	9	400	Bav; 2 of 3 sqd
Artillery:	1 battery of 4 guns			

—2nd Echelon: 1400 cavalry

Alt-Werth ARK	1621	-	200	Bav; 3rd sqd
Salis CR	1644	5	300	Bav; 2 of 3 sqd
Fleckenstein	1620	-	200	Bav; 3rd sqd
Sporck ARK	1638	-	400	Bav; 2 of 4 sqd
Schoh DR	1638	6	100	Bav; 1 sqd
Lapierre KUR	1635	-	200	Bav; 3rd sqd

TOTAL: 8800 infantry in 18 bns; 7200 cavalry in 39 sqds; 28 guns = 16,000

French-Hessian Army—Conde

Center—Marsin: 800 cavalry in 5 sqds; 3600 infantry in 10 bns; 18 guns
—1st Echelon—Marsin: 2500 infantry in 7 bns & 18 guns

UNIT	ESTSTR	NOTES
Persan IR	300	French
Enghien IR	300	French
Conti IR	300	French
Mazarin IR	300	French
Mazarin IR	500	Italian
Oisonville IR	500	French
Bellenave IR	300	French
Artillery:	3 batteries, 2 of 7 & 1 of 4 guns	

—2nd Echelon—La Moussaie: 1100 infantry in 3 bns
Montausier IR	500	French
Havre IR	300	French
Gramont IR	300	French

—3rd Echelon: 800 cavalry in 5 sqds
Carabiniers CR	450	French; 3 of 4 sqd
Gendarmes CR	350	French; 2 sqd

Right—Gramont: 2575 cavalry in 14 sqds, 1200 infantry in 4 bns; 4 guns
—1st Echelon: 1000 cavalry in 6 sqds & 4 guns
Enghien CR	350	French; 2 sqd
Fabert CR	150	French; 1 sqd
Wall CR	150	French; 1 sqd
Carabiniers CR	150	French; 4th sqd
Garde Coy	200	French; Conde Guards; 1 sqd
Artillery:	1 battery of 4 guns	

—2nd Echelon: 600 cavalry in 4 sqds
La Claviere CR	150	French; 1 sqd
Boury CR	150	French; 1 sqd
Chambre CR	150	French; 1 sqd
Gramont CR	150	French; 1 sqd

—3rd Echelon—Chabot: 975 cavalry in 4 sqds & 1200 infantry in 4 bns
Marsin CR	300	French; 2 sqd
Garnison IR	300	French; "garrison" bn
Fabert IR	300	French
Du Val IR	300	Irish
Trousses IR	300	French
Neu-Rosen CR	675	German; ex-Weimar; 2 sqd

Left—Turenne: 5775 cavalry in 21 sqds; 3000 infantry in 6 bns; 5 guns
—1st Echelon—Turenne: 1275 cavalry in 5 sqds & 5 guns
Turenne CR	300	German; 1 sqd
Tracy CR	300	French; 1 sqd
Taupadel CR	275	German; ex-Weimar; 1 sqd
Mazarin CR	150	German; 1 sqd
Russwurm CR	250	German; ex-Weimar; 1 sqd
Artillery:	1 battery of 5 guns	

—2nd Echelon: 1000 cavalry in 4 sqds
Kanoffsky CR	185	German; ex-Weimar; 1 sqd
Fleckenstein CR	315	German; ex-Weimar; 1 sqd
Alt-Rosen CR	500	German; ex-Weimar; 2 sqd

—3rd Echelon (Geiso): 3500 cavalry in 12 sqds & 3000 infantry in 6 bns
Leib CR	300	Hessian; 1 sqd
Geiso CR	300	Hessian; 1 sqd
Groot CR	600	Hessian; 2 sqd
Bruckhurst CR	600	Hessian; 2 sqd
Kotz IR	500	Hessian
Stauf IR	500	Hessian
Wrede IR	500	Hessian
Uffel IR	500	Hessian

Lopez IR	500	Hessian
Franc IR	500	Hessian
Schwert CR	600	Hessian; 2 sqd
Rauchhaupt CR	600	Hessian; 2 sqd
Ohm CR	500	German; ex-Weimar; 2 sqd

TOTAL: 7800 infantry in 20 bns; 9200 cavalry in 40 sqds; 27 guns = 17,000

Each of the 5 batteries was supported by a detachment of musketeers.

Some oddities are apparent in this deployment, notably, those involving the left. Over half the troops were on this wing, especially in the third, reserve echelon—which included the whole Hessian army. This probably owes less to a deliberate plan than the personal relations between the generals. Conde and Geiso hated each other, but both trusted Turenne implicitly. Geiso would not want his contingent broken up or under Conde; Conde may have indulged hopes of winning without Hessian assistance.

Conde himself had no fixed post, so that he could supervise the whole action, but in fact he spent the battle with the center. Turenne placed himself at the head of his favorite Fleckenstein Cavalry Regiment.

THE BATTLE OF 2nd NORDLINGEN-ALLERHEIM, AUGUST 3, 1645

Like 2nd Breitenfeld and Rocroi; 2nd Nordlingen was a very "linear" battle; in its combination of field fortifications and battle lines it presages Malplaquet, Poltava, and Fontenoy. The actual maneuvers were comparatively simple and straightforward, but the timing of the various attacks and counterattacks and the use of reserves were critical to the outcome—characteristic of a linear battle.

Impatient to come to blows, Conde began his attack at 5:00 P.M. rather than waiting for the next day. The battle evolved as three separate actions, Conde against Mercy, Gramont against Werth, and Turenne against Geleen.

The signal to advance was the firing of 14 guns in the center. Marsin led the main assault directly against the village, 7 battalions and 14 guns. The Bavarian artillery tore at them as they came slowly forward. Conde saw that the bulky guns were holding them back, so he ordered the infantry to pass them by—thus, the assault had neither the impetus of a rapid approach nor the support of their guns. Amazingly, through sheer determination and *furia francese* they reached their target, overran the forward works, and drove into the village itself. Mercy fed infantry forward, counterattacking the battered French. The Bavarian guns continued to pour fire into their ranks. Marsin was struck down, badly wounded. The French broke.

At this point (about 6:00), Conde, too late, ordered forward the 3 battalions of La Moussaie's 2nd echelon. He led them himself, passing miraculously through the hail of musketry and cannon fire. Despite his bravery, this attack failed to duplicate the success of the first. By 7:00, the first two echelons of the center had ceased to exist.

When Mercy saw Conde throwing away his second line in a hopeless attack, he was ecstatic. "They have delivered themselves into our hands!" he gloated.[22] A major counterattack, launched just as the last battalions dissolved, would rip

Map 6.2
The Battle of 2nd Nordlingen, August 3, 1645

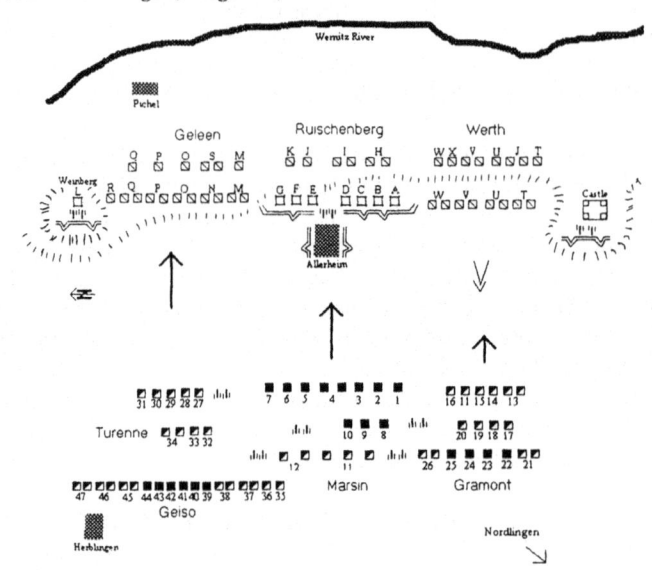

Bavarians (Mercy)
A - Mercy
B - Cobb
C - Rouyer
D - Gold
E - Bournonville
F - Halir
G - Govo
H - Free Companies
I - Jung-Kolb
J - Salis
K - Gil de Haas

L - Mandelslohe -Plettenberg
M - Alt-Kolb
N - Cosalky
O - Gayling
P - Beck
Q - Holstein
R - Croats
S - Stahl

T - Alt-Werth
U - Fleckenstein
V - Sporck
W - Lapierre
X - Schoh

French & Hessians (Conde)
1 - Persan
2 - Enghien
3 - Conti
4 - Mazarin
5 - Mazarin
6 - Oisonville
7 - Bellenave
8 - Montausier
9 - Havre
10 - Gramont
11 - Carabiniers
12 - Gendarmes

13 - Enghien
14 - Fabert
15 - Wall
16 - Garde
17 - La Claviere
18 - Boury
19 - Chambre
20 - Gramont
21 - Marsin
22 - Garnison
23 - Fabert
24 - Du Val
25 - Trousses
26 - Neu-Rosen

27 - Turenne
28 - Tracy
29 - Taupadel
30 - Mazarin
31 - Russwurm
32 - Kanoffsky
33 - Fleckenstein
34 - Alt-Rosen
35 - Leib
36 - Geiso
37 - Groot
38 - Bruckhurst
39 - Kotz
40 - Stauf
41 - Wrede
42 - Uffel
43 - Lopez
44 - Franc
45 - Schwert
46 - Rauchhaupt
47 - Ohm

the French line in two and secure the victory. But before he could give the necessary order, he was killed by a fluke cannon shot. Ruischenberg failed to rise to the occasion.

To the south, Gramont had suffered an even more ignominious defeat than Conde. Upon reaching Werth's first echelon, the French squadrons were suddenly counterattacked, Werth's 1600 on Gramont's 1000. Despite their reputation—Conde's own regiment was there and a squadron of gardes—the French were routed. Gramont put himself at the head of 2 regiments from the 2nd echelon[23] and counterattacked, breaking through the Bavarian front. He was promptly encircled by elements of Werth's 2nd echelon, overwhelmed, and captured. Marshal Chabot, commanding the 3rd echelon, tried to salvage the situation, but the routed horse of the first two lines pouring through his position swept his people away as well. Werth indulged in a furious pursuit, himself at the head of his horse, harrying the French from the field.

On Turenne's wing, however, the attack was better handled. The advance of the French 1st echelon was halted by that of Geleen—the Bavarians had the advantage of ground—at which Turenne regained the initiative by throwing in his 2nd echelon. Geleen, like the competent veteran he was, countered with his own 2nd echelon. But then Turenne ordered in his 3rd line, the 6500 men of the Hessian army.

Had Mercy still been in command, he might have responded with the 5000 men of the center reserve. But he was dead, and no one was in charge. Technically, Geleen should have taken over, but he didn't know what had happened; anyway, he was by now in French hands, captured trying to hold his wing together. Werth came next, but he didn't know it either; he was miles away, still exploiting his success. Ruischenberg was unfit even to command the center, let alone the army.

Despite Geleen's best efforts, his exhausted troops could not withstand Geiso's attack. They fled, leaving the Weinberg in Turenne's hands. The Bavarians still had the edge, but panic engulfed the center—many of whom had not even been engaged. They withdrew in such disorder that they left behind their artillery; moreover, Turenne was able to cut off one of the Gil de Haas battalions and some hundreds of men from Rouyer Infantry Regiment. Werth could perhaps have redressed the balance by falling on the nearly-nonexistent French center, but by the time he returned—to find himself suddenly in command—his men were too tired to do more than cover the retreat. Ruischenberg and Werth had managed to snatch defeat from the jaws of victory.

This French "victory" was a disaster for both sides. The French lost 4000 men and no less than 70 flags; among the dead were Colonels Boury, Fabert, and Schwert; Gramont was captured. The Bavarians lost 2500 killed and wounded, plus 1500 captured, including Geleen, Holstein, Hiller, Rouyer, Cobb, and Stahl. They also lost 7 cornets—from Geleen's people—and 8 ensigns[24]—Gil de Haas and Rouyer—as well as at least 12 guns. The most serious loss was Mercy.

AFTERMATH

Nordlingen surrendered immediately after the battle, so Conde resumed his interrupted siege of Dinkelsbuhl, which place fell August 20. Conde had contracted dysentery during the siege, so he returned to France leaving Turenne in command. He fell back to Hall to reprovision and consider his next move. While there, he received word that Archduke Leopold had joined the Bavarians with 8000 horse and dragoons borrowed from the Swedish front—Torstensson's Jankow offensive had ended in failure.[25] By October 5, the Imperials had 18,000 at Nordlingen. Turenne realized that he couldn't stop them with 12,000, so he hastily retired to Philippsburg. The captured strongholds, even including Wimpfen, were lost, and the French ended 1645 back where they'd started.

Although the French and Swedes had gained little in 1645, the two defeats of Jankow and 2nd Nordlingen had fatally undermined Imperial prestige and morale. Ferdinand III admitted privately that the war was lost—the new goal in the ongoing peace negotiations was to minimize losses. Had the French been less greedy in their demands, the war would have already been over.

ALLERHEIM CHRONOLOGY, 1645

March 6	Battle of Jankow	Jul 8	Capture of Wimpfen
March 24	Turenne begins campaign	Aug 3	2nd Nordlingen
May 5	Action of Marienthal	Aug 20	Conde departs
Jul 1	Conde-Turenne Link Up	Oct 5	Turenne retires

THE CAMPAIGNS OF 1644 AND 1645

The linear character of the Battle of 2nd Nordlingen was an indication of the way that warfare was evolving. Equally significant was the character of the strategy. The quick-thinking "move-countermove" activity of Mercy and his opponents demonstrated a "chess grandmaster" style of generalship foreshadowing that later demonstrated by Turenne and Montecuccoli, Marlborough and Villars, Eugene and Vendome. Mercy was both the heart and the brain of his army, in a way that even Tilly or Gustavus had not been. The Bavarians were helpless when he was lost, just as helpless as the French at Sassbach in 1674 when Turenne was killed.

Mercy was undoubtedly the best Imperial army commander of the later war, and his loss was one that the Imperial cause could not afford. He was succeeded by Gronsfeld.

SOURCES

It is strange to admit that the best English account of the 1644–45 campaigns is probably a work of fiction, G. A. Henty's *Won by the Sword* (1904). In German, the principal works are Schaufler's *Die Schlacht bei Freiburg im Breisgau 1644* (1979) Heilmann's *Feldzuge* (1851),and the relevant sections of his *Kriegsgeschichte von Bayern* (1880–82). See also Wrede and Gonzenbach. For those who have a little French, Turenne's memoirs contain much of interest.

APPENDIX A: MERCY AT FREIBURG

The Bavarian forces at Freiburg consisted of 11 infantry regiments, 4 cuirassier regiments, 3 arkebusier regiments, 2 dragoon regiments and 20 guns, mustering (at the start of the campaign) 9927 foot and 9713 horse, of which 8300 foot and 8200 horse actually took part in the battle. There is some dispute about these figures. Most sources give the Bavarian strength at 14–16,000, while Heilmann says 21,000. These figures are based on the Schaufler study, the most recent and detailed.

Of the forces available, 300 foot from Enschering Infantry Regiment and 40 horse from Cosalky Arkebusier Regiment were detailed to garrison Freiburg itself. Of the balance, Schaufler indicates that only 6600 mounted cavalry and 1600 dismounted remained.

Chart based on Schaufler and Heilmann.

Unit	Date	Coy	Strength	Notes
Ruischenberg IR	1620	11	917	ex-Anholt, Geleen
Holz IR	1620	8	977	ex-Mortaigne, Comargo
F. Mercy IR	1620	10	1031	ex-Herliberg, Gronsfeld
Miehr IR	1620	9	951	ex-Bauer, Alt-Tilly, De Buich
Rouyer IR	1620	8	862	ex-Haimhausen, Jung-Tilly, Albert
Enschering IR	1620	10	929	ex-Schmidt, Reinach, Hagenbach
Winterscheid IR	1621	8	850	ex-Springen, Hubner, Pappenheim
Wahl IR	1624	6	705	ex-Erwitte, Gallas
Hasslang IR	1631	8	741	ex-Fugger
Fugger IR	1632	8	900	ex-Ruepp, Eblinstetten
Gold IR	1638	8	1064	New
K. Mercy KUR	1620	8	—	ex-Erwitte, Horst
Gayling KUR	1620	9	—	ex-Kratz, Cronberg, Keller
Alt-Kolb KUR	1634	8–10	—	ex-Binder
Lapierre KUR	1635	9	—	ex-Gotz
Alt-Werth ARK	1621	8–9	—	ex-Eynatten, Salis
Cosalky ARK	1634	9	—	ex-Lohn, Truckmuller
Sporck ARK	1638	10	—	New
Wolf Dragoons	1638	6	—	New
Kurnreuter DR	1644?	—	—	New?

Heilmann gives the Bavarians 28 heavy guns. Schaufler states that there were 4 demicannon (24 pdr), 5 demiculverins (12 pdr), 8 falcons (5 pdr), 3 falconets (1–3 pdr), and 3 mortars, plus a wagonload of petards under, GZM von Vehlen.

As regards casualties, there is a vast discrepancy between French assertions and Bavarian admissions. Most sources give the Bavarian loss as 5000, one going as high as 9000(!). Heilmann admits only 1500, and Schaufler 2400–2500. French claims include alleged losses from August 8–10, plus the Freiburg garrison; Bavarian figures are confined to August 3–5. This question is integral to the ongoing controversy over who won the battle.

APPENDIX B: THE FRENCH AT FREIBURG

The French army, by way of contrast, is universally set at 20,000—no doubt an approximation. The strengths of the individual regiments, however, are not known.

The French were divided into two separate corps, the "Army of Germany" under Turenne, and the "Army of France" under Conde and Marshal Gramont, both of 10,000. Turenne had 5000 each, horse and foot, and 20 guns; Conde had 6000 foot, 4000 horse and 17 guns. Turenne's army was divided between Royal French units, who made up most of the infantry, and the remnants of the Weimar army, under Major Generals Rosen and Taupadel, who constituted most of the cavalry. The 2 remaining Weimar infantry regiments plus Schmidtberg formed a separate "German Brigade"—most of the Weimar foot had been lost at Tuttlingen.

ARMY OF FRANCE

Unit	Date	Notes
Enghien IR	1635	French; D'Espenan Brigade; 800 men
Persan IR	1636	French; D'Espenan Brigade; 800 men
Mazarin IR	1644	French; Tournon Brigade; 800 men
Conti IR	1636	French; Tournon Brigade; 800 men
Le Havre IR	1636	French; Marsin (AKA Marchin) Brigade; 800 men
Bussy IR	1616	French; Marsin Brigade; 800 men
Guiche IR	1629	French
Desmartes IR	1644	French
Fabert IR	1641	French
9 IR		6000 infantry
Garde	—	French; Conde Guard coy
Gendarmes	—	French; 6 coys?
Cheveauleger CRs	—	French; included Enghien, La Claviere CRs
		4000 cavalry

ARMY OF GERMANY

Unit	Date	Notes
Hattstein IR	1634?	Weimar; German Brigade
Bernhold IR	1634	Weimar; German Brigade
Schmidtberg IR	1634	German: German Brigade
Du Tot IR	1636	French; 1st Brigade
Aubeterre IR	1635	French; 1st Brigade
La Couronne IR	1638	French; 2nd Brigade
Montausin-Melun IR	1636	French; 2nd Brigade
Mezieres IR		French; 3rd Brigade
Mazarin IR	1642	Italian; 3rd Brigade
9 IR		5000 infantry
Turenne CR	1644	French-German
Guebriant CR	—	French
Tracy CR	—	French
Alt-Rosen CR	1634	Weimar (German)
Taupadel CR	1634	Weimar (German)
Erlach CR	1644	Weimar (German)
Kanoffsky CR	1634	Weimar (German)
Fleckenstein CR	1634	Weimar (German)
Baden CR	1644?	Weimar (German); AKA Margrave
Witgenstein CR	1634	Weimar (German)
Russwurm CR	1634	Weimar (German)
Neu-Rosen CR	1634	Weimar (German)
Scharfenstein CR	1634	Weimar (German); AKA Ohm
Berg CR	1639	Weimar (German)
14 CR		5000 cavalry

The artillery included 6 demicannon and 29 falconets.

The 11 Weimar cavalry regiments were mainly, but not entirely, the same as those in 1639. Caldenbach, Schon, and Rotenhan are to be identified with the later Fleckenstein, Russwurm, and Neu-Rosen. Muller and Nassau were shattered at Tuttlingen and their remnants were probably used to form Turenne Cavalry Regiment, which the French paid as a German regiment. Erlach Cavalry Regiment was expanded from the Breisach garrison coy, and Margrave of Baden Cavalry Regiment was new.

Note that Mazarin (French) Infantry Regiment and Mazarin (Italian) Infantry Regiment were two separate units. Cardinal Mazarin's colonelcies were purely honorary.

The French appear to have favored 2 battalion brigades of about 1600. These were ad hoc collections, casually rearranged between actions according to the tactical situation.

The French rank of marechal de camp must not be confused with marshal. The marechal de camp was roughly equal to a Swedish/Weimarian major general or an Imperial/Bavarian generalwachtmeister. Marechals de camp at Freiburg included D'Espenan, Tournon, Marsin, Palluau, De Chouppes, L'Eschelle, Roqueserviere, D'Aumont, and D'Ognone. Lower in rank was the marechal de bataille (De Mauvilly).

French casualties are variously estimated at 5000–6000 and 8,000–10,000. Heilmann says 5000–6000. Schaufler, on the other hand, places them as high as 5600–7900. Most set the French higher than the Bavarian thus, 10,000–5000; 8000–5000; 5500–1500, and 7750–2450. The exception is 9000 Bavarians to 6000 French (a misprint?). While the higher figures may include the whole period August 3–10, losses during the retreat were very light.

APPENDIX C: MERGENTHEIM/MARIENTHAL

Turenne fielded 15 cavalry regiments and (at least) 8 infantry regiments for his 1645 offensive, the Turenne, Fleckenstein, Taupadel, Kanoffsky, Ohm, Baden, Wittgenstein, Alt-Rosen, Neu-Rosen, Russwurm, Mazarin, Betz, Tracy, Beauveau, and Duras cavalry regiments, and the Hattstein, Schmidtberg, Bernhold, Mezieres, Aubeterre, Mazarin (It.), Oisonville, and Montausier infantry regiments, a total of 5000 cavalry, 5000–6000 infantry, and 10 guns. Betz was probably the previous Berg Cavalry Regiment. Mazarin Cavalry Regiment was a new German unit, possibly split off from Turenne Cavalry Regiment. The Beauveau and Duras cavalry regiments were new French units, 1 of which may have been the former Guebriant Cavalry Regiment. Another new German unit, the Rosen Dragoons, appears only in a 1645 muster; it was probably expanded from earlier dragoon companies and did not take part in either Marienthal or 2nd Nordlingen.

Turenne's forces were divided between these cantonments:

Fleckenstein CR	Aub	Tracy CR	Rottingen
Taupadel CR	Staten	Beauveau CR	Curtzelbach
Kanoffsky CR	Wurzburg Bishopric	Alt-Rosen CR	Krautheim
Ohm CR	Boxberg	Neu-Rosen CR	Feuchtwang
Turenne CR	Grunsfeld	Russwurm CR	Gerlingen
Mazarin CR	Ballenberg	Duras CR	?
Betz CR	Buchen	Rosen DR	?
Baden CR	Kirchberg	Mazarin (It) IR	?
Witgenstein CR	Langenburg	Montausier IR	?
Oisonville IR	Niedernhall		
Hattstein, Schmidtberg, Bernhold, Mezieres, & Aubeterre IRs		Marienthal	

Only 7 cavalry regiments and 5 infantry regiments were able to reach Mergentheim before fighting started: Kanoffsky, Ohm, Mazarin, Betz, Baden, Witgenstein cavalry regiments, and probably Turenne Cavalry Regiment; Hattstein, Schmidtberg, Bernhold, Mezieres, and Aubeterre infantry regiments. These totaled some 3000 foot in 5 (?) battalions and 3000 horse in 9 or 10 squadrons. The 2 squadron cavalry regiments were probably Turenne and Ohm. The 2 squadrons forming Rosen's 2nd echelon were most likely from Ohm Cavalry Regiment.

Mercy's army was probably much the same as the Bavarian contingent at 2nd Nordlingen (see Appendix D). The infantry regiments would have been Rouyer, Gold, Marimont, De Puech, Mercy, Cobb, Ruischenberg, Winterscheid, and Gil de Haas, of which Gil de Haas probably formed 2 battalions. The cavalry were Fleckenstein KUR (3 sqd), Gayling KUR (3), Kolb KUR (3), Lapierre KUR (3), Werth ARK (3), Cosalky

ARK (2), Jung-Kolb ARK (2), Sporck ARK (4), Stahl CR (2), Salis CR (3), Schoh DR (1), and the free companies (2) = 31 squadrons. Of these forces, all but Rouyer, Gold, Marimont, De Puech, Stahl, Salis, Schoh, and the free coys were part of the Jankow expedition and no doubt incurred heavy losses there. Holz Infantry Regiment was at Jankow, but not 2nd Nordlingen; it may have been at Marienthal. It is likely that the 2 squadrons left to guard the baggage were the dragoons free coys. Due to Mercy's rapid march, the 9 guns were probably falcons and falconets.

APPENDIX D: MERCY AT 2ND NORDLINGEN

The Bavarian-Imperial forces at 2nd Nordlingen consisted of 18 infantry battalions, 39 mounted squadrons, and 28 guns totaling some 15,000–16,000. Of these, 10 battalions were Bavarian, 6 Imperial, and 2 other (?). Of the horse, the Bavarians counted 31 squadrons, the Imperials 8. The Imperial contingent is estimated at 4500, leaving 11,500 Bavarians—essentially the Marienthal army. As for unit strengths, the available musters are for January and November. The Jankow units would have been especially weakened.

Chart based on Heilmann and Wrede.

Unit	Date	Coy	Strength: Jan	Nov	Est	Notes
Ruischenberg IR	1620	10	837	817	600	Bavaria; Jankow
Mercy IR	1620	10	827	685	600	Bav; Jankow
Cobb IR	1620	8	748	705	550	Bav; ex-Miehr; Jankow
Rouyer IR	1620	8	771	925	600	Bav
Winterscheid IR	1621	9	701	806	500	Bav; Jankow
Marimont IR	1624	9	557	873	450	Bav; ex-Wahl
De Puech IR	1631	8	609	693	500	Bav; ex-Hasslang
Gold IR	1638	8	891	717	700	Bav
Gil de Haas IR	1644	10	2000	1048	1150	Bav; 2 bn; Jankow
Gallas IR	1626	10	—	—	400	IMP-Gr; exPallant;Jankow
Mandelslohe IR	1630	10	—	—	400	IMP-Low Ger; ex-Holk
Fernemont IR	1631	10	—	—	400	IMP-Wall;exSuys;Jankow
Mercy IR	1633	4	173	—	200	IMP-Low German
Bournonville IR	1636	10?	—	—	400	IMPPole;Hennin;exButler
Waldstein IR	1643	10?	—	—	200	IMP-Bohemia; only a det
Plettenberg IR	1644	10	—	—	400	IMP-German
"Halir IR"	?	?	—	—	400	IMP?
"Govo IR"	?	?	—	—	400	IMP?
Fleckenstein K	1620	8	671	—	600	Bav; ex-Mercy; 3s;Jankow
Gayling KUR	1620	9	872	—	600	Bav; 3 sqd; Jankow
Alt-Kolb KUR	1634	8	732	—	600	Bav; 3 sqd; Jankow
Lapierre KUR	1635	9	918	—	600	Bav; 3 sqd; Jankow
Alt-Werth ARK	1621	9	886	—	600	Bav; 3 sqd-Jankow
Cosalky ARK	1634	9	689	—	400	Bav; 2 sqd-Jankow
Jung-Kolb ARK	1634	8	681	—	400	Bav; ex-Werth; 2 sqd
Sporck ARK	1638	10	1153	—	800	Bav; 4 sqd; Jankow
Schoh DR	1638	6	857	—	100	Bav; ex-Wolf?; 1 sqd
Stahl KUR	1628	5	451	—	400	IMP-Bav; ex-Collerd; 2 sq
Salis CR	1644	5	517	—	500	Bav; 3 sqd
Free Coys	—	5?	479	—	400	Bav; 2 sqd
Beck KUR	1634	?	—	—	500	IMPexHorrich;3sqd;Hillin
Holstein KUR	1642	?	—	—	500	IMP-German; 3 sqd
Gil de Haas KU	16—	?	—	—	200	IMP; 1 sqd
Marcovich Croat	1641	8	—	—	100	IMP; 1 sqd

11,500 Bavarians; 4500 Imperials = 16,000
8800 Infantry; 7200 Cavalry = 16,000

The tiny Mercy Infantry Regiment and the Waldstein detachment probably formed a single battalion. The identities of the Halir and Govo battalions recorded by Heilmann are unclear—no such units appear in the Imperial, Bavarian, Westphalian, or Saxon lists. They could be irregular units or minor allies, possibly from Wurzburg or Bamberg, or Spanish, or simply recorded under an unfamiliar name. Stahl appears in both IMP and Bavarian lists.

As regards the 28 guns, these were probably 4 demicannon (24 pdr), 6 demiculverins (12 pdr), 12 or so falcons (5 pdr), and the rest, 6 falconets (2–3 pdr). They were deployed in 7 batteries, 1 of 6 guns in Allerheim, 1 of 5 on the Weinberg, 1 of 3 in the castle, 1 of 4 with Werth, 1 of 3 with the center infantry, and 2 of 4 and 3 with Geleen's horse. The latter 4 would be falcons and falconets.

Some of the unit positions indicated are conjectural.

APPENDIX E: THE ALLIES AT 2ND NORDLINGEN

The Allied forces under Conde consisted of three contingents, the remnants of Turenne's Army of Germany, 5000 strong; Gramont's Army of France, set at 6000, and the 6000 men of the Hesse-Cassel army under Geiso. Although the distinction between the two French armies was of less importance than in 1644, the "Weimarian" Germans still regarded themselves as different and were so paid and treated. The Hessian army had been formed in late 1631 and some of its units had been in continuous existence since. It still used the Swedish system of organization. Most of its experience had been gained in the Westphalian theater; it had taken part at Wolfenbuttel in 1641. By comparison with the French, the Hessian units were large, near full paper strength. Gramont's regiments, by way of contrast, were quite small—possibly he had failed to repair the losses of Freiburg.

ARMY OF FRANCE:

Unit	Date	Notes
Enghien IR	1635	French
Persan IR	1636	French
Mazarin IR	1644	French
Conti IR	1636	French
Fabert IR	1641	French
Haure IR	1636	French; AKA Le Havre?
Gramont IR	1626	French; AKA Guiche
Bellenave IR	1644	French
Trousses IR		French; ex-Desmartes?
Garnison IR	—	French; bn formed from Lorraine garrisons
Irish IR	1640?	Irish; AKA Du Val
11 IR of 300 each		3300 infantry
Enghien CR	—	French; Leib regiment; 2 sqd
Gendarmes CR	—	French;; 2 sqd
Gardes CR	—	French; Conde Guard; 1 sqd
Carabiniers CR	—	French; 4 sqd
Fabert CR	—	French; 1 sqd
Wall CR	—	French; 1 sqd
La Claviere CR	—	French; 1 sqd
Boury CR	—	French; 1 sqd
Chambre CR	—	French; 1 sqd

Gramont CR	—	French; 1 sqd
Marsin CR	—	French; 2 sqd
11 CR		17 sqd = 2700 cavalry

ARMY OF GERMANY

Montausier IR	1636	French; AKA Montausin-Melun
Mazarin IR	1642	Italian
Oisonville IR		French
3 IR of 500 each		1500 infantry
Turenne CR	1644	French-German; 1 sqd
Tracy CR	—	French; 1 sqd
Taupadel CR	1634	German; 1 sqd
Mazarin CR	1645	German; 1 sqd
Russwurm CR	1634	German; 1 sqd
Kanoffsky CR	1634	German; 1 sqd
Fleckenstein CR	1634	German; 1 sqd
Alt-Rosen CR	1634	German; 2 sqd
Neu-Rosen CR	1634	German; 2 sqd; May -371 men
Ohm CR	1634	German; 2 sqd
10 CR		13 sqd = 3500 cavalry

HESSIAN ARMY

Kotz IR	Hesse-Cassel
Stauf IR	Hesse-Cassel
Wrede IR	Hesse-Cassel
Uffel IR	Hesse-Cassel
Lopez IR	Hesse-Cassel; AKA Lopels
Franc IR	Hesse-Cassel
6 IR of 500 each	3000 infantry
Leib CR	Hesse-Cassel; 1 sqd
Geiso CR	Hesse-Cassel; 1 sqd
Groot CR	Hesse-Cassel; 2 sqd
Bruckhurst CR	Hesse-Cassel; AKA Baucourt; 2 sqd
Schwert CR	Hesse-Cassel; 2 sqd
Rauchhaupt CR	Hesse-Cassel; 2 sqd
6 CR	10 sqd of 300 each = 3000 cavalry

TOTAL: 7800 infantry; 9200 cavalry; 27 guns = 17,000

Most of the guns would be of the new 4 and 8 pdr types.

There are some differences between Heilmann's reconstruction and the diagram in *Documenta Historica Bohemica*. In that source, du Tot Infantry Regiment forms a battalion with Oisonville, Aubeterre with Bellenave, and Roze with Trousses. Boury Cavalry Regiment forms a single squadron with Camarche Cavalry Regiment. The second squadron of Alt-Rosen becomes Margrave Cavalry Regiment, that of Ohm, Betz. Beauveau Cavalry Regiment, Rosen Dragoon Regiment, and Oisonville Cavalry Regiment are added to Turenne's force. Finally, it makes it 3 squadrons of gendarmes, 2 of gardes, 1 of carabiniers.

APPENDIX F: THE ACTION OF WOLFENBUTTEL

After the death of Baner in May 1641, command of the Swedish army devolved on three "directors, " Generals Wrangel, Pfuhl, and Wittenberg. All of the hatreds and rivalries of Baner's regime came home to roost: the directors quarreled bitterly, and all

Mercy and Turenne 231

three were challenged by a major mutiny, led by a fourth general, Mortaigne. Nevertheless, the arrival of Guebriant's French and Hessians plus the Brunswick-Luneburg army under Klitzing persuaded them to join the siege of the Imperial-held fortress of Wolfenbuttel.

A relieving army under Archduke Leopold Wilhelm and Piccolomini arrived, only to find the besiegers both superior in numbers and well entrenched. Nevertheless, they attempted to dislodge them—perhaps aware of the disunity amongst the Swedes—in the Action of Wolfenbuttel, June 29, 1641.

The Swedes numbered 13,000, 7000 foot and 6000 horse; the French 4000 foot and 2000 horse; the Brunswickers 7000 in all for a total of 26,000. The Swedes were formed into 13 infantry brigades, 42 cavalry squadrons, and 26 guns; the allies had 6 brigades, 37 squadrons, and 5 guns. The Swedes stood on the west or right, Konigsmarck commanding the right wing cavalry, Wrangel and Pfuhl the infantry center, and Wittenberg the left wing cavalry. Guebriant's French and Weimarians stood to his left, then Klitzing.

The Imperials had some 22,000 in 11 infantry battalions, 57 squadrons, and 11 guns. Among these forces were the Matthey, Grana, Suys, Bourri, Ranfft, and Fernemont infantry regiments; the Alt & Neu Piccolomini, Montecuccoli, Sperreuter, Gonzaga, Wintz, Geleen, Harrach, Pompeji, Wolframsdorf, Jung, Rodovan, Vera, Altieri, Hatzfeld, Bruay, Caba, Ulhefeld, and Mislik KURs; the Munster and Grodetzky ARKs; the Gallas and Gall a Burk Dragoon Regiments; the Foldvary, Reikowitz, and Losy Croats, plus the 2 companies (1 cuirassier + 1 dragoon) of Piccolomini Leib. A strong Bavarian-Westphalian contingent was commanded by FM Wahl. Piccolomini commanded the right wing cavalry, the archduke the infantry center, and Wahl the cavalry left wing.

Wahl and the archduke struck at the allied right, held by Wrangel (4 brigades), Pfuhl (3 brigades), and Konigsmarck (15 squadrons). They held, with the assistance of 7 Weimar squadrons under Taupadel. Guebriant and Klitzing countered by threatening the Imperial right with 30 squadrons. As the probe had failed and seeing the danger to his own flank, Piccolomini opted to disengage and withdraw. The Swedes sullenly refused to follow up, so the action ended after only 3 hours. The allies lost 2000; the Imperials 3000—1800 Imperials and 1200 Bavarians—plus 7 guns and 16 flags.

APPENDIX G: HESSE-CASSEL ARMY, 1631-48

March 16, 1632	November 1632	July 1633	July 24, 1645	1648
Leib CR	Leib CR	Leib CR	Leib CR	Leib CR
F.Dalwigk CR	F.Dalwigk CR	—	Groot CR	Groot CR
K.Dalwigk CR	K.Dalwigk CR	Dalwigk CR	Barcourt CR	Ernst CR
Seekirch CR	Seekirch CR	Seekirch CR	Schwert CR	Wied CR
Uslar CR	Uslar CR	Melander C	Geiso CR	Geiso LeibCoy
Mercier CR	Mercier CR	Rostein CR	Rauchhaupt C	Tarent CR
2 Free Coys				6 Free Coys
Scharrkopf DR	Dragoons	Dragoons	Ohm CR	LG Leib Coy
Mtd Jagers				
Leib IR	Leib IR (Green)	Eberstein IR	Ros IR	Wartenburg IR
Dalwigk IR	Dalwigk (Red)		Stauff IR	Stauff IR
Geiso IR	Geiso (White)			Geiso IR
Uffeln IR	Uffeln IR (Blue & White)		Uffeln IR	Uffeln IR
Riese IR	Gersdorff IR (ex-Riese)		Wrede IR	Gunterade IR

Uslar IR	Uslar IR	Franc IR	Thungen IR
	1 Free Coy		14 Free Coys
		Lopez IR	Willich IR
			Wurtemberg I
			St Andreas IR
			Benthon IR
			Stemfels IR
			Motz IR
			Ahlfeld IR

NOTES

1. In theory the Bavarian and Saxon "armies" were now (after the Peace of Prague), merely corps of the Imperial Army, but in fact they remained independent.
2. See Chapter 2.
3. See Appendix G.
4. The same Hatzfeld who lost Wittstock and Jankow.
5. The same Lamboy who hampered Gotz at Breisach.
6. 1000 cavalry, Wolf Dragoon Regiment, 600 musketeers under Gold.
7. See Appendix F.
8. 600 soldiers, 200 wounded, 100 horses and 2 guns.
9. They were also discouraged by repeated defeats.
10. Possibly Tournon's brigade.
11. The flexibility of ad hoc forlorns was balanced by lack of cohesion, particularly if, as in this case, the unit was composed of men from a number of different regiments. It was a risky command; note that, at Freiburg alone L'Eschelle, Roqueservieres, and De Mauvilly were all shot leading forlorns.
12. Couronne and Montausin-Melun infantry regiments.
13. An odd choice after their sufferings on the 3rd!
14. For a pro-French interpretation see, Derek Croxton, *Peacemaking in Early Modern Europe* (Selinsgrove NJ: Susquehanna University Press, 1999), pp. 124–27; also see Appendix A.
15. Mercy, like a German, considered cavalry superior in field battles, infantry for sieges and defense. Conde, as a Frenchman, still followed the pre-1635 doctrine of infantry as predominant—despite his own cavalry victory at Rocroi.
16. Gayling was acting as Kaspar Mercy's replacement as cavalry second-in-command.
17. He later denounced their "faint-heartedness."
18. A demicannon, a falconet, and a mortar.
19. See Chapter 4.
20. They were especially short of forage, a serious lack in a cavalry-oriented army.
21. See Appendix C for details.
22. But see the skeptical comments in Wedgwood; C. V. Wedgwood, *The Thirty Years War* (New York: Anchor, 1961), p. 467.
23. Probably Gramont and Chambre cavalry regiments.
24. Heilmann says that 15 flags and "most" of the guns were lost, but Gonzenbach, 40 flags and 12 guns.
25. Leopold joined Geleen (exchanged for Gramont) and Werth at Regensburg on September 28.

7

The Battle of Zusmarshausen: The End of the Thirty Years War

From 1630 on, the Imperials had been under continuous pressure from a succession of unusually gifted generals: Gustavus, Bernhard, Baner, Torstensson, Wrangel, Konigsmarck, Guebriant, Turenne, and Conde. This was not entirely due to chance; while the French generals, taken as a whole, were no better than the Imperial—maybe not as good—those trained or advanced by the king of Sweden were exceptional. Whatever the longterm effects on his nation of Gustavus's obsession with war, it certainly gave them an edge. There were some excellent officers serving the Empire—Mercy, Piccolomini, Montecuccoli —but too often the Imperials had to rely on second-raters like Hatzfeld, Gotz, or Melander, if not out-and-out incompetents like Gallas, Savelli, or the archduke. Mercy, of course, was killed inopportunely, while Piccolomini and Montecuccoli were obstructed by the very intrigues that advanced Hatzfeld and the others. As Italians, they were opposed by the numerous "German" or "anti-Spanish" bloc in both army and court. Piccolomini was blamed for the archduke's blundering at 2nd Breitenfeld, and Montecuccoli was made the scapegoat for Brandeis (1639). It was more this imbalance in talent than any of the social, economic, political, diplomatic, financial, or organizational details favored by the "New History" that had brought the Hapsburg cause to ruin.

THE CAMPAIGNS OF 1646 AND 1647

Despite his dubious record, Archduke Leopold was still in command in 1646. It would be his responsibility to deal with both Turenne and the new Swedish commander, Wrangel. The Bavarians were commanded by the old veteran, Geleen.

The allied plan for 1646 somewhat resembles that of Gustavus in 1632, that is, to knock the Bavarians out of the war much as Torstensson had done to the

Saxons. More subtle than the Swedish monarch, Mazarin hoped to accomplish this through diplomacy as well as force. Unfortunately, the vicissitudes of these negotiations hampered Turenne's operations. When, however, he learned that a Bavarian corps had joined the Imperial army facing Wrangel (June, near Hanau), he abandoned restraint and marched at once, via Hesse, to join the Swedes (Wetzlar, August 10). Rash as he was, the archduke realized that he was no match for these combined forces; he fell back before their advance, skirmishing but avoiding direct contact. The allies besieged and took Aschaffenburg (August 21), occupied Nordlingen (September 8), then pushed on for the Danube and Bavaria. Rain fell September 21. Their next target was Augsburg, where they were rebuffed by a small force under Werth. The archduke lay nearby but was unable to prevent them from capturing Landsberg, devastating Bavaria, and threatening Munich itself. Outrage at this Imperial impotence as much as the actual destruction drove Maximilian back to the negotiating table. On March 14, 1647, Bavaria unilaterally abandoned the war, the Truce of Ulm.

In 1647, the allies would go their separate ways, Wrangel against Austria, Turenne against Spain. The French marshal's plans went badly from the start. The remnants of the old Weimar army had many grievances against their employers: pay not received, promotions denied, privileges set aside, discrimination in favor of French troops. The order to leave Germany for Flanders was the last straw. On June 15, the Weimarians mutinied. After 2 months of bargaining and skirmishing, the mutineers, 3000 strong, deserted to the Swedes.[1]

Reduced to his French troops—having lost most of his cavalry—Turenne failed to conquer Luxemburg, being repelled by 5000 Spanish under Beck.

The Swedes did no better. Wrangel launched another Bohemian offensive, via Hesse and Thuringia, opposed by the new Imperial commander Melander. He was defeated at the Action of Triebl (near Pilsen, August 19–20) and fell back to winter quarters in Oldendorf in Westphalia. Melander followed him cautiously, going into quarters in Hesse.

Momentous events occurred in Bavaria as well. Enraged at Maximilian's betrayal of the cause, Generals Werth, Sporck, and Holtz resolved to take the whole Bavarian army over to the emperor. The plot was exposed, but the generals escaped and were made Imperial field marshals. To add to Maximilian's troubles, Mazarin overplayed his hand with outrageous demands; the elector was forced to conclude that renewed warfare would be less disastrous than acquiescence. He terminated the truce on September 14.

THE CAMPAIGN OF 1648

Melander left Hesse on January 5 for Schwabach, near Nuremberg. Gronsfeld, in winter quarters in Kitzingen, joined him February 21. Together they had 24,000 men, 10,000 under Melander (3000 horse, 7000 foot), and 14,000 under Gronsfeld (9000 horse, 5000 foot). Melander, as Imperial lieutenant general, held overall command, but he had no way of enforcing his authority over the recalcitrant Gronsfeld; their forces did not unite but remained two separate armies merely moving together.

Wrangel broke quarters in February, advancing south, via the Fulda gap with 15,000 horse, 7000–8000 foot and 60 guns. Konigsmarck commanded the vanguard, a semi-independent corps of 4000–5000 horse. They occupied the Arnstein-Neustadt-Kitzingen-Remlingen-Schweinfurt area near Wurzburg and stayed there until March 13. At the same time, Turenne crossed the Rhine at Mainz, 9000 strong, and took up a position at Aschaffenburg.

Melander and Gronsfeld retired before the enemy advance to the Ingolstadt area and remained there until March 23. Nervous at the enemy approach, Gronsfeld started detaching small garrisons to the towns and castles north of the Danube.

Wrangel lay siege to Windsheim (north of Ansbach) on March 11. It was held by 250 dragoons from Creuz Dragoon Regiment and 9 guns and held out 2 days, surrendering on the 13th. The prisoners joined the victorious Swedes, the first of many.

On the 18th, the Swedes and French linked up at Dinkelsbuhl, together over 30,000 strong.

Melander and Gronsfeld left Ingolstadt on March 24, marching west, crossing the Lech, and occupying the area west of the Lech and south of the Danube. This maneuver was partially defensive, securing the Danube against the allies, and partially mere foraging. The Bavarians secured the crossings of Donauwerth and Lauingen on the 28th.

At the same time, Turenne and Wrangel moved against Donauwerth, quickly capturing it and half a dozen smaller places, Wallerstein Castle, Vorberg Castle, Harburg, Pappenheim, Katzenstein, and Moosbach—Gronsfeld lost over a thousand men in less than a week. On March 26, Turenne and Wrangel held a council of war at Nordlingen. The Swedes proposed securing their supplies before undertaking serious operations, by conquering the Upper Palatinate and looting it thoroughly. Turenne preferred to overrun the Imperial strongholds west of the Lech, in Swabia and Wurtemberg. The argument became invidious: the Swedes accused the French of sacrificing war strategy to Mazarin's diplomacy, of secret negotiations with Bavaria—which was true. The French accused Wrangel of looting for his own profit—which was also true. The acrimonious question of the Weimarian deserters was rehashed. In the end, they compromised; first Wrangel would occupy the Upper Palatinate, while Turenne remained at Ansbach. Then they would move into Swabia.

Wrangel marched into the Upper Palatinate and quickly secured the strong town of Neumarkt (April 5). He concentrated on the Bavarian garrisons nearby, while Konigsmarck's corps was dispatched against the capital at Amberg. When they learned that Wrangel was marching east, Melander and Gronsfeld did the same,[2] taking up a defensive position at Regensburg. On April 8, they sent a force of 1700 horse under Truckmuller across the river to operate against the Swedes in the Upper Palatinate. He discovered that the enemy offensive had fizzled out. Wrangel had taken a number of Gronsfeld's microgarrisons but had achieved only a small foothold around Neumarkt. Konigsmarck, rebuffed at Amberg, had wandered up to the Imperial fortress of Eger, where, in turn, he had skirmished with some Imperial cavalry under Puchheim. By the 14th, he was back at Neumarkt.

Turenne had had rather better luck in the Ansbach area, taking 5 or 6 strongpoints and 100,000 talers.

Melander's strategy was essentially the same as he'd used in 1647; the army would avoid direct contact with the enemy, harassing their operations with skirmishes and cavalry from a safe position. Gronsfeld vociferously disagreed. They should, he said, take advantage of the division between the allied armies to fall on each in turn. Gronsfeld's plan did not appeal to Melander, who was preoccupied with the unwieldy and divided character of his forces. The scheme could have succeeded, provided that the enemy could be forced to battle before they could reunite—a dubious proposition in itself—but Gronsfeld was more interested in demonstrating his "aggressiveness" than in actually executing this plan.

On April 16, Wrangel abandoned his Upper Palatinate offensive; he rejoined the Turenne near Dinkelsbuhl the next day.[3] That town was held by 500 of Gronsfeld's Bavarians, 300 foot and 200 horse. The allies besieged it on the 19th; after a sharp action costing the Swedes 100 men and the defenders 30, it surrendered on the 21st.

This failed to solve the allies' supply problems. The Upper Palatinate project had failed, and the north Danube area was nearly exhausted. It appeared that Melander's stomach strategy had succeeded. On April 27, the allies pulled out, marching west and south to Wurtemberg. Turenne established himself at Reutlingen; Wrangel, at Goppingen. Melander countered by reoccupying the Donauwerth-Neuburg area. He disposed his forces on a line Gunzburg (on the Danube)-Augsburg, the Bavarians centering on the village of Burgau, the Imperials on that of Zusmarshausen (May 1).

Melander's position at Zusmarshausen was well chosen from the standpoint of stomach strategy. It was in hostile/neutral territory, which reduced the strain on Bavaria. It lay across the enemy's line of advance—the allies had already devastated the north Danube area, so if Melander now did the same for Swabia, he would have encircled Bavaria with a sort of artificial desert, as fatal to the Swedes as Jutland had been to Gallas in 1644. He dispersed his forces, which not only reduced the strain on individual areas but enabled him to ravage a wider area. Keep in mind that Melander had to feed not only his 20,000 men but an alleged 100,000 camp followers.

The posture had military drawbacks. He did not, unlike Mercy at Freiburg, concentrate his forces at a defensible site or entrench a fortified camp. In fact, his dispositions more closely resembled that of Turenne at Marienthal. If the enemy advanced, Melander intended to retire. However, he would have to stay alert; if he were surprised, it would be another Tuttlingen, another Marienthal.

The next 2 weeks were occupied with minor skirmishing against Swedish screening forces. Gronsfeld retook Harburg. FM Sporck with 1500 horse bumped into a superior Swedish corps and was chased back to Gunzburg with heavy losses—the Swedes pursued with such elan that they had to be ejected from Gronsfeld's artillery park. Raiders on both sides looted the unfortunate inhabitants, but no advantage was gained by either. On May 12, Gronsfeld reported that Wrangel was at Langenau, less than 10 miles from Gunzburg—but Gronsfeld was always "seeing Swedes," and there were plenty of Swedish cavalry around anyway.

This time, though, he was at least partially correct. On the 16th Wrangel and Turenne crossed the Danube (north to south) at Lauingen, less than a day's march from the Imperial position.

THE COMMANDERS

Henri de la D'Auvergne, Viscount of Turenne (1611-75)—as noted in Chapter 6, did not reach his military peak until the 1650s. However, after his schooling under Conde and Mercy, he was already one of the best generals in Europe; he certainly had nothing to learn from Melander or Gronsfeld. There would be no more Marienthals, no more Freiburgs or Allerheims. His operations were somewhat hampered by Mazarin's diplomatic meddling and his dependence on Wrangel's superior numbers.

After the end of the war, an uprising called the Fronde broke out inside France. Turenne supported the royalists and was instrumental in their victory, overcoming Conde in the process. He went on to defeat Conde and the Spanish at the Dunes, 1659. By this time, he was the best general in Europe. During the Louis XIV wars, he conducted several "classic" linear campaigns, notably, his strategic duel with Montecuccoli 1672-75. He was killed by a stray cannonball, July 27, 1675, at Sassbach, ending the "duel."

Field Marshal Karl Gustav von Wrangel (1613-76) was arguably the weakest of the "great" Swedish commanders of war, being compared unfavorably with his own subordinate, Konigsmarck. A very junior officer under Gustavus, he was one of a generation of generals advanced under Baner, becoming colonel in 1637 and major general in 1639. After Baner's death in 1641, he briefly commanded at Wolfenbuttel (1641) but was unable to quell the mutiny until Torstensson arrived. During the 1644 war with Denmark, he was appointed admiral and commanded the Swedish squadron at the victorious Battle of Femarn. He succeeded Torstensson as army commander (1645) and was made field marshal (1646). He operated in cooperation with Turenne 1646-48. Wrangel was not favored by the peace-minded Queen Christina but resumed command under her successor, Karl X, in his wars with Poland and Denmark, 1655-58, winning the Battle of Warsaw, July 28-30, 1656.

Wrangel was an effective tactician and battlefield commander but an indifferent strategist. He more than anyone else gave "stomach strategy" a bad name; he was more concerned with loot and keeping his army fed than in winning the war, and his operations tended to meander in search of plunder. Militarily, he deviated from Swedish battle strategy into excessive emphasis on "small war," cavalry skirmishes, and raiding. He was accused, with justice, of conducting his strategy for personal gain and of prolonging the war to enrich himself. Personally, he was avaricious and ambitious, unpopular with his men, and distrusted by his government.

Field Marshal Count Peter (Eppelmann) Melander von Holzapfel (1585–

1648) was the most successful of the war's "upstarts." A Calvinist peasant, he rose to supreme command under the Catholic emperor. Melander was already a professional soldier when the war broke out, having served his "military apprenticeship" in the Dutch army of Maurice of Nassau (Melander was from Nassau himself), then regarded as the best in Europe. After the truce with Spain (1609), he became a free agent, first as a captain in Basel, then as a colonel for the Venetian Republic, 1620–30, before rising to general in Hesse-Cassel, 1631–40. Upon Uslar's defeat, he assumed effective—but not official—command. In 1633, he led the left wing at the victorious Battle of Oldendorf. He intrigued with the emperor 1635–36, attempting to get Hesse-Cassel to accept the Peace of Prague and to take his force into Imperial service. He was disgruntled when the Landgravine opted to support France instead. His disapproval of the French alliance, plus the Landgravine's refusal to make him official commander caused their relationship to deteriorate, peaking in a bitter quarrel with Baner and Klitzing of Brunswick-Luneburg in 1640. Melander resigned his position, with much bad feeling on both sides, and remained in retirement for almost 5 years.

In 1645, Melander accepted the post of Imperial commander in Westphalia (in succession to Geleen, who had succeeded Hatzfeld) and tried to organize an army of 14,000 there. In 1647, he was promoted to lieutenant general and assumed command of the main army. This promotion was mainly due to the intrigues of the "German" faction in the army.

As supreme commander, Melander found things very different from his accustomed Westphalian theater.[4] He, in common with later historians, especially disapproved of the swollen baggage train, which he considered a dangerous hindrance to mobile operations. Keep in mind that the small field forces that he was used to were seldom more than a week's march from home, whereas the main army had to range the length of the Empire. He quarreled bitterly with his chief subordinate, Montecuccoli, an adherent of the Italian faction, and, in 1648, with Gronsfeld. Melander tried, on the whole successfully, to apply the principles of "small war" that he'd learned in Hesse and Westphalia in the main theater of war.

Politically, Melander represented those Germans, of all three religions, who favored uniting behind the emperor against the foreigners. He distrusted the Swedes and loathed the French and held to this stand in spite of personal cost.

Melander was a man of real, albeit limited, military ability and was recognized as such by his contemporaries, if not by historians. Despite somewhat narrow experience, he proved a match for Wrangel, though not Turenne. Personally, he was an assertive, aggressive personality, ambitious and very shrewd financially—his estate of 1,500,000 talers was one of the largest private fortunes in the Empire. In spite of these traits and his "upstart" status, he was well respected by his contemporaries.

Field Marshal Count Jobst Maximilian von Gronsfeld (1598–1662) had been one of Tilly's best colonels and an able second-in-command to Pappenheim, but less satisfactory as an independent commander. He badly mismanaged the defense of the Weser in 1633, with heavy loss. He was not, however, responsible for the subsequent defeat of Oldendorf, where his wing was routed by Melander. The quarrelsome Gronsfeld next fell out with Gallas, whom he accused, justly, of mishandling the 1635–36 campaign against France; he resigned in protest and did not resume his career until 1645. He succeeded Geleen as Bavarian commander in 1647; the 1648 campaign was his only major operation. He was released from imprisonment 1649 but left Bavarian service.

Gronsfeld was a capable subordinate, but too abrasive and indecisive for independent command. He held Imperial, League, and Bavarian commissions but got along badly with Imperial generals—Merode, Bonninghausen, Gallas, Melander—refusing to acknowledge their seniority. He especially disliked Melander, holding a grudge over Oldendorf. Gronsfeld was constantly "playing up" to Elector Maximilian, and this, plus his personal animosity, accounts for his strategic disagreements with Melander—he was actually even more defensive-minded. Both Gronsfeld and Melander had developed a predilection for "small war" based on their experiences in Westphalia.

Lieutenant General Count Raimondo Montecuccoli (1609–80) was a younger son of a military family of Modena, Italy. He entered Hapsburg service in 1625 and took part in the battles of Breitenfeld, Nordlingen, and Wittstock, rising to colonel in 1635 and general in 1642. As an Italian, however, he ran afoul of the "German" faction and was unfairly blamed for the defeat of Brandeis (1639). He commanded successfully on secondary fronts 1642–45 and thus avoided the disasters of 2nd Breitenfeld, Jankow, and 2nd Nordlingen. He became Melander's second-in-command in 1647. The friction between the two was largely his fault; Montecuccoli was doubtless correct in arguing that Piccolomini would have been a better choice, but Melander was at least an improvement over Gallas and Archduke Leopold.

Montecuccoli remained in the Imperial army after 1648, becoming—like Turenne in France—a major figure in the transition to linear warfare. He distinguished himself in the Northern War against Sweden (1657–58), the Turkish War (1661–64), and the French War (1672–74), winning the battles of St. Gotthard (1664) and Altenheim (1674). He was considered the only general able to match Turenne—in fact he outmaneuvered the French commander in 1673. Montecuccoli was to prove a thoroughly able commander, both strategically and operationally, but he had not yet reached his peak in 1648.

THE ARMIES
Imperial Army—Melander

UNIT	DATE	COY	NATION	NOTES
Melander KUR	1647	1	—	Leib Coy
Jung-Nassau KUR	1625	10	German	Nassau-Dillenburg
Merode KUR	1625	10	German	Merode-Boccarme.
Gonzaga KUR	1626	10	German	Louis Gonzaga
Lannoy KUR	1627	5	German	AKA Lanan
Schaff KUR	1628	10	German	Schaff von Havelsee
Piccolomini KUR	1629	10	L.Ger	
Kaplir KUR	1630	10	German	
Bocamaggiore KUR	1631	5	—	AKA Gropelli
Vernier KUR	1631	10	L.Ger	
Montecuccoli KUR	1632	10	German	

Unit	Date	Coy	Type	Notes
Pless KUR	1632	10	German	
Khevenhuller KUR	1632	—	German	
Beck KUR	1633	9	German	
Furstenberg KUR	1634	8	German	
Sporck KUR	1635	—	—	
Alt-Nassau KUR	1635	—	—	Nassau-Dillenburg
Konigsegg KUR	1637	—	L.Ger	Westphalia
Kapaun KUR	1638	—	—	AKA Capaun
Pompeii KUR	1639	—	—	
Tapp KUR	1640	—	Silesia	ex-Waghi ARK
Warfuse KUR	1640	—	Saxon	ex-Saxony
Pallavicini KUR	1641	8	H.Ger	Upper Austria
Luttke KUR	1641	—	German	ex-Brandenburg
Kolowrat KUR	1642	6	Bohemia	
Lutzelburg KUR	1646	6	—	
Bonninghausen KUR	1647	4	German	AKA Boninghausen
Paconchay DR	1641	—	—	
Someda DR	1645	—	—	
Colombo Croats	1632	10	Croat	

29 CR = 3000 Cavalry

Unit	Date	Coy	Type	Notes
Baden IR	1618	10	H.Ger	
Ranfft IR	1618	10	H.Ger	
Puchheim IR	1619	10	German	
Ruischenberg IR	1619	10	L.Ger	
Zuniga IR	1625	10	Bohemia	
Gallas IR	1626	10	L.Ger	
Hauser IR	1628	6	German	
Mercy IR	1630	10	H.Ger	
Mandelslohe IR	1630	10	L.Ger	
Fernemont IR	1631	10	Walloon	
Wachenheim IR	1631	8	German	
Mercy IR	1632	4	L.Ger	
Conti IR	1639	10	German	5 coy present
Starhemberg IR	1642	10	H.Ger	
Fernberger IR	1642	—	H.Ger	Lower Austria
Melander IR	1646	—	German	

15 IR = 7896 Infantry
Artillery: 6 x 3 pdr; 3? x 12 pdr; 3? x 24 pdr
Total: 7896 infantry; 3000 cavalry; 12 guns = 10,896 men

Bavarian Army—Gronsfeld

UNIT	DATE	COY	ESTSTR	NOTES
Fleckenstein KUR	1620	9	779	
Gayling KUR	1620	10	941	
Alt-Kolb KUR	1634	10	805	
Jung-Kolb ARK	1621	10	904	
Truckmuller CR	1633?	6	505	
Bartl DR	1641/2	10	189	ex-Creuz; dispersed
Guscheniz Croats	1635	5	207	Unit dispersed
Wurtemberg Croats	1642	10	845	

8 CR = 5175 Cavalry

The Battle of Zusmarshausen

Cobb IR	1620	9	628		
Rouyer IR	1620	7	684		
Elter IR	1638	8	842		

3 IR = 2154 Infantry
Artillery: 2 x 24 pdr, 4 x 8 pdr, 4 x 6 pdr, 12 x 4 pdr, 6 x 3 pdr & 2 mortars
Total: 2154 infantry; 5175 cavalry; 30 guns = 7329
10,896 Imperials + 7329 Bavarians = 18,225 men & 42 Guns.

Swedish Army—Wrangel

UNIT	COY	ESTSTR	SQD/BN	NATION	NOTES
Kruse CR	4	450	1	Swede	W.Gothland
Wrangel CR	4	365	1	"	Uppland CR
H. Horn CR	8	620	2	Finn	
Wrangel Leib CR	13	700	3	German	
Wrangel Leib DR	9	535	-	"	
Axel Lillie CR	8	280	1	"	
Konigsmarck CR	13	1000	3	"	
Konigsmarck DR	8	700	-	"	
Baner CR	8	500	2	"	
Douglas CR	8	420	1	"	
Stenbock CR	8	370	2	"	
Hesse CR	16	802	2	"	Darmstadt
Goldstein CR	8	398	1	"	
Hammerstein CR	8	414	2	"	
Horn CR	8	353	2	"	
Baden CR	8	400	2	"	Bd-Durlach
K.Lewenhaupt CR	8	457	2	"	
D'Avangour CR	8	250	1	"	D'Avancourt
Lettmat CR	8	329	1	"	
Wittkopt CR	8	372	1	"	
Per Andersson CR	8	342	2	"	
Frolich CR	8	393	2	"	
Hundelhausen CR	8	346	1	"	
Bottiger CR	8	344	2	"	
Poley CR	8	351	1	"	
E. Pentz CR	8	358	2	"	
Fritz CR	8	255	2	"	
Gortski CR	8	270	1	"	
Endt CR	8	300	2	"	
Kurck CR	8	300	1	"	
Kettler CR	8	450	2	"	
Jordan CR	8	339	2	"	
Pfuhl CR	4	228	2	"	
Pege CR	8	220	-	"	ex-Weimar
Mohr CR	8	250	-	"	ex-Weimar
Plaunitz CR	8	450	-	"	ex-Weimar
Qwast CR	4	220	-	"	ex-Weimar
36 CR + 2 DR		15,241			12,000 horse
Sack IR	8	600	1	Swede	bn w Paikull.
Paikull IR	2	200		German	bn w Sack
Nehren IR	4	400	1	Swede	bn w Alt-Blau

UNIT	COY	ESTSTR	SQD/BN		NOTES
Alt-Blau IR	12	615		German	Gustavan vets
Gladstein IR	8	820	1	Swede	East Botten
F.Knorring IR	8	700	1	Finn	Tavastehus
Konigsmarck IR	12	500	1	German	bn wLewenht
G.Lewenhaupt IR	8	300		"	bn w Konigk
Stenbock IR	12	400	1	German	bn w Doring
Doring IR	8	460		"	bn w Stenbck
Linde IR	12	700	1	"	bn wSteinckr
Steinacker IR	2	100		"	bn w Linde
Forbes IR	8	460	1	"	bn wVolkman
Volkmann IR	8	400		"	bn w Forbes
12–14 IR		6655			5000 foot

Artillery: 5 x 24 pdr, 15 x 12 pdr; 40 x 3 pdr = 60 Guns
Total: 5000 infantry; 12,000 cavalry; 60 guns = 17,000 men

French Army—Turenne

UNIT	COY	ESTSTR	SQD/BN	NOTES
Duras CR	12	300	2	French
Tracy CR	8	300	2	"
Meispas CR	8	300	2	"
Beauveau CR	8	150	1	"
Olipart CR	8	254	2	"
Turenne CR	12	400	3	German
Mazarin CR	8	350	2	"
Betz CR	8	330	2	"
Ohm CR	8	320	2	" Weimar
Fleckenstein CR	8	115	1	" "
Taupadel CR	8	137	1	" "
Erlach CR	8	248	2	" "
Russwurm CR	7	200	2	"
Buchenau CR	8	296	2	"
Turenne DR	10	100	1	"
15 CR		3800	27 Sqd	
Turenne IR	20	600	1	French
Montausier IR	14	500	1	"
Vaubecourt IR	30	600	1	"
Netancourt IR	12	300	1	" 1 bn w La Couronne
La Couronne IR	12	300		" w Netancourt
Passagie IR	12	300	1	" 1 bn w Du Tot
Du Tot IR	12	300		" w Passagie
Duval IR	12	300	1	" 1 bn w Erlach
Erlach IR	10	200		Weimar; 1 bn w Duval
Mazarin IR	12	500	1	French-Italian
Schmidtberg IR	12	200	1	German; 1 bn w Kluge
Kluge IR	12	300		"
12 IR		4400	8 bns	

Artillery: 25 x 12 & 24 pdr + 17 x 4 pdr = 42 guns
Total: 4400 infantry; 3800 cavalry; 42 guns = 8200 men
8200 French + 17,000 Swedes = 25,000 & 102 guns

THE BATTLE OF ZUSMARSHAUSEN, MAY 17, 1648

Turenne indicates that the allies were not deliberately trying to ambush Melander, that, in fact, when they began their advance from Wurtemberg, they had only a vague idea of his location. Apparently, both sides were blinded by the other's covering forces. The allies were advancing along the *north* bank of the Danube. When they reached the crossing at Lauingen (May 16), Turenne dispatched some scouts to the south bank. These reported that the main enemy encampment was only 3 hours' march away. Wrangel, Konigsmarck, and Turenne immediately set themselves at the head of a strong body of horse for a reconnaissance in force, the balance of the army being directed to cross to the south bank and await orders.

Melander had become aware of the allies slightly before. It would, he considered, be madness to confront their 25,000+ with less than 20,000, leaving aside that over 2000 of his horse were on foot and 600 of his foot were sick. He directed that both his army and Gronsfeld's at once fall back to Augsburg.

Melander was betrayed by his lack of experience. Back in Westphalia, an army could cover the 10 or 20 miles to safety in a few hours of hard marching. But here, things were different; he had not realized just how much the camp followers and baggage train would hinder the escape. Also, he had not properly prepared his route. Augsburg was not far away, but the intervening terrain was unfavorable, woods, hills, streams, marsh. The road involved a number of bottlenecks that would reduce movement to a crawl. Melander therefore established a special rearguard under Montecuccoli, consisting of 1500 cavalry—Melander had less than 2000 still mounted—800 detached musketeers under Col. Starhemberg, and four guns. The line of march was thus: Gronsfeld and the Bavarians first, the Imperial foot, Melander with a few horse, the baggage train, and Montecuccoli last. They set off the night of the 16th—the darkness did not improve their mobility.

One would have expected the 5000 Bavarian horse to form the rearguard, but apparently Gronsfeld was not feeling cooperative.

The allied vanguard consisted of 3000 cavalry, 3 French cavalry regiments—including Turenne Leib—and 6 Swedish. When they arrived at Zusmarshausen on the morning of the 17th, they found the Imperial camp deserted. Casting about, they discovered Montecuccoli at 7:00 A.M. Turenne then sent word back to the main force to join them at once.

Melander's route to Augsburg was a narrow road confined by three bottlenecks or passes, the last being the longest, then opening into the valley of the Schmutter, a large stream running parallel to the Lech. The retreating army would have to traverse all three passes, then cross both the Schmutter and the Lech. Unfortunately, movement of the train had slowed to a crawl. If Melander expected the rear guard to hold the allies long enough for the baggage to escape, he was being overly optimistic.

Montecuccoli approached the problem with his usual skill and courage; both sides praised his handling of the retreat. At the first pass, he presented his 1500 cavalry, tightly arrayed. Wrangel tried to outflank his right, the north, via a bypass route, but Montecuccoli withdrew to the second position before he could be cut off. This pass was protected by a marsh (the Zus stream) to the south and thick brush to the north. Unfortunately, on arriving Montecuccoli found that the tail of the train was still lagging between the second and third bottlenecks. It would be necessary to make a serious stand. Despite his best efforts, he could not stop 3000 crack horse with 1500—he must have wished for the Bavarians then! He was pushed back to the third pass, losing the rearmost 60 baggage wagons.

Montecuccoli had planned his main stand for the third pass. This was the strongest of the positions, narrow with thick woods on both flanks and a marshy stream along the front. However, it was also the longest and most awkward, and the baggage train was still entrapped along it, en route to the Schmutter.

Montecuccoli had "dug in" Starhemberg's 800 musketeers and 4 guns to hold this position, but by the time he had come up, his horse were battered from the fight at the second pass. Moreover, the lead element of the main allied army, 1000 French cavalry, reinforced Turenne at about the same time (9:00 A.M.). Turenne fell upon the defenders with an overwhelming frontal assault, while Wrangel, unnoticed, again attempted to envelop them by crossing the marsh to the south, the Imperial left. The already weakened Imperial horse were giving way when Melander appeared with a small reinforcement, 400 cavalry, 500 musketeers, and 2 more light guns drawn from the main army. There resulted a renewed cavalry melee, a desperate hand-to-hand fight. Melander was shot and killed. At the height of the strife, Wrangel reappeared in the Imperial rear. The musketeers' works were penetrated; the defense dissolved. About half the fleeing cavalry got away through the woods—Montecuccoli himself escaped by wading the marsh on foot—the musketeers were all killed or captured, and the guns were lost. At this point, their very success worked against the allies; the captured baggage train blocked the pass as effectively as an army.

Aside from Melander, the Imperials lost 1300 musketeers, 900 cavalrymen, six 3 pdr guns, 6 flags, 353 baggage wagons, and over 700 horses. Of the cavalry who escaped with Montecuccoli, many were dismounted and all were scattered and demoralized. Allied loss was light.

Not satisfied with this success, Turenne pressed after the main body of the enemy. However, Gronsfeld had prepared a surprise for him. After emerging from the third pass and crossing the Schmutter, the Bavarians had broken off their retreat and adopted a defensive position behind the stream. The infantry and guns entrenched on a fair-sized hill, the 5000 cavalry forming to their right, the north. A sharp exchange developed (2:00 P.M.), to Turenne's disadvantage. Gronsfeld was deployed, entrenched, and ready, whereas the allies had to funnel their forces up the road. Also, the defenders were relatively fresh, whereas the aggressors were suffering the effects of the earlier action. Gronsfeld put them under fire from some 30 guns, plus the Elter Infantry Regiment. Turenne dragged up 6 guns to reply, but the imbalance was too great. The Bavarian horse, the Fleckenstein, Truckmuller, Alt-Kolb, Jung-Kolb, and Wurtemberg cavalry regiments engaged and cut up the allied van. Regretfully, the allied commanders put off further action until the rest of the army could be brought up. The Bavarians slipped away that night and were safely across the Lech by morning.

The "Battle" of Zusmarshausen was actually just an unusually bloody rearguard action. It is clear that Melander's decision to retire preserved his army from the fate of Turenne at Marienthal. Nevertheless, he should have planned more carefully. In the event, he might have done better to abandon the baggage and preserve the rearguard; still he had succeeded in extracting the army almost intact from a very dangerous situation.

The action on the Schmutter showed Gronsfeld at his best, a competent veteran taking proper action. Melander being dead, command of the Imperial contingent had devolved on the relatively junior Montecuccoli, Gronsfeld assuming overall charge of both forces. Now he had a chance to show what he could do.

THE 2ND BATTLE OF THE LECH, MAY 26–7, 1648

Counting up the survivors in both corps, Gronsfeld found that he now had 8750 foot, of whom 600 were sick, and 7224 horse, of whom 4224 were mounted. This force was obviously incapable of facing Turenne and Wrangel on even terms; the defense of Bavaria depended on holding the line of the Lech. An allied attempt to cross near Augsburg was warned off by the approach of the Bavarian-Imperial host. On May 19, the allies marched away north; Wrangel detached Konigsmarck with 1500 men to attack Bohemia. This weakened the main allied concentration, of course, but it also alleviated their logistical situation, and it would prove a valuable diversion. The allies positioned themselves at Oberndorf, on the west bank of the Lech just a mile from Rain.

Gronsfeld, meanwhile, was repeating the mistakes that he'd made defending the Weser in 1633; he dispersed his troops in detachments scattered between Augsburg and Rain. By the 25th, his main body was at Ober-Peiching, east of Rain. The two armies stood in much the same positions as Gustavus and Tilly at the Battle of the Lech in 1632. Wrangel hoped to reprise his old master's triumph, whereas Gronsfeld believed that he could avoid Tilly's errors. The allies mustered 23,000, 9000 foot and 14,000 horse; the Germans had 7000 cavalry—not all mounted—and 7500 infantry.[5] Shrewdly, Gronsfeld had erected a sconce to guard the crossing at Rain.

Tilly had been blamed for placing his defenses too close to the riverbank; the superior Swedish artillery had shot his troops to pieces before the crossing began. Gronsfeld, by way of contrast, kept his main body (of 14,500) well back and deployed only a light screen along the river, mostly cavalry patrols and the aforementioned earthwork. When the allies attempted to cross, he would counterattack, catch them with only a part of their forces across, and crush that division against the river. This was a workable plan, but it would require exact timing; if he struck too soon, he would be exposed to their cannon, but if he delayed too long, the enemy would be able to establish themselves and the defense would be undone.

Wrangel spent May 26 in preparations for the crossing. He raised a battery of 12 heavy guns to bombard the Bavarian defenses and built a large portable bridge to be extended in sections along the river. The battery killed few, as

Gronsfeld had kept his main force well back and out of its range, perhaps too far back as it turned out. Thus the bank was "cleared" for the crossing. Wrangel planned to cross on the 27th; by way of further preparation, he had small parties of horse swim the river and recon the opposite side. As luck would have it, some of these groups encountered one of Gronsfeld's patrols (around 5:00 P.M.); these reported to the marshal that the Swedes had already crossed. Gronsfeld realized that without the advantage of the river, no defense was possible, so, on the night of May 26–27, he abandoned the Lech line altogether and fell back toward Ingolstadt.

On the 27th, Wrangel, unaware of Gronsfeld's departure, began his operation. First, he threw some covering squadrons across to secure the bank. These probed inward, bypassed the defenses at Rain, and discovered the retreating Bavarians. Gronsfeld, mistaking them for the whole allied army, redoubled his speed. They harassed his rear guard for several hours, causing the loss of 8 guns and some infantry.

Wrangel then dropped the bridge to bring the main force across. Amazingly, the tiny garrison at Rain managed to set it afire. For a moment, the whole operation seemed in doubt, but Turenne's people extinguished the blaze without serious damage. They quickly secured Rain, and the invasion of Bavaria commenced.

The "2nd Battle of the Lech" scarcely deserves the name of skirmish; had it not been for the abandoned garrison at Rain, the allies would have crossed entirely unopposed. 2nd Lech shows Gronsfeld at his worst.

Slight as it was, the Lech action was catastrophic to Bavaria. The allies proceeded to wreak such havoc on the unfortunate inhabitants as to cause comment even in those hardened times. Turenne's uncharacteristic brutality derived from policy; the peace negotiations were in their final stages, and Mazarin hoped to force the elector to surrender.

Hopelessly outnumbered, Gronsfeld could do nothing but continue his retreat. On June 3, he was relieved of command and placed under arrest, pending court-martial. GZM Hunoldstein assumed temporary command until a successor could be appointed. Gronsfeld was subsequently convicted; his career was over.

Considering the skill and dash of Melander and the solid competence of Gronsfeld, it is tempting to suggest that they could have avoided their tragic fates. Had Gronsfeld showed Melander the same loyalty he'd given Pappenheim... But some partnerships are not to be. Given their differences in background and outlook, the political strain between their masters, and the bad blood between them, it is remarkable that they cooperated as well as they did.

The Zusmarshausen campaign furnishes some interesting examples of the pluses and minuses of varying solutions to similar situations. At Marienthal, Turenne opted to stand and lost most of his army; Melander, by way of contrast, retreated, losing his rearguard and baggage. Tilly, defending the Lech, was too far forward and exposed to hostile fire. Gronsfeld was too far back and allowed the enemy to cross unopposed. Christian of Denmark, at Lutter, succeeded in catching a small force cut off from its friends but was both unable to crush the detachment *and* was cut up by hostile artillery. Some commanders, such as

Melander, Turenne, Wrangel, and Hatzfeld, favored an "up-front" approach, even conducting their own reconnaissances. As a result, Melander was killed. Similarly, Tilly was nearly killed at the Wiesloch action. On the third day at Freiburg, Turenne and Conde were away reconnoitering at a critical moment; the same time happened to Hatzfeld at Jankow. At Wittstock, Hatzfeld got so caught up in the immediate fighting that he neglected the overall situation. On the other hand, at 2nd Lech, Gronsfeld stayed well back and relied entirely on his scouts—so that a single erroneous report undid his whole plan. Montecuccoli wrote (in 1642),

> "It is clear that a commander who subjects himself to excessive hazards and who rushes into danger inappropriately not only risks his own life but also compromises everyone else's....Where only slight benefit will be derived from the success of some personal undertaking but where all would be lost should he fare badly, he must not act like an ordinary private.... Nevertheless, when it is really imperative...[he} must not be sparing of his own person."[6]

This, it could be argued, was begging the question. Melander did not need to lead the counterattack at Zusmarshausen, as any competent colonel could have handled it. On the other hand, Gronsfeld should have checked the Lech report for himself.

ZUSMARSHAUSEN CHRONOLOGY

	Gronsfeld	Melander	Turenne	Wrangel	Konigsmarck
Jan 5	Kitzingen	Hammelburg	Strassburg	Oldendorf	Oldendorf
	"	Arnstein			
	"	Retzbach	Landau		
Feb 7			Mainz		
12	leave	Schwabach		Fulda	
16	Uffenhein	"		Gemunden	Neustadt
21	Schwabach			"	
Mar 3				"	
4	Berching			Arnstein	Kitzingen
	Kipfenberg		Wiesbaden		
	Beilngries		Aschaffenbrg		
	Kosching on Danube		Remlingen	Kitzingen	Schweinfurt
13			Bischofsheim	Ickelheim & Windsheim	
18			Crailsheim	Leutershausen in Ansbach	
			Ellwangen	Feuchtwang	
			Dinkelsbuhl		
24	Ingolstadt & Reichshofen		Funfstetten	Donauwerth	
25	Pottmes		"	Neuburg	
26	Thierhaupten		Nordlingen		
28	Donauwerth &Lauingen				
			Moosbach	Donauwerth	
			Ansbach	Weissenburg	
			Markdorf	Heideck	
Apr 4		Ingolstadt	Kretzberg	Frenstadt	
5	Pfeffenhasn		Donauwerth	Neumarkt	Amberg
6				"	to Eger

	Regensburg		"	
14	Schwandorf	Castel	Neumarkt	
15		Iphofen	Gunzenhausen	
16			Altmuhl	
17		Dinkelsbuhl	Durrwang	
18		Dinkelsbuhl	Gunzenhausen	
26		Dinkelsbuhl		
27		Wurtemberg		
	Donauwerth & Neuburg	Reutlingen	Goppingen	
	Wertingen	"	"	
	Gunzburg	"	"	
May 1	Burgau Zusmarshausen	"	"	
12	Gunzburg "	Lauingen	Langeneck	
16	Zusmarshausen	Lauingen		
17	Augsburg Zusmarshausen			
18	Augsburg	Augsburg		En route to
25	Ober-Peiching	Oberndorf		Bohemia
28	Landshut	Rain		Neumarkt
Jun 2	"	Freising		Up Pal
5	*Hunoldstein* Passau	Freising & Landshut		Weiden
9	Passau *Piccolomini*	" "		Mies
Jun 14–July 6	Inn Operations	Inn Operations		Falkenau
July 27–Aug 28	Mamming	Dingolfing		Prague
Sept 2–Oct 8	Geisenhausen	Moosburg		"
Oct 1	"	Moosburg Feldmoching		"
Oct 9–16	Munich-Ingolstadt	Retire from Bavaria		"
Oct 24–Nov 3	*End of war*			

THE ISAR-INN CAMPAIGN

The Imperial command had not much benefited from Gronsfeld's departure: his successor, Hunoldstein, was equally defensive-minded and, moreover, was on bad terms with Montecuccoli.[7] At least he lacked his predecessor's obsession with detachments. While no great intellect, Hunoldstein was at least energetic. Immediately upon assuming command, he began to implement a new defensive strategy.

Bavaria has one great defensive advantage against attack from the west, a series of rivers, tributaries of the Danube, flowing south-to-north. Also, the terrain grows increasingly mountainous and barren as one moves south. The Lech being lost, Hunoldstein resolved to hold at the Isar river line. This line was defined by four strong points, north-to-south, Landshut, Moosburg, Freising, and Munich. Each of them already had its own garrison, courtesy of Gronsfeld; the main body was concentrated at Landshut. Between detachments recalled and such Imperials as remained with the Bavarians, Hunoldstein deposed of something over 15,000, while the allies, having left 2000 Frenchmen at Rain, were down to not more than 22,000. However, their advantage in cavalry was at least 2–1, so no defense was possible in the open.

Under Wrangel's direction,[8] the allied army made for Freising, the weakest link in Hunoldstein's chain. It may seem strange that they neglected the opportunity to take Munich, but thus were Turenne's instructions. It must be remembered that the final peace terms were even then being negotiated. Mazarin believed that the destruction of his capital would only embitter the elector, whereas the constant threat would weaken his resolve. In any event, Freising was invested on June 2 and surrendered on the 3rd. An allied corps advanced on Landshut; Hunoldstein cautiously retired to the next line, the Inn River. The Swedes raised 2 siege batteries on the 6th, but the town was blockaded only on the west bank.

Wrangel wasted the week in Freising, looting and terrorizing the district and penning several bombastic missives to the Bavarian cabinet, full of gruesome threats of what he would do to the Bavarian people if the elector failed to "see reason." These threats were subsequently executed in full.

While Wrangel was so engaged, Piccolomini arrived at Passau as successor to the late Melander as Imperial commander-in-chief (June 9). With his "immense energy and tenacity" he set about reassembling the defeated armies. Their stand would be made on the Inn.

On the 12th, Wrangel finally moved out, crossing to the east bank of the Isar at Freising, then taking Landshut. The Isar had proven as feeble a defense as the Lech; the Inn, he hoped, would follow. He made for the townlet of Wasserburg-on-Inn, east of Munich and well south of the main Imperial concentration at Passau (June 14). Although weakly held, the place rebuffed the bombardment of his 3 batteries. On the 18th, he switched to Muhldorf, about halfway between Wasserburg and Passau. This was a mistake; Hunoldstein had fortified it with a strong earthwork, well garrisoned and supported by the Bavarian militia. Wrangel persisted; Piccolomini reinforced Hunoldstein. On June 22, 2954 Imperials arrived under Wachenheim. The allies' luck had turned. Even the weather turned against them as heavy rains swelled the Inn to double its normal size. The offensive was broken off July 6.

Wrangel next established a fortified camp at Eggenfelden, midway between the Isar and the Inn (July 9–21), from which stronghold he ravaged the west Inn district. As noted, the Swedish conduct in this campaign was among the most brutal of the war; the sack of Erding was the last great atrocity, "worse than Magdeburg." When Landshut failed to raise 20,000 florins on demand, he burned the suburbs—they then found the cash! While he was so engaged, he received a reinforcement, 4500 men under Baden-Durlach.

Piccolomini had been more industriously engaged. Between the old units and reserves he'd scraped up, he built the army up to 24,000,[9] at least as large as Wrangel's force. On July 17, he went over to the offensive, crossing onto the west bank. Around the same time (July 19), a Bavarian raiding party blew up the French-held bridge at Rain.

Learning of Piccolomini's advance, Wrangel fell back to the Isar (July 22), establishing a new camp at Dingolfing (July 27). Piccolomini established himself at Landau, less than 10 miles downriver. Neither side was willing to risk a field battle. Piccolomini had always regarded the Swedish army with great respect and hoped to force them back through stomach strategy. Turenne knew that the risk of a setback at this point in negotiations far outweighed any possible advantage. Wrangel didn't care about the negotiations, but he knew that a major defeat would give his pro-peace queen the excuse that she wanted to relieve him of command. By establishing a base on the east bank of the Isar, the allies would devastate that region as they had the Inn, at once punishing the elector and feeding themselves at Bavaria's expense.

On August 2, Enkefort, an officer very attached to the Imperial cause, assumed the position of Bavarian commander[10] in succession to Gronsfeld. Piccolomini's authority was now absolute. On the 3rd, he established a new camp at the tiny village of Mamming, less than a mile opposite Wrangel's position at Dingolfing. His plan was to use his superior light cavalry (Croats) to hamper the allied subsistence and, ultimately, force them to retreat, even abandon Bavaria altogether.

The armies spent most of August in this confrontation. While avoiding open battle, they tried to weaken each other by maneuver and skirmishes. On August 1, Wrangel had taken a couple of squadrons on reconnaissance when he was ambushed by 1500 Bavarian horse under Truckmuller and Wurtemberg; 151 Swedes were taken prisoner. On August 12, Werth raided the allied camp with 5000 cavalry; they counterraided with 2000, and a large-scale cavalry action developed, lasting 7 hours and costing both sides several hundred men. No real advantage was gained by either. On August 17, Wrangel perceived a threat to one of his bridges, so he strengthened its protection with several redoubts, backed up by cavalry. They proved well sited for harassing the Imperial camp with artillery fire. Piccolomini raided them that night, overrunning the works and capturing 95 French, but Wrangel retook them with an immediate counterattack. Whether because of these guns or lack of provisions, Piccolomini pulled back to Landau on August 24.

The Imperials were further discouraged by reports of Konigsmarck's advances in Bohemia and of Conde's destruction of a Spanish-Imperial army in Flanders (Battle of Lens, August. 20, 1648).

The operation had not been in vain, however, for Wrangel found his own provisions exhausted by the 28th. Things were no better in Landshut (August 28–September 2), so he established his third base camp at Moosburg (September 2)—a very strong site protected by the town walls and the angle formed by the confluence of the Amper and Isar rivers. The allies strengthened it with earthworks and three military bridges.

Piccolomini's next scheme, an attempt to surprise Landshut, was blocked by prompt countermeasures. On September 8, he set up a new forward camp at Geisenhausen near Moosburg and on the 10th, overran a minor strong point, taking 115 Swedes. The action of Moosburg on the 11th was bloodless and unimportant, but the allied deployment was well recorded.[11]

It was becoming increasingly difficult for Wrangel to feed his army. He attempted a cavalry raid into the Munich area, still relatively intact, but was met and defeated by Werth and Enkefort at the Action of Feldmoching (October 1), losing 700–800 men, a number of cornets, and all his booty. The Moosburg position could no longer be maintained. On October 8, the allies retired to Landsberg, crossing the Lech back into Swabia on the 10th. Bavaria had been preserved, but at heavy cost.

After separating from Wrangel (May 18), Konigsmarck had moved north through the Upper Palatinate to invade Bohemia. En route, he drew in detachments to bring his force up to 2000 horse and 1000 foot. The Imperial defenses, no more than adequate to begin with, had been depleted to reinforce Piccolomini. Konigsmarck quickly sacked the small towns of Taus, Klattau, Schuttenhofen, Bischofsteinitz, and Falkenau. These easy successes encouraged the independent corps of Palsgrave Karl Gustav (in Saxony) and Field Marshal Wittenberg (Silesia) to promise support. Knowing that they were on their way, Konigsmarck resolved to surprise Prague itself.

An Imperial lieutenant colonel, a Protestant, had defected to the Swedes[12] with Imperial information. This officer led a false flag party inside the town (July 26). As there were only a few hundred soldiers inside, success seemed assured. Unfortunately for Konigsmarck, the advance party started looting; the townspeople ejected them from within the walls. The Imperials rushed a reinforcement into the town before it could be fully invested, 3500 men under General Puchheim.[13] Obstinately, Konigsmarck tightened his grip on the Bohemian capital. Prague was not a strong fortification, nor were its inhabitants militaristic. In 1620, 1631, and 1632, the town had surrendered without resistance. Things were different in 1648. So horrific had the Swedish reputation become, that the whole population, Catholics, Protestants, Jews, clergy, even students, formed ad hoc companies and manned the walls.

Wittenberg arrived July 30 with 2000 horse, 2000 foot 16 guns, and 2 mortars, raising the investing force to 7000—rather weak for a serious siege. However, he soon lost interest in the slow reduction of a bitterly defended town. He first struck at the nearby strongpoint of Tabor (August 15–23) then Tetschen (September 3–26), before forming the plan of attacking Linz in hopes of sparking an uprising in Upper Austria. The scheme was foredoomed; there may well have still been anti-Hapsburg elements in Upper Austria,[14] but they were no more eager to welcome the Swedes than the Bohemians had been. Wittenberg marched south with 4000 horse—practically all the available cavalry—and 8 light guns (September 18). Despite an alleged success, the Action of Frauenberg (September 23), his offensive was halted by Imperial forces near Krummau.

Karl Gustav joined Konigsmarck at Prague on October 3, with 6000 men and 16 guns[15]—the foot and artillery that they needed for a proper siege. The Swedes stormed the town on October 25 but were beaten off.

Wrangel, having been forced out of Bavaria, resolved to join Konigsmarck and redeem his losses by sacking Prague. He crossed the Danube at Donauwerth, moving north and east toward the Upper Palatinate. Piccolomini was shadowing him to the east; he hoped to somehow cut Wrangel off, then lift the siege. Before the strategy could be concluded, news arrived (November 3) of the conclusion of peace (October 24). Fighting was broken off; Turenne withdrew to Swabia, the Swedes to Nuremberg. Konigsmarck remained encamped near Prague, but the siege was lifted. The beleaguered town had held out for over 3 months, inflicting over 1200 Swedish casualties for 694 Bohemian.

Piccolomini's reconquest of Bavaria was an excellent example of stomach strategy as a defense; in his capable hands it proved much more than the aimless plundering of a Brunswick or a Wrangel. However, while he virtually reversed the allied gains from Zusmarshausen and 2nd Lech, he could not, by that point, similarly reverse the strategic imbalance between the two sides. Even without considering the defeat of Lens, the emperor was fortunate to obtain peace on such reasonable terms.[16]

SOURCES:

The principal English source is Gindely (1884). Wedgwood (1961) and Barker (1975) deal with Zusmarshausen in passing. Turenne has some useful details, but the principal source for the fighting is Heilmann (1868). The Swedish study, *Från Femern och Jankow till Westfaliska freden* (1948), while not as detailed as the earlier works on Gustavus, is still well worth reading.

APPENDIX A: THE IMPERIAL ARMY

The Imperial Army in 1648 consisted of 96 regiments, 43 infantry regiments, 40 cuirassier regiments, 5 dragoon regiments, 6 Croats, and 2 of Polish Cossacks. There was in addition a handful of free companies, both horse and foot, mostly acting as minor garrisons. Of these regiments, 44 accompanied Melander to Zusmarshausen, 29 remained in the Bohemia-Moravia-Silesia area watching secondary Swedish forces, 3 were with the Spanish in Flanders, 9 were in Westphalia, and 8 infantry regiments were acting as garrisons. Melander's field army consisted of 15 infantry regiments, 26 cuirassier regiments, 2 dragoon regiments, and 1 Croat, plus a small artillery train.

When Melander assumed command in 1647, he was exchanging the relatively static Westphalian theater for an army suffering from repeated defeats and from 15 years of leadership by the nearly incapacitated Gallas. He was shocked at the contrast. The men, he said, "did not know what pay was"; over a quarter of the cavalry was on foot; what mounts they had were too often plowhorses, mules, or worse expedients, not proper warhorses; there was no money, and the train of camp followers had grown so large as to hamper operations—supposedly, of 127,000 mouths there were fewer than 30,000 combatants. There were other problems that he didn't notice: fine veteran regiments being disbanded because it was cheaper to raise new units than to rebuild the old, confusion and dissension among the officers, rates of desertion threatening unit integrity. Some of this was due to Gallas's neglect, some to lack of resources, some to misguided attempts at reform. Nevertheless, the core of the army retained its fighting spirit, and most units were, individually, in fair condition.

The infantry were in better shape than the cavalry or artillery, in that they were adequately equipped and organized. The infantry regiments averaged over 500 in the field forces, two-thirds musketeers and one-third pike. They retained a hard core of 15 old units formed prior to 1632, and these played a vital role in field operations. Imperial garrison policy, unlike Bavarian, avoided using field infantry in fortresses. Instead, a local governor would form a garrison company or regiment according to how much he thought was needed and how much the area could afford. Field units would reinforce them only in the immediate presence of the enemy—Prague had actually been entered by the Swedes before more troops were dispatched. Of the 43 infantry regiments, at least 6 were immobile garrisons. This allowed a higher proportion of field forces to concentrate for field operations.

The Battle of Zusmarshausen

The cavalry had undergone great changes. The arkebusier regiment, already in disfavor in 1633, had been finally discredited by the defeat of 2nd Breitenfeld. The last arkebusier regiment was disbanded by 1644. Of 40 cuirassier regiments, at least 8 were converted arkebusier regiments—4 others were transfers from other armies. This did not, however, radically raise the heaviness of the horse, as an increasing proportion of them were so-called "demi-cuirassiers" with light armor and a carbine. The tendency in both Imperial and Swedish armies was toward a non-specialized generic "cavalry" capable of both formal battle and skirmish. Some of the duties of the arkebusier regiment devolved onto the dragoons, who were now often employed for scouting and raids—however, these retained their predilection for fighting on foot. Fortunately, there were still plenty of Croats, hussars, and Cossacks. Indeed, Polish light horse appeared by the thousand in the last 3 years of fighting in Bohemia. The cavalry lacked the continuity of the infantry regiments—of 40 cuirassier regiments only 9 were older than 1632 and 5 of these were ex-arkebusier regiments. Only 1 of 6 Croats and none of the 5 dragoon regiments could make this claim. Strength was low, less than 150 per regiment. Their effectiveness was further degraded by lack of mounts.

Aside from Wallenstein, none of the Imperial commanders were artillery-minded, and the innovations favored by the Swedes and French had largely passed them by. Except for a larger proportion of light guns, the train in 1648 was practically the same as in 1618. The Imperials made no effort to organize or regularize the arm; it remained a guild of expert gunners hired to operate a miscellaneous collection of cannon.

Chart based on Wrede and the Imperial *Krieglisten*:

Unit	Date	Coy	Nation	Notes
Melander KUR	1647	1	—	Leib Coy
Jung-Nassau KUR	1625	10	German	ex-Neu-Saxon; Nassau-Dillenburg
Merode KUR	1625	10	German	ex-AltSaxon ARK;Merde-Boccarme
Gonzaga KUR	1626	10	German	Louis Gonzaga
Lannoy KUR	1627	5	German	AKA Lanan; ex-Bernstein-Trappola
Schaff KUR	1628	10	German	ex-Colleredo ARK; von Havelsee
Piccolomini KUR	1629	10	L.Ger	ex-Alt-Piccolomini ARK
Kaplir KUR	1630	10	German	ex-Bonninghausen ARK
Bocamaggiore KUR	1631	5	—	ex-ARK; Boccamagiore de Gropelli
Vernier KUR	1631	10	L.Ger	ex-Neu-Trcka
Montecuccoli KUR	1632	10	German	ex-Neu-Piccolomini
Pless KUR	1632	10	German	ex-Hasenburg/Assenburg (League)
Khevenhuller KUR	1632	—	German	ex-Westfalen (Catholic League)
Beck KUR	1633	9	German	ex-Harrich/Harrach/Horrich
Furstenberg KUR	1634	8	German	ex-S.Piccolomini-Lammersdorf
Sporck KUR	1635	—	—	ex-Kaspar Mercy
Alt-Nassau KUR	1635	—	—	Nassau-Dillenburg
Konigsegg KUR	1637	—	L.Ger	ex-Ohr, Westphalia
Kapaun KUR	1638	—	—	AKA Capaun
Pompeii KUR	1639	—	—	
Tapp KUR	1640	—	Silesia	ex-De Waghi ARK
Warfuse KUR	1640	—	Saxon	ex-Wolframsdorf, ex-Saxony
Pallavicini KUR	1641	8	H.Ger	ex-Archduke L.W. Leib, Up Austria
Luttke KUR	1641	—	German	ex-Sax-Lauenburg, ex-Brandenburg
Kolowrat KUR	1642	6	Bohem	
Lutzelburg KUR	1646	6	—	
Bonninghausen KUR	1647	4	German	AKA Boninghausen
Paconchay DR	1641	—	—	
Someda DR	1645	—	—	

Unit	Date	Coy	Nation	Notes
Colombo Croats	1632	10	Croat	ex-Dornberg

29 CR = 3000+ horse at Zusmarshausen

Unit	Date	Coy	Nation	Notes
Baden IR	1618	10	H.Ger	ex-Alt-Saxon
Ranfft IR	1618	10	H.Ger	ex-Alt-Breuner
Puchheim IR	1619	10	German	ex-Collato
Ruischenberg IR	1619	10	L.Ger	ex-Tiefenbach
Zuniga IR	1625	10	Bohemia	ex-Colloredo
Gallas IR	1626	10	L.Ger	
Hauser IR	1628	6	German	ex-Zweyer
Mercy IR	1630	10	H.Ger	ex-Hardeck
Mandelslohe IR	1630	10	L.Ger	ex-Holk
Fernemont IR	1631	10	Walloon	ex-Suys
Wachenheim IR	1631	8	German	ex-Schlick
Mercy IR	1632	4	L.Ger	
Conti IR	1639	10	German	ex-Gil de Haas; 5 coy in Prague
Starhemberg IR	1642	10	H.Ger	ex-Schifer
Fernberger IR	1642	—	H.Ger	Lower Austria
Melander IR	1646	—	German	ex-Zaradetzky

(Note that no. of coy fluctuated annually, and that the original nationality of the older units would not mean much by 1648)

15 IR = 7000 foot at Zusmarshausen.

The only guns that took part in the fighting were six 3 pdrs.

Total: 3000 cavalry + 7000 infantry = 10,000 men.

The other forces:

Unit	Date	Coy	Nation	Theater	Notes
Renz KUR	1636	—	—	Bohemia	ex-Hanensee
Velradt KUR	1636	—	—	"	AKA Fellrath
Donepp KUR	1639	5	—	"	ex-Wiedemann ARK
De Waghi CR	1642	8	Silesia	"	6 KUR + 2 Drag Coy
S.Gotz KUR	1643	—	—	"	
Schneider KUR	1644	7	—	"	
Liechenstein KUR	1645	4	Austria	"	ex-Archduke L.W. II
Creutz KUR	1645	3	Moravia	"	ex-Wrbna
Zriny KUR	1647	3	German	"	
Dohna KUR	1648	4	German	"	
Gallas DR	1634	10	German	Bohemia	
De Waghi DR	1642	—	—	"	
Palffy Croats	1631/2	10	Croat	"	ex-Corpes
Marcovich Croats	1641	—	Croat	"	
Palffy Croats	1647	1	Croat	"	
Lubetich Croats	1647	4	Croat	"	
Schaffelitzky CR	??	??	Poles	"	Cossacks
Przichowski CR	??	??	Poles	"	"
Souches IR	1629	10	Bohemia	"	ex-Waldstein
Moncado IR	1631	12	H.Ger	"	ex-Illow
Montevergues IR	1636	—	German	"	
Waldstein IR	1643	—	—	"	
Locatelli IR	1644	—	—	"	AKA Eulenburg
Wallis IR	1644	10	German	"	AKA Wallace
Rochow IR	1646	5	Silesia	"	ex-garrison coys
Strassoldo IR	1647	—	Silesia	"	

Zeillern IR	1647	6	Bohemia	"	ex-garrison coys	
Morder IR	1647	—	Silesia	"		
Warlowsky IR	1647	4	Bohemia	"		
Rantzau KUR	1645	—	Walloon	Flanders		
Beck IR	1626	9	German	"	ex-Neu-Saxon	
Wrede IR	1645	—	German	"		
Holstein KUR	1642	—	German	Westphal		
Gotz KUR	1643	—	—	"	ex-Goldacker	
Salm KUR	1647	—	Hesse	"	ex-Melander	
Reumont IR	1636	—	L.Ger	"	Cologne	
Arco IR	1641	5	Tyrol	"		
Plettenberg IR	1644	—	German	"		
Fehlberg IR	1644	—	Cologne	"		
Lamboy IR	1647	—	Trier	"		
Holstein IR	1647	4	Dane	"	Ex-Danish	
D'Espaigne DR	1632	10	German	?		
Zrinyi Croats	1642	6	Croat	Serinvar Garrison		
Enkefort IR	1631	9	German	Memmigen Garrison; ex-Funk		
Spieckh IR	1632	10	L.Ger	Ehrenbreitstein Gar; ex-Hatzfeld		
Bournonville IR	1636	—	Silesia	Trier Gar; Bournonville-Hennin		
Sparr IR	1636	10	German	South Germany		
Wolfsegg IR	1638	8	German	Lindau Garrison; ex-Vitzthum		
Bunigen IR	1639	—	H.Ger	Bregenz Garrison; Carinthian		
Schaumburg IR	1639	—	German	Offenbach Garrison		
Rubland IR	1645	—	Italy	Tyrol		

There were 2 free companies in the field forces and 1 in Lower Austria. There were 24 in garrisons, 3 in Bohemia, 6 in Moravia-Silesia, about 6 in Germany, and about 9 in Hungary. To these must be added the venerable Vienna Stadt Guard, the standing (since 1526) garrison of the capital, a mixture of militia and about 1000 regulars.

In addition to regulars in Westphalia, there were at least 12 infantry regiments and 3 cavalry regiments of local forces. Some of the Catholic rulers, such as Cologne and Bamberg, had independent units not included in Imperial or Bavarian lists.

APPENDIX B: THE BAVARIAN ARMY

The Bavarian Army in 1648 consisted of 13 cavalry regiments, 14 infantry regiments, and 6 free companies of infantry, which acted as garrisons. On the whole, the Bavarians enjoyed a slight qualitative edge over the Imperials—better organized, better paid, better equipped—but were otherwise similar. There were differences in approach. The Bavarians, confronted with different opponents and strategic situations, had retained the arkebusier; they were, however, imitating the Imperial use of light cavalry with Croats of their own. More problematic was the matter of garrison policy. The theory was the same as the Imperials'; free companies and militia would hold normally, to be reinforced by regulars during a crisis. In fact, however, the Bavarians entrusted much less freedom of action to garrison commanders and placed much more reliance on field force supplements. This was possibly due to the attitude of Elector Maximilian, who paid great attention to finances—a major contrast with his Hapsburg allies—and was greatly concerned with defense and strongholds. Thus, when the enemy approached the Bavarian heartland—as in the period 1645-48—there was pressure to disperse the field forces into garrisons. This was bad enough under an able commander like Mercy; at 2nd Nordlingen he deployed only 9 of his 13 infantry regiments, the rest being in garrison. Asofar as that goes, the field battalions were weakened by detachments for the same purpose. Under a defensive minded general like Gronsfeld, the army practically disappeared—of 14 infantry regiments only 3 went to Zusmarshausen. Dispersal of cavalry, while excessive, was less egregious. As Gronsfeld regarded cavalry as the decisive arm, he did not view the dissipation of his infantry as important.

Unit	Date	Coy	1647	March	Dec	Notes
Fleckenstein KUR	1620	9	824	—	779	ex-Erwitte; Schmutter
Gayling KUR	1620	10	942	—	941	ex-Kratz; at Lech
Alt-Kolb KUR	1634	10	917	—	805	ex-Binder; Schmutter
Lapierre KUR	1635	9	935	—	898	ex-Gotz
Jung-Kolb ARK	1621	10	911	—	904	ex-Eynatten;Schmutter
Cosalky ARK	1634	8	704	—	664	ex-Neuenheim
Zink ARK	1639	10	1034	—	961	ex-Sporck
Waldott CR	1642	8	701	—	584	ex-Sperreuter
Truckmuller CR	1633?	6	—	—	505	at Schmutter
Modersbach CR	1645	5	—	—	433	
Bartl DR	1641/2	10	723	—	689	ex-Creuz; at Lech
Guscheniz Croats	1635	5	477	—	427	at Lech
Wurtemberg Croat	1642	10	1070	—	845	at Schmutter
Enkefort IR	1620	10	704	736	645	ex-Anholt
Holz IR	1620	8	657	688	655	ex-Mortaigne
Mercy IR	1620	10	603	609	691	ex-Herliberg
Cobb IR	1620	9	628	628	615	ex-Bauer; at Lech
Rouyer IR	1620	7	740	684	554	ex-Haimhausen; Lech
Gronsfeld IR	1620	10	720	793	—	ex-Schmidt
Winterscheid IR	1621	9	528	711	—	ex-Springen
Marimont IR	1624	9	605	681	—	ex-Erwitte
De Puech IR	1631	10	924	808	—	exFugger;AKABuiche
Fugger IR	1632	8	519	660	—	ex-Ruepp
Elter IR	1638	8	830	842	735	ex-Gold; at Schmutter
Horst IR	1644	6	819	818	—	
Beltin IR	1644	10	653	660	695	ex-Gil de Haas
Ners IR	1645	10	687	720	—	AKA Nersen
Free Coys	1645?	6	—	586	—	Garrisons

Gronsfeld set his force at the beginning of the campaign at 5000 foot and 9000 horse, probably Mercy, Cobb, Rouyer, Winterscheid, De Puech, Fugger, Elter, and Ners infantry regiments (a nominal 5662), plus Fleckenstein, Gayling, Alt-Kolb, Lapierre, Zink, Jung-Kolb, Cosalky, Truckmuller, Bartl, Guscheniz, and Wurtemberg (a nominal 8418). By Zusmarshausen, however, he was down to 5000–6000 horse and 2000–3000 foot: Cobb, Rouyer, and Elter (2154); Fleckenstein, Gayling, Alt-Kolb, Jung-Kolb, Truckmuller, Bartl, Guscheniz, and Wurtemberg (5895). By July, they were back up to 4000 foot and 6000 horse, presumably by regrouping some of Gronsfeld's detachments.

Heilmann gives two artillery lists:

April 1646
2 Demicannon
6 Quarterculverins
14–15 Falcons
6 Field Guns
1–2 Mortars

June 27, 1648
4 Demiculverins
4 Sakers
8 Heavy Falcons
4 Falconets
2 Howitzers

Gronsfeld's guns were 30: 2 demicannon (24 pdr). 4 demiculverins (8 pdr), 4 sakers (6 pdr), 12 falcons (4 pdr), 6 falconets (3 pdr), and 2 mortars. The 8 guns lost after the Lech action were 2 demicannon, 4 falcons, and 2 falconets.

APPENDIX C: THE SWEDISH ARMY

The Swedish Army in Germany in 1648 mustered a nominal 62,950 men in 954 companies, 20,736 cavalry; 39,760 infantry, and 2645 dragoons; 17,744 Swedes and 45,206 Germans. These were divided into a field force of 37,511— 22,821 horse and 14,690 foot—and 25,440 in garrison. The Swedish garrisons extended the length of Germany, from the Baltic to Westphalia in the northwest; Alsace, Uberlingen, and Rain in the south; Bohemia, Silesia, and Olmutz in the southeast. The Swedish army was the largest in Germany, dwarfing the Imperials, the Bavarians, and the French contingent under Turenne.

The Swedish army consisted of two parts, the permanent native army, raised by conscription, of 23 infantry regiments and 8 cavalry regiments, and more temporary mercenary forces. At this time these "foreign" troops were mostly Germans. The Swede and Finn units serving in Germany were technically battalions or detachments of the real regiments remaining at home. While the standing army was supported by taxes, tolls and so on, only a tiny proportion of this domestic revenue went to the forces in Germany. These, both Swedes and Germans, were maintained by local kontributions, French subsidies, and loot.

Of the nominal field force of 37,511, Wrangel invaded Bavaria with about 23,000— 15,000 horse and 8000 foot—and posted at least 10,000 in the secondary Bohemia-Silesia, Saxony, and Westphalia fronts. In May, Konigsmarck was sent north with 1500; he acquired another 3000 en route and was subsequently joined by Wittenberg with 4000 and Palsgrave Karl Gustav with 6000, implying 13,000 operating in Bohemia. At the same time, Baden joined Wrangel with 4500. Mankell's lists do not tell us which units were with Wrangel, which were at Zusmarshausen, and which with Konigsmarck. The units at Moosburg in September were mostly with Wrangel the whole campaign, but this does not mean that others were not.

Tactically, the Swedes were still much the same as they had been in 1636 under Baner. The infantry fought in fair-sized battalions, "brigades," and the cavalry in small squadrons. The infantry relied on the musket, the cavalry, who were still the best in Germany, relying on the charge. The artillery had lost a bit of the luster that it enjoyed under Gustavus and Torstensson, but it was still the best in Europe.

Organizationally, however, there had been changes. The infantry, who had formed over half the army under Baner and 40–50% under Torstensson, had dwindled to a third. Wrangel was cavalry-minded and, like his opponents, treated the foot as a support arm. Cavalry sweeps and skirmishes had superseded strategy. The once-prominent Scots were no longer significant in the army—the supply had dried up with the outbreak of the British civil wars. There was at this time a large contingent of native Swedes, 9128, about a quarter of the field force—they were especially numerous among the foot, 6070 to 8620 Germans. The prejudice against German officers was wearing down: Konigsmarck was second in command; there was 1 German lieutenant general to 2 Swedes and a Scot, and 3 major generals of 7.

The mobile army was composed of five corps: Wrangel, Konigsmarck, Wittenberg, Karl Gustav, and Baden. It seems that Baden separated from Wrangel before Zusmarshausen but rejoined in time for Moosburg; there is no way of determining which units these were. Therefore, most of Baden is included under Wrangel. Konigsmarck's original 1500 consisted of his personal dragoon regiment, 4 ex-Weimar cavalry regiments, plus his Leib coy—the first coy of his cavalry regiment. All these units were at Zusmarshausen. The units listed under Wittenberg and Karl Gustav were (probably) all part of those corps, but not all of them. The units listed as "Uncertain" would mostly be from Karl Gustav and the extra units acquired by Konigsmarck. These listings are approximate, as the Swedish commanders were constantly shifting units between corps and garrisons. Thus, as Wrangel advanced, he left field units in garrison and drew on rear garrisons for supplements; Konigsmarck, detached with 1500 horse, acquired 500 horse and 1000 foot from garrisons and detachments; Wittenberg, in turn, took most of these horse for his Austrian operation, leaving behind his own foot.

Fourteen infantry regiments were definitely with Wrangel on May 4: Sack, Gladstein, Nehren, Knorring, Alt-Blau, Linde, Steinacker, Forbus, Volkmann, Paikull, Doring, Lewenhaupt, Stenbock, and Konigsmarck, in 9 brigades. All were present at Moosburg, several of them in the same brigades. The West Gothland Cavalry (Kruse) seems to have been divided into 2 squadrons, one under Wrangel, and the other with the Palsgrave.

Chart based on Mankell (Field Force):

Wrangel's Corps:

Unit	Coy	Strength	Notes
Wrangel CR	4	365	Swede; Uppland; Moosburg-1 sqd
Kruse CR	4	450	"W.Goth AKA L.Cruus; Mbg-1 sq
H. Horn CR	8	620	Finn; Tavastehus; Moosburg-2 sqd
Wrangel Leib CR	13	700	German; Moosburg-3 sqd
Wrangel Leib DR	9	535	
Konigsmarck CR	13	1000	" Moosburg-3 sqd
Baner CR	8	(500)	" Moosburg-2 sqd
Axel Lillie CR	8	280	" Moosburg-1 sqd
Douglas CR	8	420	" Moosburg-1 sqd
Stenbock CR	8	370	" Moosburg-2 sqd
Landgrave Hesse CR	16	802	" Darmstadt; Moosburg-2 sqd
Goldstein CR	8	398	" Moosburg-1 sqd
Hammerstein CR	8	414	" Moosburg-2 sqd
Horn CR	8	353	" Moosburg-2 sqd
Margrave Baden CR	8	400	" Durlach; Moosburg-2 sqd
K. Lewenhaupt CR	8	457	" Count Karl; Moosburg-2 sqd
D'Avangour CR	8	250	" D'Avancourt; Moosburg-1 sqd
Lettmat CR	8	329	" Moosburg-1 sqd
Wittkopt CR	8	372	" Moosburg-1 sqd
Per Andersson CR	8	342	" Moosburg-2 sqd
Frolich CR	8	393	" Moosburg-2 sqd
Hundelhausen CR	8	346	" Moosburg-1 sqd
Bottiger CR	8	344	" Moosburg-2 sqd
Poley CR	8	351	" Moosburg-1 sqd
U. Pentz CR	8	500	" Moosburg-2 sqd
E. Pentz CR	8	358	
Fritz CR	8	255	" Moosburg-2 sqd
Gortski CR	8	270	" Moosburg-1 sqd
Endt CR	8	300	" Moosburg-2 sqd
Kurck CR	8	300	" Moosburg-1 sqd
Geischwitz CR	8	450	" =Kettler? Moosburg-2 sqd
Jordan CR	8	339	" Moosburg-2 sqd
Pfuhl CR	4	228	" Moosburg-2 sqd
Sack IR	8	900	Swede: Moosburg-1/2 bn
Nehren IR	4	400	" Moosburg-1/2 bn
Gladstein IR	8	820	" East Botten; Moosburg-1 bn
F. Knorring IR	8	700	" Tavastehus; Moosburg-1 bn
Konigsmarck IR	12	900	German; Moosburg- 1/2 bn

Unit			
Alt-Blau IR	12	615	" Gustavan" vets; Msbg-1/2 bn
Stenbock IR	12	700	" Moosburg-1/2 bn
G. Lewenhaupt IR	8	600	" Moosburg-1/2 bn
Linde IR	12	700	" Moosburg-1/2 bn
Volkmann IR	8	700	" Moosburg-1/2 bn
Doring IR	8	460	" Moosburg-1/2 bn
Forbes IR	8	460	" Moosburg-1/2 bn
Paikull IR	8	1150	" Erfurt garrison; Msburg-1/2 bn
Steinacker IR	12	(750)	" Schweinfurt gar; Msburg-1/2 bn
Bulow IR	8	900	" Nordlingen garrison
Konigsmarck's Corps:			
Konigsmarck DR	8	700	German
Pege CR	8	220	"
Mohr CR	8	250	"
Plaunitz CR	8	450	"
Qwast CR	4	220	"
Palsgrave Karl Gustav's Corps:			
Kruse CR	4	550	Swede; W.Gothland AKA L.Cruus
Oxenstierna CR	4	443	" Smaland CR
Kruse CR	8	920	Finn; Karelia, AKA E. Kruse
Royal Leib CR	12	1000	1/2 Swede & 1/2 German
Prince's Leib CR	3	350	German
De la Gardie CR	4	400	"
De la Gardie DR	9	600	"
Mecklenburg CR	8	319	"
Fitinghof IR	4	550	Swede; Sodermanland
Skytte IR	6	700	" Kronborg, AKA Fleetwood
Kagge IR	4	400	" West Gothland
Gordon IR	4	500	Finn; Viborg
Royal Leib IR	8	850	German
Wittenberg's Corps:			
Wittenberg CR	8	450	German; ReichsZeugmeister
Free Coys	10	600	" cav
Hamilton IR	8	1150	Swede; Uppland
G. Knorring IR	8	(500)	" West Nylands
Barclay IR	4	300	" Varmland & Dal
Sabel IR	4	330	Finn; Helsinki
Ritter IR	5	500	" Tavastehus
Wittenberg IR	12	800	German
Uncertain:			
Lewenhaupt CR	6	260	Swede
Muller CR	8	350	German
G. Lewenhaupt CR	8	189	"
Ulfsparre CR	8	398	"
Arendson CR	8	211	"
Kanneberg CR	8	450	"
Douglas DR	8	500	"
Ekeblad	2	250	Swede
Nilsson IR	4	600	" Smaland
Axelson IR	6	520	Finn; Abo
Axel Lillie IR	12	635	German
Mellin IR	8	500	"

Persin IR	9	700	"

Wrangel had 60 guns, about 20 heavy—mostly 12 pdr, a few 24 pdr—and 40 light 3 pdr.

The Swedish garrisons:

6 garrison cavalry coys	400 (German)
Swabia-Donauwerth-Rain-Nordlingen	1,931 infantry
Alsace	1,000 "
Upper Palatinate	500 "
Franconia	1,284 "
Bohemia	600 "
Moravia	1,860 "
Silesia	2,700 "
Saxony	3,313 "
Brandenburg	1,160 "
Westphalia	4,135 "
Bremen	1,120 "
Mecklenburg	1,390 "
Pomerania	3,756 "

Of the native standing army, the 8 cavalry regiments were Uppland, East Gothland, Smaland, West Gothland, Noble Levy, and 3 Finn regiments. To these may be added a militia unit and a dragoon regiment. The 23 infantry regiments included 14 Swedish (Uppland, Westmanland, Dalarna, Nerike, Sodermanland, West Botten, East Botten, Norrland, 3 Smaland—Kronborg, Kalmar, Jonkoping—and 3 from West Gothland), and 9 from Finland. Each of three Finnish regions, Abo, Tavastehus, and Viborg, supplied 3 infantry regiments and 1 cavalry regiment.

APPENDIX D: TURENNE'S FRENCH ARMY

Turenne's army was a comparatively small part of the estimated 120,000 French troops in service, and not typical of the whole. Like the Swedes, the French contingents in Germany were divided into French and German units, both field force and garrison. Turenne's numbers varied less than Wrangel's, so the order of battle would have been much the same for Zusmarshausen and Moosburg. The field force numbered about 9,000 at the start of the campaign, 4000 horse and 5000 foot, but by Zusmarshausen it was down to 7000–8000. Two infantry regiments and a cavalry regiment had been detached.

Chart derived from Mankell and Gonzenbach:

Unit	Coy	1649 Str	Notes
Duras CR	12	300	French; Moosburg 2 sqd
Tracy CR	8	300	" " 2 sqd
Meispas CR	8	300	" " 2 sqd
Beauveau CR	8	300	" " 1 sqd
Olipart CR	-	—	" " 2 sqd
Turenne CR	12	700	German; " 3 sqd
Mazarin CR	8	350	" " 2 sqd
Betz CR	8	330	" " 2 sqd
Ohm CR	8	320	" Weimar; Moosburg 2 sqd
Fleckenstein CR	8	315	" " " 1 sqd
Taupadel CR	8	274	" " " 1 sqd
Erlach CR	17	1100	" " " 2 sqd
Russwurm CR	7	200	" " " 2?
Schutz CR	8	354	"
Buchenau CR	8	296	" Moosburg 2 sqd
Turenne DR	10	400	" " 1 sqd

The Battle of Zusmarshausen

Turenne IR	20	—	French? Moosburg-1 bn
Montausier IR	14	—	French; " 1 bn
Vaubecourt IR	30	—	" " 1 bn
Netancourt IR	12	—	" " 1/2 bn
La Couronne IR	12	—	" " 1/2 bn
Passagie IR	12	—	" " 1/2 bn
Du Tot IR	12	—	" " 1/2 bn
Duval IR	12	—	" " 1/2 bn
Mazarin IR	12	—	French-Italian; Moosburg 1 bn
Schmidtberg IR	12	—	German; Moosburg 1/2 bn
Kluge IR	12	—	" " 1/2 bn AKA Kluck
Erlach IR	10	—	" Weimar; Moosburg 1/2 bn
Breisach Garrison	43	2671	Erlach, Charlevois, Bernhold IRs
Alsace	5	414	
West Bank of Rhine	15	—	
Spires	15	—	Plus 2 cav coy
Palatinate	9	—	
Lauingen	13	—	
Wurtemberg	11	243	Plus 3 cav coy
Swabia	6	—	
Mainz	12	—	
Baden	3	196	

The French also had available the Hesse-Cassel army.

Leib Coy	1	Landgrave Wilhelm
Leib CR	10	
Groot CR	10	
Landgrave Ernst CR	10	
Wied CR	10	
Taranto CR	10	"Prince of Taranto"
Geiso Leib Coy	1	LtGen of Hesse-Cassel
Free Coys	6	cavalry
Geiso IR	12	
Wardenburg IR	12	
Gunterade IR	12	
Wurtemberg IR	12	Duke Friedrich of Wurtemberg
Thungen IR	12	
Willich IR	12	
St Andre IR	12	
Stauf IR	12	
Benthon IR	12	
Stemfels IR	12	
Ufflen IR	12	
Motz IR	12	
Ahlfeldt IR	8	
Free Coys	14	infantry

Hessian total: 58 cavalry coys & 166 infantry coys = 10,000–15,000 men.

APPENDIX E: ALLIED O.B. AT MOOSBURG (MANKELL)
Right Wing:

1st Echelon		2nd Echelon	
Baner CR	Swede;2 sqd	Wittkopf CR	Swede-1 sqd

J. Wrangel CR	" 1	Goldstein CR	" 1
H. Horn CR	" 2	P. Andersson CR	" 2
Lifregement CR	" 3 "Leib"	Lettmat CR	" 1
Jordan CR	" 2	Axel Lillie CR	" 1
Margrave CR	" 2	Poley CR	" 1
Landgrave CR	" 2	Kruse CR	" 1 Which?
Hammerstein CR	" 2	Hundelhausen CR	" 1
Konigsmarck CR	" 3	Pentz CR	" 2 Both?
Douglas CR	" 1	Gortski CR	" 1
		Endt CR	" 2
	20 Sqd		14 Sqd

Center:

1st Echelon		2nd Echelon	
Nehren & Alt-Blau Bn	Swede	Forbes & Volkmann Bn	Swede
Knorr IR	"	Lewenhaupt & Konigsmarck Bn	"
Linde & Steinack Bn	"	Stenbock & Doring Bn	"
Netancourt & La Couronne Bn	French	Schmidtberg & Kluge Bn	French
Turenne IR	"	Mazarin IR	"
Vaubecourt IR	"	Passagie & Du Tot Bn	"
Montausier IR	"		
	7 Bn		6 Bn

Left Wing:

1st Echelon		2nd Echelon	
Horn CR	Swede-2 sqd	Fritz CR	Swede-2 sqd
Stenbock CR	" 2	Pfuhl CR	" 1
D'Avancourt CR	Swede?-1	Kurck CR	" 1
Olipart CR	French?-2	Bottiger CR	" 2
Count Carl CR	Swede?-2	Beauveau CR	French-1
Duras CR	French-2	Erlach CR	" 2
Tracy CR	" 2	Ohm CR	" 2
Meispas CR	" 2	Mazarin CR	" 2
Betz CR	" 2	(Russwurm CR)	(2)
Taupadel CR	" 1		
Buchenau CR	" 2		
Fleckenstein CR	" 1		
Turenne CR	" 3		
Dragoons	" 1		
	25 Sqd		15 Sqd

Reinforcement:

Gladstein IR	(Swede)	Kettler CR	Swede-2 sqd
Sack & Paikull Bn	"	Frolich CR	" 2
Duval & Erlach Bn	(French)		
	3 Bn		4 Sqd

Total: 16 battalions & 78 squadrons. Therefore, the battalions averaged about 500, a squadron a bit less than 200.

APPENDIX F: THE FRANCO-SPANISH WAR TO 1648

French operations in 1646 were characterized by limited success in Flanders, inertia in Italy, and failure in Spain-Catalonia. The Lerida campaign in Catalonia proved insoluble both to the able Harcourt in 1646 and to Conde in 1647. Italy showed some signs of improvement in 1647, first with the victory of the Oglio, then with a major anti-Spanish uprising in Naples and Sicily. The strain of war had sent half the Spanish empire—Portugal, Catalonia, Sicily, Naples—into revolt. But the opportunity was lost—Mazarin again managed to overreach himself—and the Two Sicilies returned to loyalty to Spain.

In Flanders, things went differently. Archduke Leopold Wilhelm (the loser at 2nd Breitenfeld) was appointed governor of the Spanish Netherlands—the Spanish hoped that this would reinforce their weakening ties with Austria, even divert Imperial resources to Flanders. With great energy and enthusiasm, he began a major counteroffensive, 1647–48. Turenne's effort to intervene was cut short by the Weimarian mutiny and Beck's defense of Luxemburg. Leopold enjoyed considerable success at first, retaking the lost fortresses of Armentieres, Comines, Landrecies, and Lens. Unfortunately for him, Conde, fresh from his failure in Catalonia, was appointed to the Flanders command. The resultant massacre, the Battle of Lens (August 20, 1648), cost Leopold 8000 men and his reputation.

APPENDIX G: TURENNE'S ARMY 1647–49

Garrisons 1647–48:

Garrison	1647	1648	Notes
Breisach	1789	1789	Charlevois Fr IR (10 coy)= 933
			Erlach Ger IR (9 coy)= 856
Landskron, Pfeffigen, Hunigen	414	122	
Dachstein	101	—	
Lichtenegg & Limburg	66	—	
Stollhofen	196	196	
Rheinfelden	414	422	Bernhold German IR
Lauffenburg	340	340	
Hohentwiel	262	243	Wiederhold IR
Neuburg	—	298	
Thann	—	116	
Total:	3552	3526	

Turenne's Cavalry 1649:

Unit	Coy	Str	Nation
Turenne CR	12	700	German
Fleckenstein CR	—	315	"
Schutz CR	9	354	"
Ohm CR	8	320	"
Mazarin CR	8	350	"
Buchenau CR	8	296	"
Taupadel CR	6	274	"
Betz CR	8	330	"
Russwurm CR	4	200	"
Erlach CR	17	1100	"
Dragoons	10	400	"
Duras CR	9?	300	French
Tracy CR	9?	300	"
Beauveau CR	9?	300	"
Meispas CR	9?	300	"
Total:		5839	"

APPENDIX H: RAISING AND PAYING UNITS

Most of the units employed during the war were raised by "military enterprisers" under contract to the "warlords," the ruling princes. The enterpriser would give the recruits a full month's pay in cash, some additional cash for expenses (called *liefergeld* or *laufgeld*, subsistence money, for infantry, but *anritt*, mounting costs, for cavalry), weapons, and sometimes clothing. Of the expenses involved, some were billed to the warlord and some deducted from the men's pay over the next year.

The tem *handgeld* (cash in hand) properly refers to an additional bonus for signing up, but it could be applied to expense money and/or the month's pay.

A League (Wurzburg) bill of 1625 for a company of 300 foot (Heilmann):

1 flag (ensign)	91.5 florins
2 fifes at 6 fl each	12
1 partisan	3
10 halberds at 1.5 fl each	15
80 pikes and armors, at 7.5 fl each	600
201 muskets with accessories, at 4.5 fl each	904.5
1 barrel (cwt.) gunpowder	60
1 barrel (cwt.) bullets	9
2 barrels (cwt.) match at 9 fl each	18
1 month's pay	3375
Raising costs (*liefergeld*)	1749
Total:	6837 florins

From a bill submitted to the emperor in 1627 (Redlich):

Laufgeld for 10 infantry coys	4,500 florins
Their first month's pay	28,100
10 flags (ensigns)	400
Anritt for 400 KUR	6.000
Their first month's pay	7,760
10 flags (cornets)	400
Anritt for 600 ARK	9.000
Their first month's pay	10,560

A League table of equipment of 1625 for a regiment of 3000 (Heilmann):
10 flags (ensigns)
10 officers' partisans
50 NCO halberds
1200 suits of armor (for pikemen)
1000 pikes
200 ordinary halberds
200 pairs of armored gauntlets
1500 muskets
1500 musket rests
1500 bandoleers and powder flasks
31 drums
20 fifes
300 arquebuses
300 arquebus flasks and accessories
1851 jackets

Note that jackets were issued to musketeers, but not pikemen, who received armor instead. Officers were responsible for most of their own equipment.

A 1610 bill to Cologne for 1500 Dutch muskets with bandoleers and accessories ran 4 florins each. A 1611 price list (Bavaria) ran (Heilmann):

Ornate partisan for officer	6 florins
Musket	3 fl
Musket rest	.167 fl (10 kr)
Powder flasks and belts	1.5167 fl (91 kr)
Bullet mold for the musket	.083 fl (5 kr)
Arquebus	2.25 fl
Arquebus flask and accessories	.7167 fl (43 kr)
NCO halberd	.45 fl (27 kr)
Drum	4 fl
Fife	2 fl

A League (Bamberg) bill for muskets (Heilmann):

1619	Musket	2.05 florins
	Musket rest, bandoleer, and accessories	1.3 fl
1622	Musket with all accessories	2.25 fl

Pay Rates (florins/month) (Redlich):

Imperial 1619	KUR	15
	ARK	12
Saxony 1619	Infantry	9.6
Baden 1621	KUR	16
	ARK	14
Mansfeld 1621	Cavalry	15
Bavaria 1622	KUR	18
	ARK	16.5
	Pike	8
	Musket	7.5–8
Brunswick 1622	KUR	18
	ARK	15
	Pike	9
	Musket	7
Imperial 1626–28	Infantry	9–10
Imperial 1629	Cavalry	12
	Infantry	7.5
Imperial 1625–36	Croats	4–5
Imperial 1630	KUR	15
	ARK	12
	Infantry	6.67
Sweden 1631	KUR	16.5
	Infantry	6
Imperial 1630	KUR	9+food
	ARK	6+food
	Infantry	4+food
Imperial 1640	KUR	15
(half in food)	ARK	12
	Infantry	6.5

A bill of the Heilbronn Bund, 1633 (Kretzschmar):

Unit	Coy	Monthly Cost (florins)
Birkenfeld CR	8	4,050

Rhinegrave CR	8	4,050
Birkenfeld IR	8	1,425
Vitzthum IR	7	1,275
Courville CR	8	4,050
Mitzlaff IR	4	645
Rosen IR	1	142
Muffel IR	7	1,355
Total:	51	16,992 florins/month

At about the same time, Oxenstierna estimated the cost of troops at 44 talers/year per infantryman, and 123 per cavalryman. This would be at the half pay rate used by Sweden throughout the war.

An Imperial (Westphalia) account of June 1638 (*Documenta*):

	Foot	Horse
Hatzfeld	1000	—
Georg of Brunswick-Luneburg	2000	2000
Hesse-Darmstadt	1000	1000
Westerhold	1000	1000
Vehlen	2000	—
From the Main Army	—	4000
Total:	7000	8000

Powder	3000 Barrels (cwt.)
Bullets	2000 Barrels
DemiCannon	14
Artillery Horses	600
Cannonballs	4000
Provisions	50,000 gulden = 50,000 florins

Powder	500 Barrels
Match	1000 Barrels
Provisions	30,000 fl
Artillery	30,000 fl
Total:	60,000 florins

An Imperial account of January 5, 1641, cash issued to cover recruiting and remounts for the coming campaign year (*Documenta*):

Quarters	Arm	Regiment	Coys	Florins
Vienna	Cavalry	Alt-Piccolomini	12	12,000
		Jung-Piccolomini	10	10,000
		Montecuccoli	6	9,000
		Nicola	10	11,000
		Bruay	7	7,000
		Mislik	8	8.000
		Capaun	6	6,000
		Puchheim (Gissenburg)	8	8,000
		Ramsdorf	8	9,000
		Gil de Haas	10	6,000
	Infantry	Gonzaga	11	5,000
		Caretto	10	5,000
		Savelli	10	6,000
		Soye	10	4,000
		Suys	12	5,000

Regensburg	Cavalry	Bourre	10	5,000
		Waldstein	10	4,000
		Leib Gardes	10	13,000
		Gonzaga	12	12,000
		Braganza (Desfurs)	8	10,000
		Spiegel	6	6,000
		Heister	8	8,000
	Infantry	Geleen	10	10,000
		La Fosse	10	3,000
		De Mors	8	3,000
		Mercy	-	3,000
		Beck	7	4.000
		Gil de Haas	10	3,000
Total:				75,000

A Bavarian Army estimate of April 1643 for 3 months' expenses (Heilmann):

2646 horses for remounts, with saddles and trappings	150,000 florins
New clothes for 4000 men	55,000
2000 pairs of cavalry pistols, with holsters and accessories	18,500
2000 cavalry swords	2,500
Artillery equipment, munitions, 152 horses	23,705
Provisions and fodder	20,000
Miscellaneous expenses	10,000
Total:	279,705 florins

These remounts and expenses were needed to field the army for the new campaign year. The cost of clothing and equipment issues was deducted from the soldier's pay. The implication of this bill is that the army had 12,000 men in winter quarters, but wished to recruit another 4000 (2000 cavalry and 2000 infantry).

A Bavarian bread bill of 1643: 1.5 pound bread daily for 16,000 men = 80 Schaffels (300 pound barrel). 2400 Schaffels at 5.5 florins each = 13,200 florins a month (Heilmann).

Bavarian Army expenses for 1645 (entire year) (Heilmann):

Remounts, provisions, and fodder	997,088 florins
Artillery and munitions	225,000
Recruitment expenses	36,000
Miscellaneous	34,969
Provisions for Imperial troops in Bavaria	26,000
Militia expenses	27,242
	1,346,501 florins

In the Swedish army, it early became customary to issue part of a soldier's pay in clothing, and this practice was not at all uncommon in Germany in the 1630s and 40s. When a unit was raised, the enlisted men (not the officers) might be issued a suit of clothes, the cost to be deducted from their pay. Similarly, in winter quarters each year, another suit might be issued, again as part of the pay. If, as was not always the case, the purchasing colonel selected a particular color scheme, the unit would assume a uniform appearance. As the issues were not mandatory and were often replaced and supplemented on an ad hoc basis, these were not yet true uniforms, as the term was understood during the linear period.

After about 1631, it became increasingly common for local commanders to exchange prisoners with their counterparts, rather than incorporate them into their own units (although that always remained an option). Under the "cartel" system, prisoners in excess of the other's number would be ransomed back to their own side at so much a head. The following were cartel rates for rankers (florins) (Redlich):

Signing Parties	Year	Cavalry	Infantry
Imperials-Swedes	1626	12	7
Imperials-Hesse-Cassel	1633-4	12	6
Imperials-Weimar	1635-9	7.5	3
Imperials-Hesse-Cassel	1643	9	4.5
Imperials-Swedes	1644	12	6 (dragoon=9)

APPENDIX I: THE PEACE OF WESTPHALIA

Emperor Ferdinand III had begun peace overtures in 1643, following the disasters of 2nd Breitenfeld and Rocroi. Nevertheless, it took over five years to reach a settlement, the French and Swedish demands being unacceptable to the Germans.

By 1648, the situation had changed. Repeated defeats had rendered the Imperial cause precarious, making "unthinkable" concessions possible. Even more important, powerful pro-peace factions had come to power in Sweden and Holland. Events had demonstrated to these allies that the French were using them as catspaws for their own ends (!). The Dutch signed a separate peace (January 30, 1648). The Swedes threatened to do the same. But what finally decided Mazarin was the growing threat of civil war in France. On October 24, the war between the Empire, France, and Sweden ended; that between Spain and France dragged on until 1659.

NOTES

1. Not all the German units were involved. The mutineers were mostly lesser officers and rank-and-file; the senior officers remained loyal to their employer. However, some units had to be completely rebuilt.

2. Gronsfeld detached Jung-Kolb Arkebusier Regiment to hold the riverbank.

3. He left 700 men behind to garrison Neumarkt.

4. See Appendix A.

5. Turenne—5000 infantry and 5000 cavalry; Wrangel—4000 infantry and 9000 cavalry; Gronsfeld—2000 infantry and 5000 cavalry; Montecuccoli—5500 infantry and 2000 cavalry.

6. Barker, *Military Intellectual*, p. 158.

7. Representing, as they did, the rival German and Italian factions.

8. Turenne, having the smaller corps, was content to play a subordinate role at this time—provided that Wrangel respected the goals of French diplomacy.

9. Imperials: 6000 infantry and 8000 cavalry; Bavarians: 4000 infantry and 6000 cavalry.

10. Hunoldstein had been only interim commander.

11. See Appendix E.

12. This sort of treachery was considered dishonorable.

13. Waldstein, Mercy, and Conti infantry regiments; Kaplir, Pless, and Renz cuirassier regiments; Gallas and Paconchay dragoon regiments, and the Schaffelitzky and Przichowski Cossacks.

14. There had been a series of Protestant uprisings in Upper Austria, 1619-26.

15. 3000 infantry, 3000 cavalry, two 24 pdrs, six 12 pdrs, eight 3 pdrs, 8 petards, and 1000 hand grenades.

16. See Appendix I.

Glossary

Action: or skirmish; a combat not large enough to be considered a battle.
Alt: "old"; when two regiments shared the same name, the senior was prefixed as *Alt-*, the junior either *Jung-* or *Neu-*.
ARK: abbreviation of *arkebusier*, normally refers to an *arkebusier* regiment.
Arkebus: short-barreled, muzzle-loading cavalry smoothbore, a *firelock*. Carried by an *arkebusier*, a *dragoon*, or a *demicuirassier*.
Arkebusier: medium cavalry armed with swords and *arkebus*.
Arquebus (harquebus): short-barreled, muzzle-loading infantry smoothbore, usually a *matchlock*. Carried by an arquebusier.
Art: abbreviation for artillery.
Bastion: in a fortress, an artillery position projecting from the wall with an improved field of fire. More generally, any defensive *work*.
Battalion: (abbreviated bn) infantry **tactical** unit, containing both *pike* and *shot*, sometimes referring specifically to the *pikemen*. Also a subdivision of an infantry *regiment*.
Battery: (abbreviated batt) a group of artillery pieces; an artillery **tactical** unit.
Bav: abbreviation of "Bavarian."
Bn: abbreviation of battalion.
Body: of pike, the *pike* formation at the core of a *battalion*, flanked by the *sleeves*.
Brigade: a **tactical** grouping of several *battalions* or *squadrons*.
Caliver: a large-caliber arquebus.
Camp Followers: nonmilitary persons attached to an army, primarily wives and prostitutes; also includes offspring, servants, grooms, and peddlers.
Cannon: a short-barreled, thin-walled, muzzle-loading artillery piece. The most common type was the 24 *pounder* demicannon (i.e., "half-cannon").
Caracole: a cavalry tactic emphasizing firepower as opposed to shock action.
Carbine: or carabin; a type of *arkebus*.
Cav: abbreviation for cavalry.

Col: colonel.
Company: (abbreviated coy) basic unit of organization, usually 50–100 cavalrymen or 100–200 infantrymen under a captain.
Contribution or "contributio": a war tax voted by a legislature.
Cornet: a cavalry flag; could also refer to the company carrying the flag or to the officer bearing the flag.
Corselet: infantry body armor; a breastplate and backplate.
Cossacks: Polish light irregular cavalry armed with lances.
Covered Way: the ditch or moat between a fortress wall (or trace) and the *glacis*.
Coy: abbreviation for company.
CR: abbreviation of cavalry *regiment*.
Croat: light irregular cavalry recruited in Croatia, *arkebusiers* and *dragoons*.
Cuirass: body armor worn by heavy cavalry, called cuirassiers.
Culverin: a long-barreled, thick-walled, muzzle-loading artillery piece. The most common type was the 12 *pounder* demiculverin.
Demicuirassier: a "light" heavy cavalryman armed with sword, pistol, and arkebus.
Demilune: a curved outwork, open in back so that it could not protect the attacker from defensive fire.
Detachment: (abbreviated det) an **ad hoc** grouping detached from their parent regiment.
DR: abbreviation of *dragoon regiment*.
Dragoon: (abbreviated drag) a mounted infantryman, normally armed with an *arkebus* or similar weapon.
Echelon: a line of tactical units abreast with intervals between. Normally there would be 200 meters or so between *echelons*.
Ensign: an infantry flag; or the officer bearing it.
EstStr: estimated strength.
File: men formed in line ahead.
Firelock: as opposed to a *matchlock*, a firearm that used sparks to detonate the powder charge instead of a match. Firelock types were *wheellocks* and *snaphances*. A few of these were rifled.
FM: field marshal.
Forlorn or Forlorn Hope: a formation of *shot* unsupported by *pikemen*.
FZM: feldzeugmeister, "chief of artillery."
Garde: guard.
Gen: general.
Glacis: earthen ramp placed in front of a fortress wall to screen it from fire.
Guidon: a cavalry flag, term particularly used by dragoons.
Gun: an artillery piece.
GWM: generalwachtmeister, roughly equivalent to major general.
GZM: generalfeldzeugmeister, "general of artillery," a senior rank.
Half-pike: short pike seven to nine long, often carried by officers/cadre instead of a full pike. Partizans, halberds, and spontoons also played this role.
HG: High (South) German.
Hornwork: a more elaborate outwork than a demilune or a ravelin, with two or three sub-bastions. It was, however, also open in the back.
Hussars: light irregular cavalry recruited in Hungary and Transylvania.
IMP: abbreviation of "Imperial."
Inf: abbreviation of infantry.
IR: abbreviation of infantry *regiment*.
Jung: "young"; prefix used for a junior regiment of the same name.
Kontribution: a tax in cash or kind levied by an army in an occupied area; a form of

organized plundering. The term "kontributions" refers to the proceeds.
KUR: abbreviation for kurassiere; normally refers to a cuirassier regiment.
League (the League): the Catholic League
Leib: (English: Life Guard) a personal company or regiment of a commander. Some leaders distinguished between leib, household, and guard units.
LG: Low (North) German.
LtCol: abbreviation of lieutenant colonel.
LtGen: abbreviation of lieutenant general.
MajGen: abbreviation of major general.
Matchlock: a firearm where the gunpowder was detonated by a match, a length of smoldering cord. Most muskets, arquebuses, and calivers were matchlocks.
Mine: in sieges, an underground chamber filled with powder; the detonation was intended to destroy defensive works.
Mortar: a siege weapon with a high trajectory; it fired explosive shells rather than iron balls.
Musket: a long-barreled, muzzle-loading, infantry smoothbore, normally a *matchlock* requiring a *rest*. Carried by musketeers.
Neu: "new"; prefix used to distinguish the junior regiment of the same name.
Outwork: parts of a fortification lying outside the main defenses. Outworks included demilunes, hornworks, ravelins, sconces, and independent fortlets. The purpose of an outwork was to delay an enemy's attack on the main defenses.
Pdr: abbreviation of *pounder*.
Pike: a long spear, normally 14–18 feet, primarily used as a defense against cavalry.
Pikemen: heavy infantry armed with the *pike,* often armored.
Pistol: short cavalry firearm, normally a *wheellock*.
Pounder: (abbreviated pdr) classification of the caliber of an artillery piece by the weight of its projectile. A "12 pdr" fired a 12 pound ball.
Quarters: area where a force or unit was housed (quartered), normally also where it was drawing its subsistence from. "Winter Quarters" would have to be capable of supporting the force for three to five months.
Rank: A line abreast.
Ravelin: similar to a *demilune* but more angular, like a shallow "v.".
Regiment: standard **administrative** unit for both infantry and cavalry; consisted of three or more *companies* under a colonel.
Rest: a fork supporting a musket; the musketeer held the rest in his left hand, balanced the barrel in the fork of the rest, and pulled the trigger with his right hand.
Rifle: as opposed to a smoothbore, longer ranged but slow loading; rarely used except for jager ("hunter") units. Most were firelocks.
Sap: a narrow trench used to approach hostile fortifications.
Sconce: a fully detached outwork with all-around defense; most were quite small.
SgtMaj: abbreviation of sergeant-major.
Shot: light infantry carrying firearms, including musketeers and arquebusiers.
Sleeves: Supporting shot on the right and left sides of a "body" of *pikemen*.
Snaphance: firearm similar to the later flintlock; the charge is detonated by sparks from a flint against a steel striker.
Squadron: cavalry **tactical** unit, also a subdivision of a cavalry *regiment.*
Str: strength, number of men in a unit.
Subsistence: that portion of a soldier's pay intended to cover food, often issued in kind.
Tercio: Spanish term for an infantry regiment; less specifically, a *battalion* formation in which the *pikemen* are two ranks to one file, the *shot* composing both *sleeves* and some ranks in front of the pike.

Train or Baggage train: the wagons accompanying the army on the march.
Wheellock: firearm where the charge is detonated by sparks from pyrites on a spring-wound wheel grinding against steel.
Wing: a major division of a army in battle order; such an army would be divided into right wing, left wing, and center. The center was normally infantry; the wings, cavalry.

Bibliography

PRINTED PRIMARY SOURCES

Abelinus et al. *Theatrum Europaeum*. Frankfurt, 1635–50.
Barwick, Humfrey. *Concerning the Force and Effect of Mauall Weapons of Fire*. London, 1594?
Cruso, John. *Militarie instructions for the Cavallrie*. Cambridge, 1632.
Davies, Edward. *The Art of War and Englands Traynings*. London, 1619.
De Gheyn, Jacob. *The Exercise of Arms*. The Hague, 1607.
Du Cornet, Louis de Haynin. *Histoire Générale des Guerres de Savoie, du Bohême, du Palatinat, & des Pays-Bas, 1616–27*. Brussels: Société de l'Histoire de Belgique, 1868.
Gualdo Priorato, Galeazzo. *History of the Late Warres*. London, 1648.
Ludlow, Edmund. *Memoirs*. 1692.
Markham, Gervase. *The Souldiers Exercise*. London, 1639.
Monro, Robert. *Monro: His Expedition with the Worthy Scots Regiment Called Mac-Keys*. London, 1637.
News from Germanie. London, 1642.
Overton. *True and Brief Relation of the Bloody Battle*. London, 1638.
Polisensky et al. *Documenta Historica Bohemica*. Vol. 1–7. Prague, 1971–81.
Repgen, Konrad, et al. *Acta Pacis Westphalicae*. Munster: Aschendorff, 1962–84.
The Swedish Discipline. London, 1632–34.
Turenne, Henri de la. *Memoires du marechal de Turenne*. Paris: Renouard, 1909–1914.
Turner, James. *Pallas Armata*. London, 1683.
Vincent, Philip. *The lamentations of Germany*. London, 1638.
Watts, William. *The Swedish Intelligencer*. Parts I–IV. London, 1633–34.
Williams, Sir Roger. *The Works of Sir Roger Williams*. Oxford, 1972.

SECONDARY SOURCES

Albrecht, Dieter. "Der Finanzierung des Dressigjahrigen Krieges," *Zeitschrift fur*

bayerische Landesgeschichte. 19 (1956), pp. 534–567.
Ardant du Picq, C.J.J.J. *Battle Studies.* Mechanicsburg PA: Stackpole, 1958.
Asch, Ronald. *The Thirty Years War.* New York NY: St. Martin's Press, 1997.
Barbe, Marie-France. *La Bataille de Rocroi, 19 Mai 1643.* Rocroi: Syndicate d'Initiative de Rocroi, 1977.
Barker, Thomas. *The Military Intellectual and Battle.* Albany NY: SUNY Press, 1975.
———. *Army, Aristocracy, Monarchy.* New York: Social Science Monographs, 1982.
Belaubre, Jean. "The Troops of Electoral Saxony during the Thirty Years War." Condray, 1982.
Benecke, Gerhard. *Society and Politics in Germany 1500–1750.* London: Routledge, 1974.
———. *Germany in the Thirty Years' War.* New York NY: St. Martin's Press, 1978.
Bireley, Robert. *Religion and Politics in the Age of the Counterreformation.* Chapel Hill NC: University of North Carolina Press, 1981.
Bjorlin, Gustaf. *Sveriges Krighistoria.* Vol. 1. Stockholm: Pahlmans, 1914.
Black, Jeremy. *The Origins of War in Early Modern Europe.* Atlantic Highlands NJ: Humanities Press, 1987.
Bodart, Gaston. *Militar-historisches Kriegs-Lexikon, 1618–1905.* Vienna: Stern, 1908.
Bonney, Richard. *Political Change in France under Richelieu and Mazarin.* Oxford: Oxford University Press, 1978.
———. *The King's Debts.* Oxford: Clarendon, 1981.
Bruijn, J. *The Dutch Navy of the Seventeenth and Eighteenth Centuries.* Columbia SC: University of South Carolina Press, 1990.
Burckhardt, Carl. *Richelieu and his Age.* New York NY: Harcourt, 1970.
The Cambridge Modern History. Cambridge: Cambridge University Press, 1934.
Canovas del Castillo, Antonio. *Estudios del reinado de Felipe IV.* Madrid, 1888.
Chudoba, Bohdan. *Spain and the Empire, 1519–1643.* New York NY: Octagon, 1969.
Clarke, Jack Alden. *Huguenot Warrior.* The Hague: Nijhoff, 1966.
Croxton, Derek. *Peacemaking in Early Modern Europe.* Selinsgrove NJ: Susquehanna University Press, 1999.
Cust, Edward. *Lives of the Warriors of the Thirty Years' War.* Freeport NY: Books for Libraries Press, 1972.
D'Aumale, Henri. *Histoire des Princes de Condé pendant les XVIe et XVIIe Siècles.* Paris: Calmann Lévy, 1886.
Delbruck, Hans. *History of the Art of War.* Vol. 4. Westport CT: Greenwood, 1985.
De Peyster, John W. *The History of the Life of Leonard Torstensson.* Poughkeepsie, NY: Platt and Schram 1855.
Droysen, Gustav. *Bernhard von Weimar.* Leipzig: Duncker and Humblot, 1885.
Duffy, Christopher. *Siege Warfare.* London: Routledge, 1985.
Duffy, Michael. *The Military Revolution and the State, 1500–1800.* Exeter: Exeter University Press, 1980.
Dupuy, R. Ernest, and Trevor N. *The Encyclopedia of Warfare.* New York NY: Harper, 1970.
Egler, Anna. *Die Spanier in der LinkRheinischen Pfalz 1620–32.* Mainz: Selbstverlag der Gesellschaft fur mittelrheinische Kirchengeshichte, 1971.
Elliott, John H. *The Revolt of the Catalans.* Cambridge: Cambridge University Press, 1963.
———. *Imperial Spain, 1469–1716.* New York NY: St. Martin's Press, 1964.
———. *Richelieu and Olivares.* Cambridge: Cambridge University Press, 1984.
———. *The Count-Duke of Olivares.* New Haven CT: Yale University Press, 1986.
Elster, Otto. *Die Piccolomini-Regimenten wahrend des dressigjahrigen Krieges.* Vienna,

1903.
Engelbert, Günther. *Das Kriegsarchiv des Kaiserlichen Feldmarschalls Melchior von Hatzfeldt (1593–1658)*. Düsseldorf: Droste, 1993.
Ernst, Hildegard. *Madrid und Wien, 1632–1637*. Munster: Aschendorff, 1991.
Fischer, E. L. *The Scots in Germany*. Edinburgh: Schulze, 1902.
Frauenholz, E. von. *Prinz Eugen und die Kaiserliche Armee*. Munich: Beck, 1932.
Generalstaben, Svensk Armen. *Sveriges krig, 1611–1632*. Stockholm, 1936–39.
———. *Meddelanden fran Generalstabens Krighistoriska*. Stockholm, 1939.
———. *Gustaf II, Adolf*. Stockholm, 1938.
Geyl, Pieter. *The Netherlands Divided*. London: Williams and Norgate, 1936.
Gindely, Anton. *History of the Thirty Years War*. New York NY: Putnam, 1884.
Glete, Jan. *Warfare at Sea 1500–1650*. London: Routledge, 2000.
Gonzenbach, August von. *Hans von Erlach*. Bern: Eyss, 1880–82.
Griffith, Paddy. "Cavalry Melees." *Courier*. 6/6, p. 20.
Guilmartin, John. *Gunpowder and Galleys*. London: Cambridge University Press, 1974.
Gunter, Heinrich. "Die Habsburger-Liga, 1625–1635." *Historische Studien*. Berlin (1908).
Gush, George. *Renaissance Armies*. UK: Patrick Stephens, 1975.
Guthrie, William P. "Naval Actions of the Thirty Years War," *The Mariner's Mirror*. 87/3 (August 2001), pp. 262–280.
———. *Battles of the Thirty Years War*. Westport CT: Greenwood, 2002.
Hale, John R. *War and Society in Renaissance Europe, 1450–1620*. Leicester: Leicester University Press, 1985.
Hall, Bert S. *Weapons and Warfare in Renaissance Europe, Gunpowder, Technology, and Tactics*. Baltimore MD: John Hopkins University Press, 1997.
Heilmann, Johann. *Die Feldzuge der Bayern 1643, 1644, 1645*. Leipzig: Goedsche, 1851.
———. *Kriegsgeschichte von Bayern, Franken, Pfalz, und Schwaben, 1506–1651*. Munich: Cotta, 1868.
Henty, G. A. *Won by the Sword*. New York NY: Scribner, 1904.
Hoeven, Marco van der (ed.). *Exercise of Arms, Warfare in the Netherlands, 1568–1648*. Leiden: Brill, 1997.
Huater-Ammann, F. von. *Geschichte kaiser Ferdinand II*. Schaffausen: Hurtersche, 1850–64.
Hutton, Ronald. *The Royalist War Effort, 1642–1646*. London: Routledge, 1982.
Israel, Jonathan I. *The Dutch Republic and the Hispanic World, 1606–1661*. Oxford: Clarendon, 1982.
———. *The Dutch Republic, Its Rise, Greatness, and Fall 1477–1806*. Oxford: Clarendon, 1995.
Jennings, Brendan. *Wild Geese in Spanish Flanders*. Dublin: Irish Manuscripts Commission, 1964.
Kagan, Richard, and Parker, Geoffrey. *Spain, Europe and the Atlantic World*. Cambridge: Cambridge University Press, 1995.
Kapser, Cordula. *Die bayerische Kriegsorganisation in der zweiten Hälfte des Dreissigjährigen Krieges 1635–48/49*. Munster: Aschendorff, 1997.
Keegan, John. *The Face of Battle*. New York NY: Vintage, 1977.
Krebs, Julius. *Aus der Leben des kaiserlichen Feldmarschalls Grafen Melchior von Hatzfeld*. Breslau: W. G. Korn, 1910–26.
Kretzschmar, Johannes. *Der Heilbronner Bund 1632–1635*. Lubeck: Rahtgen, 1922.
Loewe, Victor. *Die Organisation und Verwaltung der Wallensteinischen Heere*. Freiburg: Mohr, 1895.
Lundkvist, Sven. "Svensk krigsfinansiering 1630–1635." *Historisk Tidskrift* 86 (1966),

p. 377–421.
Lynch, John. *Spain Under the Habsburgs*. Oxford: Oxford University Press, 1969.
———. *The Hispanic World in Crisis and Change. 1598–1700*. Oxford: Blackwell, 1992.
Lynn, John A. ."Tactical Evolution in the French Army, 1560–1660." *French Historical Studies* (1985). pp. 176–191.
———. *Feeding Mars*. Boulder, CO: Westview, 1993.
———. *Giant of the Grand Siècle, The French Army, 1610–1715*. New York NY: Cambridge University Press, 1997
Maland, David. *Europe at War, 1600–1650*. Totowa, NJ: Rowman and Littlefield, 1980.
Mallet, Michael, and Hale, John R. *The Military Organization of a Renaissance State*. Cambridge: Cambridge University Press, 1984.
Mankell, Julius. *Uppgiver*. Stockholm: Thimgren, 1865.
Martinez de Campos y Serrano, Carlos. *España Belica, el Siglo XVII*. Madrid: Aguilar, 1968.
Mecenseffy, Grete. *Habsburger im 17. Jahrhundert*. Vienna: Rohrer, 1955.
Menédez-Pidal, Ramon. *Historia de España XXV, La España de Felipe IV*. Madrid: Espasa-Calpe, 1982.
Muir, Rory. *Tactics and the Experience of Battle in the Age of Napoleon*. New Haven CT: Yale University Press, 1998.
Murdoch, Steve (ed.). *Scotland and the Thirty Years' War, 1618–1648*. Leiden: Brill, 2001.
Naylor, Francis. *Civil and Military History of Germany 1630–1648*. London: Murray, 1816.
The New Cambridge Modern History. Cambridge: Cambridge University Press, 1968.
Noailles, Amblard de. *Bernhard von Saxe Weimar*. Paris, 1913.
Nosworthy, Brent. *The Anatomy of Victory*. New York NY: Hippocrene, 1990.
Oberleitner, Karl. *Beitrage zur Geschichte der Dressigjahren Krieges*. Vienna, 1858.
Oman, Charles. *A History of the Art of War in the Sixteenth Century*. New York NY: Dutton, 1937.
Osterreichischer Bundesverlag fur Unterricht. *Wissenschaft und Kunst, Schriften des Heeresgeschichylichen Museums in Wien*. Vol. 7. Vienna, 1976. Includes "The Hardegg IR, 1634–36," and Hoyos, "The Imperial Army 1648–50."
Pages, Georges. *The Thirty Years War, 1618–1648*. London: Harper, 1970.
Parker, Geoffrey. *The Army of Flanders and the Spanish Road, 1567–1659*. Cambridge: Cambridge University Press, 1972.
———. *Europe in Crisis 1598–1648*. Ithaca NY: Cornell University Press, 1980.
———. *European Soldiers, 1550–1650*. Cambridge: Cambridge University Press, 1977.
———. *The Military Revolution of Early Modern Europe*. Cambridge: Cambridge University Press, 1987.
———. *The Thirty Years' War*. London: Routledge, 1984.
Perkins, James B. *France under Richelieu and Mazarin*. New York NY: Putnam, 1902.
Philips, C. R. *Six Galleons for the King of Spain*. Baltimore MD: Johns Hopkins University Press, 1986.
Pleticha, Henrich. *Landsknecht, Bundschuh, Soldner*. Wurzburg: Arena-Verlag, 1974.
Polisensky, Josef. *Nizozemska politika a Bila hora*. Prague, 1958.
———. *The Thirty Years' War*. Berkeley CA: University of California Press, 1971.
———. *War and Society in Europe, 1618–48*. Cambridge: Cambridge University Press, 1978.
Raa F. J. G. ten, and Bas, F. de. *Het Staatsche Leger*. Breda-The Hague, 1911–64.
Rabb, Theodore K. *The Thirty Years' War*. Lexington MA: D. C. Heath, 1972.

Reade, Hubert. *Sidelights on the Thirty Years' War.* London: Kegan Paul, 1924.
Redlich, Fritz. *De Praeda Militari.* Wiesbaden: Steiner, 1956.
———. "Contributions in the Thirty Years' War." *Economic History Review* (1959–60), pp. 247–54.
———. *The German Military Enterpriser and his Work Force.* Wiesbaden: Steiner, 1964.
Repgen, Konrad. *Krieg und Politik 1618–1648.* Munich: Oldenbourg, 1988.
Ritter, Moriz. *Deutsche Geschichte im zeitalter der gegenreformation und des Dressigjahrigen Krieges.* Stuttgart, 1895–1908.
———. "Das Kontributionssystem Wallensteins." *Historische Zeitschrift.* XC (1902/3).
Roberts, Michael. *Gustavus Adolphus: A History of Sweden 1611–1632.* London: Longmans, 1958.
———. *Essays in Swedish History.* Minneapolis, MI: University of Minnesota Press, 1967.
———. *Sweden as a Great Power.* New York NY: St. Martin's Press, 1968.
———. *Sweden's Age of Greatness.* New York NY: St. Martin's Press, 1973.
———. *Gustavus Adolphus.* New York NY: Longmans, 1992.
Rogers, Clifford J. *The Military Revolution Debate.* Boulder CO: Westview, 1995.
Rudolf, Hans Ulrich. *Der Dressigjahrige Krieg—Perspektiven und Strukturen.* Darmstadt: Wissenschaftliche Buchgesellschaft, 1977.
Salm, H. *Armeefinanzierung im Dressigjahrigen Krieg. Der Niederrheinisch-Westfalische Reichkreis 1635–1650.* Munster: Aschendorff, 1990.
Schaufler. *Die Schlacht bei Freiburg im Breisgau 1644.* Freiburg: Rombach, 1979.
Schiller, Friedrich. *The History of the Thirty Years' War in Germany.* Weimar Edition, 1901.
Schmidt. *Die Schlacht bei Wittstock.* Halle, 1876.
Schwarz, Henry F. *The Imperial Privy Council in the Seventeenth Century.* Cambridge MA: Harvard University Press, 1943.
Steinberg, S. H. *The Thirty Years War and the Conflict for European Hegemony.* New York NY: Norton, 1966.
Stradling, R. A. *Europe and the Decline of Spain.* Boston: Allen and Unwin, 1981.
———. *Philip IV and the Government of Spain, 1621–65.* Cambridge: Cambridge University Press, 1988.
———. *Spain's Struggle for Europe.* London: Hambledon, 1994.
———. *The Armada of Flanders.* Cambridge: Cambridge University Press, 1992.
Svensk Försvarsstaben, Krigshistoriska avdelningen. *Slaget vid Femern, 1644–13/10.* Göteborg: Sjöfartsmuseets, 1944.
———. *Slaget vid Jankow, 1645–24/2.* Stockholm: Generalstabens, 1945.
———. *Från Femern och Jankow till Westfaliska freden,* Stockholm: Generalstabens 1948.
Tapie, Victor. *France in the Age of Louis XIII and Richelieu.* New York NY: Praeger, 1974.
Thompson, I. A. A. *War and Government in Habsburg Spain, 1560–1620.* London: Athlone, 1976.
Tingsten, Lars Herman. *Fältmarskalkarna Johan Banér och Lennart Torstensson såson härförare.* Stockholm: Militärlitteraturföreningens förlag, 1932.
True, Charles K. *The Thirty Years War.* New York NY: Nelson and Phillips, 1879.
Van Crevald, Martin. *Supplying War.* Cambridge MA: Harvard University Press, 1977.
Wagner, Eduard. *European Weapons and Warfare 1618–1648.* London: Octopus, 1979.
Warburton, Eliot. *Memoirs of Prince Rupert and the Cavaliers.* London: Bentley, 1849.
Warner, Oliver. *The Sea and the Sword.* New York NY: Morrow, 1965.

Webb, Henry. *Elizabethan Military Science*. Madison WI: University of Wisconsin Press, 1965.
Wedgwood, C. V. *The Thirty Years War*. New York NY: Anchor, 1961.
Weigley, Russell F. *The Age of Battles*. Bloomington, IN: Indiana University Press, 1991.
Wijn, Jan. W. *Het Krijgswesen in den tijd van Prins Maurits*. Utrecht: Druckerij Hoenenbos, 1934.
Wrede, Alphons von. *Geschichte der k. und k. Wehrmacht*. Vienna: Seidel, 1898–1905.
Young, Peter, and Emberton, Wilfrid. *The Cavalier Army*. London: George Allen and Unwin, 1974.

Index

Aalst, 188
Aardenburg, 189
Adelhausen, 208
Africa, 186
Albert, 91
Alburquerque, 170, 172, 174, 176, 177, 178, 179, 183
Aldringer, 153
Allerheim, 217, 218, 224, 229
Alps, 40, 100
Alsace, 37, 77, 78, 79, 86, 87, 92, 93, 97, 101, 102, 170, 199, 212, 257, 260, 261
Alt-Brandenburg, 44, 45, 51
Alte Veste, 27, 28, 46, 110
Altenheim, 239
Altmuhl, 248
Altsattel, 130
Amberg, 235, 247
Amersfoort, 164, 190
Amper, 250
Amsterdam, 189, 190
Andorra, 34
Anglicans, Anglicanism, 2
Angola, 186
Anholt, 201
Ansbach, 235, 236, 247
Antwerp, 158, 159, 165, 168, 180, 181, 188, 190

Archduke Leopold Wilhelm, 60, 61, 70, 105, 106, 107, 108, 109, 112, 113, 116, 119, 120, 123, 142, 142, 144, 154, 181, 191, 192, 193, 224, 231, 233, 234, 239, 263
Arendsee, 106
arkebusiers, 10, 11, 19, 20, 23, 28, 99, 117, 129, 146, 253, 255
Armentieres, 263
Arnim, 43
Arnstein, 235, 247
Arras, 168, 169, 189
artillery, 10, 14, 21, 23, 26, 28, 35, 40, 46, 48, 49, 50, 51, 56, 57, 63, 66, 70, 71, 72, 73, 80, 83, 87, 89, 90, 91, 98, 110, 111, 114, 115, 119, 127, 129, 130, 132, 134, 135, 137, 138, 139, 147, 151, 162, 172, 179, 190, 198, 199, 202, 203, 207, 209, 213, 214, 215, 218, 219, 220, 221, 223, 226, 236, 240, 241, 242, 245, 246, 250, 251, 252, 253, 256, 257, 266, 267
Artois, 168, 170
Aschaffenburg, 217, 234, 235, 247
Aschersleben, 43, 127
Augsburg, 80, 97, 234, 236, 243, 245, 248
Aurach, 86
Austerlitz, 32

Austria, 3, 4, 5, 6, 7, 29, 32, 34, 50, 62, 77, 92, 106, 107, 108, 113, 124, 128, 144, 148, 153, 182, 193, 194, 234, 258, 263
Avesnes, 100, 167, 168, 169, 190
Axel Lillie, 60, 108, 109, 112, 115, 118, 122, 144, 149

Baden, 6, 7, 14, 212, 261, 265
Baden-Baden, 153
Baden-Durlach, 249, 257
Bakos-Gabor, 143
Baltic, 27, 32, 37, 40, 59, 82, 101, 102, 106, 123, 124, 144, 154, 257
Bamberg, 27, 29, 61, 87, 215, 229, 255, 265
Baner, 37, 38, 39, 40, 41, 42, 43, 44, 45, 46, 47, 48, 50, 51, 52, 53, 54, 55, 56, 57, 58, 59, 60, 61, 63, 64, 65, 67, 68, 69, 70, 72, 74, 75, 76, 81, 82, 92, 95, 97, 105, 106, 110, 111, 112, 121, 128, 142, 144, 149, 154, 197, 198, 230, 233, 237, 238, 257
Bannstein, 203, 204, 205, 207
Barby, 43
Bardesholm, 126
Bartenstein, 216
Basel, 79, 80, 93, 99, 238
Bassompierre, 133
Basta, 17, 19
Batilly, 92
Battle of the Downs, 168, 169
Battle of the Dunes, 171, 237
Batzenberg, 199, 200
Baudissin, 43, 44, 48, 68, 74
Bautzen, 60
Bavaria, 4, 6, 7, 15, 16, 21, 29, 30, 32, 34, 39, 42, 49, 61, 70, 77, 79, 80, 81, 82, 83, 84, 87, 91, 92, 93, 94, 95, 101, 102, 106, 121, 128, 131, 132, 134, 138, 139, 140, 144, 154, 167, 182, 197, 199, 200, 201, 204, 205, 207, 208, 209, 210, 211, 212, 213, 214, 215, 216, 217, 218, 221, 222, 223, 224, 225, 227, 228, 229, 231, 232, 233, 234, 235, 236, 239, 240, 241, 243, 244, 245, 246, 248, 249, 250, 251, 252, 255, 257, 265, 267, 268
Becher Wood, 208, 209, 210, 211

Beck, 73, 150, 170, 171, 176, 177, 178, 179, 180, 181, 182, 191, 192, 193, 195, 234, 263
Beilngries, 247
Belfort, 79
Bellingwolde, 189
Belzig, 107
Benfeld, 87, 96, 99
Berching, 247
Bergen-op-Zoom, 159, 160, 166, 189
Bergh, 159, 160, 162, 163, 164, 165
Bernburg, 127, 151
Bernhard Sax-Weimar, 29, 37, 38, 40, 41, 42, 46, 77, 78, 79, 80, 81, 83, 84, 85, 86, 87, 88, 89, 90, 91, 92, 93, 95, 96, 97, 98, 99, 100, 101, 103, 121, 172, 199, 200, 201, 233, 268
Bernhold, 84
Bethlen Gabor, 6
Bettenfeld, 215
Beuthen, 108
Billigen, 87
Birkenfeld, 50, 65, 81
Biscay, 100
Bischofsheim, 247
Bischofsteinitz, 251
Bjelke, 50, 54
Black Forest, 208
Blankenberge, 188
Bleckede, 107, 153
Bodendorf, 86
Bodensee, 79, 199
Bohemia, 3, 4, 5, 6, 7, 8, 32, 35, 40, 42, 49, 60, 62, 69, 76, 101, 102, 106, 107, 108, 109, 123, 128, 129, 144, 188, 193, 196, 234, 245, 248, 250, 251, 252, 253, 254, 255, 257, 260
Bohl, 203, 204, 205, 207, 208
Bohnenkamp, 52
Bonninghausen, 239
Borneval, 68, 113, 119
Boullion, 200
Bourtange, 189
Boury, 223
Boxtel, 163, 164
Brabant, 188, 189
Brandeis, 39, 60, 69, 70, 123, 154, 233, 239
Brandenburg, 3, 7, 37, 42, 43, 44, 59, 60, 68, 71, 106, 123, 260
Brazil, 186, 195

Breda, 100, 158, 159, 160, 161, 162, 166, 168, 169, 181, 188, 189, 190, 194
Bredevoort, 189
Bregenz, 255
Breisach, 32, 42, 81, 86, 87, 90, 91, 92, 93, 97, 131, 199, 200, 212, 213, 226, 232, 261, 263
Breisgau, 86, 93, 199, 224
Breitenfeld, 16, 24, 26, 27, 28, 29, 33, 35, 37, 39, 42, 45, 46, 47, 48, 78, 84, 109, 110, 116, 118, 121, 122, 124, 132, 141, 147, 177, 180, 201, 221, 239, 268
Breitenfeld, second battle of, 39, 42, 46, 47, 105, 113, 116, 120, 121, 122, 123, 144, 146, 148, 151, 154, 233, 239, 253, 263
Bremen, 43, 260
Breslau, 107
Breze, 100, 190
Brieg, 108, 121
Britain, 194, 257
Bruay, 68, 113, 119, 127, 132, 133, 138, 139, 140, 141, 155, 231
Bruges, 165, 166, 168, 188
Brunn, 108, 123, 142, 143
Brunswick, 105
Brunswick, Christian of, 6, 7, 46, 101, 159, 188, 252, 265
Brussels, 78, 157, 163, 165, 189
Brux, 129
Buchwald, 125
Buck, 209
Bucken, 80, 84
Bucquoy, Charles, 101, 121, 195
Bucquoy, Albert, 170, 192
Budweis, 5
Bull Run, 58
Bunnigen, 87
Buntzlau, 109
Burgau, 236, 248
Burgundy, 79, 82, 88, 95, 100, 167, 174, 176, 177, 182, 183

Cadzant, 188
Callenberk, 133, 140
Calvinists, Calvinism, 1, 2, 3, 4, 5, 6, 34, 35, 47, 153, 157, 194, 238
Cambrai, 189
Cannae, 58, 108

cannon, 14, 23, 55, 56, 67, 72, 86, 127, 152, 161, 164, 190, 210, 221, 223, 245, 253
Cantelmo, 170, 180
caracole, 19, 20, 28
Cardinal-Infante, 28, 100, 102, 112, 166, 167, 168, 169, 172, 200
Caribbean, 186
Casale, 193
Castel, 248
Castro War, 82
Catalonia, 78, 100, 168, 169, 180, 184, 193, 262, 263
Catholic Church, 3, 4, 5
Catholic League, 4, 6, 7, 15, 16, 17, 19, 21, 31, 49, 62, 73, 77, 81, 93, 165, 195, 197, 201, 239, 253, 264, 265
Catholics, Catholicism, 1, 2, 3, 4, 5, 6, 7, 8, 9, 15, 17, 22, 27, 31, 34, 36, 37, 41, 42, 47, 79, 80, 81, 100, 101, 153, 157, 158, 160, 165, 172, 182, 194, 195, 198, 201, 238, 251, 255
Cerignola, 180
Ceylon, 186
Chabot, 223
Champagne, 171, 191
Charles I, 72
Charles of Lorraine, 72, 77, 78, 79, 91, 92, 198, 201
Chateau-Regnault, 170
Chatillon, 100, 190
Chemnitz, 48, 60, 69, 72, 106, 109, 110, 123, 127
China, 186
Christian IV of Denmark, 2, 6, 7, 14, 36, 43, 47, 101, 124, 125, 154, 162, 246
Christian of Anhalt, 6
Christianspreis, 125
Church Lands, 3
Cleves, 160, 167, 168, 189
Cobb, 223
Coevorden, 189
Colmar, 87
Cologne, 3, 4, 73, 190, 195, 198, 255, 265
Comines, 263
Compiegne, 100, 168
Conde, Louis, 21, 39, 99, 102, 111, 112, 121, 170, 171, 172, 173, 174, 175, 176, 177, 178, 179, 180, 181,

182, 185, 191, 192, 193, 195, 196, 200, 202, 204, 205, 207, 208, 209, 210, 211, 212, 213, 214, 217, 218, 219, 221, 222, 223, 224, 225, 229, 232, 233, 237, 247, 250, 263
Conde, Henri, 79, 100, 101, 171, 198
Corbie, 100, 168, 169
Cordoba, 121, 159, 162, 164, 165
Corsica, 184
Cossacks, 11, 114, 117, 120, 252, 253, 254, 268
Counter-Reformation, 4
Courtrai, 181, 196
Courval, 199
Crailsheim, 247
Craven, 72, 73, 74
Crequi, 100
Croats, Croatia, 5, 11, 39, 60, 68, 69, 85, 87, 94, 95, 109, 114, 115, 117, 118, 120, 123, 129, 132, 133, 143, 145, 146, 151, 153, 154, 171, 174, 183, 184, 185, 191, 196, 219, 222, 228, 231, 240, 250, 252, 253, 254, 255, 256, 265
Cromwell, 21, 39
Cuba, 162
culverins, 14
Czechs, 153

Dachstein, 263
Damme, 188
Danube, 60, 61, 106, 142, 144, 198, 234, 235, 236, 237, 243, 247, 248, 251
D'Aumont, 209, 210, 227
De Chouppes, 209, 227
De Mauvilly, 211, 227, 232
Dehne, 48, 75
Delfzijl, 189
demicannon, 14, 15, 23, 63, 64, 67, 72, 88, 89, 90, 97, 146, 152, 161, 202, 203, 209, 211, 225, 226, 229, 232, 256, 257
demiculverins, 14, 15, 23, 63, 64, 72, 89, 90, 152, 202, 225, 229, 256
Dendermonde, 188
Denmark, 2, 6, 7, 8, 24, 30, 32, 34, 36, 40, 42, 77, 101, 102, 111, 124, 125, 126, 127, 128, 129, 144, 153, 187, 188, 237
Denzlingen, 204, 213, 214

D'Espenan, 204, 205, 208, 209, 210, 211, 227
Dessau, 7, 121
Dessow, 52, 55
Deventer, 189
Dieburg, 96
Dieuze, 79
Dijon, 79, 100
Dingolfing, 248, 249, 250
Dinkelsbuhl, 217, 224, 235, 236, 247, 248
Doesburg, 189
D'Ognone, 227
Dole, 79
Domitz, 43, 44, 126, 153
Donaueschingen, 199
Donauwerth, 4, 34, 235, 236, 247, 248, 251, 260
Dortmund, 87
Dosse, 45, 51, 52, 54
Douglas, 51, 65, 67, 69, 116, 132, 134, 135, 138, 139, 140, 141, 143, 149, 155
dragoons, 10, 11, 23, 48, 52, 62, 64, 72, 74, 75, 98, 99, 117, 126, 133, 135, 137, 147, 148, 151, 152, 154, 209, 213, 224, 228, 235, 252, 253, 257, 262
Dreisam, 203, 213
Drenthe, 189
Dresden, 71, 123
Dunkirk, 181, 186, 188
Duren, 189
Durrwang, 217, 248
Dusseldorf, 164, 189

East India Company, 186
Ebringen, 203, 204
Edict of Restitution, 21, 102
Eger, 129, 217, 235, 247
Eggenfelden, 249
Ehrenbreitstein, 255
Eiberg, 73, 74
Eider, 126, 127
Eighty Years War, 2, 30, 157
Eindhoven, 163, 167
Eisleben, 44, 106, 127
Elbe, 42, 43, 44, 45, 58, 60, 69, 70, 106, 107, 109, 123, 124, 126, 127, 128

Index 283

Elector Palatine. See Friedrich, Karl Ludwig,
Ellwangen, 247
Elsterwerda, 123
Emden, 187
Emmerich, 164
England, 2, 7, 9, 11, 14, 24, 34, 39, 47, 72, 74, 102, 153, 182, 187, 194
Enkefort, 49, 62, 66, 80, 86, 127, 250
Erding, 249
Erfurt, 58, 59, 60, 61, 106, 109, 127, 147, 153, 259
Erlach, 81, 84, 86, 92, 192, 197, 204, 212
Erzgebirge Pass, 129
Escault, 191
Eschbach, 212
Eugene, 224
Europe, 1, 2, 5, 8, 11, 14, 15, 19, 22, 23, 24, 30, 34, 157, 158, 163, 187

Fabert, 223
Falkenau, 248, 251
Falkenstein, 144
Feldmoching, 248, 250
Femern, 126, 252
Ferdinand II, 3, 5, 6, 7, 15, 21, 23, 31, 37, 41, 43, 48, 77, 78, 79, 101, 112, 124, 153, 165, 238, 264
Ferdinand III, 6, 60, 83, 90, 92, 112, 126, 130, 153, 193, 197, 224, 234, 238, 252, 268
Ferentz, 74
Fernemont, 113, 114, 118, 119
Feuquieres, 190
Finland, 54, 59, 112, 148, 257, 260
Flanders, 15, 32, 34, 35, 36, 39, 60, 74, 78, 91, 99, 100, 101, 102, 112, 113, 124, 125, 157, 158, 159, 160, 162, 163, 164, 165, 166, 167, 168, 169, 171, 172, 174, 180, 181, 182, 185, 186, 188, 189, 190, 193, 194, 196, 197, 199, 200, 234, 250, 252, 255, 262, 263
Fleurus, 29, 131, 194
Fontaine, 171, 172, 174, 176, 178, 192
Fontenoy, 221
Fort Fuentes, 100
France, 2, 6, 7, 15, 17, 21, 24, 29, 32, 33, 34, 35, 36, 37, 39, 58, 59, 61, 77, 78, 79, 81, 82, 83, 87, 90, 92, 93, 97, 98, 99, 100, 101, 102, 105, 107, 110, 111, 112, 121, 123, 124, 128, 142, 143, 144, 153, 155, 157, 162, 166, 167, 168, 169, 170, 171, 172, 173, 174, 176, 177, 178, 179, 180, 181, 182, 183, 184, 185, 188, 190, 191, 192, 193, 195, 197, 198, 199, 200, 201, 202, 203, 204, 205, 207, 208, 209, 210, 211, 212, 213, 214, 216, 217, 219, 220, 221, 222, 223, 224, 225, 226, 227, 229, 230, 231, 232, 233, 234, 235, 237, 238, 239, 242, 243, 244, 248, 249, 250, 253, 257, 261, 262, 268
Franche Comte, 78, 79, 80, 100, 172, 182, 212
Franconia, 123, 260
Franco-Spanish War, 78, 102, 157, 166, 181, 262
Frankfort, 37, 78, 87
Frauenberg, 251
Frederick Henry, 160, 161, 162, 163, 164, 165, 166, 167, 168, 169, 180, 181, 187, 190
Frederick the Great, 21, 32, 40, 75, 105, 106, 154
Freiburg, 29, 52, 60, 86, 90, 99, 121, 123, 171, 195, 197, 199, 201, 202, 203, 204, 206, 207, 208, 212, 213, 214, 217, 218, 224, 225, 227, 229, 232, 236, 247
Freising, 248, 249
Fretzdorf, 45, 51, 52, 54
Fretzdorfer Heide, 51, 52, 54
Friedeburg, 109
Friedland, 109
Friedrich, 3, 4, 6, 7, 72, 101, 102, 188
Friedrichstadt, 126
Friesenheim, 87
Fronde, 171, 172, 181, 237
Fuenterrabia, 100
Fulda, 247
Furnes, 181
Furstenberg, 80
Fyen, 125

Gadau, 50, 54
Gallas, 28, 40, 46, 47, 52, 58, 59, 60, 68, 70, 75, 78, 79, 82, 94, 100, 102, 105, 112, 123, 124, 125, 126, 127,

128, 129, 131, 142, 143, 144, 154,
  167, 201, 233, 236, 239, 252
Gascony, 78, 100
Gassion, 96, 170, 171, 174, 176, 177,
  179, 181
Gayling, 213, 214
Geertruidenberg, 189
Geisenhausen, 248, 250
Geiso, 71, 217, 220, 221, 223, 229
Gelderland, 189
Geldern, 159, 167, 168, 169, 189
Geleen, 70, 201, 217, 218, 221, 223,
  229, 232, 233, 238, 239
Gelnhausen, 217
Gemunden, 247
Gennep, 160, 169
Genoa, 6, 195
Georg of Brunswick-Luneburg, 6, 37,
  43, 44, 45, 61, 63, 105, 266
Germany, 2, 3, 4, 6, 7, 8, 9, 10, 11, 14,
  15, 16, 19, 21, 23, 24, 25, 26, 27, 29,
  30, 32, 34, 35, 36, 37, 38, 40, 41, 43,
  45, 46, 47, 48, 51, 52, 54, 55, 56, 57,
  59, 60, 61, 64, 72, 73, 75, 76, 77, 78,
  80, 81, 92, 95, 98, 99, 100, 110, 111,
  112, 113, 114, 115, 131, 132, 140,
  153, 154, 157, 158, 159, 162, 163,
  164, 165, 166, 170, 171, 172, 173,
  174, 176, 177, 178, 179, 180, 181,
  182, 183, 184, 185, 187, 188, 189,
  190, 192, 193, 194, 195, 196, 197,
  199, 200, 202, 203, 204, 205, 207,
  208, 209, 213, 225, 226, 227, 229,
  230, 232, 233, 234, 238, 239, 245,
  253, 255, 257, 260, 267, 268
Ghent, 180, 188
Gipfel, 208, 211
Glogau, 107, 109, 143, 153
Glotter, 204, 212, 213
Gluckstadt, 125, 126
Goch, 159, 167
Gold, 86
Goldbeck, 55
Goldstein, 51, 65, 67, 129, 132, 133,
  135, 140, 141
Gonzaga, 49, 62, 66, 68, 69, 70, 113,
  114, 118, 119, 253
Goppingen, 236, 248
Gorlitz, 59, 72, 131
Gotz, 73, 74, 82, 87, 88, 90, 91, 92, 93,
  94, 103, 124, 128, 129, 130, 131,
  132, 133, 134, 135, 137, 139, 141,
  151, 153, 155, 198, 232, 233
Grabendonk, 163, 164, 167
Gradisca, 4
Gramont, 192, 202, 204, 205, 208, 209,
  211, 218, 220, 223, 225, 229, 232
Grave, 160, 164, 189
Gravelines, 180
Graveneck, 142
Gray, 79
Graz, 142
Gregory XV, 7
Grisons, 184
Grol, 159, 162, 163, 166, 188, 189
Groningen, 189
Gronsfeld, 94, 201, 224, 234, 235, 236,
  237, 238, 239, 240, 243, 244, 245,
  246, 247, 248, 250, 256, 268
Guben, 108
Guebriant, 87, 90, 92, 98, 99, 101, 103,
  105, 110, 123, 190, 197, 198, 199,
  200, 231, 233
Guhrau, 108
Guiche, 191
Gunzburg, 236, 237, 248
Gunzenhausen, 248
Gustavus Adolphus, 2, 6, 14, 21, 22,
  23, 24, 25, 26, 27, 28, 30, 31, 32, 33,
  35, 36, 37, 38, 39, 40, 41, 43, 45, 46,
  47, 55, 63, 70, 74, 77, 78, 81, 82, 83,
  84, 96, 101, 102, 105, 106, 110, 111,
  112, 115, 116, 118, 121, 122, 142,
  144, 146, 154, 165, 166, 172, 188,
  200, 224, 233, 237, 242, 245, 252,
  257, 259

Hagenau, 79
Hainault, 170
Halberstadt, 58, 61, 127, 153, 154
Hall, 217, 224
Halle, 122
Hammelburg, 247
Hanau, 49, 59, 96, 234
Hapsburgs, 3, 4, 5, 6, 7, 29, 32, 34, 47,
  59, 77, 78, 79, 80, 93, 100, 102, 112,
  113, 128, 141, 144, 153, 154, 182,
  193, 233, 239, 251, 255
Harburg, 235, 236
Harcourt, 101, 191, 200, 263
Harthausen, 91
Haslach, 203, 213

Index 285

Hattstein, 207
Hatzfeld, 39, 43, 44, 45, 47, 48, 50, 51,
  52, 53, 54, 55, 56, 57, 58, 60, 61, 62,
  63, 65, 66, 67, 73, 74, 75, 76, 78, 79,
  113, 125, 126, 128, 129, 130, 131,
  132, 134, 135, 136, 137, 138, 139,
  140, 141, 142, 144, 151, 154, 155,
  190, 198, 232, 233, 238, 247, 266
Havelberg, 43, 44, 45, 59, 75, 125
Heesch, 163
Heidelberg, 77, 78
Heilbronn, 214, 215, 217
Heilbronn Bund, 77, 265
Heiligenhofen, 7, 29
Helmond, 167
Henderson, 86
Henry of Navarre, 39
Hertogenbosch, 158, 163, 164, 166, 167, 188
Hesdin, 168, 169
Hesse, 27, 234
Hesse-Cassel, 6, 29, 31, 36, 46, 47, 58,
  61, 69, 112, 121, 126, 127, 131, 190,
  197, 198, 216, 217, 218, 219, 220,
  221, 222, 223, 229, 230, 231, 238,
  261, 268
Hesse-Darmstadt, 266
Heusden, 189
Hildesheim, 27
Hiller, 223
Hochst, 7, 18, 29, 42
Hofkirchen, 39, 70, 154
Hogendorf, 79
Hohentwiel, 79, 99, 199, 203, 263
Holderle Bach, 211
Holk, 28, 40
Holland, 2, 6, 7, 9, 14, 15, 17, 18, 19,
  22, 23, 26, 31, 32, 33, 34, 35, 36, 38,
  39, 78, 99, 100, 122, 125, 126, 157,
  158, 159, 160, 161, 162, 163, 164,
  165, 166, 167, 168, 169, 170, 172,
  180, 181, 182, 185, 186, 187, 188,
  189, 190, 193, 194, 195, 196, 200,
  238, 265, 268
Holstein, 47, 71, 125, 126, 153, 223
Holtz, 234
Holy Roman Empire, 2, 3, 4, 5, 12, 27,
  34, 40, 47, 60, 61, 102, 153, 233,
  238, 268
Honnecourt, 169, 172, 191
Horazdiowitz, 130, 131

Horn, 28, 37, 51, 81, 111, 124, 125, 149
Hoxter, 27
Hrin, 139
Hufingen, 199, 214
Huguenots, 142, 171
Hulst, 165, 168, 181, 188
Hungary, 2, 4, 5, 15, 34, 128, 131, 132, 142, 153, 184, 255
Hunigen, 263
Huningen, 199
Hunoldstein, 246, 248, 249, 268
hussars, 11, 109, 115, 117, 120, 143, 145, 146, 155, 253

Ickelheim, 247
Iglau, 141, 142, 144
Illow, 153
Imperial War Council, 128, 129, 130, 154
Imperials, 3, 4, 5, 6, 7, 11, 16, 17, 19,
  21, 24, 27, 28, 29, 31, 32, 33, 34, 35,
  37, 38, 39, 40, 41, 42, 43, 45, 46, 47,
  48, 53, 54, 55, 56, 57, 58, 59, 60, 61,
  62, 65, 66, 70, 72, 73, 74, 75, 77, 78,
  79, 80, 82, 83, 84, 85, 86, 88, 90, 91,
  92, 93, 94, 95, 97, 100, 102, 105,
  106, 107, 108, 109, 110, 112, 113,
  116, 117, 118, 119, 120, 121, 122,
  123, 124, 125, 126, 127, 128, 129,
  130, 131, 132, 134, 135, 136, 137,
  138, 139, 140, 141, 142, 143, 144,
  146, 148, 150, 151, 154, 155, 159,
  164, 165, 166, 167, 168, 170, 172,
  176, 179, 180, 183, 187, 190, 192,
  198, 201, 203, 214, 216, 218, 224,
  227, 228, 229, 231, 232, 233, 234,
  235, 236, 237, 238, 239, 241, 243,
  244, 245, 248, 249, 250, 251, 252,
  253, 255, 257, 263, 265, 266, 267, 268
India, 186, 195
Ingolstadt, 32, 235, 246, 247, 248
Inn, 248, 249
Inner Austria, 4, 34, 142
Innocent X, 7
Iphofen, 248
Ireland, 2, 98, 99, 101, 153, 182, 184, 192
Isar, 248, 249, 250

Isenburg, 170, 172, 174, 176, 177, 178, 179, 180, 183
Italy, 2, 6, 33, 34, 48, 49, 62, 78, 82, 100, 101, 102, 142, 153, 154, 162, 164, 172, 174, 176, 178, 179, 182, 183, 184, 191, 192, 193, 195, 202, 226, 230, 238, 239, 262, 263, 268

Jagerndorf, 124
Jankow, 29, 39, 42, 46, 47, 74, 75, 105, 131, 134, 136, 138, 142, 144, 147, 150, 151, 155, 214, 224, 228, 232, 239, 247, 252
Jankowa, 134, 139
Japan, 186
Jaromeritz, 144
Jauer, 107
Jaxt, 215
Jena, 32
Jens, 51, 75
Jews, 251
Johann Georg, 2, 4, 6, 21, 27, 42, 43, 44, 45, 47, 57, 60, 74, 80, 123, 128, 144
Julich, 4, 158, 159, 160, 162, 166, 189, 198
Juterbogk, 107
Jutland, 82, 124, 125, 126, 236

Kaiserlautern, 78
Kalbe, 127
Kallo, 168, 169, 190
Kammin, 124
Kanoffsky, 87, 90, 199, 203
Kapellhojden, 134, 135, 137, 138, 139
Karl Ludwig, 72, 73, 74
Karl Gustav X, 111, 154, 237
Karr, 47, 50, 52, 56
Katerbow, 45
Kempton, 169, 190, 198
Kenzingen, 87
Kiel, 125
King, 6, 7, 21, 36, 47, 51, 52, 55, 56, 57, 72, 73, 74, 124
Kipfenberg, 247
Kirchheim, 217
Kitzingen, 234, 235, 247
Klattau, 251
Klitzing, 44, 45, 59, 61, 63, 75, 231, 238

Kluge, 90
Kojetin, 123
Kolb, 216
Kolberg, 124, 153
Kolberger Heide, 125
Kolding, 125
Komotau, 129
Kongo, 186
Koniggratz, 123
Konigsmarck, 69, 73, 74, 106, 107, 108, 109, 111, 116, 118, 119, 122, 123, 124, 126, 127, 129, 144, 153, 217, 231, 233, 235, 237, 243, 245, 247, 250, 251, 257, 258, 259
kontribution, 30, 31
Kornenburg, 142, 144
Kosching, 247
Kosel, 7, 108
Krempe, 125
Krems, 141, 142, 144
Kremsier, 123
Krockow, 123, 124, 126
Krossen, 108, 124
Krummau, 251
Kustrin, 59
Kyritz, 43, 45

La Barre, 177, 186
La Bassee, 191, 192
La Capelle, 100, 168
La Ferte, 171, 172, 175, 176, 177
La Force, 78, 100, 200
La Motte, 200, 216
La Moussaie, 221
La Rochelle, 142
La Valette, 78, 79, 100, 101, 200
Lahnstein, 96
Lamboy, 68, 85, 91, 190, 191, 198, 232
Landau, 214, 247, 249, 250
Landrecies, 168, 181, 263
Landsberg, 234, 251
Landshut, 28, 248, 249, 250
Landskron, 263
Landwehr, 54, 55
Langenau, 237
Langeneck, 248
Langer Grund, 54
Langres, 79
Languedoc, 100
Lauenburg, 43, 60
Laufenburg, 80, 84, 98

Index

Lauffenburg, 263
Lauingen, 235, 237, 243, 247, 248, 261
Laun, 129
Le Catelet, 100, 168
Lech, 27, 29, 46, 110, 235, 243, 244, 245, 246, 247, 248, 249, 251, 252, 256, 257
Leganes, 28
Leipzig, 42, 58, 109, 110, 116, 122, 127, 143, 153
Lemgo, 72, 73, 111
Lens, 112, 169, 181, 191, 250, 252, 263
Lerida, 193, 262
L'Eschelle, 209, 210, 227, 232
Leslie, 43, 44, 47, 50, 52, 55, 56, 57, 59, 64, 92, 98, 99
Leubus, 107
L'Hopital, 170, 171, 175, 176, 177, 178, 179
Lichtenegg, 263
Liege, 184
Liegnitz, 28, 107
Ligniville, 192
Lille, 189
Lilliehook, 60, 76, 108, 112, 115, 117, 121
Lillo, 189
Limbach, 91
Limburg, 165, 263
Lindau, 255
Lingen, 159, 163, 165, 189
Linkelwald, 116, 118, 119
Linz, 251
Lippe, 74
Lippstadt, 189
Little Belt, 125
Lobkowitz, 154
Loe, 74
Lohausen, 43
Longueville, 100
Loretto, 208, 209, 210, 211, 213
Lorraine, 40, 77, 78, 79, 91, 100, 171, 184, 198, 201, 229
Louis XIII, 6, 100, 142, 168, 169, 170, 193
Louis XIV, 170, 171, 194, 196, 237
Louvain, 167, 169, 181, 189
Lowenberg, 109
Lower Austria, 4, 7, 34, 255
Lubeck, 126
Luben, 109

Luchow, 44
Luckau, 107, 127
Ludershausen, 43
Luneburg, 43, 44, 75, 105, 131, 231, 238
Lusatia, 5, 7, 60, 107, 109, 123
Lutherans, Lutheranism, 1, 2, 3, 4, 5, 6, 7, 34, 47, 63, 75, 111, 131, 153, 154, 194
Lutter, 7, 18, 29, 42, 121, 122, 177, 246
Lützen, 27, 28, 29, 32, 39, 42, 47, 55, 60, 77, 81, 84, 122, 147
Luxembourg, 39, 154
Luxemburg, 157, 170, 234, 263

Maas, 159, 163, 165, 167, 188
Maastricht, 158, 165, 166, 167, 188
Madgeburg, 27
Madrid, 6, 100, 162, 172
Magdeburg, 27, 42, 43, 44, 109, 123, 127, 249
Magyars, 153
Main, 59
Mainz, 3, 79, 96, 214, 235, 247, 261
Malplaquet, 221
Mamming, 248, 250
Mansfeld, 7, 45, 46, 81, 131, 159, 188, 265
Mansfeld (town), 127, 153
Mantua, 77, 100, 102, 163, 165, 195
Marderfelt, 155
Mardyck, 181, 188
Marfee, 169, 190
Marienbourg, 179
Mariendorf, 29
Marienthal, 143, 215, 217, 224, 227, 228, 236, 245, 246
Marlborough, 154, 224
Marradas, 153
Marrazino, 42, 43, 44, 48, 56, 58, 59, 60, 61, 63, 64, 66, 67, 68, 69, 74, 75, 154
Marsin, 205, 209, 211, 212, 218, 219, 221, 227
Matanzas Bay, 162
Mauberge, 200
Maurice of Nassau, 14, 18, 21, 22, 24, 36, 159, 160, 161, 195, 238
Maximilian of Bavaria, 4, 6, 21, 153, 234, 239, 249, 255

Mazarin, 6, 170, 171, 193, 200, 217, 227, 234, 235, 237, 246, 249, 263, 268
Mazzo, 100
Mecklenburg, 27, 42, 45, 59, 60, 75, 82, 106, 153, 260
Mediterranean, 100, 160, 186
Meissenger, 91
Melander, 113, 154, 233, 234, 235, 236, 237, 238, 239, 243, 244, 245, 246, 247, 249, 252, 254
Melnik, 123
Melo, Francisco, 169, 170, 171, 172, 173, 174, 176, 177, 178, 179, 180, 183, 191
Melo, Alvaro, 172, 174
Memmigen, 97, 255
Mercador, 179, 191
Mercy, Franz, 40, 52, 61, 70, 79, 154, 197, 198, 199, 200, 201, 203, 204, 205, 207, 208, 209, 210, 211, 212, 213, 214, 215, 216, 217, 218, 221, 222, 223, 224, 227, 228, 232, 233, 236, 237, 255
Mercy, Henrich, 132, 138, 141, 155, 201
Mercy, Kaspar, 199, 201, 202, 211, 212, 232
Mergentheim, 215, 227
Merode, 239
Merzhausen, 207, 208, 209
Metz, 79, 200
Meuse, 170
Middelfart, 125
Miehr, 207
Mies, 248
Milan, 100, 102, 166, 195
Minden, 59, 73, 153
Mistelbach, 144
Modena, 239
Moers, 189
Moldau, 129, 130, 131
Monaco, 34
Monnier, 48
Monro, 24
Montecuccoli, Raimondo, 21, 33, 36, 39, 40, 48, 57, 58, 70, 74, 108, 147, 154, 183, 224, 233, 237, 238, 239, 243, 244, 245, 247, 248, 268
Montecuccoli, Ernesto, 164
Montjuich, 193, 195

Moosburg, 248, 250, 257, 259, 260
Mooswald, 203
Moravia, 5, 7, 106, 107, 108, 123, 124, 128, 142, 153, 252, 255, 260
Morbegno, 100
Morder, 108
Mortaigne, 51, 64, 112, 115, 118, 119, 132, 133, 137, 138, 139, 140, 141, 231
Morzhausen, 204
Muhldorf, 249
Muhlhausen, 131
Mulde, 109
Muller, 141
Munich, 248, 249, 250
Munschen, 127
Munster, 68, 120, 145

Nancy, 77
Naples, 194, 263
Napoleon, 8, 15, 18, 21, 26, 30, 32, 35, 40, 41, 74, 105, 106, 194
Naseby, 122
Nassau, 84, 87, 90, 91, 92
Natte Heide, 51, 52
Naumburg, 58
Navarre, 100
Neckarsulm, 214
Neisse, 107, 108, 109
Neu-Brandenburg, 27, 64
Neuburg, 236, 247, 248, 263
Neuhaus, 141
Neukloster, 60
Neumarkt, 235, 236, 247, 248, 268
Neumunster, 126
Neunburg, 61, 70, 112
Neuneck, 86
Neusaltz, 108, 112
Neustadt, 235, 247
Nicola, 70, 95, 113, 114, 118
Nienburg, 59, 127, 153
Nieuport, 186, 188, 194
Nijmegen, 189
Nikolsburg, 144
Nolligen, 85
Nordlingen, 29, 37, 42, 46, 47, 48, 51, 52, 56, 60, 77, 78, 81, 82, 84, 95, 99, 100, 112, 121, 166, 180, 203, 217, 223, 234, 235, 239, 247, 259, 260

Index 289

Nordlingen, second battle of, 121, 155, 171, 197, 201, 221, 222, 224, 227, 228, 239, 255
Northern War, 239
Nortorf, 126
Norway, 124
Nosakow, 137, 138, 141
Nuremberg, 36, 96, 234, 251

Oberland, 4
Oberndorf, 245, 248
Ober-Peiching, 245, 248
Oder, 43, 59, 106, 108
Offenbach, 255
Ohm, 90, 92
Oldendorf, 28, 29, 47, 121, 122, 201, 234, 238, 239, 247
Oldenzaal, 159, 161, 162, 163, 166, 188
Oldesloe, 125, 126
Olivares, 6, 102, 159, 160, 164, 169, 172, 194
Olmutz, 108, 123, 129, 138, 141, 143, 144, 153, 257
Onate, 153
Oppeln, 108
Oppenheim, 214
Orleans, 180, 181
Orsoy, 189
Osnabruck, 59
Ostend, 188
Ottenheim, 87
Ottoman Empire, 34, 155
Overijssel, 189
Oxenstierna, 6, 37, 46, 60, 111, 112, 124, 125, 126, 154, 266

Paechwitz, 107
Palatinate, 6, 32, 72, 73, 165, 195, 196, 261
Palluau, 204, 209, 213, 227
Palsgrave (see also Karl Gustav X), 116, 119, 140, 155, 251, 257, 258, 259
Papacy, 6
Papenmutz, 159, 189
Pappenheim, 27, 46, 165, 195, 201, 238, 246
Paris, 100, 103, 168, 171, 181, 199, 214
Passage, 216

Passau, 248, 249
Passendale, 188
Paul V, 6
Pavia, 180
Peace of Augsburg, 3
Peace of Lubeck, 7
Peace of Prague, 29, 37, 41, 43, 47, 78, 81, 82, 95, 102, 232, 238
Pentz, 141
Perleburg, 44, 45, 51
Persan, 170, 192
Pfaffenhofen, 28, 29
Pfeffigen, 263
Pfuhl, 37, 41, 46, 75, 149, 230, 231
Pfurdthof, 208, 209
Philip III, 6
Philip IV, 6, 159, 166, 180, 181
Philippeville, 179
Philippines, 186
Philippsburg, 77, 78, 214, 216, 224
Picardy, 100, 191
Piccolomini, 28, 40, 41, 60, 61, 70, 79, 100, 101, 105, 106, 107, 108, 110, 112, 113, 116, 117, 118, 119, 121, 122, 123, 131, 153, 154, 167, 168, 170, 190, 231, 233, 239, 248, 249, 250, 251, 252
Pilsen, 5, 129, 130, 234
Pirna, 60
Pisek, 130, 131
Poland, 2, 6, 11, 14, 21, 24, 47, 59, 66, 110, 111, 124, 153, 184, 237, 252, 253, 254
Poltava, 221
Pomerania, 27, 32, 42, 43, 44, 45, 59, 60, 64, 68, 75, 106, 123, 124, 126, 153, 260
Pompeji, 132, 133, 135, 141
Ponti, 178
Portugal, 34, 158, 160, 169, 172, 180, 182, 186, 188, 193, 194, 195, 263, 268
Pottmes, 247
Prague, 5, 29, 42, 60, 106, 111, 123, 129, 130, 138, 142, 248, 251, 252, 254
Pressburg, 5
Pressnitz, 129
Pretzsch, 58
Pritzwalk, 45, 58
Protestant Union, 4, 7, 15

Protestants, Protestantism, 1, 2, 3, 4, 5, 6, 7, 8, 9, 15, 17, 19, 21, 27, 28, 29, 34, 37, 38, 41, 42, 43, 47, 73, 75, 76, 77, 78, 80, 81, 95, 97, 100, 101, 102, 112, 128, 143, 153, 157, 163, 164, 172, 188, 200, 251, 268
Prussia, 32
Puchheim, 39, 75, 109, 113, 114, 117, 118, 119, 124, 148, 154, 236, 251
Pym, 101
Pyrenees, 100

Radmeritz, 138, 139, 140
Rain, 234, 245, 246, 248, 249, 257, 260
Rakoczy, 6, 142, 143, 144
Rakonitz, 121, 123
Rantzau, 198
Rathenow, 44
Ravensburg, 144
Regensburg, 61, 70, 102, 232, 235, 248, 267
Reinach, 91, 92
Remlingen, 235, 247
Rendsburg, 125, 126
Retzbach, 247
Reuschel, 141
Reutlingen, 236, 248
Rheidt, 159
Rheinberg, 165, 166, 189
Rheinfelden, 29, 77, 80, 81, 82, 83, 84, 86, 88, 90, 93, 95, 97, 98, 199, 263
Rhine, 3, 43, 58, 59, 61, 77, 78, 79, 80, 81, 85, 86, 87, 91, 92, 93, 101, 103, 107, 128, 159, 165, 195, 197, 198, 199, 212, 214, 216, 235, 261
Rhinegrave, 37, 78, 81, 83, 84, 91, 95, 96, 98
Rhineland, 40, 92, 153, 159
Richelieu, 2, 6, 21, 77, 92, 93, 100, 101, 168, 169, 171, 190, 193, 197, 200
Rinteln, 73
Ritschke, 116, 117
Rittburg, 178
Rocroi, 29, 99, 122, 124, 157, 170, 171, 172, 173, 176, 179, 180, 181, 182, 185, 192, 193, 195, 198, 200, 204, 221, 232, 268
Rodel, 85, 86, 103
Roermond, 165, 168, 188
Rohan, 78, 83, 84, 99, 100, 102

Roqueseviere, 205, 207, 227, 232
Rosen, 85, 86, 91, 92, 98, 197, 199, 200, 209, 213, 214, 215, 216, 225, 227
Rotenhan, 91
Rothenburg, 215, 217
Rottweil, 91, 198, 212
Rousillon, 100, 101, 193
Route de Quiers, 101
Rouyer, 223
Rudolf II, 4, 5
Ruischenberg, 132, 201, 202, 203, 207, 208, 213, 214, 218, 223
Rupert, 74
Ruppin, 45
Ruthven, 43, 47, 51, 52

Saalfeld, 61
Saaz, 129
Sackingen, 80, 84, 199
Sagan, 107
Salis, 87
Salzwedel, 44, 106
Sambre, 170
San Marino, 34
Sandau, 44, 45
Santa Cruz, 165
Sas van Gent, 180, 181, 188
Sassbach, 224, 237
Sauverne, 79
Savary, 178
Savelli, 80, 82, 83, 84, 85, 86, 87, 88, 90, 91, 92, 93, 94, 95, 103, 131, 154, 233
Savoy, 6, 100, 101, 195, 196, 200
Sax-Hausen, 75
Sax-Lauenburg, 107, 108, 148, 153
Saxony, 2, 3, 4, 6, 7, 15, 21, 27, 29, 32, 37, 38, 39, 40, 42, 43, 44, 45, 47, 48, 54, 55, 56, 57, 58, 59, 60, 63, 65, 66, 68, 69, 70, 71, 72, 75, 80, 101, 102, 106, 107, 108, 109, 117, 118, 121, 122, 123, 124, 126, 127, 128, 129, 130, 131, 134, 138, 139, 140, 144, 146, 148, 153, 155, 229, 232, 234, 251, 257, 260, 265
Sax-Weimar, 6, 29, 80
Sax-Weimar, Johann Ernst, 81
Sax-Weimar, Wilhelm, 92
Scandinavia, 2
Schaffelitzky, 84, 86

Schaffgotsche, 153
Scharfenberg, 51, 52, 54, 55, 58
Scheldt, 159, 190
Schenkenschans, 163, 164, 167, 181, 189
Schlang, 50, 61, 64, 65, 67, 69, 70, 108, 111, 112, 116, 117, 118, 119, 121
Schleinitz, 122
Schlettstadt, 87
Schlick, 153
Schmidtberg, 216
Schmutter, 243, 244, 245, 256
Schnetter, 87
Schomberg, 100, 200
Schonbeck, 92
Schonberg, 80, 98, 203, 204, 205, 207
Schonickel, 50, 55, 75
Schreckenberg, 51, 54, 55, 56
Schuttenhofen, 251
Schutter, 87
Schwabach, 234, 247
Schwandorf, 248
Schweidnitz, 107, 108, 148, 149
Schweinfurt, 235, 247, 259
Schweinitz, 123
Schwert, 223
Scotland, 2, 25, 41, 43, 46, 47, 56, 73, 98, 99, 101, 132, 153, 178, 184, 186, 190, 192, 257
Sedan, 190
Seestadt, 106
Seestedt, 138, 141
Segeberg, 126
Senef, 171
Sennheim, 91
Sicily, 263
Silesia, 5, 7, 32, 42, 46, 60, 64, 76, 106, 107, 108, 111, 124, 128, 131, 142, 147, 153, 251, 252, 255, 257, 260
Silva, 190
Sirot, 170, 172, 175, 178, 179, 192
Sittard, 165
Skane, 124, 125
Slaak, 165
Sluys, 189
small war, 41, 44, 46, 52, 81, 111, 237, 238, 239
Soissons, 100, 168, 190
Sorau, 107
Souches, 142, 143

Spain, 2, 5, 6, 7, 9, 15, 16, 17, 18, 21, 22, 23, 24, 28, 29, 31, 32, 34, 35, 36, 39, 74, 77, 78, 79, 92, 100, 101, 102, 112, 121, 123, 124, 153, 157, 158, 159, 160, 161, 162, 163, 164, 165, 166, 167, 168, 169, 170, 171, 172, 173, 174, 176, 177, 178, 179, 180, 181, 182, 183, 184, 185, 186, 188, 189, 190, 191, 192, 193, 194, 195, 196, 197, 198, 200, 229, 233, 234, 237, 238, 250, 252, 262, 263, 268
Sperreuter, 37, 80, 81, 82, 83, 84, 85, 86, 95
Spinola, 81, 159, 160, 164, 194
Spires, 77, 78, 214, 261
Sporck, 141, 234, 236
St Jean de Losne, 79
St Omer, 168, 169, 190
St. Blasien, 199
St. Gotthard, 239
St. Margen, 199
St. Peter, 204, 212, 213, 214
Stade, 27, 32
Stadtlohn, 7, 18, 29, 42, 121
Stahl, 223
Stalhansk, 46, 50, 52, 56, 57, 60, 64, 75, 106, 107, 108, 111, 112, 115, 117, 118, 119, 121, 142
Starhemburg, 243, 244
Steenbergen, 159, 160
Steenwijk, 189
Steinau, 28, 29, 71, 107
Stendal, 106
Sternschanze, 203, 205, 207
Stettin, 59, 69, 153
Stockerau, 144
Stockholm, 37, 106
Stollhofen, 263
stomach strategy, 32, 40, 41, 45, 59, 60, 126, 215, 216, 236, 237, 250, 252
Straelen, 165
Strakonitz, 130
Stralsund, 59, 153, 188
Strassburg, 78, 79, 247
Striegau, 107
Stuttgart, 86, 215
Suarez, 171, 178
Suys, 70, 113, 114, 118, 132, 137, 138, 140, 141
Svarta Bergen, 134

Swabia, 4, 27, 195, 212, 214, 235, 236, 251, 260, 261
Sweden, 6, 7, 9, 21, 22, 23, 24, 25, 26, 27, 28, 29, 30, 32, 33, 34, 35, 36, 37, 38, 39, 41, 42, 43, 45, 46, 47, 48, 50, 52, 53, 54, 55, 56, 57, 58, 59, 60, 61, 64, 69, 70, 72, 73, 74, 75, 76, 77, 78, 82, 92, 95, 96, 97, 99, 100, 101, 102, 105, 106, 107, 108, 109, 110, 111, 112, 115, 116, 117, 118, 119, 120, 121, 122, 123, 124, 125, 126, 127, 128, 129, 130, 131, 133, 134, 135, 136, 137, 138, 139, 140, 141, 142, 143, 144, 146, 148, 149, 151, 153, 154, 165, 166, 167, 172, 182, 185, 187, 195, 196, 197, 198, 201, 214, 217, 224, 227, 229, 230, 231, 233, 234, 235, 236, 237, 238, 239, 241, 242, 243, 245, 246, 249, 250, 251, 252, 253, 257, 258, 260, 265, 266, 267, 268
Switzerland, 2, 99, 178, 184, 186, 195

Tabor, 131, 141, 154, 251
Tangermunde, 44, 106
Taube, 48
Tauber, 215, 216
Taupadel, 37, 81, 83, 84, 85, 86, 87, 90, 91, 103, 197, 199, 209, 210, 211, 212, 225, 231
Taus, 251
tercio, 7, 17, 18, 19, 22, 24, 25, 28, 37, 38, 122, 172, 174, 176, 177, 178, 179, 180, 182, 183, 191, 195
Tetschen, 251
Thann, 263
Thionville, 101, 112, 168, 169, 180, 181, 190, 193
Thirty Years War, 1, 2, 5, 15, 30, 31, 32, 36, 78, 144, 157, 158, 186, 200, 233
Thomas of Savoy, 190
Thuringia, 58, 106, 107, 108, 153, 234
Thurn, 5, 6, 46
Tilly, 7, 8, 10, 14, 17, 18, 19, 20, 21, 22, 27, 28, 31, 32, 35, 36, 37, 38, 39, 42, 82, 101, 102, 116, 119, 121, 122, 125, 162, 201, 224, 238, 245, 246, 247
Tirlemont, 167
Tobitschau, 123
Tonning, 125, 126
Torgau, 58, 75, 109, 123, 127
Tornavento, 100
Torstensson, 26, 40, 42, 43, 45, 46, 50, 52, 54, 55, 57, 58, 60, 68, 74, 75, 105, 106, 107, 108, 109, 110, 111, 112, 113, 115, 116, 117, 118, 119, 120, 121, 122, 123, 124, 125, 126, 127, 128, 129, 130, 131, 132, 133, 134, 135, 136, 138, 139, 140, 141, 142, 143, 144, 147, 148, 149, 152, 153, 154, 214, 224, 233, 237, 257
Tournon, 205, 210, 227
Trandorf, 58, 122
Transylvania, 2, 6, 7, 34, 123, 124, 128, 131, 142, 143
Trauditsch, 48, 60, 67, 132, 141
Traun, 91
Trautenau, 107
Treaty of Munster, 181
Treaty of Westphalia, 181, 268
Treptow, 124
Treuenbrietzen, 107
Triebl, 234
Trier, 3, 77, 102, 255
Troppau, 108, 112, 124
Truckmuller, 87, 235
Tübingen, 86
Turenne, 39, 40, 87, 90, 98, 99, 101, 103, 113, 142, 143, 144, 171, 180, 185, 193, 196, 197, 199, 200, 202, 204, 205, 207, 208, 209, 210, 212, 213, 214, 215, 216, 217, 218, 220, 221, 223, 224, 225, 227, 229, 230, 233, 234, 235, 236, 237, 238, 239, 242, 243, 244, 245, 246, 247, 249, 250, 251, 252, 257, 260, 263, 268
Turin, 101, 193
Tuttlingen, 29, 124, 198, 201, 225, 226, 236
Twelve Years Truce, 157
Tyrolia, 4, 5, 34, 255

Uberlingen, 199, 214, 257
Uffeln, 217
Uffenhein, 247
Uffhausen, 207, 208, 209, 212, 213
Ulhefeld, 48, 50, 55, 58, 67
Ulm, 97, 234
Upper Austria, 4, 7, 34, 128, 251, 268

Upper Palatinate, 235, 236, 248, 251, 260
Urban VIII, 7, 82
Uslar, 238
Utrecht, 164, 189

Valfraela, 100
Valtelline, 77, 78, 100, 102, 103, 195
Vardtorn, 54
Vauban, 23, 32, 33
Vechta, 59
Vehlen, 202, 225
Velada, 191
Velandia, 178
Vendome, 224
Venice, 6, 7, 82, 102, 238
Venlo, 162, 165, 168, 181, 188, 190
Vera, 70, 171
Vercèlli, 100
Veurne, 188
Vienna, 5, 6, 7, 16, 60, 79, 82, 91, 102, 106, 108, 113, 123, 128, 141, 142, 143, 144, 154, 197, 255, 266
Villamor, 183
Villars, 224
Villingen, 212, 214
Vingardsberg, 54, 55
Visconti, 178
Vitzthum, 37, 41, 47, 51, 52, 55, 56, 57, 75
Vivero, 178, 183, 191
Vlotho, 72, 73, 76
Volksmarsen, 27
Voltaire, 34

Wachenheim, 249
Wahl, 198, 231
Waldeck, 141
Waldkirch, 213
Waldshut, 80
Wallenstein, 7, 17, 19, 21, 27, 28, 31, 35, 38, 40, 41, 45, 46, 47, 48, 59, 66, 82, 101, 102, 113, 128, 131, 153, 154, 162, 253
Walloons 16, 113, 153, 157, 159, 163, 164, 165, 167, 170, 173, 174, 176, 177, 178, 179, 182, 183, 184, 187, 189, 191, 192, 193, 195, 201
Walschen, 153, 154
Warnemund, 59

Wasserburg, 249
Waterloo, 32
Webel, 68, 69, 113, 114, 118, 119
Weiden, 248
Weinberg, 217, 218, 223, 229
Werben, 27, 43, 44, 45, 58, 59, 75, 106, 121
Wernitz, 217
Werth, 49, 62, 66, 78, 79, 80, 81, 82, 83, 84, 85, 86, 91, 97, 100, 103, 128, 129, 130, 132, 134, 135, 138, 139, 140, 141, 167, 168, 198, 200, 201, 202, 211, 213, 214, 215, 216, 218, 219, 221, 223, 229, 232, 234, 250
Wertingen, 248
Wesel, 163, 164, 189
Weser, 73, 238, 245
West India Company, 186, 187
Westerhold, 74
Westphalia, 27, 37, 40, 43, 44, 58, 59, 72, 73, 75, 82, 87, 106, 107, 110, 111, 112, 122, 125, 126, 128, 129, 131, 144, 153, 190, 195, 197, 198, 201, 229, 231, 234, 238, 239, 243, 252, 255, 257, 260, 266
Wetzlar, 234
White Mountain, 7, 18, 29, 42, 121
Wiederhold, 79, 103, 199
Wiesbaden, 247
Wiesloch, 29, 247
Wildberg, 48, 49
Wilhelm of Hesse-Cassel, 46
Willem of Nassau, 165, 168, 190
Willemstad, 189
Wimpfen, 7, 18, 29, 42, 121, 122, 177, 217, 224
Windsheim, 235, 247
Winsen, 105
Wismar, 59, 153
Witersheim, 91
Wittenberg, 43, 58, 108, 111, 112, 115, 117, 118, 119, 123, 132, 133, 135, 137, 138, 139, 140, 141, 143, 155, 230, 231, 251, 257, 258, 259
Wittenberg (town), 127, 128
Wittenweier, 81, 82, 88, 93, 95, 97, 98, 137
Wittstock, 37, 39, 41, 42, 45, 46, 47, 48, 51, 52, 53, 54, 58, 59, 61, 63, 72, 73, 74, 75, 76, 110, 131, 135, 232, 239, 247

Wlckowitz, 137
Wolf, 84
Wolfenbuttel, 27, 105, 197, 229, 230,
    231, 237
Wolfshagen, 75
Wolfsschanze, 142, 143
Wolgast, 7
Wonnhalde, 208, 209, 210
Worms, 78, 214
Wottawa, 130
Wrangel, Hermann, 43, 59, 60, 75, 126
Wrangel, Karl Gustav, 106, 108, 111,
    112, 115, 118, 129, 144, 153, 154,
    230, 231, 233, 234, 235, 236, 237,
    238, 241, 243, 244, 245, 246, 247,
    249, 250, 251, 252, 257, 258, 260,
    268
Wurtemberg, 4, 79, 87, 102, 198, 235,
    236, 243, 248, 261
Wurzburg, 215, 227, 229, 235, 264
Wurzen, 109
Wusterhausen, 45

Ypres, 181, 196

Zandvliet, 188
Zaradetzky, 141
Zeitz, 122
Zittau, 109
Znaim, 141
Zobten Berg, 107, 148
Zuniga, 141
Zus, 244
Zusmarshausen, 29, 233, 236, 243, 245,
    246, 247, 248, 252, 254, 256, 257,
    260
Zutphen, 189
Zweibrucken, 78
Zwickau, 60
Zwittau, 123

Index of Units

BAVARIA
Cavalry
Billehe, 82, 85, 93
Cosalky, 151, 201, 219, 222, 225, 227, 228, 256
Fleckenstein, 132, 136, 151, 222, 227, 228, 240, 244, 256
Free Coys, 218, 222, 228
Gayling, 70, 82, 85, 88, 93, 132, 136, 151, 201, 219, 222, 225, 227, 228, 240, 256
Gotz, 88, 89, 91, 94
Harthausen, 87, 88, 94
Horst, 82, 85, 88, 91, 93
Kolb, 70, 88, 94, 132, 136, 151, 201, 216, 218, 219, 222, 225, 227, 228, 240, 244, 256, 268
Lapierre, 132, 136, 151, 201, 219, 222, 225, 227, 228, 256
Meissenger, 88, 94
Mercy, 199, 225
Metternich, 82, 85, 88, 89, 93, 94, 95
Modersbach, 256
Neuneck, 82, 85, 88, 93
Redetti, 87, 89, 91, 94
Sporck, 70, 132, 136, 151, 201, 219, 222, 225, 228
Truckmuller, 88, 94, 240, 244, 256
Vehlen, 89, 94
Waldott, 256
Wartenburg, 88, 94
Werth, 82, 85, 88, 91, 93, 94, 132, 136, 151, 201, 211, 219, 222, 225, 227, 228
Zink, 256
Croat
Guscheniz, 240, 256
Wurtemberg, 240, 244, 256
Dragoons
Bartl, 240, 256
Creuz, 235
Free Coys, 228
Kurnreuter, 199, 201, 225
Limbach, 88, 94
Schoh, 219, 222, 228
Werth, 88
Wolf, 82, 85, 93, 199, 201, 225, 232
Infantry
Albert, 88, 91, 94
Beltin, 256
Cobb, 150, 218, 222, 223, 227, 228, 241, 256
De Puech, 88, 94, 218, 227, 228, 256

Edlinstetten, 89, 94
Elter, 241, 244, 256
Enkefort, 256
Enschering, 202, 203, 225
Free Coys, 256
Fugger, 150, 202, 205, 225, 256
Gil de Haas, 150, 218, 222, 223, 227, 228
Gold, 82, 85, 93, 95, 202, 205, 218, 222, 225, 227, 228
Gronsfeld, 256
Hasslang, 70, 89, 94, 202, 203, 204, 207, 225
Holz, 150, 202, 203, 204, 207, 225, 228, 256
Horst, 256
Marimont, 219, 227, 228, 256
Mercy, 70, 150, 201, 202, 205, 218, 222, 225, 227, 228, 229, 256
Metternich, 89
Miehr, 202, 205, 207, 212, 225
Ners, 256
Pappenheim, 82, 85, 93, 95
Reinach, 89, 94
Rouyer, 202, 204, 205, 207, 218, 222, 223, 225, 227, 228, 241, 256
Ruischenberg, 150, 201, 218, 225, 227, 228
Schnetter, 88, 91, 94
Thun, 49, 53, 62, 66, 75
Wahl, 82, 85, 86, 93, 95, 202, 203, 204, 207, 225
Werth, 49, 62, 66
Winterscheid, 150, 202, 203, 207, 219, 225, 227, 228, 256

BRANDENBURG
  Cavalry
    Burgsdorf, 49, 63, 68
    Franz Karl, 49, 63, 66, 68
    Luttke, 113, 119, 120, 148, 151

CATHOLIC LEAGUE
  Cavalry
    Westfalen, 73
  Infantry
    Westfalen, 49, 62, 66

FRANCE
  Cavalry
    Baden, 203, 226, 227
    Beaujeu, 192
    Beauveau, 173, 175, 185, 216, 227, 230, 242, 260, 262, 263
    Beins, 192
    Berg, 203, 226, 227
    Betz, 242, 260, 262, 263
    Boury, 220, 222, 223, 229, 230
    Buchenau, 242, 260, 262, 263
    Bussy, 192
    Caldenbach, 226
    Camarche, 230
    Carabiniers, 192, 220, 222, 229, 230
    Chacks, 173, 174, 185
    Chambre, 220, 222, 229, 232
    Chaost, 173, 176, 185
    Chappes, 192
    Chemerault, 192
    Coislin, 173, 175, 185
    Conde, 173, 174, 177, 185, 192, 202, 220, 222, 223, 226, 229, 230
    Conti, 192
    Cornette Blanche, 185, 191
    Coudray, 192
    Dauphin, 191
    Du Hallier, 89, 101
    Duras, 216, 227, 242, 260, 262, 263
    Enghien, 192
    Erlach, 192, 203, 226, 242, 260, 262, 263
    Fleckenstein, 203, 219, 220, 221, 222, 226, 227, 230, 242, 260, 262, 263
    Fusiliers, 173, 175, 185
    Gassion, 173, 174, 185
    Gendarmes, 99, 173, 175, 176, 185, 202, 211, 220, 222, 226, 229, 230
    Gesvre, 192
    Gramont, 192, 222, 230
    Guebriant, 89, 101, 202, 226, 227
    Guiche, 173, 175, 185
    Harcourt, 173, 175, 185, 192
    Heudicourt, 173, 175, 185
    Kanoffsky, 199, 203, 220, 222, 226, 227, 230
    King, 192
    La Claviere, 173, 175, 185, 220, 222, 229
    La Ferte, 173, 175, 185, 192

Index of Units

La Melleraye, 192
Lenoncourt, 173, 175, 185
Leschelle, 173, 175, 185
Lillebonne, 192
Longueville, 192
Margrave, 230
Marolles, 173, 175, 177, 178, 185
Marsin, 212, 220, 222, 230
Mazarin, 192, 222, 227, 242, 260, 262, 263
Meille, 192
Meispas, 242, 260, 262, 263
Menneville, 173, 175, 185
Mestre de Camp, 173, 174, 185
Muller, 226
Nassau, 226
Netaf, 173, 175, 185
Noitlieu, 192
Ohm, 221, 222, 227, 230, 242, 260, 262, 263
Olipart, 242, 260, 262
Orleans, 190, 192
Queen, 190, 192
Raab, 173, 174, 185
Ravenel, 192
Roquelaure, 173, 175, 185, 192
Rosen, 203, 209, 211, 220, 222, 226, 227, 230
Royal, 173, 174, 185
Russwurm, 203, 220, 222, 226, 227, 230, 242, 260, 262, 263
Ruvigny, 192
Salbrick, 192
Scharfenstein, 203, 226
Schon, 226
Schutz, 260, 263
Sillart, 173, 175, 185
Sirot, 173, 175, 185, 192
St Simon,, 192
Streif, 192
Sully, 173, 175, 185
Taupadel, 203, 220, 222, 226, 227, 230, 242, 260, 262, 263
Tracy, 89, 101, 202, 216, 220, 222, 226, 227, 230, 242, 260, 262, 263
Turenne, 89, 101, 202, 220, 222, 226, 227, 230, 242, 260, 262, 263
Vamberg, 173, 175, 185
Vattronville, 89, 101
Vidame, 192
Villiette, 192
Wall, 220, 222, 229
Witgenstein, 203, 226, 227

Dragoons
  Rosen, 227, 230
  Turenne, 242

Infantry
  Aubeterre, 175, 186, 202, 210, 226, 227, 230
  Batilly, 89, 101, 103
  Bellenave, 219, 222, 229, 230
  Bernhold, 202, 207, 226, 227, 261, 263
  Betz, 227, 230
  Bies, 99
  Biscarras, 173, 175, 186
  Bourdonne, 175, 186
  Breze, 173, 175, 186
  Burgundy, 101
  Bussy, 175, 186, 202, 211, 226
  Canisy, 99
  Castelmoron, 89, 101, 103
  Cerny, 99
  Chamblay, 99
  Charlevois, 261, 263
  Conde, 192
  Conti, 192, 202, 205, 211, 219, 222, 226, 229
  Couronne, 202, 226, 232
  Desmartes, 202, 226
  Du Tot, 202, 210, 226, 230, 242, 261, 262
  Duval, 220, 222, 229, 242, 261, 262
  Enghien, 202, 204, 205, 211, 219, 220, 222, 226, 229
  Erlach, 192, 242, 261, 262, 263
  Fabert, 202, 211, 220, 222, 223, 226, 229
  Frezeliere, 99
  Garnison, 220, 222, 229
  Gesvres, 175, 186
  Gramont, 220, 222, 223, 229, 232
  Guard, 192
  Guiche, 173, 175, 186, 202, 211, 226
  Harcourt, 186
  Hattstein, 202, 207, 212, 226, 227
  Kluge, 242, 261, 262
  La Couronne, 242, 261, 262

La Marine, 173, 175, 178, 186
La Prec, 173, 175, 186
La Reine, 192
Langeron, 175, 186
Le Havre, 202, 211, 220, 222, 226, 229
Lecques, 99
Leslie, 89, 101
Mazarin, 192, 202, 205, 209, 211, 219, 220, 222, 226, 227, 229, 230, 242, 261, 262
Melun, 89, 101
Mezieres, 202, 209, 226, 227
Molodin, 173, 175, 186
Montausier, 99, 220, 222, 227, 230, 242, 261, 262
Montausin-Melun, 202, 226, 232
Navarre, 101, 190
Netancourt, 242, 261, 262
Normandy, 101
Oisonville, 219, 222, 227, 230
Orleans, 192
Passagie, 242, 261, 262
Perrault, 192
Persan, 173, 175, 186, 192, 202, 205, 211, 219, 222, 226, 229
Picardie, 101, 173, 175, 177, 178, 185, 192
Piedmont, 173, 175, 177, 178, 185, 190, 191
Rambures, 173, 175, 177, 178, 186
Razilly, 192
Rokeby, 192
Roll, 173, 175, 186
Royeaux, 173, 176, 186
Schmidtberg, 202, 207, 216, 226, 227, 242, 261, 262
Scots, 96
Scots Guard, 173, 175, 186, 192
Serres, 99
Sinot, 89, 101
Swiss Guard, 192
Trousses, 220, 222, 229, 230
Turenne, 242, 261, 262
Vandy, 99
Vardy, 89, 101, 103
Vaubecourt, 242, 261, 262
Vervins, 175, 186
Vidame, 173, 175, 186
Volunteers, 89, 101, 103

Watteville, 173, 175, 186
Wiederhold, 199, 263

HESSE-CASSEL
Cavalry
Barcourt, 231
Bruckhurst, 220, 222, 230
Dalwigk, 69, 231
Eberstein, 69
Eppen, 69
Ernst, 231, 261
Free Coys, 231, 261
Geiso, 220, 222, 230, 231, 261
Groot, 220, 222, 230, 231, 261
Leib, 220, 222, 230, 231, 261
Melander, 231
Mercier, 231
Ohm, 231
Rauchhaupt, 221, 222, 230, 231
Rostein, 231
Schwert, 221, 222, 223, 230, 231
Seekirch, 231
Tarent, 231, 261
Uslar, 231
Wied, 231, 261
Dragoons
Jagers, 231
Scharrkopf, 231
Infantry
Ahlfeld, 232, 261
Benthon, 232, 261
Dalwigk, 231
Eberstein, 231
Franc, 221, 222, 230, 231
Free Coys, 231, 261
Geiso, 231, 261
Gersdorff, 231
Green, 69
Gunterade, 231, 261
Kotz, 220, 222, 230
Leib, 231
Lopez, 221, 222, 230, 231
Motz, 232, 261
Nieroth, 69
Riese, 231
Ros, 231
St Andreas, 232, 261
Stauf, 220, 222, 230, 231, 261
Stemfels, 232, 261
Thungen, 231, 261
Uffel, 220, 222, 230, 231, 261
Uslar, 231

Index of Units

Wartenburg, 231, 261
Willich, 231, 261
Wrede, 220, 222, 230, 231
Wurtemberg, 232, 261
Yellow, 69
HOLLAND
  Cavalry
    Mountjoy, 187
    Rouillac, 187
IMPERIAL
  Cavalry
    Altheim, 68
    Altieri, 231
    Alt-Nassau, 73
    Alt-Piccolomini, 70, 94, 113, 120, 133, 136, 145, 150, 231, 239, 253, 266
    Alt-Saxon, 47
    Archduke, 70, 113, 119, 120, 144, 145, 267
    Bassompierre, 151
    Beck, 73, 132, 136, 150, 219, 222, 228, 240, 253
    Bissinger, 50, 53, 63, 66, 67, 75
    Bocamaggiore, 239, 253
    Bonninghausen, 240, 253
    Borneval, 68, 114, 119, 120, 148
    Braganza, 70, 267
    Bredow, 68
    Bruay, 68, 113, 120, 133, 136, 145, 150, 231, 266
    Brunswick, 266
    Burksdorf, 68, 114, 120, 145, 148
    Caba, 231
    Capaun, 113, 120, 145, 148, 240, 253, 266
    Creutz, 254
    Darmstadt, 50, 53, 63, 66, 266
    De Waghi, 254
    Del Maestro, 50, 53, 62, 67, 68, 75
    Desfurs, 114, 120, 145, 267
    Dohna, 254
    Donepp, 254
    Ester, 70
    Esterhazy, 146
    Falkenstein, 49, 62, 66, 67, 75
    Free Coys, 145, 148
    Furstenberg, 240, 253
    Geleen, 231, 267
    Gil de Haas, 228, 266
    Gissenburg, 68, 114, 120, 145, 150, 151, 266
    Gonzaga, 68, 70, 114, 120, 133, 145, 231, 239, 253, 267
    Gotz, 73, 151, 254, 255
    Grodetzky, 114, 120, 145, 148, 231
    Hanensee, 73
    Harrach, 50, 53, 63, 231
    Hatzfeld, 50, 53, 54, 62, 66, 67, 73, 75, 132, 136, 150, 231
    Heister, 114, 117, 118, 120, 145, 148, 267
    Hennet, 133, 136, 150
    Herlikowsky, 146
    Holstein, 47, 219, 222, 223, 228, 255
    Hussmann, 68
    Jung, 68, 114, 120, 145, 231
    Kaplir, 239, 253, 268
    Khevenhuller, 240, 253
    Knigge, 150, 151
    Kolowrat, 151, 240, 253
    Konigsegg, 151, 240, 253
    Kracht, 63, 68
    Krafft, 73
    La Coronna Traga, 113, 120, 146
    Lamboy, 68, 83, 85, 88, 95
    Lammersdorf, 115, 120, 145, 150, 151
    Lannoy, 150, 151, 239, 253
    Leittersheim, 73
    Liechenstein, 254
    Lobkowitz, 63
    Luttke, 240, 253
    Lutzelburg, 240, 253
    Madlo, 114, 117, 120, 145
    Mansfeld, 50, 53, 62, 66
    Marradas, 48, 53, 62, 66, 67, 68
    Marrazino, 66
    Melander, 239, 240, 253
    Mercy, 150
    Merode, 239, 253
    Mislik, 68, 69, 113, 119, 120, 145, 151, 231, 266
    Montecuccoli, 50, 53, 62, 66, 67, 68, 113, 120, 145, 148, 231, 239, 253, 266
    Munster, 68, 114, 120, 231
    Nassau, 114, 120, 132, 136, 145, 150, 151, 239, 240, 253

Neu-Piccolomini, 113, 119, 120, 133, 136, 145, 150, 231, 266
Neu-Saxon, 47
Nicola, 70, 88, 95, 114, 118, 120, 145, 266
Nouskowsky, 146
Novery, 114, 120
Pallavicini, 133, 136, 151, 240, 253
Piccolomini Leib, 113, 119, 120, 144, 231
Pless, 240, 253, 268
Polniskow, 50, 53, 54, 62, 66
Pompeji, 68, 114, 117, 120, 132, 133, 136, 145, 151, 231, 240, 253
Przichowski, 254, 268
Puchheim, 49, 62, 63, 67, 68, 69, 75, 266
Rantzau, 255
Ratkay, 63
Renz, 254, 268
Rittberg, 49, 62, 66, 67, 75
Rodoan, 70
Rodovan, 231
Salis, 69, 83, 85, 95, 218, 219, 222, 228
Salm, 133, 136, 150, 255
Sax-Lauenburg, 148
Schaff, 239, 253
Schaffelitzky, 254, 268
Schneider, 254
Schonickel, 50, 53, 55, 62, 66, 67, 75
Schutz, 68
Seneschal, 88, 95
Sieghofer, 68
Sparenberg, 68
Sperreuter, 83, 85, 88, 95, 113, 120, 145, 231
Spiegel, 70, 113, 120, 145, 267
Sporck, 240, 253
Stahl, 150, 151, 219, 222, 223, 228, 229
Tapp, 133, 136, 151, 240, 253
Trauditsch, 132, 136, 150
Ulhefeld, 50, 53, 62, 66, 67, 231
Velradt, 150, 151, 254
Vera, 70, 231
Vernier, 148, 150, 151, 239, 253
Vorhauer, 114, 117, 120, 145

Waldeck, 132, 136, 150
Wallenstein, 193
Wallis, 95
Walter, 150, 151
Warfuse, 240, 253
Warlowsky, 115, 120, 148
Westerhold, 73, 266
Wevin, 88
Weyer, 88, 95
Wildberg, 50, 53, 54, 62, 66, 67
Wilhelm, 94
Wintz, 48, 62, 66, 114, 120, 145, 148, 231
Wolframsdorf, 113, 120, 145, 231, 266
Zaradeszky, 64, 66, 68
Zriny, 254
Croat
  Beygott, 95
  Colombo, 240, 254
  Corpes, 87, 95
  Foldvary, 231
  Losy, 68, 231
  Lubetich, 254
  Marcovich, 145, 151, 228, 254
  Marsinay, 95
  MilliDraghi, 95
  Palffy, 151, 254
  Reikowitz, 231
  Rejkovics, 83, 95
  Tergouschlitz, 69
  Zrinyi, 151, 255
Dragoons
  Bissinger, 48, 66
  Carasco, 68
  De Waghi, 254
  D'Espaigne, 255
  Deveroux, 73
  Gall a Burke, 48, 63, 68, 115, 120, 145, 148
  Gallas, 88, 95, 115, 120, 150, 151, 231, 254
  Grana, 68
  Kratz, 88, 95
  Leslie, 48, 63, 66
  Marrazino, 48, 63, 66, 68
  Masslehner, 151
  Paconchay, 114, 120, 151, 240, 253, 268
  Schoh, 151
  Schonkirchen, 68

Index of Units

Someda, 240, 253
Infantry
Aldringer, 94
Alt-Saxon, 47
Archduke, 114
Arco, 255
Baden, 94, 150, 240, 254
Beck, 255, 267
Becker, 94
Bonninghausen, 49, 62, 66
Bournonville, 218, 222, 228, 255
Bourre, 49, 53, 62, 66, 69, 231, 267
Brunswick, 266
Bunau, 150
Bunigen, 255
Burgundian, 88
Caretto, 70, 114, 120, 266
Colloredo, 49, 53, 62, 66, 67, 68, 69, 150
Conti, 150, 240, 254, 268
Darmstadt, 49, 62, 66, 266
Enan, 49, 53, 62, 66, 75
Enkefort, 49, 62, 66, 88, 95, 114, 120, 144, 150, 255
Fehlberg, 255
Fernberger, 150, 240, 254
Fernemont, 114, 120, 145, 150, 218, 228, 231, 240, 254
Ferraris, 150
Florence, 94
Gallas, 94, 218, 228, 240, 254, 268
Gil de Haas, 267
Goltz, 49, 53, 62, 66, 68, 69, 75
Gonzaga, 49, 62, 66, 68, 69, 114, 117, 120, 136, 145, 148, 150, 266
Govo, 218, 222, 228, 229
Grana, 68, 88, 94, 95, 231
Gunter, 70
Halir, 218, 222, 228, 229
Harrach, 49, 62, 65, 66, 68, 70
Hatzfeld, 49, 53, 62, 66, 73, 266
Hauser, 240, 254
Henderson, 83, 85, 88, 95, 145, 150
Herrera, 66
Holstein, 255
Hunoldstein, 70, 150
Kehraus, 94

Knoring, 150
La Fosse, 267
Lamboy, 255
Leslie, 68
Locatelli, 254
Lombardi, 49, 62, 66
Mandelslohe, 218, 222, 228, 240, 254
Mansfeld, 49, 62, 66
Manteuffel, 49, 53, 62, 66, 75
Matthey, 231
Melander, 254
Mercy, 150, 151, 240, 254, 267, 268
Moncado, 114, 120, 254
Montevergues, 254
Morder, 255
Mors, 267
Moulin, 68
Nassau, 193
Niedrumb, 49, 62, 66, 68
Pappenheim, 49, 62, 65, 66
Plettenberg, 219, 222, 228, 255
Puchheim, 240, 254
Ranfft, 114, 120, 144, 231, 240, 254
Reich, 145, 150
Reumont, 255
Rochow, 254
Rubland, 255
Ruischenberg, 240, 254
Salis, 66, 68, 95
Savelli, 95, 266
Sax-Lauenburg, 114, 120, 148
Schaumburg, 255
Schifer, 150
Schlick, 69
Seefeld, 94
Souces, 70
Souches, 254
Soye, 73, 266
Sparr, 150
Spieckh, 255
Starhemberg, 240, 243, 244, 254
Strassoldo, 49, 62, 66, 254
Suys, 70, 114, 120, 231, 266
Tiefenbach, 94
Vehlen, 266
Wachenheim, 114, 120, 150, 240, 254

Waldstein, 49, 62, 66, 68, 88, 95, 150, 218, 228, 229, 254, 267, 268
Wallis, 254
Wangler, 68, 69, 94
Warlowsky, 255
Webel, 68, 69, 114, 120
Westerhold, 266
Wolfsegg, 255
Wolkenstein, 64, 66
Wrede, 255
Zeillern, 255
Zuniga, 68, 145, 240, 254
Zweyer, 49, 62

PALATINE
  Cavalry
    Ferentz, 73, 74
    Loe, 73, 74
    Rupert, 73, 74
  Dragoons
    Craven, 73, 74
  Infantry
    Craven, 73

SAXONY
  Cavalry
    Anhalt, 71
    Arnim, 71
    Baudissin, 49, 63, 71
    Bindauf, 71
    Bose, 48, 53, 63, 66, 67, 71
    Callenberk, 72, 115, 120, 133, 136, 146, 148, 151
    Dehne, 63, 66, 71, 75
    Elector, 63, 71, 72
    Geiso, 71
    Gersdorff, 49, 63, 66, 71, 133, 136, 151
    Hanau, 49, 63, 66, 67, 69, 71, 72, 115, 120, 133, 136, 146, 148, 151
    Hoffkirch, 71, 96
    Holstein, 71
    Kalkreuter, 49, 63, 67, 71
    Kalkstein, 48, 53, 63, 66, 67, 71
    Knoche, 72, 115, 120, 146, 148
    Leib, 72
    Masslehner, 69, 71, 72
    Milbe, 63, 66, 71
    Militia, 71
    Rauchhaupt, 71
    Reuchel, 69, 71, 72
    Rochau, 48, 53, 63, 66, 67, 71, 72
    Ruck, 49, 62, 67
    Rukert, 72, 133, 136, 151
    Sax-Altenburg, 71
    Sax-Lauenburg, 71
    Schierstadt, 48, 53, 63, 66, 67, 71
    Schleinitz, 63, 68, 69, 71, 72, 115, 120, 133, 136, 145, 146, 148, 151
    Seidlitz, 66, 71
    Steinau, 71
    Strein, 48, 63, 66, 71
    Taube, 48, 53, 63, 66, 71
    Trauditsch, 48, 63, 67, 68, 69, 71, 72
    Vitzthum, 48, 53, 63, 66, 71
    Wolframsdorf, 48, 53, 63, 66, 67, 71
  Dragoons
    Bose, 71
    Brink, 49, 62, 66, 71
    Haugwitz, 72
    Kalkstein, 71
    Kluge, 71, 72
    Lehmann, 72
    Masslehner, 63, 66, 71
    Schleinitz, 71, 72
    Schwalbach, 71
    Taube, 71
    Vitzthum, 71
  Infantry
    Arnim, 63, 66, 70, 72
    Bose, 49, 56, 62, 66, 70, 72
    Bunau, 49, 53, 62, 66, 71
    Elector, 71
    Free Coys, 71, 72
    Grubbach, 72
    Klitzing, 70
    Leib, 72
    Loser, 70
    Markenser, 70
    Mitzlaff, 71
    Monnier, 71
    Pforte, 49, 56, 62, 66, 70, 72
    Ponickau, 63, 66, 71
    Sax-Lauenburg, 70
    Schaumburg, 70
    Schleinitz, 49, 62, 66, 70, 72
    Schneider, 63, 66, 70
    Schwalbach, 63, 70, 75
    Solms, 70

Starshadel, 70
Taube, 63, 66, 70
Trandorf, 49, 62, 66, 70, 72
Vitzthum, 70
Wolfersdorf, 63, 66, 70, 71
Zehmen, 49, 62, 66, 70, 72

SPAIN
Cavalry
Balanzon, 194
Bucquoy, 191, 192
Burgy, 183
D'Epinoy, 193
Donquel, 183
Free Coys, 174, 183, 193, 194
Fuensaldana, 195
Gauchier, 193
Isenburg, 183, 193
Nassau, 193
Padilla, 183, 191
Rittburg, 183
Savary, 183, 192
Vera, 171, 183
Vivero, 191
Infantry
Aershot, 194
Alburquerque, 191
Avila, 191, 195
Balanzon, 194
Bassigny, 174, 183
Bauer, 194
Beauvoir, 194
Bentivoglio, 192
Bonifaz, 192
Bucquoy, 193
Campolattaro, 194
Castelvi, 174, 183, 191
Cordoba, 194
D'Ambise, 174, 183
Fontaine, 194
Frangipani, 174, 183
Garcies, 174, 183
Gramont, 174, 183
Granges, 174, 183
Guasco, 191
Gulzin, 194
Hennin, 193, 194
Herrera, 49, 62
Ligny, 174, 183, 191
Meghen, 174, 183
Mercador, 174, 183
Montecuccoli, 174, 183

Ponti, 178, 183, 191
Ribaucourt, 174, 183
Rittburg, 174, 183
Spinelli, 194
St Amour, 174, 183, 192
Strozzi, 173, 174, 176, 177, 183, 191
Velandia, 174, 176, 177, 178, 183, 191, 196
Verdugo, 194
Villalva, 174, 183, 191
Visconti, 173, 174, 176, 177, 178, 183, 196
Wingard, 194

SWEDEN
Cavalry
Abo, 260
Andersson, 241, 258, 262
Arendson, 259
Axel Lillie, 68, 133, 136, 149, 152, 241, 258, 262
Baden, 241, 258
Baner, 50, 65, 67, 68, 69, 75, 149, 241, 258, 261
Beckermann, 51, 65, 96
Behr, 148
Berghofer, 51, 56, 65, 67, 75
Bernhard, 95
Billinghausen, 116, 120, 147, 149
Birkenfeld, 65, 148, 265
Bjelke, 50, 65, 69
Bottiger, 241, 258, 262
Boy, 50, 65, 75
Bruneck, 50, 96
Butler, 134, 136, 152
Cappuhn, 68
Carl, 262
Courville, 266
Cratzenstein, 69, 116, 120, 147, 148
Dannenberg, 134, 136, 152, 155
D'Avangour, 134, 136, 152, 241, 258, 262
De la Gardie, 259
Derfflinger, 115, 120, 133, 136, 147, 148, 152
Dewitz, 50, 65, 67, 69, 148
Douglas, 51, 65, 67, 69, 116, 120, 134, 136, 147, 149, 152, 241, 258, 262

Duval, 51, 65, 69, 115, 120, 147, 148
East Gothland, 69, 149, 260
Endt, 241, 258, 262
Franz Henrich, 50, 65, 67, 69, 148
Free Coys, 259
Freyberg, 96
Friedrich, 148
Fritz, 241, 258, 262
Fritzlaw, 133, 136, 148, 152
Frolich, 241, 258, 262
Gadau, 50, 65, 68
Galbrecht, 133, 136, 152
Gassion, 96
Geischwitz, 258
Glaubitz, 51, 65, 67, 69
Goldstein, 51, 65, 67, 133, 136, 152, 241, 258, 262
Gortski, 241, 258, 262
Grubbe, 148
Haake, 148
Hammerstein, 134, 136, 152, 241, 258, 262
Hesse, 115, 120, 134, 147, 149, 241, 258, 262
Hoditz, 51, 65, 67, 69, 148
Hoking, 69, 115, 120, 147, 148
Horn, 134, 136, 149, 152, 241, 258, 262
Hundelhausen, 241, 258, 262
Jens, 51, 65, 69
Johann, 68
Jordan, 133, 134, 136, 152, 241, 258, 262
Kanneberg, 259
Karl Gustav, 133, 136, 152
Kerberg, 69
Kettler, 241, 262
King, 51, 65, 67, 73, 74
Kinsky, 115, 120, 147, 148
Klingspor, 50, 65, 68
Knyphausen, 69
Konigsmarck, 69, 73, 74, 148, 241, 258, 262
Krakau, 50, 65
Kruse, 241, 258, 259, 262
Kurck, 241, 258, 262
Kurland, 50, 65, 67, 69, 140, 148
Landgrave, 96, 134, 136, 147, 149, 152, 262
Leslie, 69
Lettmat, 241, 258, 262
Lewenhaupt, 241, 258, 259
Lilliehook, 116
Livonia, 50, 65, 67, 69, 148
Margrave, 133, 136, 152, 258, 262
Mecklenburg, 259
Mitzlaff, 116, 120, 147
Mohr, 241, 259
Muller, 134, 136, 149, 152, 259
Munchhausen, 148
Noble, 260
Oxenstierna, 69, 259
Pege, 241, 259
Pentz, 134, 136, 152, 241, 258, 262
Pfuhl, 51, 65, 67, 69, 75, 116, 120, 241, 258, 262
Plaunitz, 241, 259
Poley, 241, 258, 262
Polish, 115, 120, 147, 149
Prince's Leib, 259, 262
Qwast, 241, 259
Raabe, 133, 136, 152
Reichart, 134, 136, 152, 155
Reuschel, 134, 136, 152
Rhinegrave, 266
Riesengrun, 134, 136, 149, 152, 155
Rochow, 133, 136, 152
Royal Leib, 259, 262
Ruckwald, 148
Schirenhausen, 149
Schlang, 50, 64, 69, 148
Schulmann, 68, 69, 116, 120, 147, 148
Seckendorf, 116, 117, 120, 147
Seidelitz, 149
Smaland, 25, 50, 53, 64, 75, 148, 259, 260
Stakes, 69
Stalhansk, 50, 64, 65, 67, 69, 116, 120, 147, 148
Stenbock, 241, 258, 262
Stuart, 51, 65, 68
Tavastehus, 260
Tideman, 116, 120, 134, 136, 147, 149, 152
Torstensson, 50, 65, 67, 68, 69, 75, 115, 120, 133, 136, 147, 148, 152

Index of Units 305

Trotz, 149
Ulfsparre, 259
Uppland, 65, 69, 241, 258, 260
Viborg, 260
Wachtmeister, 50, 65, 67, 69, 96
West Gothland, 69, 241, 258, 259, 260
Wittenberg, 50, 64, 65, 69, 96, 116, 120, 133, 136, 147, 148, 152, 259
Wittkopt, 115, 120, 133, 136, 147, 148, 152, 241, 258, 261
Witzleben, 69, 148
Wopersnow, 51, 65, 68
Wrangel, 69, 96, 115, 120, 133, 136, 147, 148, 149, 241, 258, 262
Wurzburg, 50, 53, 64, 65, 69, 149

Dragoons
Baner, 69
De la Gardie, 259
Douglas, 259
Free Coys, 69
Goldstein, 152
Konigsmarck, 241, 259
Pegau, 152
Stalhansk, 149
Wrangel, 241, 258

Infantry
Adams, 50, 64, 67, 75
Alt-Blau, 46, 50, 64, 69, 115, 120, 123, 133, 141, 146, 149, 242, 258, 259, 262
Axel Lillie, 115, 120, 134, 136, 146, 149, 152, 155, 259
Axelson, 259
Bagge, 65, 68
Baner, 69, 115, 120
Barclay, 259
Bauer, 51, 65, 67
Bengtsson, 64
Bibau, 147, 149
Birkenfeld, 266
Blue, 25, 38, 97
Braun, 69
Bremen, 149
Bulow, 259
Burgsdorf, 96
Burtz, 149
Cratzenstein, 149
Cunningham, 50, 64, 69, 149

Dalarna, 260
Daniel, 147, 149
Doring, 242, 258, 259, 262
Dorkel, 149
Dorning, 149
Drake, 50, 64, 67, 68, 75
Drummond, 68
Dyouju, 149
East Botten,, 260
East Gothland, 69
Ekeblad, 259
Ermis, 50, 64, 147
Feldmeister, 95
Fels, 68, 69
Finn, 97
Fitinghof, 259
Fleetwood, 68, 69
Fleming, 149
Flotow, 69
Forbes, 65, 67, 149, 242, 259, 262
Forbus, 95
Gladstein, 242, 258, 262
Goltz, 50, 64, 67, 149
Gordon, 68, 69, 259
Gortzke, 96
Green, 25
Gun, 64, 68, 149
Guntersberg, 68
Hamilton, 259
Hansson, 64, 69, 147, 149
Hastfehr, 96
Haubald, 95
Herberstein, 64
Hogendorf, 96
Horn, 149
Jeschwitzki, 64, 69, 115, 120, 147
Jonkoping, 260
Jordan, 152
Kagge, 149, 259
Kalmar, 260
Karr, 50, 64, 67
Kinnemund, 68, 69
Knorring, 242, 258, 259, 262
Konigsmarck, 149, 242, 258, 262
Koppy, 134, 152
Kriegbaum, 65
Kronborg, 260
Kyle, 147, 149
Leslie, 48, 50, 63, 64, 67, 68, 69
Lewenhaupt, 134, 136, 152, 155, 242, 258, 259, 262

Lilliehook, 115, 120, 146, 147, 148, 149
Lilliesparre, 96, 149
Lind, 64
Linde, 133, 151, 242, 258, 259, 262
Lindsey, 50, 69
Mackay, 25
Maul, 115, 120, 149
Metstacke, 149
Mitzlaff, 95, 266
Moda, 64, 67
Mortaigne, 69, 115, 120, 133, 136, 138, 146, 148, 149, 151
Muffel, 266
Nehren, 241, 258, 262
Nerike, 260
Neuwad, 149
Nilsson, 259
Norrland, 260
Osterling, 69, 149
Paikull, 133, 149, 152, 241, 258, 259, 262
Persin, 260
Pfuhl, 96, 115, 120, 146, 147, 148, 149
Plettenberg, 115, 120, 149
Radike, 149
Ramsay, 96
Ratkie, 147
Red, 25
Ribbing, 134, 136, 149, 151
Ritter, 259
Rosen, 266
Royal Leib, 259
Ruth, 149
Ruthven, 51, 64, 67, 68
Sabel, 259
Sabelitz, 50, 64, 69
Sack, 241, 258, 262
Scheudorf, 149
Schlammerdorf, 97
Schlieben, 115, 120, 146, 149
Schneidwinds, 95
Schutte, 68
Seestedt, 133, 138, 152
Sincklers, 68
Skytte, 259
Smaland, 260
Sodermanland, 260
Sparr, 255

Stalarm, 134, 149, 151
Steinacker, 242, 258, 259, 262
Stenbock, 69, 147, 149, 242, 258, 259, 262
Strahlendorf, 65, 67
Teuffel, 25
Thomasson, 51, 64, 67, 149
Thurn, 96, 149
Torstensson, 69, 151
Uppland, 260
Vitzthum, 96, 266
Volkmann, 242, 258, 259, 262
Wallenstein, 97
Wancke, 149
West Botten,, 260
West Gothland, 260
Westmanland, 260
White, 123
Winckel, 97
Wittenberg, 149, 259
Wittgenstein, 96
Wolckmar, 133, 136, 152
Wrangel, 51, 64, 115, 146, 149, 151
Wurmbrand, 95
Wust, 149
Yellow, 25, 95, 96
Zerotin, 95
WEIMAR
  Cavalry
    Berg, 89, 90, 98
    Bernhard, 83, 89, 98
    Bodendorf, 83, 85, 96
    Boullion, 96
    Caldenbach, 83, 85, 89, 96, 98, 103
    Kanoffsky, 83, 85, 89, 90, 96, 98, 99
    Muller, 98
    Nassau, 83, 84, 85, 89, 96, 98, 103
    Ohm, 83, 85, 89, 96, 98, 103
    Plato, 96
    Potbus, 83, 85, 89, 97, 98, 103
    Rhinegrave, 83, 85, 89, 96, 98
    Rosen, 83, 85, 89, 91, 95, 96, 97, 98, 103
    Rotenhan, 89, 98, 103
    Schon, 98
    Taupadel, 83, 85, 89, 91, 95, 98
    Villefranche, 96

Witersheim, 89, 98, 103
Witzleben, 96
Wurtemberg, 83, 85, 96, 98, 102
Zillert, 96

Infantry
Bernhard, 89, 98
Bernhold, 96, 98
Flersheim, 89, 97, 98, 99
Forbus, 83, 85, 89, 95, 96, 97, 98, 99
Hattstein, 83, 85, 89, 97, 98, 99, 103
Hodiowa, 89, 96, 98, 99
Kanoffsky, 96
Lolson, 96
Moser, 89, 90, 98, 99
Quernheim, 96, 98, 99
Rhinegrave, 96
Schaffelitzky, 96, 99
Schmidtberg, 89, 96, 97, 98, 99, 103
Schonbeck, 89, 95, 96, 98, 99, 103
Wiederhold, 98, 99
Wurtemberg, 96

About the Author

WILLIAM P. GUTHRIE is an independent researcher. Since receiving his Ph.D. in 1992, he has written extensively on military history and the 17th century. This is his second book.